Jacobite
SPY WARS

MOLES, ROGUES AND TREACHERY

Also by Hugh Douglas

The Underground Story (Robert Hale)
Crossing the Forth (Robert Hale)
Portrait of the Burns Country (Robert Hale)
Edinburgh, a Children's History (Longman)
Burke and Hare, the True Story (Robert Hale)
Charles Edward Stuart, the Man, the King, the Legend (Robert Hale)
Robert Burns – a Life (Robert Hale)
Burns Supper Companion (Alloway Publishing)
Hogmanay Companion (Neil Wilson Publishing)
Flora MacDonald, the Most Loyal Rebel (Sutton Publishing)
The Private Passions of Bonnie Prince Charlie (Sutton Publishing)
Robert Burns: The Tinder Heart (Sutton Publishing)

Jacobite SPY WARS

MOLES, ROGUES AND TREACHERY

HUGH DOUGLAS

SUTTON PUBLISHING

First published in 1999 by
Sutton Publishing Limited · Phoenix Mill
Thrupp · Stroud · Gloucestershire · GL5 2BU

British Library Cataloguing in Publication Data
A catalogue record for this book is available from the British Library

ISBN 0 7509 1425 4

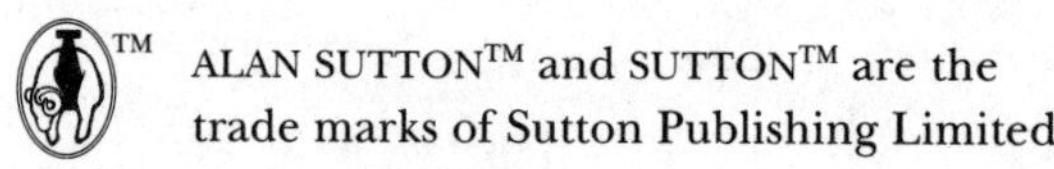

Typeset in 10/12pt New Baskerville.
Typesetting and origination by
Sutton Publishing Limited
Printed in Great Britain by
MPG, Bodmin, Cornwall.

John M.B. Stocks
1929–86
In memoriam

Contents

List of Illustrations

Acknowledgements

The darker side of the long Jacobite war that plagued Britain for a century is difficult to trace for the simple reason that much of the correspondence was destroyed in case it might fall into enemy hands. Nevertheless, surviving Jacobite and government correspondence is permeated with gossip and intelligence, which combine to give an accurate picture of the espionage war that was waged alongside the military and naval one.

Much has been written in the past about the Jacobite movement generally and about Charles Edward Stuart, but recent research has moved Jacobite history on from the realm of myth and legend of gloomy James, the Old Pretender, and his hero son, Prince Charlie. Historians have done much to uncover this new dimension of Jacobitism. Eveline Cruickshanks, Bruce Lenman and Allan I. Macinnes have discovered new material on the movement generally and in the Highlands, and Paul Monod has minutely researched its impact in England. Frank McLynn's work on the Cause and Prince Charlie is always interesting but his studies on the '45 rising in relation to England and France make a particularly valuable contribution to our knowledge of the movement. John S. Gibson's work on shipping during in the '45 is well known and has been of value to me. I am indebted to all of these and many others, and have acknowledged their work within the book where it has been of help. I express my general thanks to all of them here.

The only previous books on espionage during Jacobite times are Andrew Lang's *Pickle the Spy* and *Companions of Pickle*, written more than 100 years ago. They remain valuable sources and a great 'read' today.

Many libraries, organisations and individuals have helped me. The Stuart Papers in the Royal Archives at Windsor Castle contain many letters to and from the Pretenders, and I acknowledge my thanks to Her Majesty the Queen for graciously permitting me to quote from these.

I must thank the staff of my local library, Peterborough Central Library, and the London Library for continuing generous help. The British Library, Public Record Office, National Library of Scotland, Scottish Record Office, University Libraries of Aberdeen, Cambridge and Nottingham, the Mitchell Library, Glasgow, and Guildhall Library, London, have provided material, and the Librarian of the Catholic Central Library went out of his way to assist me.

Queries have been answered and documents supplied by public libraries in Bristol, Canterbury, Carlisle, Derby, Forfar, Edinburgh, Elgin,

Exeter, Fort William, Inverness, Harwich, Lichfield, Manchester, Newcastle-upon-Tyne, Oxford, Rochdale, Stafford and Stirling. The Archivist at the Highland Council, HM Customs & Excise, Kintyre Antiquarian Society, the National Postal Museum, Scottish National Trust Culloden Centre, United Services Museum, Edinburgh, and West Highland Museum, Fort William, have assisted with answers to specific queries.

Efforts to contact the copyright holders of the pictures of James II being welcomed at St Germain, of Young Glengarry and of the 1753 portrait of Charles Edward have failed. I should be pleased to hear from them.

Abroad, the Archives Nationales and Musée de l'Arsenal, Paris, Bibliothèque Municipale, Avignon, and the Osterreichische Nationalbibliotek, Vienna, welcomed me with great courtesy and supplied information and copies of documents in their collections. Florence Pluvinage, Eleanor Baha, Annie and Terry Rogers, Joyce Hall and H.J. Grüber all smoothed the way in overseas researches.

At home I would like to extend special thanks to Keeta and John Campbell and Clive Burton who read and commented on the text as the book progressed, and I must also thank Myrtle Anderson-Smith, A.A. Bond, Pat and James Bruce, Iain Coates, Michael Cumming, John Douch, Peter Ewart, Alison G. Finlay, Wendy Glavis, Sally Harrower, Ian Hutchison, H.J.K. Jenkins, Helen Litchfield, Donald F. MacDonald, Dr Rosalind Marshall and Dr Louise Yeoman. Last but by no means least, I express deep gratitude to my publishers, to Anne Dewe, to my wife, Sheelagh, and all my family and friends, whose steps have been dogged by Prince Charlie's spies for more time than I would care to admit to. They have been very patient, and I hope they will enjoy reading the book as much as I have enjoyed researching and writing it.

Preface

The Jacobite movement began with the Glorious Revolution of 1688 when James II of England and VII of Scotland fled and his daughter, Mary, and her husband, William of Orange, took over the two thrones. It ended in 1788 with the death of Prince Charlie, who ruled as Charles III, King over the Water. His brother, Cardinal Henry, proclaimed himself Henry IX, but no one – not even his closest friends – recognised his claim. Although the Jacobite Cause had been 'killed off' several times – by the defeat of risings in 1708, 1715, 1719 and 1745, and the wrecking of several attempted invasions by France and Spain, it proved remarkably resilient and always returned to haunt the Hanoverian government.

There is thus much more to the Jacobite story than the tale of Bonnie Prince Charlie, his unlucky father and grandfather, and a handful of battles – the Boyne, Sheriffmuir, Preston, Prestonpans, Falkirk and Culloden. It is one of history's longest-running spy sagas. *Jacobite Spy Wars* unravels an intricate intelligence war on and off the battlefield that drew in people as far flung as Sussex smugglers and Highland clansmen. Across Europe 'moles' dug for secrets at every court, and kings, ambassadors, soldiers, cardinals and royal mistresses all participated, from the great Duke of Marlborough to Madame de Pompadour and the devious King Louis XV. Even Young Glengarry, heir to a Highland chieftainship, sold himself to Prince Charlie's enemies. Sir Robert Walpole proved a compulsive master mole-catcher, Baron Philip von Stosch combined art collecting with spying, and the Irish adventurer, pimp and card sharper, Dudley Bradstreet, claimed with justification to have wrecked Prince Charlie's 1745 rising.

As for the Prince, in his character lurked all the virtues of a great spy and the faults of a bad one. He was a master of disguise and intrigue, which fooled his enemies, yet his arrogance and impetuosity contributed greatly to the Jacobites' eventual defeat in the espionage war. In the final analysis all the battles won and lost during the Jacobite century do not account for the failure of the Stuarts to be restored to the kingdoms they lost at the Glorious Revolution – ultimate defeat lay in their failure to win the intelligence war.

Chronology

1688 The Jacobite movement was born out of the Glorious Revolution when King James II of England and VII of Scotland fled to France and his daughter, Mary, and her husband, William of Orange, were proclaimed joint monarchs.

1689–98 First Jacobite restoration bids failed in Scotland, Ireland and England, and James made his last attempt in **1698**. When plots against his life were foiled, William began to build up an effective espionage network.

1701 James II and VII died and was succeeded by his son, James III and VIII, King over the Water to his friends, and the Pretender to his enemies.

1702 William was succeeded by Queen Anne.

1707 Union of Parliaments of England and Scotland led to young James's first restoration attempt in Scotland supported by France (**1708**). Frightened off by the Royal Navy, the French would not allow him to land.

1713–14 Under the Treaty for Utrecht James had to leave France and settled first at Avignon and later in Rome. Agents were busy in England and France and at one point it appeared that Anne might will her crown to James, if he were prepared to renounce his Catholic faith, but he was not.

1714 On Anne's death George of Hanover succeeded peacefully as King George I, but the following year James mounted a major rising, the '15, which was badly organised. It failed virtually before he set foot in Scotland. A second rising in the Highlands backed by Spain was defeated in **1719**.

1720 James's son, Charles Edward Stuart, the Young Pretender was born. A second son, Henry Duke of York, was born five years later.

1721–43 Whigs ruled and Sir Robert Walpole built up an effective espionage and counter-espionage system in Britain and across Europe. English Jacobites were neutralised after Atterbury/Layer Plot failed in **1722**. Scots followers in France and the Highlands talked much of a rising and in **1739** formed an Association to promote this.

1743–4 King Louis XV of France planned an invasion of England, using the Stuarts as his excuse. Charles Edward hurried from Rome only to find the British Navy and storms had wrecked the French fleet, and the plan was abandoned. Deserted by France, the angry Prince set out to plan a Scottish rising in secret.

1745 Charles sailed with only two ships, one of which was intercepted and had to return to France. With few arms and men he arrived in Scotland on **23 July**. Having persuaded a few clans to join him he raised the Stuart standard at Glenfinnan on **19 August**, then made a bold strike south to seize Edinburgh and proclaim his father king. Having won a victory at Prestonpans he marched south to Derby, but found little support among English Jacobites. The English spy Dudley Bradstreet persuaded Charles's leaders that the Hanoverians were closing in, thus influencing their decision to retreat to Scotland and await French help, which never came.

1746 Back in Scotland Prince Charlie won another victory at Falkirk, but retreated, demoralised and disorganised, into the Highlands. At Culloden on **16 April** his army was routed, and Charles was hunted among the mountains and islands while the Hanoverians ravaged the Highlands. After five months the Prince escaped to France on **19/20 September**.

1747 Neither France nor Spain would support a new rising and in high secrecy Henry deserted his brother to Rome to become a cardinal of the Roman Catholic Church.

1748 Under the terms of the peace treaty of Aix-la-Chapelle, which ended the War of the Austrian Succession, Charles was ordered to leave France, but refused. When he was arrested and expelled he defied Louis XV and went to Avignon.

1749–53 Prince Charlie became the 'Wild Man' of Europe, moving from country to country, drinking and womanising, and pursued by King George's and King Louis's spies. A secret visit to London (**1750**) was followed by the Elibank Plot to kidnap the Hanoverian royal family (**1752**). Thanks to Pickle the Spy the plot was betrayed and Dr Archibald Cameron, the last man to die for the Cause, was executed (**1753**).

1752 Charles took Clementine Walkinshaw as his mistress and she bore him a daughter, Charlotte, the following year.

1753–9 Followers in England, Scotland and Europe deserted in droves because they believed Clementine was the traitor who had betrayed the Elibank Plot, yet Charles refused to send her away. In **1759**, during the Seven Years War, France again mounted an invasion of England, but its fleet was defeated at Quiberon Bay. Spies once again kept the Hanoverians well informed of France's plans.

1760 George II died and George III succeeded peacefully. Having been treated cruelly by the Prince for years, Clementine fled to a convent the same year with the connivance of the French authorities and Charles's father in Rome. She took their daughter, whom Charles adored, with her.

1766 James Stuart died and Charles returned to Rome, where he proclaimed himself King Charles III, but even the Pope refused to recognise him. From then until **1788**, agents spied on every move he made at his little court, first in Rome then Florence – his disastrous marriage to Louise of Stolberg (**1772**), her elopement with the Italian poet Alfieri (**1780**), the return of his beloved daughter and acknowlegement of her legitimacy (**1784**).

1788 Charles died and his cardinal brother proclaimed himself King Henry IX, but no one took any notice. The Cause was dead even in its heartland, and Scottish Episcopalians, who had prayed loyally for the Stuarts all through the Jacobite century, felt they could no longer pray for the exiled ancient royal house.

CHAPTER ONE

A Cause to Spy For

> The story of Jacobitism contains many an example of treachery and double-dealing in high places, but it is also illuminated by numerous instances of the most sublime self-sacrifice.
>
> Sir Charles Petrie, *The Jacobite Movement*[1]

Revolutions and civil wars have been bloody businesses all through history, as Charles I, Louis XVI, Tsar Nicholas of Russia and numerous others discovered. That makes the Revolution of 1688 not just glorious, but remarkable for being bloodless and a piece of sleight of hand so smoothly accomplished that it was completed before the people of England, Scotland or Ireland were properly aware of what was taking place. Without a drop of blood being shed King James VII of Scotland and II of England fled his kingdom and settled into exile in one of King Louis XIV's castles at Saint-Germain-en-Laye in France – with such speed that he was left feeling shocked and cheated, but not defeated. The Glorious Revolution was in no sense a spontaneous rising with the common people, the nobility or anyone else clamouring for King James's blood. The arrival of his son-in-law, William of Orange, and his installation as joint monarch with James's daughter Mary was accompanied by plenty of panic, posturing and pamphleteering, but it really made little immediate difference to the daily life of the people. And it has to be admitted that if James had expended as much energy holding on to his crowns in the first place as he spent thereafter trying to win them back, there might never have been a Glorious Revolution at all.

James was dethroned with the minimum of disruption. His departure marked the start of a century of Jacobitism that history looks on today as little more than a persistent irritation to the established government, but which at the time was a life-threatening canker within the wellbeing of Britain – a 100-year-long struggle that could have been called the War of the British Succession, similar to those other great eighteenth-century power conflicts, the Wars of the Spanish, Polish and Austrian Succession, which consumed practically all of Europe, and the Seven Years War and War of American Independence, which took the search for power to the ends of the earth.

But for the accident of prehistory that created the English Channel and North Sea, the War of the Stuart Succession might have turned into something much more devastating than a series of unsuccessful invasion attempts, which created a legend whose principal character is a bonnie, kilted prince who adorns shortbread tins and whisky bottle labels today, the hero of a story laced with bravery, treachery, love, adventure and above all faithful followers who sacrificed homes, families, and their own lives for his Cause. The reality of Jacobitism is not Bonnie Prince Charlie, but a century of a tragic family barred from its inheritance by an efficient army and the greatest navy in Europe supported by battalions of spies, rogues and traitors.

James Stuart's campaign to return did not begin well. At the time of his flight at the end of 1688, Scotland was still embattled in the conflict against Stuart attempts to impose episcopacy – a struggle marked by the kind of bitter intransigence and bloodshed that has been a mark of religious wars throughout history. Now the hated John Graham of Claverhouse, 'Bluidy Clavers' of the 'killing times', rode north and raised a Highland army for King James. Claverhouse, Viscount Dundee, led his Jacobite followers to victory at Killiecrankie in July 1689, only to be killed in his moment of triumph. It was first blood of the Jacobite century to the exiles, but without Dundee to hold the Highlanders together, James's hopes in Scotland were at an end; only one brave little group managed to hold out on the Bass Rock off the East Lothian coast for another five years.

Catholic Ireland appeared a better prospect, since the French king and James were surrounded in France by Irish emigrés who were desperate to see the Catholic king re-estabished in their homeland. James sailed to Ireland but his campaign ended in disaster in spite (or perhaps because) of the fact that he himself was leading the Jacobite army. He was no match for his son-in-law, who was a capable general if a dull man, and the Battle of the Boyne shattered his every hope. Although he was never to set foot in Ireland again James returned to France unshaken in his belief of ultimate restoration.

Now he turned his thoughts to England only to discover his Cause there to be a hive of conspiracy and plot producing little action, which is virtually how the English movement remained all through the Jacobite century. Campaigns there were fought over the dinner table rather than on battlefields, and if claret had won wars the Stuarts would have been carried back on a tidal wave to restoration: but it did not; it merely loosened tongues, which made the work of the English government intelligence agents easier.

James's timing for seeking French support for an English invasion was perfect, since it suited Louis to distract William's attention from the Netherlands where he had greedy eyes on grabbing land to extend France's dominions. The invasion scheme began well with a victory over William's navy off Beachy Head, but on land nobody drew a sword for the King over the Water, and soon a combined British and Dutch fleet defeated the French at La Hogue. The first English attempt was over.

Three Jacobite failures in all three countries may have left William and Mary firmly on the throne, but they still felt far from secure since the exiled James's efforts now turned to a series of plots against William's life and a campaign of espionage and counter-espionage that was to continue into the reign of the last of the Stuarts, Queen Anne, and beyond to the first three Georges after the British crown was settled on the House of Hanover at Anne's death in 1714.

Espionage was at a low ebb in England during the years leading up to the Glorious Revolution since James had inherited an intelligence system in which mistresses mattered more to the king than his ministers. Charles II, with his roving eye, had set the standard: his many courtesans were regularly recompensed from monies earmarked for the running of his secret service, and as a result he actually ended up footing the bill to supply his own secrets to France. When the beautiful innocent face of the young Frenchwoman, Louise de Kéroualle, appeared at Charles's court – in all probability sent by Louis XIV purposely to spy – Charles wanted her for his bed. She coyly contrived to resist at first but eventually surrendered and was soon passing state secrets she learnt on the King's pillow back to Paris.

The secrets of King Charles's bed cost both Charles and Louis dear: Louise milked the two kings so successfully that it was said she earned no less than £600,000 from the two of them in the year 1661 – as Bernard Newman, an authority on espionage, commented: 'a fantastic figure for a society prostitute'.[2] She also received a title from each of her royal masters, Duchess of Portsmouth from Charles and Duchesse d'Aubigny from Louis. It is appropriate that Louis chose Aubigny as Louise's title for this town, located almost exactly in the geographical centre of France, still calls itself the city of the Stuarts: its streets are hung with banners proclaiming the Auld Alliance between France and Scotland and every year a great Scottish festival is held to mark the link with the royal house of Stuart which stretches back to the Middle Ages. The Alliance, used by the French to divert the English at that time and ever after, was in reality an 'auld illusion' so far as the Scots were concerned. Undoubtedly it added new dimensions to Scottish culture, but poor Scotland paid dearly for everything she received – from Flodden to Culloden. As the Jacobites were to discover, nothing had changed and as far as France was concerned the Auld Alliance was still only designed to threaten England's back door.

As a result of Charles II's bedtime 'alliances' with France, James II found at his succession in 1688 that such enormous amounts of money had been siphoned off to maintain his brother's mistresses that he had no secret service to speak of to keep him informed of what crafty Louis XIV was up to. He was not even able to monitor his own officials' conduct. Dutch William, on the other hand, had surrounded himself with an efficient army of 'moles' who not only supplied information about his father-in-law's activities but also were able to subvert many officials so that when the time came to choose, James found himself deserted.

The aristocracy and ambitious men at James's court who aspired to power were no heroes. 'Few of them were even honest men,' G.M. Trevelyan commented. 'But they were very clever men, and, taught by bitter experience, they behaved at this supreme crisis as very clever men do not always behave, with sense and moderation.'[3] Many lesser men followed James into exile at the Glorious Revolution, but few of the key figures in English government joined him immediately. And because of threats from the Jacobites in Ireland and Scotland and the French invasion scare in England, Whigs and Tories in the English Parliament were brought together closely enough to produce the Revolution Settlement.

Aware of the insecurity of his position, William became obsessed with the Jacobite threat to his life, since undercurrents of rebellion continued right through his reign. Serious plots began to be hatched from the moment he and Mary were accepted as joint sovereigns, so he set one of his closest friends, William Bentinck, to upgrade his secret service. Bentinck quickly gathered together an efficient espionage network and, after James's Irish defeat John Macky was sent to Paris, as he put it himself, 'to see what they were doing'.[4] He returned to London to report plans of the abortive French invasion hard on the heels of James's Irish defeat. The French were planning to create a diversion by sending two ships to Eilan Donan in Scotland while they landed James in England with 32,000 men. The result of the early warning was the French defeat at La Hogue and, as his reward, Macky was appointed inspector of the coast from Harwich to Dover to prevent treasonable correspondence from passing between England and France. In this capacity he claimed that he had made 'such discoveries as rendered King William entirely Master of the Jacobite Correspondence, and pointed out every Person concerned in both Kingdoms'.[5] He kept his own man to carry mail between the British ambassador in Paris and Dover, and thus prevented the French from intercepting mail for the government in London.

Macky used women to spy for him too. 'There were two Women that were permitted to go to St German's with Gloves, and other Trinkets, which the [Stuart royal] Family wanted from England, who were very useful in giving an Account of those Lords and Gentlemen who privately waited on King James from England, which they never failed of, and were entertained by Mr Macky, as is well known to Secretary [Edward] Vernon.'[6] This may not have been spying on the scale of the gorgeous Duchess of Portsmouth's pillow talk, but it was invaluable to King William.

Early success did not mean that the intelligence war brought London easy victory. William's spy network was as full of holes as James's, and much of the time he knew little of what the Jacobites were up to. The problem was that for all his work to improve the gathering of information, spying remained an amateur business, with agents working on their own and guarding the secrets they had uncovered even from their friends. There were plenty of 'moles' out there, but rivalry often rendered their digging worthless.

In the years following the Glorious Revolution a declaration of loyalty to William and Mary, opposition to Roman Catholicism or even preferment to high office were no bar to supporting the exiled James, or simply keeping in touch with him to wait and see whether the revolution was permanent or merely a brief interruption in King James's reign. Even the Quaker leader, William Penn, was arrested no fewer than four times between 1689 and 1691 on suspicion of being a Jacobite. On the last occasion he was detained as a result of the arrest of Richard Graham, Viscount Preston, who was caught on the Thames in a boat belonging to a Quaker woman from Wapping, carrying two letters from Penn to King James. Preston said later that Penn, the Earl of Clarendon who was the new Queen's uncle, the Countess of Dorchester, Bishop Turner of Ely and Penn's barrister friend, Charlwood Lawton, were all involved in a restoration plot, which was set in train the moment William departed for Ireland to deal with James's uprising there, and the French plan to invade England got under way. Details of this plot were sent from France by two Jacobite messengers, one of whom (unknown to Saint-Germain) was a double agent; the other, Matthew Crone, broke down under threat of execution and confirmed its details. As a result, John Ashton, one of Preston's accomplices, was executed for his part in the plot.[7]

While the landed classes fought their claret wars, plenty of shady characters further down the social scale filled the London public houses throughout the 1690s – cashiered officers, thieves and cut-throats, fighting and attaching themselves to any plot that might turn a dishonest penny. Bentinck's agents kept careful watch on them, too, since even a whisper might prove to be a shadow of darker treachery. This was exactly the situation in March 1696 when one of Bentinck's spies was warned to make sure the King did not go hunting at Richmond the following day: as a result of this remark a plot to waylay William at Turnham Green as he returned from hunting was uncovered and it was found to involve a great number of important people including Sir John Fenwick, who was beheaded.

But William was not the only person surrounded by men who could not be trusted: James Stuart had as many enemies and false friends in France, and had he been a better judge of character he would have realised that his search for betrayers ought to have begun no further away than the gates of Versailles where Louis XIV was first in a long line of Judases of the Jacobite Cause.

It suited Louis to have the exiled Stuarts within his control to help him to play a trump card in Scotland, Ireland or among the discontented in England whenever he wished to divert England's attention from Flanders. The exiled Stuarts could provide new opportunities to launch full-scale attacks to divert British troops or simply to cause annoyance by tweaking the lion's tail at opportune moments; but neither Louis XIV nor his successor, Louis XV, really cared whether the Stuarts returned to London or not. They had sympathy for the disinherited king simply because James was a monarch and if this exile who shared their faith and belief in absolute kingship could be forced to abdicate, what might happen to a king of France? And yet, at heart the Sun King was well aware that under a restored Stuart monarchy England would remain his enemy just as she had been for centuries past.

It is not too cynical to say that the French were prepared to support almost any restoration attempt by the Kings over the Water – but never to commit quite enough backing for an attempt to succeed. Time and again throughout the Jacobite century, the movement proved its worth to France and as a reward received enough sweet words and cash to underpin the petty little exiled court, pay pensions to indigent followers, and provide a modicum of unreliable support in the form of men and arms for future risings. But James and his successors could never be assured of sufficient French aid at the very times they needed it, as in 1714 after Queen Anne died, or again in 1744 when a shameful betrayal by the French angered Charles Edward Stuart so much that he set out on the 'rash adventure' of the 1745 rising without adequate men or money. At other times Louis made encouraging noises, but never gave the Pretenders, Old or Young, the backing they needed to succeed.

In 1689 James II was taken in by French duplicity: Louis XIV welcomed him like a reigning monarch and a returning friend, for James Stuart had spent his formative years in France and even served as a soldier in the French service at the time of the Civil War. He was given one of Louis's own châteaux to live in: it consisted of two castles, the *château vieux* and the *château neuf*, set in sumptuous gardens and with a terrace more than a mile long running alongside its fine parklands. James settled into the new castle, while his former army officers and their families were given the old one, which, it has to be said, they soon turned into a 'ramshackle barracks' to the great annoyance of the fastidious French.[8] Although Louis had gone to great pains to provide James with a home, sumptuous gifts and a generous allowance that enabled him to set up a court far more splendid than anything he had known in London, James's memories of the twin castles of Saint-Germain could never have been happy. This was where he had stayed in exile with his mother as a boy, and it was here he learned of the execution of his father, King Charles I.

Life as a pensioner of the Sun King at Saint-Germain was agreeable enough for James II, living in regal splendour with a wife and child he loved, receiving fawning subjects who were arriving in droves (eternally begging money) and hunting to his heart's content in the best forests of France. James wanted more though, so that Saint-Germain quickly became a boiling pot of intrigue to drive Dutch William out of England.

The overt manoeuvring was only the visible tip of a very large and imperceptibly melting iceberg of Jacobitism. Hidden from sight, but a constant danger to William and Mary, widespread and dangerous currents of dissent permeated every aspect of life, political, religious, and social, a threat which William realised had roots in France as well as England. To counteract Jacobite intelligence activities in France and the extensive French espionage system that supported them, William set about broadening the scope of his own secret service, by organising an efficient English spy network in Paris, using his ambassadors to control it, first the Earl of Portland and later the Earl of Jersey. The intelligence web was woven by the ambassador's secretary, the poet, diplomat and highly accomplished spy, Matthew Prior.

London poured out large amounts of money to keep abreast of what was happening at Saint-Germain, and to monitor all the secrets passing between there and Versailles – and there were plenty of these since James was constantly slipping morsels of information to Louis to tempt him to lend his weight to yet another anti-Williamite plan. Prior, who masterminded all this information gathering, was helped enormously by the fact that nobody at either Saint-Germain or Versailles could hold their tongue, and consequently both courts leaked secrets like sieves. There was now so much information passing between Jacobites in England and Scotland, and Saint-Germain and Versailles that Prior had to recruit an army of moles, composed of genuine informers, trouble-makers and impostors who simply made up what they did not know: between them these spies kept Prior amply supplied with valuable, accurate intelligence as well as a mass of half-truths and lies, all of which was listened to avidly in London.

Not content with what others could give him, Prior himself spent much time in Paris coffee houses, 'becoming acquainted,' as he said, 'with half the starving English and Irish about Paris'. The Jacobites were already beginning to squabble among themselves and at times these quarrels ended in bloody fights, which Prior was always pleased to report. 'Three or four fellows have been killed last week at Saint Germains by their countrymen and comrades,' he told his master in July 1698, 'thus disorders and murders reign where this unhappy man lives, and his domestic affairs are governed just as his three kingdoms would have been.'[9]

The remit of every British envoy was to manoeuvre for James Stuart to be thrown out of France, but this was not easy to achieve since James always had powerful friends at court, especially the mighty Madame de Maintenon, the King's mistress. He was further hampered by the fact that protocol ordered that he should never come face to face with the Stuart king or any of William's enemies, but Prior ignored that and enjoyed several close encounters with James and his son, although they never actually spoke. It amused him that gentlemen of the French court referred to James as 'le roy d'Angleterre' when speaking to Jacobites but as 'le roy Jacques' when talking to Prior.

Ambassadors were not always lucky or efficient in choosing their agents. Portland at one point used a French Catholic, a former court hanger-on who had access to the Pretender but used the information he collected to build great fantasies about English nobles crossing to France. On another occasion Portland chose Richard Kingston, one of the best agents the government ever had, but it was also he who hired the Jacobite double agent, John Simpson, and the perjurer, John Taafe.[10]

Many in high places in England continued to play their cards cannily: almost everybody was hedging his bets in case William and Mary should be overthrown, a cautious practice which continued through the reign of Queen Anne. Day-by-day political divisions were seldom clear-cut, although Whigs favoured the new regime and Tories automatically supported the Stuarts. And the Jacobites played cleverly on this confusion.

Even John Churchill (soon to become the great military commander, the Duke of Marlborough) played the treachery game and spent six weeks in the Tower of London on a charge of high treason as a result of an incredible Jacobite plot around the time of the threatened French invasion at the start of William and Mary's reign. With London in a high state of nervousness, a master forger named Robert Young drew up a document purporting to be a plan to capture King William dead or alive and restore James: on it he forged the signatures of Churchill and several others. The paper was then hidden – of all crazy places – in a flowerpot at the house of the Bishop of Rochester and the government was duly tipped off. Churchill was arrested but fortunately searchers missed the pot containing the note and the truth came out after the invasion scare passed. Churchill was then freed.

On the word of three Jacobite spies, a Roman Catholic Bishop, Edward Dicconson, accused Admiral Edward Russell, Lords Godolphin and Halifax and John Churchill, of carrying complaints about the Williamite regime to Saint-Germain.[11] With the help of Dicconson's accusation, the historian Lord Macaulay turned Churchill's suspected treachery into a drama of a shameful deserter begging to be brought back into the Jacobite fold. In the words of Macaulay, Colonel Edward Sackville, one of James's agents in England, was treated to 'the edifying spectacle of such an agony of repentance as he had never before seen'.

'Will you,' said Macaulay, quoting Dicconson, 'be my intercessor with the King? Will you tell him what I suffer? My crimes now appear to me in their true light; and I shrink with horror from the comtemplation. The thought of them is with me day and night. I sit down to table: but I cannot eat. I throw myself on my bed: but I cannot sleep.'

Having given the priest's version verbatim, Macaulay (in the words of Marlborough's descendant and biographer Sir Winston Churchill) then 'snaps at the hands of Dicconson, from which he had hitherto fed with such relish'. Sir Winston comments, 'The truth was that when Marlborough told the Jacobites that his sense of guilt prevented him from swallowing his food by day and taking his rest at night, he was laughing at them. The loss of half a guinea would have done more to spoil his appetite and to disturb his slumbers than all the terrors of an evil conscience.'[12]

Marlborough has also been accused of double-dealing and of passing secrets to the enemy, particularly over a letter betraying a planned British attack on Brest, which ended disastrously. This has all the hallmarks of another piece of Jacobite skulduggery, based on a letter which never existed or which, if it did, could not have been seen by James in advance of the attack. The Camaret Bay Letter, as it is known, 'had a good run for several generations' down to 'Ossian' (James Macpherson) and Macaulay. It is interesting to note that Admiral Russell, victor of La Hogue, was similarly suspected.

At worst all that can be said is that Marlborough did contact Saint-Germain, and his conscience may well have troubled him since he had been a close friend of James II but deserted to William's side. His correspondence was partly prompted by remorse but it may also have been a kind of insurance policy in case of restoration, a hedging-of-bets that was common enough among highly-placed Englishmen at the time.

Much of the correspondence between Marlborough and all the others who remained in contact with Saint-Germain was destroyed, so it is impossible today to assess whether it was treacherous or not. But the dramatic confessions and heart-searching of which Macaulay and Ossian made so much, are hard to believe. Marlborough's conscience did trouble him and he certainly continued to hold James Stuart in high regard after the Revolution: he also sought forgiveness and promised future loyalty, but he always remained faithful to England in spite of the fact that his relationship with William was never a warm one. The two had no love for one another, but William was well aware that a number of his subjects apart from Marlborough were playing safe by keeping close to James's court. He persuaded himself that this contact with Saint-Germain was good counter-espionage, which raises the other question about Marlborough – did he betray military secrets at this time or later when he was Captain-General of the British army in Flanders and Germany?

The historian Frank McLynn offers a credible explanation: he was simply divulging medium-level information in return for pre-dated pardons in case of a Stuart return.[13] This echoes Sir Winston Churchill's suggestion that it was a deliberate plan to lure the Jacobites into letting slip secrets that helped his campaigns. According to Sir Winston it was a game in which Marlborough gave the enemy hints about his intentions, then 'a month or perhaps a week later – a swift march, a sudden assault, thrusting out of a cloud of honeyed words and equivocation, changed fortunes in the field. Webs of intrigue, crossings, double-crossings, stratagems, contrivances, deceit; with smiles, compliments, nods, bows, and whispers – then *crash!* sudden reversion to a violent and decisive military event. The cannon intervene.'[14]

For whatever reason, the Jacobites – and their French allies – received more than they bargained for from the Captain-General. Sir Winston draws self-interest as the bottom line under the questions about Marlborough's actions. 'It is affectation,' he claims, 'to pretend that statesmen and soldiers who have gained fame in history have been indifferent to their own advancement, incapable of resenting injuries, or guided in their public action only by altruism. . . . The test is whether he was false in intention or in fact to the cause of Protestantism and constitutional freedom, and above all whether the safety of England or the lives of her soldiers and sailors were jeopardised by his actions.'[15] Alas, the correspondence that would prove this has not survived, but perhaps the Captain-General's victories at Blenheim, Oudenaarde and Malplaquet speak just as eloquently as any of the lost letters could have done.

Although the first great thrust of the Jacobite war lasted only until the turn of the century, the pattern of the whole Jacobite century was now set – intermittent military campaigns alongside gossiping, backbiting and unending spy wars, in which the government in London gradually won the upper hand, but the Jacobites never gave up. Eveline Cruickshanks sums it up: 'It was a game in which the British government held most of the trump cards, buying information from Jacobite exiles with either money or hopes of pardon, posting spies round the Jacobite courts and bribing influential foreigners in exchange for intelligence or for blocking pro-Stuart projects.'[16]

Plot after plot failed after young James Stuart, the boy whose birth had triggered the Glorious Revolution, grew up and succeeded as King James VIII and III on his father's death in 1701. Scotland became the focus of the majority of these plots and of the Cause itself because relations between the two kingdoms, in spite of their shared monarchy, were at a very low ebb during the first years of Queen Anne's reign. The English put it down to Scots intransigence; to the Scots it was fuelled by English arrogance. The Scots were divided as always by their age-old watersheds of Highlands and Lowlands, religion, tradition and culture. But they were united as no other part of the kingdom was, bonded by a feeling that the English were not treating them as part of a shared monarchy.

The trouble was that the Scots had for centuries been an outward looking nation, a European nation, which shared a tradition of learning and trading with all of Europe, whereas their southern neighbours had only much more recently come to realise the power of colonisation and overseas trade, and had selfishly tried to exclude the Scots from sharing the benefits. As a result the Scots set up their own colonisation scheme at Darien in the isthmus of Panama in 1695 with disastrous results – the Darien disaster ended in ruin and bankruptcy and humiliation for the whole country.

William died in 1702 and was succeeded by Anne; an Act of Settlement was then passed to secure the Protestant succession on Anne's death through the line of the Electors of Hanover, who were descended from the daughter of James VI and I. The London parliament expected the Scots to follow its lead and pass a similar Act, but Scotland still remained a separate and independent kingdom, with a shared monarch it is true, but with its own parliament, which was in no mood to follow meekly at England's heels. Parliament in Edinburgh flatly refused to pass an Act, even threatening to break off the 100-year-old union of the monarchies. London retaliated sharply and as a result of much dark manoeuvring and manipulation a treaty of total Union between the two kingdoms was devised, debated and pushed through, so that on 1 May 1707 the two kingdoms were merged into the United Kingdom of Great Britain.

Although the Union guaranteed Scotland's Presbyterian religion and the country soon began to benefit commercially from the dropping of the laws that had barred her merchants from trade with the colonies, many felt the price was too high – they had paid for these benefits with their independence. Furthermore, their nationhood, which had been something beyond price since the days when William Wallace and Robert the Bruce won it, was 'stolen' by the duplicity of many of their own nobles and 'moles' planted by the English government. The worst of these was none other than Daniel Defoe, a prolific anti-Jacobite pamphleteer, already an agent of proven ability, who had learnt his trade in England and used much of the material he gathered on his travels to write his *Tour Thro' the Whole Island of Great Britain.* His rose-tinted accounts of Whig Britain were excellent practice for the fictional *Robinson Crusoe* and *Moll Flanders.*

He was a machiavellian character, two-faced, and has been described by a journalist of today as 'a sort of eighteenth-century spin-doctor, a familiar figure in the corridors of power'.[17] Like most spin-doctors Defoe made enemies and paid for his indiscretion in criticising establishment figures by being put in the pillory and gaoled in Newgate. He talked his way back into favour by acting as a government agent in Scotland at the time the Treaty of Union was being negotiated.

In 1706 Defoe turned up in Edinburgh with a tale that he had come to set up a glass factory or a salt works, but later he changed his story to the much more plausible one that he was gathering material to compose a new version of the psalms or a history of the Union. Under cover of these lies he worked ceaselessly to persuade the Scots to accept the Union, and at the same time to smear the Jacobites with Whig propaganda. He was so confident of himself that he was able to write to his master, Robert Harley (later Earl of Oxford), 'I act the part of Cardinal Richelieu. I have my spies and pensioners in every place and confess 'tis the easiest thing in the world to hire people here to betray their friends. I have spies in the Commission, in parliament and in the Assembly, and under pretence of writing my history I have everything told me.' The Union was a triumph for the master agent, and at the same time proved just how far behind the Scots – and the Jacobites too – were in the intelligence game.

The resentment that resulted from the Union confirmed the whole ethos of Jacobitism as a Scottish Cause. People who would never have supported the return of the exiled Stuarts hitherto – especially as such a monarch was certain to be Roman Catholic – now felt a desire for change and the Pretender represented a chance for the overthrow of those they blamed for their misfortune. As a result of the discontent leading up to the passing of the Act of Union, Jacobite hopes ran high between 1702 and 1708, the first six years of Queen Anne's reign. And young James Stuart showed more spirit than his father.

When James was only fifteen Simon Fraser, a member of the great Lovat clan, came to France with a scheme to raise an army of 12,000 men who would rise against Queen Anne with the help of 5,000 French soldiers. The French were suspicious of the Scots' ability to field so many men and Lovat was sent back to Scotland, where he betrayed the plot to the Duke of Queensberry. It was then arranged for Lovat to return to the Highlands to discover exactly which chiefs were involved in the plot and there clan rivalries took over. He accused the Marquis of Atholl, who just happened to be an enemy of himself and Queensberry, and although Atholl was never put on trial, the conspirators' cover was blown and a number of leaders on both sides of the Border were arrested. Fraser himself then returned to France to act as a double agent, but found himself a prisoner in the chateau of Angoulême.

Sir Winston Churchill summed up the Scottish situation at the time of the Union: 'Highland clansmen, Lowland Jacobites, Whig noblemen, Covenanters, Catholics, and Presbyterians, were all ripe for rebellion, though with different objects. Now, if ever, was the hour for the rightful heir to Scotland's ancient crown to set foot upon Scottish soil.'[18]

Although King Louis was well aware of this simmering national feeling, he exploited it only to his own ends, which meant using it to divert the British from Marlborough's campaign against him in Flanders. The war was going badly there for Louis, so he planned to encourage the clans to rise while he invaded with an army 6,000 strong. By committing a relatively small force he would thus relieve pressure on his armies in Flanders and at the same time create an opportunity to rid himself of all those troublesome Jacobites, who were perpetually knocking at his door asking for money.

In the spring of 1705 and early autumn of 1707 he sent an intelligence agent to Scotland to persuade the clan chiefs to organise a rising backed by a French invasion force. With typical disregard for Scottish feelings, Louis chose Colonel Nathaniel Hooke, a vain Irishman who had been 'palmed upon the court of Saint-Germain . . . as one who would follow his [King Louis's] directions and be true to his interest'.[19] George Lockhart of Carnwath, whose description that was, added sourly that the French King was not disappointed 'for the Colonel showed more concern to raise a civil war at any rate (which was what the French King chiefly wanted) than so to manage and adjust measures as tended most for King James's service and to encourage his subjects to do something for him'.[20]

Hooke brought back a wildly optimistic assessment of the situation in Scotland: 'I found all the nation extremely exasperated against the English, even to a degree beyond expression,' he told the King's Secretary of State in Paris. 'Particular interests of different parties were in a manner all laid asleep, and every one in general thought of nothing but of shaking off the English yoke.' For confirmation, Hooke brought with him a memorial, which he claimed was supported by 'the richest and the most powerful chiefs of that kingdom', with only the dissenting voices of the Duke of Hamilton and one of his friends.[21]

On the strength of this report and knowledge of the genuine feeling of unease that pervaded Scotland at the time, Louis began to assemble a fleet at Dunkirk early in 1708, and sent the Earl of Wigtoun ahead to warn Scottish leaders to expect an invasion by young King James and to arrange a code of signals by which contact could be made when the French fleet arrived.

James had the usual ill luck of the Stuarts on both sides of the English Channel – the London government soon had wind of the plan, and ministers in Paris were far from enthusiastic about it: the naval commander in charge, the Comte de Forbin, was not only lukewarm but incompetent as well. Then James went down with measles, but insisted on sailing with the French fleet. Lastly the weather and poor seamanship turned against the expedition – Channel storms and the Royal Navy penned the fleet up in Dunkirk, then poor navigation delayed it further, so that it was towards the middle of March before the French reached the Firth of Forth. By then the British Navy had caught up with them. Forbin lost one of his ships in an untidy scrap, which convinced him that he dared not take on the British fleet. James begged to be put ashore, but the French admiral would not allow it, and he was taken back ignominiously to France. He was to have no better luck in future attempts.

All the government's intelligence efforts failed to prove treason against any of the Scottish nobility following the 1708 invasion attempt, but that did not prevent it from suspending the *Habeas Corpus* Act and rounding up the great chiefs, virtually at random, without account of age or alibi, and throwing them into Edinburgh Castle. Although held simply on suspicion, many had to provide bonds for large sums to guarantee their future good behaviour before they were freed. The 1708 rising struck such fear into the authorities in London and Edinburgh that their response foreshadowed what was to happen after the '15 and '45 risings.

In the south the Wapping Quaker wife's boat and other vessels continued to carry subversive letters and secret agents between Britain and France for as long as the Stuarts lived at Saint-Germain. Every morsel of information they carried was chewed over, savoured and digested because the Jacobite and French courts were both so riddled with counter-spies that security hardly existed. King James did not help: he was willing to talk to anyone, especially if he thought they could persuade King Louis to supply ships, men and money for new invasion attempts in England or Scotland. But Louis never really delivered.

James continued to wage a war of nerves against his half-sister Anne's ministers. During the closing years of her reign he became a familiar figure, riding his white horse on the battlefront in Flanders, easily identified by British soldiers, who took off their hats and cheered him whenever he appeared. They hurrahed but did not desert to him. The Jacobites may not have been winning the espionage war, but they had considerable success in the campaign during Anne's last years and the beginning of the reign of George I, when it took little to upset the equilibrium of the London government. When James had a medal struck, displaying a bust of himself, and distributed it widely among friends and enemies alike, one found its way to the Faculty of Advocates in Edinburgh, where it caused great consternation among Whigs. He even sent a conciliatory letter to Anne, which went unanswered, yet brought him closer to regaining his throne than at any time before or after. 'This was the moment . . . when an almost bloodless revolution and restoration might have taken place,' wrote Sir Charles Petrie, 'and had James possessed the initiative of his elder son he would have paid a surprise visit to the British camp, in which event the course of history might well have been changed; but James III was not Bonny Prince Charlie.'[22]

Religion was always seen as the great bar to restoration, yet even on this subject the Pretender lived in cloud-cuckoo land, believing that a mere undertaking to allow his subjects freedom of worship would be sufficient for him to be invited back. But it was not, and all the overtures the Tories in London continued to make brought him no nearer to a peaceful restoration. Spies reported every move, through innumerable leaks from Saint-Germain and the vast French espionage web, as well as hints from dissident Tories. On the Jacobite side wishful thinking kept James's hopes alive and in London too many sympathisers, who should have known better, remained hopelessly addicted to believing that something would turn up, which, of course, it never did. And in 1713 the terms of the Peace of Utrecht forced James to leave France, taking him further away from his goal than ever.

He moved first to Lorraine, next to the papal city of Avignon, and finally to Rome; thereafter Italy was the exiled Stuarts' home, which tied them so securely to the Vatican's coat-tails that they would never be accepted back in Protestant England. This arrangement pleased Britain.

The drawing up of the Utrecht treaty was not a pretty business politically, but it certainly provided its negotiators with plenty of sexual adventures. It was negotiated secretly in France, largely by the high Tory, Viscount Bolingbroke, and Matthew Prior, behind the backs of Whigs in London, and poor Marlborough, who was trying at the time to fight the war in Flanders, ended up being dismissed and discredited. As for Bolingbroke and Prior, they negotiated their peace against the background of a highly compromising social life: Bolingbroke flirted openly with the beautiful Claudine de Tencin and Prior associated with a number of women at Louis's court. Naturally rumour had it that the secrets Bolingbroke whispered in Madame de Tencin's ear found their way to French ministers and vice versa.

Bolingbroke tried hard to follow up his successful Utrecht treaty negotiations with a hush-hush scheme to restore James Stuart on Anne's death, but failed. The plotting and conniving involved a number of high Tories, including the Duke of Ormonde, who had supported William of

Orange at the Glorious Revolution and had followed Marlborough as Captain-General only to find his Flanders campaign a disaster largely because of Bolingbroke's double-dealing. Ormonde might just have pulled off the restoration coup, but in the opinion of the Duke of Berwick, who was in a position to know since he too was up to his neck in the plotting, he just was not statesman enough to achieve it. 'Pour exécuter un pareil projet, il falloit un autre génie,' Berwick wrote, 'de si grands desseins ont besoin d'un Héros, et c'est ce que le Duc d'Ormond n'étoit pas.'[23]

The end was a great disappointment for James: in England the Tories were triumphant and there was much secret support for his return in spite of the Act of Settlement, although Whigs postured and created commotions, while pamphleteers screamed against a Catholic king and supporters of the restoration made little progress. At the end of 1713 events overtook the plotting and posturing of both sides: the Queen took ill and the pro-Jacobite faction in government pressed hard for James to turn Protestant or at least to 'dissemble'. But James refused.

With the succession unresolved many feared civil war would follow the Queen's death, yet in spite of intense lobbying and manoeuvring after the last Stuart monarch passed away at seven o'clock on the morning of Sunday 1 August 1714 the Elector of Hanover was proclaimed and crowned King George I with much local dissent and rioting, but no coordinated nationwide opposition.

A story was told afterwards of a packet of the Queen's private papers, which George I's representatives said they had burned in accordance with the Queen's instructions on her deathbed. Papers were certainly burnt but was one of them a document bequeathing the crown to James Stuart? The answer to this intriguing royal mystery will probably never be known.

And as for James Stuart, another tale claims that the Duke of Ormonde, Bishop Atterbury and the Earl Marischal discussed proclaiming him king at Charing Cross but decided that the moment was not right. While they dithered the Whigs proclaimed George, Elector of Hanover, King of Great Britain and Ireland.

The Cause had come a long way in its first twenty-five years, yet had achieved nothing in spite of all the military attempts. The spy war had come a long way, too, but it still had much further to go before the Stuarts would abandon their claim.

CHAPTER TWO

In the Jacobite World and Underworld

Flushed with success these lawless vagrants come;
From France their maxims, and their Gods from Rome
Ruffians, who fight not in fair Honour's cause,
For injur'd Rights, or violated Laws;
But, like the savage race, they roam for prey,
And where they pass Destruction makes their way.

New Prologue written for *The Beggar's Opera* subscription production in December 1745.[1]

Up to the moment Queen Anne drew her last breath and the will leaving her crown to her half-brother was destroyed (if it ever existed), return of the Stuarts remained a possibility – for a brief moment even a probability, had young James Stuart himself not ruined his chances by his determination to cling to his Roman Catholic faith. Instead, the Elector of Hanover was peacefully installed, with little real opposition, as King George I.

All restoration plots to date had failed and a half century of almost absolute Whig power began, leaving the architect of restoration, Bolingbroke, to face impeachment and charges of treason. He wisely 'took fright and fled in disguise to Paris to throw himself into the cause of the Pretender and into the arms of Madame de Tencin again'.[2] It looked like a piece of good fortune to be able to take the lovely Claudine de Tencin into his bed once more, but Bolingbroke now found he had to share her with the Abbé Dubois, who was not only one of Louis's ministers but also a fervent supporter of George I. The affair with Claudine ensured that Jacobite secrets continued to reach London.

Even without the ill fortune of having to share his mistress with the Abbé, Bolingbroke was not at ease in France or with the Pretender, because he despised James for his failure to make the compromises that would have won him his crown. 'He trembles before his mother and his priest,'[3] Bolingbroke said angrily. He did leave Jacobite service, but not of his own free will: the Pretender dismissed him without so much as discussing the decision with any of his inner circle of advisers because he believed that, as his Secretary of State, Bolingbroke had been negligent in not sending arms to him during the rising in Scotland the year after George's accession. Bolingbroke abandoned the Cause with ill grace. 'May my arm rot off if I ever use my sword or my pen in their service again!' he raged.[4] And he meant it. With Bolingbroke's departure, James Stuart lost the best adviser he ever had but it was the end of Bolingbroke's career too; he ended his days out of office and out of favour with both sides.

Ormonde was threatened with impeachment also and had to flee to France, where he offered himself to the Cause. He organised a landing by a small force in Devon at the time of the '15 rising but was betrayed by his own confidential agent, Colonel Maclaine, and had to return to France without even disembarking.

Macky, who had given yeoman service to the government on the southern coasts, was another who came unstuck as a result of the attempted manipulation of the succession before Anne's death. His espionage became too successful for his own good: he learned that a boat had arrived at Calais secretly and dutifully passed the information on to Bolingbroke, who ordered him to keep his mouth shut about what he had heard. What Macky did not realise was that this part of the Tories' restoration plan and this mysterious boat had arrived to bring some of their fellow conspirators to England. On learning that the boat had returned to Deal with three persons on board, all carrying passes issued by Bolingbroke, and that one of them was none other than the Abbé Gaultier, who was deeply involved in the negotiation of the Treaty of Utrecht, Macky could not resist dashing to Canterbury to tell the Duke of Marlborough what he had discovered. Marlborough passed the information back to Bolingbroke, and when the Secretary of State discovered 'who had laid the Train that sprang to Mine' – Macky's own description of his action – the Inspector of the Coast was threatened with hanging. In the end his life was spared, but his packet-boat contract was taken away and he was thrown into prison where he remained until George I's accession. He was eventually given the Dublin packet-boat contract but that earned him so little that he ran into debt. Such was the security that moles enjoyed in the espionage business.

After Anne's death Bolingbroke advised James against an immediate attempt on the throne but the decision was taken out of the Pretender's hands by the Earl of Mar, who richly earned his nickname 'Bobbing John' and his reputation of being a traitor to the Cause. Mar had helped to put down the 1708 rising, but now crossed over to the Jacobites and, without waiting for the right moment, raised King James's standard at Braemar in August 1715. Within weeks he had gathered an army of 12,000 clansmen, but then he sat down at Perth to await the arrival of the King. A small group that marched south was defeated at Preston while Mar's own army neither won nor lost a running fight at Sheriffmuir in November. By the time James landed at Peterhead more than a month later the '15 rising was all but over and there was nothing left to do but return to France.

The retribution that followed the '15 was a rehearsal for the aftermath of the '45 – more than a score of nobles were attainted and lost their lands, several being brought to trial for treason. The Earl of Derwentwater and Viscount Kenmure were executed and the Earl of Nithsdale only escaped the execution block because his wife, having petitioned the King without success, helped him to escape from the Tower of London dressed in women's clothes. Prisoners taken at Preston were tried at London and Liverpool and, to the outrage of Scots, those captured in Scotland were marched across the Border to Carlisle for trial. Many were executed.

It took a further four years to find a 'sponsor' for another attempt. By sheer bad luck Louis XIV died at about the same time as Queen Anne, and the Duc d'Orléans, who became Regent to the young King Louis XV, had no desire to stir up trouble with the old enemy so soon after the end of the War of the Spanish Succession, and the long, wasteful campaign against Marlborough. At last, in 1719, the Pretender found new sponsors in Charles XII of Sweden, who had his own quarrel with the Hanoverians and disliked them intensely, and Philip V of Spain. Both agreed to support another invasion attempt but, unfortunately for James, Charles XII died and it was left to Spain to mount the expedition of 1719. There was to be a landing in north-west Scotland led by Earl Marischal, coupled with a rising organised by the Earl of Lucan in Ireland and an invasion in the west of England.

The Stuarts never had luck with seaborne attacks, and the '19 invasion was no exception: a terrible storm off Cape Finisterre destroyed part of the fleet, and damaged the rest of it so badly that all it could do was limp back to Spain. As a result the '19 amounted to no more than a small rising in the north of Scotland, which was quickly brought to an end by a battle at Glenshiel. James rushed to Corunna enthusiastically as soon as he learned of the planned expedition, only to arrive in time to see the half-wrecked invasion fleet returning to port. It was the last major attempt in which James was to be involved personally.

From then until Prince Charlie raised the standard in his father's name in 1745 the Cause lay virtually becalmed through twenty despairing years during which no military attempts were made to oust King George I or – after 1727 – his successor, George II. In England the Cause was left largely to claret-drinkers, lawbreakers, smugglers or others looking to the main chance to claim to be acting on behalf of the King over the Water. In Scotland there was a sullen quiet but the Stuarts were not forgotten.

Alas, from the start to the finish of the Jacobite century the Kings over the Water faced many hurdles in the way of their return but none higher nor harder to clear than the varying degrees of enthusiasm with which each faction of their supporters wanted to see them restored. Each and every group of followers had its own agenda right from the day James II sailed to France – Roman Catholic hearts were set on creating a Catholic monarchy; high Anglican churchmen could not bring themselves to swear an oath of allegiance to the new King and Queen; Tory landowners opposed increasingly oppressive Whig control; Whigs loathed the treachery they fancied they saw in the soul of every Tory; and there were far too many people around with nothing to do but cause mischief. These were joined by the idle rich, the idle poor and the criminal classes, all of whom had something to gain from paying their own peculiar form of allegiance to the Stuarts – money, in many cases!

The only factor common to supporters of each faction was self-interest, which led to betrayal and distrust that ran through British and Jacobite politics. The exiled King James and then his son, Charles Edward, faced a constant stream of complaints from Highland chiefs and Lowland lairds who carried on their age-old internecine feuds, which could go as far as to betray comrades who were fighting for the same cause. Lord Lovat's sense of grievance has been described as 'one of his best-developed faculties'.[5] His sense of having the world against him drove him from one side to the other and, coupled with his determination to support the winner of the Jacobite war, it led him to the execution block in the end.

With so many malcontents at large in England as well as in Scotland, it is hardly surprising that there were plenty of people ready to turn a dishonest penny spying for the Pretender and as many again simply bent on creating trouble for the government by living riotously, stirring up discontent and meeting in secret to drink the exiled King's health. This undercurrent of dissatisfaction played an important part in keeping Jacobitism alive from the birth of the movement right up to Prince Charlie's rising in 1745, although it did little to further the real hopes of the Pretenders. Naturally, such simmering rebellion also provided the government with a weapon to use against them.

At the core of this dissent in the south after the Revolution was a large number of James II's army officers who had lost their commissions and officials dismissed by the new regime. It has been estimated that as many as a third of these cashiered army officers followed the exiled King James II to Ireland to fight for him there, or to Europe in the hope of joining the Jacobite court at Saint-Germain or of being given a commission in the French army or the armies of Spain, the Empire, Sweden and Russia. James Keith, a son of the great Marischal family from north-east Scotland, achieved high rank in both the Russian and Prussian armies; a descendant of Aeneas MacDonald – a man who helped to arrange Prince Charlie's escape over the sea to Skye with Flora MacDonald – became one of Napoleon's most famous marshals; others served with honour in the Scottish and Irish Brigades in the French army and faced their own countrymen in Flanders and in Scotland during the '45 rising. And for the remainder of the century, whenever France was at war – which was often as Britain was 'the enemy' much of the time – they fought under the French flag.

Other exiled supporters of the Cause made new lives for themselves across Europe as diplomats, bankers, teachers and merchants, who made great profits in trade, both legitimate and privateering. George Keith,

10th Earl Marischal, who led the '19 rising, was Prussian ambassador to France during the 1750s, while the Waters family were the Pretenders' bankers, and two Irish Jacobite merchants, Antoine Walsh and Walter Rutledge, lent Charles the ships which took him to Scotland at the start of the '45. Walsh also arranged the Prince's rescue at the end of the rising a year later. All along the northern coast of France and Spain displaced Jacobites lived and worked as traders, just as French Huguenots had settled in southern England during the previous century.

An underclass was born out of the Glorious Revolution in England among the cashiered officers and although they were not all poor, since a number were the younger sons of aristocratic families, they had too much energy and time on their hands and consequently caused great trouble for the authorities. Their exploits were widely reported in newspapers of the day and much talked about, thus providing the government with a valuable propaganda weapon against the Stuarts.

They set out to shock, and succeeded, especially when the government presented itself as a holier than thou, pure (and puritanical) body. And not surprisingly, they became caught up in plots against King William, often not so much from conviction but rather to make 'flamboyant gestures, and from their love of intrigue and violence'. Writing of the notorious 1696 Turnham Green plot to assassinate King William, Paul Kléber Monod comments: 'The assassins were products and victims of a swashbuckling Cavalier mentality, and their plot was the finale of a drama they had been acting out for years.'[6] Yet, although ten or so were executed following the failure of the attempt on the King's life, the plotters could by no means be dismissed merely as a discontented band of underworked young captains cashiered from the army. Their riots and posturing reflected a genuine wish to have their king – and their commissions – restored.

Between the extremes of hot-headed poverty-stricken young troublemakers and such public figures as Bolingbroke and Marlborough whose double-dealing was all too evident, Jacobites in England and Wales came in many political shades and degrees of commitment: the trouble was that no one group would trust or confide in another.

Even the Church was riven from top to bottom when more than 400 clergy refused to take an oath of allegiance to William and Mary because it meant breaking the oath they had previously taken to James. A number of bishops, including the Archbishop of Canterbury, William Sancroft, were among those Non-Jurors who refused to accept the new regime, and the Bishop of Chester actually chose to follow James into exile because of it. The great majority walked out of their rectories and vicarages to face poverty and want, an action which Sir Charles Petrie, an historian of the Jacobite movement, called one of the great sacrifices in the entire history of the Jacobite century. The Church of England had seen nothing like this before and has seen nothing comparable since. In fact in the whole of Britain the only similar mass exodus was that of Scottish ministers at the great Disruption of 1843. In a quieter, but equally selfless, way, the Episcopal Church in Scotland, which was disestablished at the Revolution, continued to pray for the Stuarts until 1788 when the succession of the Pretender's younger son, a Roman cardinal, proved too much even for these staunch loyalists and the name of George III was substituted in relevant prayers.

From the first the Jacobites provided a popular 'cause' for all who felt unfairly done by as a result of the Glorious Revolution, and there were riots and disorders in many parts of the country, which Tories often encouraged in order to annoy their Whig opponents. Bristol saw some of the worst of these demonstrations, which went so far that supporters of the exiled King James rang bells and danced in the streets when they heard of the death of Queen Mary. As the Whig city fathers prepared to celebrate the accession of George I 'a horde of colliers, hired for the purpose and primed with liquor by some fanatical Tories, burst into the city, where they were joined by great numbers of the lowest class, and soon worked serious havoc to the cty of "Sechaverell and Ormond, and damn all foreigners"'.[7] Similar riots took place in other English towns as far apart as Norwich and Taunton, and George's coronation sparked off further demonstrations. During an election the following year Bristol 'was still seething with faction and disorder'.[8]

Rather than genuine pro-Jacobite demonstrations, many of these marchings and counter-marchings were nothing more than Tories baiting Whigs, shouting, damaging property, sometimes injuring those who opposed them and singing old songs from Civil War days – 'The King Shall Enjoy his Own Again' was always popular at King James's birthday. Effigies of the villains of both sides were burned publicly, but it is hard to know just how much some of the dissidents really wanted the Stuarts back, or if they were simply making a protest against the establishment.

Manchester became a notorious Jacobite centre, and Oxford was convenient enough to London for dissidents in fear for their lives to slip away and find shelter there, but there was trouble all over England throughout the Jacobite century, often tied to Jacobite or Hanoverian anniversaries or to discontent over some local complaint totally unconnected with politics. Typical of these was an incident at Harwich in 1724 when the anniversary of the King's succession was being celebrated by the mayor and members of the council in the Guildhall. 'A great noise and huzza' was heard in the street and when the councillors rushed to the window they saw 'a person dressed up with horns and carried on People's shoulders attended by a mob to a number of 100 persons.' Someone rushed out and pulled the 'devil' down, only to discover it was a local sailor named John Hart.[9] Hart's fate is not recorded but he was no doubt severely punished, for to speak well of the Jacobites or ill of the Hanoverians anywhere in Britain during this time was a serious offence punishable by imprisonment, fines, the pillory or whipping. Even that failed to silence those who resented the new regime.

Britain simmered with dissatisfaction from end to end, but while the Pretender provided malcontents with a vehicle to display their dissent, he did not give them the focus they needed to change their government or king. Perhaps he could never have achieved that focus since the time was not ripe for the Jacobite movement or any other organisation to produce its own internal revolution within Britain. One historian has suggested that the Cause was too far ahead of its time historically to succeed. 'A genius at political mobilisation could, in another era, have welded together an overwhelming anti-regime coalition from the disparate "out" groups who were prepared to see the "Pretender" back on the throne,' wrote Frank McLynn, 'but the capacity for forming mass movements did not appear in European history until the French Revolution. It would be truly anachronistic to look for such a capability during the Jacobite century.'[10]

In other words, a cruel mistiming by history was added to the Pretenders' many other misfortunes – their inbred defects of character, their penchant for making wrong decisions, their ability to choose the least able leaders and fall out with the best ones, all militated against them. Added to that was the ill luck of requiring the support of an ally in Europe, which gave the Whigs yet another propaganda weapon against them.

The Jacobites were identified with Britain's enemies abroad. But when they found an ally to support them the Stuarts still failed: even with the power of France or Spain behind them, the Royal Navy wrecked every seaborne invasion attempt, ably assisted by those contrary Protestant winds that seemed to blow up in the English Channel or Atlantic just as French or Spanish fleets put to sea. The Stuarts were indeed unlucky to have genes, allies, enemies and even the weather against them. Few royal houses met such unending misfortune.

With so many uncontrollable factors to hinder them, the Pretenders needed unity within the movement, but they were denied that too. They always faced that insuperable problem of a unifying aim to weld their followers into a single force which would provide momentum that could overthrow the might of Hanover.

That did not mean the Stuarts had no friends in Britain: even after the Whigs held power securely there were many who would gladly have seen the back of German George, and might just have been tempted to accept a return of the Stuarts.

And so it remained for the next twenty-five years up to the time Prince Charles Edward arrived in Scotland in 1745. If every person in Britain who would gladly have seen the back of King George had rallied to their support in the intervening years or to their standard when the rising broke out, the ancient royal house could probably have been restored. Had those who took pledges of support to the Pretender's court in exile, or who sent him money, fulfilled a fraction of their promises, the Germans might well have been packed back to Hanover a dozen times over. But the truth was, too many paid no more than lip service to the

Cause and lifted nothing more than a glass of wine to drink to the health of the King over the Water.

Ireland and Scotland each had their own national agenda, which was coloured by the fact that they were thoroughly disliked by the English. Ireland remained strongly Catholic, and her people had not forgiven England for having confiscated so much of her land and forced her people to leave during the seventeenth century. The final defeat of the Jacobites by William at the Boyne and Limerick completed the 'flight of the wild geese', which deprived the country of natural leaders. As a result Ireland might have been expected to be the most disaffected part of Britain during the Jacobite century, but with a large British army presence and without its land resources or pro-Jacobite leaders, the island remained quiet while virtually all the action to restore the Pretenders was confined to Scotland. The 'wild geese' provided a ready-made nucleus of loyal subjects for the King over the Water, although it must be said that almost all put their own careers first and the Cause second – but then the same can be said of other supporters.

By the mid-point of the Jacobite century the Irish around Europe were legion, and their influence substantial. Four of the Seven Men of Moidart, who accompanied the Prince to Scotland at the start of the '45 were Irish. Sir Thomas Sheridan was one of the most honest and trustworty followers the Prince ever had: he had been one of the Prince's governors and his confidant throughout his youth. Charles trusted him and a close bond existed between them, but Sheridan was an old man by the time he stood at Charles's side at Culloden on 16 April 1746. Father George Kelly was an elderly renegade, an experienced hand at the spying and plotting game, who had acted as courier during previous plots. Sir John Macdonnell, an ill-tempered drunkard, was found a job as instructor of cavalry during the '45 campaign – although there was hardly any cavalry to instruct, which was perhaps just as well. And the last of the Moidart Irishmen was John William O'Sullivan, who had gone to France to study for the priesthood but became a tutor and then a soldier; Charles appointed him quarter-master and adjutant-general, a disastrous choice for O'Sullivan was not fitted for the job by training or natural ability. Charles showed great love for those Irishmen who surrounded him: they pleased him by giving him the answers he wanted to hear rather than the often unpalatable advice his dour Scots leaders offered. Small wonder then that the Scots had little time for them during the 1745–6 campaign.

The Prince's remaining companions on the voyage to Moidart were two Scots, Aeneas MacDonald, the Paris banker, who had an 'investment' in the enterprise, and the titular Duke of Atholl, who in theory should have been able to raise a large number of fighting men, and a single Englishman, Sir Francis Strickland, who came from Westmorland.

The Scots had many reasons for casting their lot with the Stuarts, but the single strongest strand, which ran all the way through Scottish society, was the loathed Treaty of Union. It drove diverse groups together, who could never have found common ground otherwise, to carry the movement through the first half of the century right on to the battlefield of Culloden. Yet, while Scots could always put forward a reason for supporting the Stuarts, they tended to split into factions just as the clans had quarrelled over the centuries. This bickering led to backbiting and betrayal and to chiefs running to the Pretender with complaints that they expected him to put right. Solomon himself could not have pronounced judgements to please them, and James Stuart was no Solomon. He could never have found a right time for them all to come together to fight for him as Charles Edward was to discover when he arrived among them in 1745. To the Prince's bitter disappointment, the clans who stayed at home were more numerous than the ones who rallied.

It is often suggested that in the '45 rising, the final great confrontation between the Stuarts and the Hanoverians, the Jacobite army was largely Highland and Catholic but the truth was very different. Protestants were in the majority, although their exact ratio to Catholics is difficult to assess since nobody took the trouble to count them. Even that enthusiastic young spy, John Home, a devout Presbyterian, who went out to Duddingston to count the number of soldiers the Prince had in his army when it was encamped just outside Edinburgh, did not differentiate. George Hilton Jones summed this up: 'The populace of the eighteenth century did not take time for study, but burned at once Pope, Devil, and Pretender without cogitation. Historians followed where party-writers led, and the myth of overwhelming numbers of Catholics in the party has come down to our own day.'[11]

Religion was an important force in the Jacobite movement when the time came to act for the King over the Water, but the Roman Catholics did virtually nothing for the Catholic Stuarts in 1745 – in fact the Presbyterians helped him more. The Episcopalians made the greatest contribution, as Prince Charlie's best recruiting ground lay in the Episcopalian heartland running from Montrose through Aberdeen and along the Moray Firth to Ross-shire, as well as parts of Perthshire, Angus and Fife, and south to the Borders. In Glasgow and the old Covenanting West support was meagre. Religion apart – and in the predominantly Protestant south of Scotland the Stuarts' Roman Catholicism was a strong motivator against Jacobitism – Lowlanders had a further incentive to make them wish Prince Charlie had never come: they were prospering economically, in spite of rumbling discontent over the 1707 Union and a malt tax, imposed because the southern government thought Scotland was not paying its share to the Treasury. This tax had caused riots in even sober, well-doing Glasgow, but even that was not enough to tempt the Lowlanders to defy the government and throw away their greater gains from the Union. Nevertheless, in relation to their numbers the people of the Lowlands did make a vital contribution to the '45 campaign by providing the Prince with a higher proportion of leaders than actual numbers of their fighting men justified.

When King James's standard was raised at Glenfinnan in August 1745, the Episcopalian clans were strongly represented, and Roman Catholic ones too. Among the clans who rallied were the Camerons, Mackinnons, MacLeans, Macphersons and many MacDonalds including Morar, Glengarry, Keppoch, and Glencoe, but within individual clans loyalties were divided, especially among the Gordons, Grants, Mackenzies, Murrays of Atholl and Mackintoshes. The Campbells and the majority of the MacLeods of Dunvegan and MacDonalds of Sleat in Skye followed their chiefs' lead and did not join the Prince. Clanranald stayed at home too in order to save his estates from being confiscated, as had happened in 1715, but he sent his son to join the prince. The Mackays, Sutherlands and Munros in the far north also stayed away, while in the middle sat crafty old Lord Lovat, waiting as always to choose the winning side. At Glenfinnan to watch the aged William Murray, Jacobite Duke of Atholl, raise the Stuart standard was Rob Roy MacGregor's son, James Mohr, who brought the Prince the good news that the MacGregors would join him, and at the same time collected every scrap of information he could to pass back to the government in Edinburgh, As usual nobody could be quite sure what side anyone was on – or indeed whether they were double-dealers assisting both.

The Mackintoshes were one of the divided clans, at heart Jacobite, but unable to come out for the Prince because their chief's Hanoverian sympathies had persuaded him to accept a commission in one of the recently-raised Black Watch companies. In his absence his wife rode around the country to raise 300 men for the rebel army and she entertained Charles at the clan seat of Moy Hall. The Atholl Murrays were another divided family, with two rival claimants to the chief's title. The man who raised the standard at Glenfinnan, the titular Duke William, who had been out in the '15 and '19 risings, had been attainted and deprived of his titles in favour of his younger brother, Duke James, a faithful supporter of King George. The Duke's second brother was none other than the best leader Charles Stuart ever had (and never appreciated) – blunt, outspoken Lord George Murray.

In spite of the failure of so many clans to follow the Prince, and the self-seeking of many of their chiefs that kept them at home, the '45 rising and the movement itself became identified as Scottish and Highland, perhaps due to the fact that the most colourful Scots on the Jacobite side were clansmen, and it was the Highlands that suffered the greatest and most lasting revenge of the southern government, which destroyed whole communities and the clansmen's way of life.

Throughout the century the word Jacobite was anathema to English ears, with all Scots assumed to be Jacobites and loathed accordingly. In spite of more than a century of shared monarchy, the age-old Anglo-Scottish enmity flourished, and continued to do so long after the Jacobite Cause was dead and buried. Nor was appalling treatment of Scots confined to the ignorant masses: in 1745, after Charles Edward made his triumphant entry into Edinburgh, a London Scot complained to Lord President Duncan Forbes about the treatment Scots were receiving in the south. 'I am really in deep distress,' he told Forbes. 'Already every man of our country is looked on as a traitor, as one secretly inclined to the Pretender, and waiting but an opportunity to declare. The guilty and the innocent are confounded together, and the crimes of a few imputed to the whole nation.'[12] He added that this attitude was not limited to the mob. 'I wish I could say that they were confined to the lower sort of people; but I must fairly own, that their betters were as much touched as they. Their reflections were national; and it was too publicly said that all Scotland were Jacobites.'[13]

A significant number of Scots *were* supporters of the Cause, but the great majority remained as loyal in 1745 as any Englishman: the trouble was that Scotland and England were countries with totally different outlooks that transcended complaints against the perceived injustices of day-to-day relations. The Scots tended to be dour, and the kirk spoke with a loud, joyless voice on many subjects – was Allan Ramsay not at that very time struggling to stop it from banning the theatre in Edinburgh? And did not Burns sing out against its stultifying narrowness only a generation later?

Of course genuine complaints could be made against the Scots, and Sir Robert Walpole, when he came to power in 1721, could find reasons to justify the introduction of an unpopular malt tax in Scotland, while at the same time considering Scotland so irredeemably opposed to his government that he gave her little in return. The truth was that Scots were laughed at as poor, ignorant and lacking in southern refinement – a view that seeped through every layer of English society.

A feeling of unease existed among Jacobites on the Continent, where followers had their own aims just as those at home did. Many had by now made careers for themselves and were to all intents and purposes Frenchmen, Spaniards, Germans or Italians. The Cause was no longer first on their list of priorities and while they still remembered the Pretender warmly and wished him well (and some even sent him money), it was no longer of vital importance to them that he should be restored.

There was still much coming and going between supporters in Britain and the Pretender's court, now at Rome, with the Highlanders quarrelling among themselves, and agents continuing to search out every detail, useful or otherwise, that might be of interest to report back to London. James's visitors from Scotland kept him informed of every scheme or scrap of news that reflected well on the movement, but what they told him tended to be tailored to fit what they thought he wanted to hear. And of course they brought their complaints too.

Life at the court always had a certain edge – a frisson of wariness which invariably permeated the King's presence as each man watched carefully in case he was losing out. Backbiting remained a part of life as his advisers eyed one another up like prizefighters, ready to light out whenever an opportunity presented itself. Back-stabbing too was the order of the day. This vein of downright treachery and unreliability was well established during the first five years of George I's reign when the Jacobite movement took on the shape that was to define it for the following twenty-five years until Prince Charlie arrived.

Meanwhile the Hanoverian government had much to feel contented about. Between 1715 and 1720 two attempts had failed, even when the Pretender found new friends in Sweden and Spain to support him. As for France, young Louis XV's ministers were as well disposed towards Britain as they were ever likely to be. But that was not how the Hanoverians saw matters in 1720; to them the French remained a threat, inactive at that moment, but always dangerous. With Britain looking more and more to trade and colonial power there was still much to fight about and the Jacobites were always useful as an excuse to attack the old enemy. At home, the Jacobite movement remained little more than a Cause to which the common people could turn when they had a grievance to air, but in higher echelons of society, among the nobility and political leaders, it was a weapon in their war against Whiggery. These were the opponents who were to prove harder to tame.

The government felt it could not relax, and politicians, hitherto only fearful of the Pretender, now became paranoid about the threat. Sir Robert Walpole now came to power, and began a great new campaign, which revolutionised the whole spy war and effectively silenced the Jacobites for the next twenty years.

CHAPTER THREE

Secrets of the 'Secret Man'

How can I learn Jacobite designs but from themselves?

Sir Robert Walpole on being asked why he employed Jacobites as spies.[1]

By the 1720s when the Tories had been proscribed and the Whigs held total power, James Stuart found that little had changed for his cause either in its military campaign or its espionage war. George I sat securely in London, although he still preferred to spend much of his time in Hanover which he always considered home. However, in spite of vast expenditure of cash and effort, his gathering of Jacobite intelligence was far from efficient. The truth was simply that spying on both sides remained as inexpert and undeveloped as it had been the day James II left England. Money ruled, and intelligence gathering was rotten with money-grubbers who cared little about which cause they supported, Hanoverian or Stuart, so long as they were well rewarded for their work. Blackmail, bribery and threats were the tools of information-gatherers, but as much information was acquired through careless talk, betrayal by outwardly loyal supporters, or from mistresses who were good listeners, as through clever intelligence-work. Few secrets could be kept for long.

The year 1719 brought bad news and good news to James Stuart: on his arrival at Corunna to join the Spanish expedition to Ireland and Scotland he found Spain's invasion attempt to help him had already failed. This disappointment was, however, more than compensated for by the arrival of a pretty young Polish princess, Clementina Sobieska, who became his wife. Clementina was rich and well connected, with aunts who were queens of Spain and the Holy Roman Empire and a sister married to the powerful Duc de Bouillon. The Pope was one of her godfathers.

The fillip the King's marriage brought to Jacobites everywhere was nothing to that which followed on the last day of 1720, when Clementina presented them with an heir who would carry the Cause into the next generation. The Stuart Cause exploded in joy as a royal salute fired from the Castel Sant'Angelo in Rome announced the birth of Charles Edward Stuart, the child who was to grow into the legendary Bonnie Prince Charlie. The message of the guns of Sant'Angelo resonated throughout the Catholic world and the Pope himself called at the Palazzo Muti to bless the child. In France ten-year-old king Louis XV danced for joy on hearing the news and in Britain there were many who drank secretly to the health of the new prince, and some who even whispered that one day this boy might come 'home' as their king.

The Hanoverians were much discomfited, and even an assurance from one of their spies in Rome that the baby was malformed and that his mother could never bear another child did little to cheer them. In due course both Charles and his mother proved the spy wrong – Charles turned into a lively boy and Clementina produced a second son, Henry Benedict, five years later.

No one was more acutely aware of the threat this new Jacobite generation heralded than Sir Robert Walpole, who became King George's most powerful minister less than a year after Prince Charlie was born. Walpole feared the menace of Jacobitism to an ever-growing degree, until his fear turned to obsession and then paranoia. As a result he began to build up an impressive 'espionage machine', which worked hard for him throughout Europe but nowhere more diligently than in Rome, where the closest Jacobite secrets were to be uncovered.

With an enormous shifting population of Jacobite sympathisers, King George's loyal subjects on the Grand Tour and churchmen visiting Rome or settled in the city, there were always plenty of sources of intelligence available to both sides but especially to the Hanoverians. The great problem was always to know who the traitors were, and for which side they were gathering intelligence. Abbé Grant was typical of many: Lord Elcho believed he was all things to all men, a Jacobite to the Jacobites, a Georgite to the Georgites, and an agreeable companion to everyone. The unanswered question is – was he one of Walton's agents?[2]

In discovering Walton, Walpole was blessed with great good fortune. John Carteret, Earl Granville, head of the Southern Section of the Foreign Department at the time, had recruited a German Baron, Philip von Stosch, as his agent there, and von Stosch – using the pseudonym John Walton – kept London informed of everything that happened at the Stuart court – and a great deal that never took place as well! The Baron had perfect credentials for a spy – he belonged to an old Silesian family, noble enough to provide him with introductions to important people, and he was an obsessive bibliophile and collector of manuscripts and works of art, so was able to mix freely in the gossipy, cultured, political world of Italy, where he was totally unscrupulous about the way in which he obtained both his artefacts and his information. The scale of his art thieving only emerged more than a century after his death when the Vatican discovered that some of the manuscripts from his collection, which it had bought from his heirs after his death, had actually been stolen from its own library in the first place.[3] Stosch was a plausible man, a Protestant, yet managed to wring a pension from Pope Clement XI, and mercilessly milked his Vatican friends, Cardinal de Polignac and Count Renato Imperialii, for information, which he passed back to London.

Sir Horace Mann, then British representative in Florence, was always suspicious of von Stosch, and although Walpole himself was happy to purchase works of art from von Stosch the collector, he never trusted John Walton the spy. Once he wrote of the Baron: 'Stosch used to pretend to send over an exact journal of the life of the Pretender and his sons, though he had been sent out of Rome at the Pretender's request and must have had very bad or no intelligence of what passed in that family.'[4]

Between them von Stosch and Cardinal Alessandro Albani covered both the Stuart court and the Vatican. Fed by stories circulated by members of the Stuart household, they kept London well informed. Mrs Sheldon, who became Prince Charles's governess, was in an ideal position to spread rumours about disagreements between the King and Queen over the bringing up of the child. Under the evil influence of the Earl of Mar – another of those overt friends who were secret traitors – she inflamed Clementina into new quarrels and sowed the seeds of the slander that James was having an affair with Marjorie Hay, the wife of his staunchest supporter in Rome. Rumours of adultery were nothing new – they had been blowing through the corridors of the Muti since the Pretender's marriage was months old – but Mar succeeded in reviving them through this sinister woman and von Stosch passed them on.

There is not a shred of evidence that James Stuart was ever unfaithful to his wife but that made no difference: at a moment when Clementina's mind was becoming less stable and she was turning manic depressive, such gossip undermined the marriage and led to quarrels, reconciliations and yet more quarrels until Clementina's mind snapped and she fled to a convent. Young Charles responded to the uncertain situation at home by throwing tantrums and becoming such a wilful child that he once mortified every Catholic Jacobite by refusing to kneel when presented to the Pope.

Eventually von Stosch was forced to leave Rome and settle in Florence, but from there he was unable to monitor the Pretender's movement and his reports from then on contained much fiction.

Diplomats at foreign courts remained the principal source of intelligence and counter-intelligence for all governments at this period, the efficiency of British intelligence being hampered by the inept manner in which foreign affairs were organised in London. Relations with overseas countries were run along much the same antiquated, inefficient lines as they had been since the reign of Henry VIII with neither a foreign office nor a foreign minister to coordinate policies and actions. Instead, responsibility was divided geographically between two Secretaries of State, each located in his own separate building and following his personally-inspired policies, with his own staff to implement them. The Northern Secretary had charge of Sweden, Germany, Poland, Russia and Holland, while the Southern Secretary's area of power ran through France, Spain, Italy, Portugal and Turkey. Home and colonial affairs were shared, and the senior of the two secretaries at any particular time gave orders to the Lord Lieutenant of Ireland. Separate Foreign and Home Offices were not established until 1782.[5]

In such a divisive climate, rivalry between the secretaries was inevitable, and the constant jockeying for supremacy led to ludicrous competition and bickering, with very little coordination of the King's policies. Once, early in Sir Robert Walpole's 'reign', the Northern Secretary, Lord Townshend, and Southern Secretary, Carteret, both insisted on accompanying King George on one of his frequent extended visits to Hanover, leaving the astute Walpole free to outmanoeuvre all three of them back home in their absence. Such a cumbersome, inevitably farcical system naturally led to inefficiency among envoys abroad, which was aggravated by the fact that they were given inadequate instructions or at times none at all.

The choosing of ambassadors was as eccentrically haphazard as the system, so it is hardly surprising that Britain's interests at the courts of Europe were often badly served by self-seekers ranging from ambitious men plotting to build a better future for themselves back home, to inadequate dilettantes for whom a stay at a foreign court was little more than an extended pause on the Grand Tour, during which they enjoyed a lavish lifestyle and indulged their interest as collectors of art and antiques.

However, an ambassador's life was not always easy, especially financially, since although salaries were usually paid, out-of-pocket expenses – which included the payment of bribes and rewards to spies for intelligence – often fell so far into arrears that envoys ran up huge debts. A British ambassador was once driven to sell a diamond and a gold snuffbox to meet his expenses and it was not unknown for others to be marooned abroad, unable to return home after being replaced, because they could not pay their debts to enable them to leave the country.

Jacobite sympathisers managed to infiltrate the system from time to time. Certainly George Hay, Earl of Kinnoull – brother of the Old Pretender's right-hand man, John Hay, Earl of Inverness – who was sent to Turkey as ambassador during a key period shortly before the '45 rising, had been imprisoned during the '15 rising, and was accused of involvement in a plot hatched by Bishop Atterbury and Christopher Layer in 1722. Perhaps the London government thought Kinnoull could do little harm politically by the 1730s when he was in Turkey because he had become a quarrelsome character by then, with a complicated personal life, 'fond of lying on a sofa with women', it was said.[6] Kinnoull was unique even by the standards of eighteenth-century diplomats: he did exactly as he chose regardless of orders from London and stayed on in Constantinople for the best part of a year after his replacement arrived in 1737, causing much bother to his successor.

Since an essential part of any ambassador's duties was the gathering of intelligence, Jacobite matters consumed much of every envoy's time. He was expected to bribe local officials, pay spies, compromise whoever had a secret of value, or simply wheedle confidential information out of vain nobles and politicians by flattery. And since government officials could often be bought easily, there was always plenty of intelligence to be had, some true, large amounts of it false, but every scrap of interest to London – especially if it concerned the Stuart Pretender. But there was little or no coordination between the foreign departments and those in Britain who could use the intelligence.

As the century progressed, the threat from the Stuarts showed no sign of receding, making the London government ever more nervous of new Jacobite threats to invade, until Robert Walpole became so obsessed that he began to build up a vast counter-espionage system and intercepted mail inside the country and between Britain and the Continent. All this cost money – vast amounts of it – for the ideologically-motivated spy was unknown in the eighteenth century. No agent risked his life simply out of patriotism, and 'amateurs' came expensive. The going rate for a single spy was several hundred pounds, four or five hundred if he was good at his work; thus the Northern and Southern Secretaries had to set aside large amounts to buy information and pay bribes. And in times of crisis spies cashed in and demanded more. At such times the intelligence purchased at such a high price was often inaccurate or worthless.

Censorship of correspondence was nothing new in the 1720s – it had been going on for centuries and William III had been well aware of its value – but Walpole developed and refined the practice to a remarkable degree as a highly secret arm of the Post Office, which was a royal monopoly. Under an official who was never named but was merely referred to as 'the Secret Man', Walpole operated both a Secret Office and a Deciphering Branch. Through this official, whose very existence was denied, he was able to intercept letters from suspected individuals, have them opened, copied, read and translated or decoded, then resealed and forwarded. The work was carried out so expertly that the recipients usually had no idea that the contents of their correspondence were known to the government, so they continued to use the same cyphers and special inks long after the Deciphering Branch had cracked the codes and discovered the secret of the inks.

William of Orange had done much to improve the breaking of codes and uses of special inks. He had been fortunate enough to inherit a deciphering genius, the mathematician, Dr John Wallis, who had served the Parliamentarians well in the Civil War; in the post-Glorious Revolution years he became the King's decipherer. But he was now an old man, so William ordered him 'to train a young man in the art of deciphering that it may not die with him'.[7] Wallis taught his grandson, and in due course the business of deciphering was taken over by Edward Willes, who was succeeded in due course by his own three sons and then his three grandsons. Willes, an Oxford clergyman, and Anthony Corbière gave expert evidence against Bishop Atterbury in 1722. Willes was well rewarded by a grateful government, who presented him with a rectory, then a canonry, a bishopric, and finally a tomb in Westminster Abbey. Corbière was given the lucrative sinecure of Commissioner of Wines Licences and was appointed naval officer in Jamaica, but never left England.

Helping the 'Secret Man' was a rewarding business for anyone with a nose for breaking a code. The family of decipherers provided the British government with a succession of experts who made the Jacobites' task of keeping secrets virtually impossible, even though the latter improved their skills in devising cyphers so successfully that Willes once complained that some letters were 'unusual and difficult and would take him two or three days to decipher'.[8] None the less, it has to be said that Wallis and his successors had such expertise that they could unpick even the most complicated of codes – although it sometimes cost days of work to do so. Wallis once toiled for three months over a single letter, and on another occasion took ten weeks to decode one.[9] In time techniques so improved that the contents of letters were often on the desks of the government in London as soon as, or even before, they were read by the recipient in another part of England and Scotland.

Aware of the decipherers' tricks, governments evolved ever more complicated cyphers, up to a couple of thousand characters in one case, but even so the codes could usually be broken quickly. Much money was spent on bribing officers in foreign post offices to obtain cyphers. This was a two-way traffic: 'During the years 1735 and 1736,' wrote postal authority, Basil Williams, 'it appears that Lord Waldegrave obtained ten cyphers from a clerk at the French Foreign Office, at the rate of 100 louis d'or for each cypher.' The tables were sometimes turned: about the same time, the Duke of Newcastle had suspicions that his cyphers had been obtained from a clerk in the office of Benjamin Keene, Minister in Madrid. The only safe course in such circumstances was to send despatches by special messengers or servants of the ambassadors, but even that was not totally secure. Mention is made in one despatch of *billets* from the French Chargé d'Affaires, 'taken out of Mr Coetlongen's pocket June 17th, 1737', by one John Hutchins.[10] If there was any suspicion that mail was being tampered with, a simple means of finding out was to plant a piece of false information in a letter and wait to hear from a mole at the recipient's office that it had been reported.

Special inks, which became visible when treated with acidic reagents or held close to a flame, were in popular use among Jacobite correspondents too. Walpole also employed these and to help his agents he had a corn-factor in Southwark, 'a person well affected', produce reagents 'which would make writing both invisible and visible again'.[11]

Spying was a dirty game, and in spite of all the secrecy, the work of 'the Secret Man' was known and disapproved of by Jonathan Swift who attacked the Secret Office and Deciphering Branch bitterly in *Gulliver's Travels*. 'It is first agreed and settled . . . what suspected Persons shall be accused of a Plot,' Gulliver explained:

> Then, effectual Care is taken to secure all their Letters and other Papers, and put the Owners in Chains. These Papers are delivered to a Set of Artists very dextrous in finding out the mysterious Meaning

> of Words, Syllables and Letters. For Instance, they can decypher a Close-stool to signify a Privy Council; a Flock of Geese, a Senate; a lame Dog, an Invader; the Plague, a standing Army; a Buzzard, a Minister; the Gout, a High Priest, a Gibbet, a Secretary of State; a Chamber pot, a Committee of Grandees, a Sieve, a Court Lady; a Broom, a Revolution; a Mouse-trap, an Employment; a bottomless Pit, the Treasury; a sink, a C–t, a Cap and Bells, a Favourite; a broken Reed, a Court of Justice; an empty Tun, a General, a running Sore, the Administration.

As for the cyphers themselves, Gulliver explained these:

> So, if I should say in a Letter to a Friend, *Our Brother Tom hath just got the Piles*, a Man of Skill in this Art would discover how the same letters . . . may be analysed into the following Words: *Resist, – a Plot is brought home – The Tour.*[12]

Mails from France, Spain, Prussia, Poland, Saxony and Sweden were all intercepted regularly and Walpole made good use of the services of Richard Wolters, a merchant in Rotterdam, who ran an espionage empire that stretched half way across Europe. Even after the '45 Wolters continued to intercept correspondence and supply London with information on the Jacobites from his correspondents in Paris, Madrid and every naval base between Ostend and Toulon.[13] Wolters's wife took over her husband's spy ring in 1770, but she was hardly a Louise de Kéroualle or a Madame de Tencin.

Walpole's success in trapping Francis Atterbury, Bishop of Rochester, one of those behind the Jacobite plot of 1722, turned him into an even more obsessive spy-catcher and, although it proved impossible to obtain a conviction against the bishop, Atterbury was forced to leave the country and settle in Brussels, from where Walpole continued to have his correspondence monitored through Wolters. Walpole even sent John Macky, still one of the chief spies in spite of the fall from grace at the time of Queen Anne's death, to Brussels specially to keep watch on him. Through Macky and an almost limitless chain of intelligence gatherers planted at every key point across the Continent, Walpole was able to monitor the gossip and plotting, not just of Atterbury, but of Britain's Jacobite enemies, right up the scale of Jacobite influence to Daniel O'Brien (Lord Lismore) and General Arthur Dillon, two of James Stuart's closest agents.

Walpole had many triumphs, but his greatest was probably the recruitment of 'Agent 101', a Frenchman whose real name was François de Bussy. De Bussy, a greedy young clerk in the French Foreign Office, had been recruited to the British secret service by the ambassador in Paris, Lord Waldegrave, who had lent him money. He was sent to meet Walpole 'as he spoke fluent English and Walpole bad French', and in return for £1,000 became a British agent. De Bussy was completely without scruple. Sent to Hanover in 1741, 'he reduced George II to tears for fear of an invasion of Hanover by a French army massed on its frontiers and bullied him into signing the convention affirming the neutrality of Hanover, a treaty he later disavowed under pressure from his English ministers when the threatening army was withdrawn'.[14] De Bussy cost Walpole a great deal of money in return for little useful intelligence, until a real threat came in the 1740s when he proved his worth.

Paris remained a key centre for the business of spying, and Sir Robert's brother, Horace Walpole, who was Britain's envoy in Paris, was a valuable recruiting agent for spies. Horace's successor was less skilful and among those he recruited were a Scotsman called Conna, who at the same time provided information to the other side, and a fire-eating Colonel Gamberini, who made great promises but had to flee the country when he called the Elector of Saxony an imbecile. Walpole was more successful with the Swedish ambassador, who passed on everything the French ministers told him.[15] Even ambassadors could be bought.

Walpole read every report that came in avidly, and was prepared to risk his personal reputation to meet his spies, or correspond with them. Once when asked why he employed a certain Jacobite he replied, 'Who should I employ else? How can I learn Jacobite designs but from themselves?'[16] But playing games with Jacobites was a dangerous business, even for a man as patently loyal as Walpole, so Sir Robert was always careful to handle every contact very cannily. He would invite them secretly to his home or hold hole-in-wall conversations with them in taverns and such unexpected places. That was how he hooked Colonel William Cecil, the Jacobite agent in London, to work for him when Charles Edward was growing up and during the period that Bolingbroke evolved a plan for James to renounce his claim to the throne in favour of the Prince of Wales, who would be brought up a Protestant in Switzerland. Needless to say the devout Catholic Pretender would have nothing to do with such an idea, but Walpole got wind of the secret scheme and persuaded Cecil to give his advice on the matter. Walpole and the Colonel met secretly, and of course the result was that Cecil was compromised into helping the British. It was a typical piece of Walpolery.

But espionage traffic was not all one way. The King in Rome had many contacts in England and Scotland, as well as a remarkably efficient network of informants throughout Europe. Money bought information, and there were few highly placed officials who did not have junior members of their staff or servants willing to sell intelligence. Sometimes even those in the highest places were not to be trusted: in London, Carteret himself was not free from suspicion, and doubt fell also on the Earl of Mar, that disastrous leader who wrecked the '15 rising and betrayed his former friends. Even during and after the '45 rising there were others who sold themselves to the enemy.

Walpole's counter-espionage work during the 1720s and 1730s made it much more difficult for James's supporters in both England and Scotland to organise a rising during the 1740s. The turning point in England had been the 1722 Bishop Atterbury/Christopher Layer Plot, which ended in the trial and expulsion of Atterbury and the execution of Layer. From then on, most of those who might have led the movement had to flee or lie low, terrified to lift more than a wine glass in favour of the King over the Water. Walpole did his work well and the movement in England was left without a single charismatic or even competent leader during those vital years. But absence of active Jacobitism did not mean the Cause itself was moribund in England or that it did not form a focal point of anti-Whiggism and political dissent. It did, especially among the land-owning classes. However, the bogey of the Pretender was used by Walpole and his successors to put such fear into supporters of the Cause that they were terrified to be seen to have close contact with each other, let alone with the Pretender in Rome. When rioting or civil disturbances broke out in London or the provinces, the Jacobites were blamed, which set the majority of the people more determinedly against the Stuarts than ever.

Throughout the 1730s there was plenty of political scheming in both London and Rome, with a steady stream of letters in cypher passing between the Pretender and English Jacobites. But it was a campaign conducted in whispers, rather than a beating of the drum by English Jacobites, who were always afraid they might be upstaged with a rising in Scotland without their being consulted. When a bewildered King James sent Colonel Arthur Brett to assess the situation in England, the reply he received was that, while the English leaders were 'as full of good inclinations as ever, it was absolutely impossible to form any plan of business with them'.[17]

Because of English half-heartedness James was forced to cast around Europe in search of backing in the 1730s but hard as he tried, one country after another from Spain to Russia refused to support a rising. As for France, there he was left in the wilderness by Louis XV thanks to old Cardinal Fleury, who blew hot and then cold on the Cause and never came forward with any help.

Yet Walpole's fears grew because, he said, the Pretender's supporters would not come into the open, but remained 'real but concealed Jacobites' while they hid behind the pretence of espousing liberty.[18] Walpole, despite all he had done to keep the Jacobites at bay over two decades, was forced to resign early in 1742, but even that brought James Stuart no nearer to his goal of restoration in England.

CHAPTER FOUR

Travellers and Fellow Travellers

To Gibbet and Gallows your Owlers advance,
That, that's the sure way to Mortifie France.

A 1701 verse quoted in the *Oxford Dictionary* definition
of the word owler: a smuggling Boat.

After the fall of Robert Walpole the era of the Pelhams began, and both Thomas Pelham, Duke of Newcastle, and his brother Henry proved earnest spy masters who continued the espionage practices Sir Robert had refined so carefully. A huge amount of Newcastle's foreign correspondence was devoted to spying and, like Walpole, Newcastle kept his own motley collection of spies in his pay with de Bussy one of his most prized operatives, especially after Cardinal Fleury sent 'Agent 101' to London, where he had the easy task of negotiating with his English paymaster.

Among Newcastle's other moles were two Italians, named Carracciolo and Platania, always referred to as the Sicilian Abbots, who had been thrown out of Spain by Queen Elizabeth Farnese when she thought they had become too great an influence on her husband, King Philip. From France the pair continued to keep the Spanish king informed until his wife discovered some of their letters in his pocket, but by that time the Sicilian Abbots had been recruited by Sir Robert Walpole's brother, Horace, then British representative in Paris. Horace Walpole arranged for the pair to make a secret journey to London, asking Newcastle to find lodgings for them near St James's or the Cockpit but adding that an upper storey would be quite good enough for them. Abbots, however valuable their information, clearly did not stand high on a social level. During the years leading up to the '45, these two provided excellent value in return for the 300 louis d'or a year they were paid by their masters in London. They not only uncovered invaluable information but also were skilled at giving sound political advice on both French and Spanish plans.

The English Channel was a busy stretch of water throughout the eighteenth century. It was filled with packet-boats carrying wealthy travellers on the Grand Tour, government officials, young men on their way to study in Europe or people simply making legitimate commercial journeys to and from the Continent. But it was also filled with small boats used by smugglers, spies or those escaping from justice in Britain, or – in the view of persecuted Jacobites – fleeing from the Hanoverian and Whig injustices.

These small vessels carrying forbidden passengers or contraband were known as owlers because, like owls, they moved under cover of night between places like Romney Marsh in Kent, or other secluded creeks along the southern coast, and France. The smuggling trade itself was known as owling, and the free traders who carried on the business, like their boats, were called owlers. From the seventeenth to nineteenth centuries there was a brisk secret trade with France in high quality English wool and even sheep; taxable goods came in the opposite direction. Rudyard Kipling summed up the owling trade in his 'Smuggler's Song':

Brandy for the Parson,
'Baccy for the Clerk;
Laces for a lady, letters for a spy,
Watch the wall, my darling, while the Gentlemen go by!

Owlers smuggled wool to France by night, and brought back French brandy, lace, tobacco, tea and other goods that were heavily taxed in Britain especially in times of war. Huguenots, who had settled in England to avoid religious persecution in France, ran much of the south coast trade with the help of their kinsmen across the Channel. In time, transporting Jacobite spies, money and illicit letters became a part of the free traders' business as well.

Large communities of expatriate Britons, most with strong Jacobite leanings, based in seaports all along the French Channel coast, were involved too, supported by French officialdom, which allowed them easy access to northern ports and turned a blind eye to their activities. The smugglers thus provided Louis with an inexpensive additional means of destabilising Britain at key moments to suit his own political and militaristic plans. This was especially true of the period around the time of Prince Charlie's '45 rising when the smuggling gangs stirred up considerable trouble in every coastal county from Kent to Dorset.

Smuggling and carrying Jacobites and intelligence was by no means confined to the southern-most counties of England, however. Both were practised from end to end of the country, especially by way of those offshore islands where tax laws were more lenient. The Channel Islands provided a base for the south, while the Isle of Man supplied north Wales, north-west England and southern and western Scotland. Anyone who was an enemy of England was readily helped in Ireland, so free traders were doubly welcome there – all of which made it hard for customs and security men to control illegal trading.

In the words of one authority, 'Foreign vessels, known as "*coopers*", lay for days off our south and east coasts, and even within the Tyne and Humber estuaries, acting as floating supermarkets. Although no statistics exist to prove it, it is believed that by 1740 something like a quarter of all Britain's overseas trade was being smuggled'.[1] One thing *is* sure, however: the smuggling trade was beyond price to the Jacobites.

Transporting spies, escapees and correspondence for the exiled Stuarts proved an even greater boon for smugglers than its mere earning power. This subversive trade helped to unsettle the London government, so the French authorities were always willing to encourage the owlers' trade. Nevertheless, the Channel coast was well guarded by the King's customs men and the sea was controlled by the Royal Navy, making owling always a perilous game. To be caught meant a grisly death on the gibbet – an innkeeper at Lydd, captured smuggling letters to the French fleet during the invasion attempt at the start of William and Mary's reign, was hanged, drawn and quartered. Others weighed up the risk but still considered it worthwhile because profits matched the dangers.

At the beginning of the eighteenth century most smugglers of Jacobites were 'loners', who earned a formidable reputation even among their colleagues. From 'Farmer' Hunt, one of the most notorious operators, to the Quaker woman from Wapping, whose boat was captured carrying letters from William Penn to the Pretender, carriers of secret cargoes, like spies, were in the business for one thing only – money. But there was a point beyond which even hard men like 'Farmer' Hunt refused to go: he told one of his passengers once that 'he would not be hanged for any B— in Christendom'.

Those who needed to deliver intelligence or counter intelligence to or from the Jacobite court at Saint-Germain were prepared to pay well for the owlers' service, and as for sympathisers who had to make a quick and surreptitious exit from England, the captains of the little boats could charge them sweetly. It cost the Earl of Ailesbury ten guineas for a passage to France, yet he had to lurk for ten miserable days on the coast waiting for a boat, with practically no food and only 'a runlet of thin gut wine from Calais, and sour, so I was forced to boil it'.[2]

Nobody was to be trusted, and even 'Farmer' Hunt once found himself kidnapped and spirited away to France by the Jacobites because they feared he would reveal too much if he was taken.[3] With such distrust among their own kind and their customers, as well as the Royal Navy controlling the English Channel and customs men watching every move made on land, the men and women who smuggled for the Jacobites remained in a high-risk business. Inevitably, the rewards attracted criminal gangs, so that by the 1730s the business had fallen largely into the hands of a series of mafiosi-type groups, powerful enough to take on the customs authorities in pitched battles. They were sympathetic to the Pretender's Cause, not from political conviction but because it was profitable to them, and the Whig government feared their power.

Alongside this clandestine traffic there was the steadily growing movement of legal travellers, especially students on their way to study at universities such as Leyden and Montpellier, or young men and women setting off on the Grand Tour, that great social phenomenon which burgeoned in the eighteenth century. Growing numbers travelled across Europe, sightseeing, visiting the courts of kings and princes, talking, viewing and buying art, whoring and spying. For them leaving England may have carried less risk but their voyage to Europe was not a great deal more agreeable than that of fugitives sailing in owlers. The packet-boats were uncomfortable and unreliable, and passengers often found themselves becalmed or blown off course by contrary winds so that the journey lasted many hours longer than expected. Seasickness turned even the calmest journey into a nightmare and many brave men who crossed the North Sea or English Channel were terrified by the propect of having to make the return journey.

Even though Europe suffered upheaval during the Jacobite century, with wars and all the fear the Jacobite threat whipped up in Whig governments, travel was seldom seriously curtailed. In times of war it still remained relatively easy for anyone, except perhaps a serving member of His Majesty's forces, to leave Britain. The only impediment was that if Anglo-French relations were strained or broken, it might not be possible to travel from Dover to Calais, so the crossing had to be made by the longer route to Ostend or from Harwich to Holland although, of course, many Scottish travellers made the journey by that route anyway, rather than by the way of southern English ports.

Passports or some form of permission was needed for many countries, especially those well disposed towards the Stuarts, but these seem to have been granted with little difficulty and travellers were seldom forbidden by governments. If trouble arose, it was usually caused by over-zealous officials at local level, rather than by actual government policy or intervention.

Even the old rival, France, presented few problems: in spite of Marlborough's wars and the Spanish and Austrian Succession Wars, there were relatively long periods of calm in Anglo-French relations – the years from 1716 till about 1740 were quiet. Calm, too, was much of the time after the end of the Austrian Succession War in 1748 when Prince Charlie was banished from French territory, and from the end of the Seven Years War in 1763 up to the French Revolution. At other times, even while Europe's monarchs were brawling with one another, tourism from Britain continued: in fact, travellers were even able to visit battlefields and watch battles!

Paris was a regular first stop for tourists, and when the British ambassador, Horace Walpole, gave a great feast there in 1728 to mark the birthday of the newly crowned King, George II, he commented that the company included 'fifty Lords and Gentlemen of the British Nation'.[4] Lord Waldegrave noted regularly in succeeding years that the town was swarming with English. There were sufficient women among them for him to add to his usual comment about the large numbers: 'This town swarms with English of both sexes.'[5]

Although they journeyed as far afield as Russia, Austria, Greece, Spain and Portugal, the goal for the majority was Italy, a long and difficult journey by way of Lyon, then down the Rhône valley and on by sea to Genoa, or over the Alps to Turin, which involved being carried across the mountain passes on a sort of sedan chair while the coach was dismantled and manhandled into Italy. It was a long, hard journey but well worth it for the many cultural experiences and art treasures to be discovered at its end. 'The appeal of Italy,' wrote Jeremy Black, historian of the Grand Tour, 'was composed of various factors: the opportunity for sexual adventures, the climate, devotional reasons for Catholics, and the variety of occasions for enjoyment that the tolerant and civilised society of Italy presented.'[6] Black did not add, though he might have done, '*and for Protestants to flirt with Roman Catholicism and the Jacobites*'.

Although visiting the Jacobite court in Rome was technically a capital offence under English law for a British traveller, no real obstacles were put in the way of the Grand Tourists who wanted to see the two handsome young Stuart princes. The only restraint was that they must meet them outside the Muti Palace, which was easily arranged by finding out where the Pretender and his sons were due to appear in public. It was in London's interest for British subjects to see Jacobites, since information they happened to bring back would be of value. No doubt hints were dropped that they should eavesdrop on gossip from the Muti Palace, and talk about more than art with von Stosch and others. But by and large travellers proved inefficient moles and uncovered nothing much of value.

London had little to fear from the Grand Tourists since few returned converted either by Catholicism or by the divine right views of the Pretender. In 1728 the London newspaper, *The Craftsman*, commented on the opinions of one newly returned traveller from Italy: 'I was extremely pleased to find, that notwithstanding his travels into countries of slavery and arbitrary power, he was still full of those noble and virtuous sentiments, which are so peculiar to us Englishmen and so much to our honour'.[7] The Grand Tour demonstrated that Britain was best.

Anyone brave enough to visit the Pretender's court was disappointed by the experience: both James himself and the Muti Palace in Rome and the castle at Urbino, where Pope Clement XI settled him, were boring in the extreme. Urbino was a fourteenth-century building superbly set among the Apennine hills but isolated from reality and Highlanders found the magnificence of the Apennine scenery no fair exchange for the mountains of their homeland. The Earl of Mar bemoaned the absence of the Highlands: 'The house is an excellent one,' he conceded, 'but for the part of the country it stands in there are few places of the Highlands of Scotland that are not champaign level countries in respect of it . . . walking about the large rooms and galleries of the house to me is a much more agreeable exercise.' The tedium of Urbino was broken only once, when the Earl of Peterborough turned up from England and a rumour spread that he had been sent to murder James. The Pope clapped the Earl in jail until the British government put pressure on him to release the prisoner. Eventually it was all found to be an unfortunate mistake.

In Mar's opinion eating at the King's table was far from pleasurable. 'We shall certainly grow very dull and insipid for want of a little good wine to enliven us, and even give a fillip to our spirits now and then,' he complained.[8] Back in Rome the Pretender was no better company even after his marriage to Clementina Sobieska. Visiting 'subjects' were granted audiences and often were invited to dine with the Pretender, but these royal dinners were neither generous nor jolly. James was not a drinker and, as the rule was that nobody drank before the King raised his glass, guests usually went short of wine. Conversation was equally meagre – and what there was of it was hardly nourishing. At Easter 1721 one young visitor on the grand tour accepted the royal invitation to dinner with James and Clementina in defiance of his father, who had warned him to avoid the Pretender's circle. He confessed his disobedience and described the event to his family:

> There is every day a regular table of Ten, or Twelve Covers, well serv'd, unto which some of the qualify'd Persons of his Court of Travellers are invited: It is supplied with English and French Cookery, French and Italian Wines, but I took notice that the PRETENDER Eat only of the English dishes, and made his Dinner of Roast Beef and what we call Devonshire Pie: He also prefers our March Beer, which he had from Leghorn, to the best Wines.[9]

By and large few travellers on the Grand Tour were spies, but their letters nevertheless provided interesting sidelights on life on the Continent generally and on Jacobite activities in particular. The Grand Tour 'spy' was an amateur, in the words of Frank McLynn, 'drawn into the secret service orbit . . . asked to keep his eyes and ears open and report on anything of interest he found on his travels. In this respect he was a close cousin of the twentieth-century Western businessman in Eastern Europe who "drops into" the embassy afterwards.'[10]

Although espionage was not the objective of the Grand Tour, there can be no doubt that young members of aristocratic families were asked quietly to keep their eyes open and report anything of interest they saw, and it provided part of the training of young men who would soon be in positions of power, probably even members of the government. As an opportunity to acquire political skills, spending time at foreign courts was invaluable – even a visit to the Stuart court in Rome provided useful experience. London, therefore, was never especially alarmed to learn of a visit to the Muti Palace by some young aristocrat to dine with the Pretender.

What did worry people back home much more was contact with the Roman Catholic Church. Young Protestant aristocrats were fascinated by Catholic ritual and relics, and a few even went so far as to be presented to the Pope. They were also not averse to admiring and buying religious paintings, many of which can still be found in great houses of Britain.

In the final analysis, antipathy to Catholicism was the prime force that worked against the Stuarts in Britain during the Jacobite century – it was the principal reason for the Stuarts losing their crowns in the first place, it was the cause of their rejection after Queen Anne's death, and it remained an insurmountable obstacle to the end. That, allied to their unshakeable belief in divine right, meant they were never to be trusted in Protestant Britain. Travellers were always astounded by the credulity of Roman Catholic believers, yet remained fascinated by the exiled Stuarts' religion.

While most grand tourists returned home convinced that the Protestant King George was preferable to Catholic James Stuart, there were a great many travellers who made the long journey across Europe specifically to pay homage to the King in Rome and to plot some means of restoring him. After the birth of Princes Charles and Henry, this journey turned into a kind of pilgrimage to venerate the new generation of the royal house. Visitors to Rome frequently brought the King encouraging news from Scotland and England, where, James was constantly assured, his Cause was in excellent heart, and he drank in all this gossip and intrigue – it was all the poor man had to encourage him after the failure of the Layer plot, since neither Spain nor France would agree to mount another attempt during that dead period between the early 1720s and 1740 in spite of all James's nagging and begging. His troubles multiplied when his marriage broke down and his wife left him to bring up his young sons alone. Then Clementina died in 1735, leaving him to dote on his sons, who were all he had left of his kingdom or family.

It was especially gratifying to the Pretender to find visitors admiring Prince Charles, now given the title Prince of Wales and growing into a fine young man: James watched proudly as the boy danced at court balls, handsome and resplendent in Highland dress sent from Scotland by the Duke of Perth. The spy Walton reported this sensation back to London immediately. And when Lord Elcho, roughly of an age with Charles, arrived in Rome in 1737, James made the two youths stand back to back and naturally the young prince stood proud as any Scottish chief.

Supporters saw what they wanted to see in Charles Edward, but there is no doubt that John Murray of Broughton spoke from the head as well as the heart when he said of the Prince, just turned twenty: 'There is indeed such an unspeakable majesty diffused through his whole mien, and such as it is impossible to have any idea of without seeing; and strikes those that have with such an awe as will not suffer them to look on him for any time, unless he emboldens them to it by his excessive affability.'[11]

At last John Gordon of Glenbucket brought news of burgeoning discontent in the Highlands and Lord Sempill, the Stuart agent in Paris, assured James that English Tories were also ready to rise, so the Pretender cautiously sent William Hay to Scotland to spy out the situation. The news Hay brought back simply dashed the Pretender's hopes once more – but not for long.

Europe was in ferment again, with the war of the Austrian Succession breaking out in 1739 and, although Britain was not involved at first, the turmoil did raise Jacobite hopes that she soon would be drawn in and that first Spain and then France might take up the Pretender's cause once more.

To prepare for such an eventuality Scottish Jacobite leaders formed an association of sympathetic leaders, but it was an odd assortment of 'loyal' chiefs – Lord Traquair who 'drank loyal healths enough to float a ship',[12] the bankrupt Campbell of Auchenbreck, William MacGregor, known as Drummond of Balhaldy because the name MacGregor was proscribed, Lord Lovat, who turned his coat several times to be sure of supporting the winning side but chose the wrong one in the end, and Donald Cameron of Lochiel, described as the only honest man among them. They were not an attractive bunch, and between them contributed little manpower, weaponry or money to the Jacobite Cause. In the words of Victorian historian Andrew Lang, 'The Scots were loyal, but, as a rule, would not part with a bawbee.'[13]

By the early 1740s, when the Prince came of age, James had a new concern – to find a wife for his son: but he had no more success in that than in preparing Charles for an attempt to recover his inheritance. James felt thwarted on every side when he found the outbreak of the War of the Austrian Succession brought neither help for a new attempt in Britain nor an opportunity for Charles to gain military experience in France or Germany. Apart from serving briefly alongside the Duke of Liria at the siege of Gaeta when he was only fourteen, the lad had seen no military service whatever and his father was desperate for him to do so as part of his training to prepare him to take over the Cause in due course. Nobody in the governments of Europe wanted the Prince as a soldier any more than they wanted him as a claimant to the British throne – least of all the French.

It was stalemate at every move until January 1743 when the aged French Cardinal Fleury, who had been the greatest obstacle to French backing for a new rising, died. Then everything changed to suit the Jacobites, not least when rumours arrived from England that a revolution might be on the cards provided the French weighed in with an invasion. James even hoped that Cardinal de Tencin, whom he had helped to win his cardinal's mitre, might be appointed one of Louis's key ministers and help him, but here again hopes were dashed when the wily French King began to ignore his ministers and run the country without them.

Jacobites, buzzing around the French court like flies, brought news that Scotland too was ready to rise, but all this to-ing and fro-ing led to backbiting among the Scottish leaders, especially between MacGregor of Balhaldy and Murray of Broughton, who became sworn enemies.

In England George II remained unloved apart from a brief moment of popularity when he led his armies to victory at Dettingen – the last battle in which a British king led his troops on the field – but that soon waned when he showed partiality to his Hanoverian soldiers over his British ones. In the light of what he was hearing, Louis decided to sound out the position in England for himself, so he sent his master of horse, James Butler, across under pretext of buying horses but in reality to talk to leading supporters of the Cause. Butler returned full of enthusiasm and confirmed that men like the Duke of Beaufort, Lord Orrery, Lord Barrymore, Sir John Hinde Cotton and Sir Watkin Williams Wynne were all enthusiastic about the Cause. What was not made clear was that, like many of the Scots, they were unwilling to raise men to fight. And they were every bit as canny with their bawbees.

Louis, however, believed what he heard and now made up his mind to invade England: the war was going badly for him in Germany, where his army had just been beaten at Dettingen, and he needed a 'new front'. Invasion of neutral England would suit him nicely and the Jacobites would lend credibility to the project. Louis liked his plan and set it in hand at once, without telling his ministers any more than was necessary and, of course, without informing the Stuarts in Rome in spite of the fact that they were to be a key element in the scheme.

Devious to the last, Louis set about orchestrating the scheme. As Charles Edward's biographer, Frank McLynn put it: 'The trick was to acquire the Jacobite manifestos and declarations to the people of England without having Charles Edward in tow. By a sleight of hand Louis could contrive it so that the prince arrived in Paris only after the expedition's commander-designate, the Comte de Saxe, had captured London. Charles Edward would then cross the Channel to ratify the French conquest.'[14]

Such a momentous scheme was not a secret which could be kept, especially in that sieve of insecurity, the French court, and soon it was known in Rome – in Britain too. However, Louis knew nothing of that.

Charles was desperate not to be left out of this wonderful opportunity to win back his father's kingdom but his father, suspicious to the last, cannily held back in case the French once again were using his Cause for their own selfish purposes and would let him down at the last minute. That set the scene for one of the greatest pieces of double-crossing and double-double-crossing in which the Jacobites and their French friends indulged during the entire Stuart century. In retrospect it all looks petty, but it achieved much for both: it diverted the British to permit Louis to pursue his campaign to grab more land in Flanders and it provided Charles Edward Stuart with the opportunity to mount what is arguably the greatest attempt the Jacobites were to ever to make to win back their inheritance. The '45 rising arose directly from trickery of 1744 – and the Scots have a word for that, *joukery-pawkery*.

Balhaldy was to be Louis's go-between. The French king decided to send him to Rome with news of the plan and an invitation for Charles Edward to participate – but only when the time was right. In fact, at this stage the French King wanted nothing more than the Stuart King's approval and he had no intention of setting a date for the Prince to come to France. He wanted nothing in writing and refused to give Balhaldy so much as a letter to take to Rome. Naturally Balhaldy was unhappy about the vagueness of the message he was instructed to take to the Pretender, especially the vagueness of the timing of when Prince Charles was to come to France. Louis would not be drawn further, but eventually the French Foreign Minister, Amelot, mentioned when pressed that if the Prince wished to make his way to Paris on his own after 12 January 1744, he was free to do so. With nothing more than that vague date, plucked from the air by the minister, Balhaldy set out on the difficult winter journey via Switzerland and across the Alps, the route on which he was least likely to be seen by British agents. He arrived in Rome shortly before Christmas 1743 and James drafted a declaration of regency in favour of his son, as the French asked. But doubts remained: James still wanted some written commitment from the French King. 'He dashed off a letter to Louis, thanking him for Balhaldy's message and telling him he had postponed Charles Edward's departure until he got a clearer light from France,' McLynn writes. 'Here was another error. If James had written directly to Amelot, he might have received an express from the Foreign Minister, telling him on no account to send the prince. But this letter to Louis was never answered, either through the king's indolence or because the missive got snarled up in French bureaucracy (either is plausible).'[15]

Charles, now twenty-three, was to have a say in his father's affairs and he refused to wait for the French reply – 12 January had been mentioned and in any case Balhaldy believed the French meant business this time, so he would go to Paris and he would do so now. James gave in and in great secrecy plans were laid. The first problem was to decide by which route he should travel since it was winter and the Alpine passes would be almost impassable: worse, much of northern Italy was virtually closed to travellers because plague was raging all through southern Europe at the time. In the end it was decided that Charles should travel overland to Genoa, then by sea to Antibes and up the Rhône Valley to the French capital.

The ground for the 'escape' was prepared during the first days of the new year by arranging for the gates of Rome to be opened for Charles whenever he went hunting at any hour or the day or night. That would enable him to slip out of the city at a time when he was least likely to be observed. As the hunting season was due to begin on 9 January and the Duke of Caserta had invited Charles to hunt on his lands, members of the Prince's household were sent ahead on 7 January to prepare for the Prince's arrival. Naturally, he let his intention to go hunting be known openly, so it would reach the ears of Mann, the British agent in Florence, quickly. On the following evening Charles took supper with his brother, then announced that he intended to leave before first light and that he proposed to retire early. The early departure was no surprise as it was well known that Charles Stuart never needed much sleep They would meet at Cisterna in a day or two he told Henry. Instead of going to bed the Prince slipped to his father's room by a secret passage and there they said their farewells. That was the last time father and son were ever to see each other.[16]

As arranged the Porta San Giovanni was opened without questions to allow the post-chaise in which the prince rode with his old tutor, Sir

Thomas Sheridan, to pass out of the city, escorted by one servant, Stafford, and a groom, Vivier, who led three black horses. No sooner were they safely through the gate than Charles ordered the chaise to stop and announced to Sheridan that he intended to ride to Albano first and then across to Cisterna. Sheridan argued that this would not be wise and a loud discussion followed, every word clear enough to be heard by the postillion and members of the Prince's staff. It was all part of a carefully stage-managed plot to put agents off the scent – and exactly the kind of subterfuge that Charles Stuart relished. Shouting that he would be in Cisterna ahead of his tutor, Charles rode off into the dark morning, Stafford at his heels, clearly making for Albano.

A little further along the road Charles changed clothes with Stafford and, while the servant hurried on to Frascati, the Prince rode all the way round the walls of the city, across the Tiber and on to Caprarola, where he met up with the groom, Vivier, as had previously been arranged. Charles had left by the southern gate of the city and was now riding northwards – he had covered forty miles but was still able to change horses and set out for Massa without rest.

Sheridan arrived at Cisterna but of course found no Prince of Wales awaiting him and even after Henry joined him there was no sign of Charles. Only old Tom Sheridan knew the reason but he kept it to himself. Then Stafford joined them with the news that his master's horse had fallen at Albano and the Prince had suffered a bruised rib so would have to rest for three days. Just to make the story sound more plausible he produced a note from Charles asking Henry not to worry their father with news of the accident because the King was a worrier, always warning his son about riding on dangerous Italian roads, and now would say I told you so.

While Henry waited at Cisterna Charles himself pushed on with Vivier to Massa, then over treacherous icy roads to Genoa, which he reached on 13 January, only five days after leaving Rome. He had ridden close on 300 miles without change of clothes, with only a few hours' sleep and nothing but a few eggs to eat. Long days of riding and hunting in the hills around Rome and Albano had prepared Prince Charles well for the challenge of this, his first attempt on his father's kingdom.

Unfortunately his route to Genoa took him through Florence, where the Austrian Minister, Count de Thun recognised him and tipped Horace Mann off. The news went off to London in a letter written on 21 January,[17] but by that time the Prince was practically in Paris. The marvel is that in Italy, a country thick with spies waiting to report every breath the Pretender and his sons drew, everyone failed to catch up with him until he was beyond Florence. Perhaps the description Mann sent to London and no doubt circulated to his acolytes threw all the British agents off the scent. 'The young man is above the middle height and very thin,' he wrote. 'He wears a light bag-wig. His face is rather long, the complexion clear, but borders on paleness; the forehead very broad, the eyes fairly large, blue, but without sparkle, the mouth large, with the lips slightly curled, and the chin more sharp than rounded.'[18] Or perhaps the suggestion of that lack of sparkle misled his enemies, for Charles's eyes must have shone at that moment with the thrill of the chase.

At Finale on the coast north of Genoa, Charles tried to hire a *felucca* to take him to France but every vessel there was stormbound, so he had to push on to Savona where he at last found a captain willing to take him – ironically, a man based at Finale, so there was no option but to return there! It took almost a week for the storms to abate sufficiently to enable him to bribe the captain with extra money to leave and they reached Monaco on 21 January.[19] But by this time the British had managed to get the news to Admiral Thomas Matthews, the irascible 68-year-old seadog who had been dragged out of retirement to command the Royal Navy fleet in the Mediterranean and was busy playing cat-and-mouse with the French and Spanish fleets anchored in Toulon. Matthews broke off his watch at Toulon to go after this better game.

Friends and enemies alike had been totally outmanoeuvred by now, giving the Prince a good start; to their credit both his father and old Tom Sheridan had played their parts superbly, so well that even Prince Henry was taken in by the tale of the riding accident and in Rome everyone, from British and French spies right up to the Pope himself, was flabbergasted to learn what had happened. The leading British spy, Mann, was the most confused of all and in desperation clutched at every straw that blew past his windows. He sent message after message, never coming anywhere near to the truth: at first Charles was on his way to serve with the Emperor's army in the Austrian Succession War, then he was to join a French invasion of Scotland. He went further off the mark with a report first that Charles's bride was to be the French King's daughter, then the Princess of Modena. But he was wrong every time.[20]

By the time the Prince was making his way along the Mediterranean coast, however, the hounds were closing in and he had a narrow shave as he approached Antibes. While he was delayed by yet another storm, the British followed him, coming so close that by the time he entered the port of Antibes one of the Royal Navy pinnaces was within hailing distance of his little *felucca* – so close that at one point it nearly collided with the stern of the Prince's boat.

The pursuit, and the arrival of two vessels in a port quarantined because of the plague outbreak, caused such a stir in Antibes that de Villeneuve, the port Governor, rushed down to the harbour to investigate the instant he learned the identity of the new visitor. Fortunately it had not occurred to Paris that the Prince might take this route – indeed, they had not expected him to leave Rome at all as soon as he did – so no instruction had been sent to Antibes advising what to do if he turned up in the port. Quick thinking by the Prince saved the day: he told the governor that a great secret would be revealed to him if he would just get rid of the British pinnace. Governor Villeneuve made the judgment of Solomon – he ordered both to leave, but the pinnace should depart first because he had further inquiries to make concerning the *felucca.*

With the pinnace gone, the Prince explained the reason for his urgent journey to Paris, so the governor immediately arranged for him to transfer to a larger ship, which was fortunate since yet another British ship now arrived in port, pretending to need to revictual. While supplies were being loaded Villeneuve acted out a charade so similar to the one Charles used to fool the authorities at the gates of Rome that the Prince must be handed the credit for thinking of it. He furiously demanded that the *felucca* should leave at once and when the British vessel had completed loading she set out in pursuit of the poor *felucca* captain. She was chased all the way back to Monaco only to find no Prince on board. Poor Matthews resumed his blockade at Toulon and when the enemy fleets emerged a fortnight later he engaged them. In the fight at Huyères his second-in-command, Richard Lestock, who was barely on speaking terms with the admiral, ignored Matthews' signals and the enemy escaped. Matthews and Lestock were both court martialled and the admiral was cashiered from the navy at the age of seventy-one. Lestock, who was mainly at fault for the débâcle, was honourably acquitted.

While Matthews returned to his war with France, Spain and his fellow admirals, Charles sat safe at Antibes but not free, for Villeneuve decided to detain him while he sought instructions first from his immediate superior, the Marquis de Mirepoix, then, after he had come to realise the importance of the Prince's arrival, from Foreign Minister Amelot in Paris. The Prince's luck held. Mirepoix's reply arrived first and said simply that the Prince should be held for the regulation eight days' quarantine, thereafter he was free to depart. That was enough for Charles Stuart – using his tremendous powers of persuasion he prevailed on the governor not to wait for Paris's answer, but to allow him to leave and he was on his way at first light on 29 January. King Louis had been outmanoeuvred once again.

A superhuman race up the Rhône followed – all day and all night the Prince rode to Aix-en-Provence almost without pause, then on to Avignon and Lyon, where he arrived on 3 February, but again was on his way before dawn the following morning. He arrived in the French capital on 8 February, in his own words *rendu,* but triumphant

Paris was as astounded as Rome to learn the news – but, while ordinary people in the city went mad with joy over the unexpected arrival of this hero prince, King Louis and those in on his plan were appalled that Charles's arrival might wreck the whole secret of their scheme, which was now at a very delicate stage involving English Jacobites. But with such acclaim for the Stuart heir in the streets of Paris, they had no option but to go through the motions of welcoming him. Charles was probably too tired and too excited about the prospect ahead to appreciate the delicacy of the situation. However, had he done so, it would have made little difference. He would have been too impetuous to care.

Preparations for the invasion were well under way on both sides of the Channel now. As part of the French scheme, attempts were made during the early part of 1744 to destabilise England further by encouraging those smugglers along the English south coast who had been so useful in the early days of the movement. Now, using France's northern ports, free traders were able to operate more openly and declare themselves so pro-Jacobite that John Collier, Surveyor-General for Kent Customs, was told by his clerk in May 1744 that smugglers in the area had been 'so impudent as to publicly drink to the Pretender and his sons' health, and wish success to their arms and confusion to his Majesty's King George'.[21]

Smuggling by now had become so profitable it was no longer simply a business for enterprising individuals; yet it is questionable exactly how closely it was linked to the Cause. Illicit trade certainly fed upon Jacobitism and vice versa, so that together they frightened the authorities to the extent that in 1745 Admiral Vernon complained that 'this smuggling has converted those employed in it, first from honest industrious fishermen, to lazy, drunken and profligate smugglers, and now to dangerous spies on all our proceedings'.[22] That may have been something of an exaggeration but it does demonstrate the depth of fear which prompted the British to deploy several army units to the Channel ports.

Law and order was not easy to maintain elsewhere in Britain at this time. Feelings ran high everywhere, so that little excuse was needed for anti-Whigs to mount a protest in which many of the protesters wore tartan, forbidden since 1716 under the Disarming Act as a kind of badge of defiance.[23]

All this may have meant very little in terms of restoring the Stuarts, but it did trigger panic in London when ministers learned what was afoot on the other side of the Channel. The French plan was to send their Brest squadron to sea under Admiral de Roquefeuil to draw the Royal Navy further down the Channel, thus allowing Saxe's army to cross from Dunkirk and land in Essex near the mouth of the Thames. There they were to be joined by a force raised by the English Jacobites.

The British had no idea of any of this until de Bussy, 'Agent 101' whom Walpole had recruited a few years earlier, brought them the shattering news. By now the greedy Frenchman had been appointed His Most Christian Majesty's representative in London, where he played the dual role of envoy privy to French aims and intentions in England, and at the same time purveyor of this same information to His Britannic Majesty's ministers.

The news 'Agent 101' brought on 14 February 1744, just a week after Charles Stuart's arrival in Paris, was nothing less than the entire plan for the invasion of England, naming English Jacobites involved, including the Duke of Beaufort, Lord Barrymore, Sir Watkin Williams Wynn and Sir John Hynde Cotton. In London the panic button was pressed and within days a loyal address to the King had been passed in Parliament, army reinforcements were summoned from Ireland and the Netherlands, and

English Jacobite suspects were being rounded up by the score. And 'Agent 101' was £2,000 better off in return for this information.

At almost the same moment as the British government became aware of the invasion plan, Charles, impatient to be into the action, arrived in Gravelines on the Channel coast under the pseudonym Chevalier Douglas. His feelings were mixed: some worry about the reception French officialdom had given him, but also such elation at the prospect of leading an invasion of England that he pressed his allies to push ahead faster. Here he was, a soldier at last, in the midst of frantic preparations for war, mixing with ordinary people for the first time in his life – unrecognised and accepted simply as another young nobleman preparing to fight.

What Charles did not realise yet was that even before the secret of the invasion was passed to London, nothing had been going according to plan: the English Jacobites were proving difficult and in the end it was doubt over the effective support they would give that helped Louis make up his mind to call the whole thing off. On the naval side, pilots could not even be found to guide the ships into English landing places, and now, with Britain aware of the French plan to attack at a time when the two countries were at peace, a declaration of war was inevitable. And it was very convenient to blame Prince Charlie's dramatic appearance in Paris for it all. Worst of all from the Prince's point of view was the fact that Louis XV's council of state in Paris had changed, and with changes of key players in French politics, opinion was swinging towards a campaign in Flanders instead of an invasion of England – a campaign led by King Louis himself.

At sea the expedition had collapsed by now too. French naval organisation was a shambles and the fleet was only saved from being humiliated by the British under Admiral Sir John Norris because a storm blew up and scattered it first. Admiral Roquefeuil could only watch his ships being tossed about like corks, masts swept away and one sunk without a shot being fired by Norris's fleet. The Protestant winds, which had already spoilt so many Jacobite attempts, did their work well, also destroying the vessels loaded with supplies and men, all ready to sail when the storm struck. A number of men and a large quantity of supplies were lost, making the invasion impossible. Roquefeuil himself raced off towards Brest.

Even before the Protestant winds had done their work in the English Channel, Saxe had written to the Prince, telling him the invasion was off. Charles showed that mercurial side of his character which was to surface so often throughout his life: in an instant the carefree young soldier, in whom the adrenalin was flowing, turned to a haughty royal prince outraged that his divine right was being challenged. He wrote to Saxe demanding to know why the winds managed to devastate the French fleet yet leave the British unscathed?[24] It was a good question and Saxe, already furious with everybody – his own navy, English Jacobites, Charles Edward, and every other person who got in his way – defended himself strongly. There followed cold, childish exchanges that reflected no credit on either correspondent.

Worse was to come: without telling the Prince in advance, Louis XV declared war on Britain, and Saxe was ordered to march his army off to Flanders, leaving only a token force at the coast in the hope of misleading the Hanoverians into thinking the invasion was still on. The scheme may have failed but it had fallen in with Louis's overall strategic plan very nicely by taking his army to within a short march of Flanders where it could drive a wedge between Britain and her allies. One can understand the assessment of Saxe's biographer, Jon Manchip White: the invasion, he said, had been 'nothing more than military vaudeville'.[25]

The Prince was left alone at Gravelines with no one to comfort him but a handful of supporters, the principal of whom was the aged Earl Marischal, a veteran of the '15 and '19 risings and totally the wrong person to advise and guide an angry, disappointed and impetuous young man. Although a lifelong Jacobite, Marischal never really liked Charles – or his father – and now at Gravelines he failed to understand Charles's frustration. Nor was he capable of offering an alternative idea or supporting anything the Prince proposed at this time of crisis.

Marischal's negative attitude, following hard on the heels of betrayal by Saxe and King Louis, drove Charles towards his destiny. Stranded at Gravelines he sat down and wrote to Lord Sempill that if King Louis would not help him further he would hire a fishing boat and sail to Scotland where he was sure his faithful Highlanders would rally to him. 'I would rather die at the head of these brave men,' he told Sempill, 'than languish in exile and dependence.'[26] He was to get his wish to lead his Highlanders within the year.

CHAPTER FIVE

With Such Friends, Who Needs Enemies?

> I cannot but mention a parabale here which is: that if a Horse which is to be solde if spurred does not skip, nobody would care to have him even for nothing; just so my friends wou'd care very little to have me if, after such usage as all the world is sensible of, I should not show I have Life in me . . . I have presumed to take upon mee the management of all this without even letting you suspect there was any such thing a-brewing . . . had I failed to convince you, I was then afraid you might have thought what I was going to do to be rash, and so to have absolutely forbidden my proceedings . . .
>
> Letter from Charles Edward to his father, sent immediately prior to sailing for Scotland in July 1745 and justifying his secrecy.[1]

Of the many words that could be used to describe the conduct of Louis XV between the autumn of 1743 and the end of 1744, deceitful, dishonest, disgraceful and despicable come most readily to mind. The French King chose the Stuarts to provide justification for his invasion of England, yet he concealed the plan from them for as long as he could; then when Charles Edward arrived in France he was ignored and humiliated – and, to add final insult, was blamed when the whole enterprise fell apart. The French broke their promises to him, they let him down and then they tried to get rid of him when he became a nuisance to them. With King Louis of France for a friend, the Stuarts did not need to look far for enemies.

This may sound a harsh judgment on the Bourbons, for there were faults on the Jacobite side of the relationship too, not least the fact that its supporters were constantly at loggerheads. But, without doubt, Louis's devious method of governing and incompetence in carrying out what policies the government of France had, meant that Prince Charles Edward did not receive the help he might reasonably have expected when he needed it. The world of French politics was every bit as deceitful as anything experienced in the Jacobite court at Rome.[2]

Charles was beside himself with rage and ranted against everybody – the perfidy of Louis, the French navy's incompetence and Marshal Saxe. He demanded to see Saxe to face him with all these accusations including the delicious morsel that prior to the débâcle a couple of captains in the British fleet had already been subverted by the Jacobites. A splendid battle of words followed, in which Saxe tried to defend the French Navy, and Charles contemptuously reduced the Marshal to the level of a banker by demanding 500 louis d'or of the money he had been given for the Stuart Prince's use. The correspondence only ended when Saxe announced that he had been commanded to return to court and the matter was now closed.[3] Old, curmudgeonly Earl Marischal took the wrong tack as usual: he tried to calm the angry young Prince, and find excuses for the French behaviour. Charles Stuart simply could not cope with that – just as he could never handle criticism. Whoever was not totally for him was against him. His upbringing, with parents who could not understand each other let alone their son, bred in him an inability to handle relationships with others and now when princely statesmanship was required he could only respond with despotic rage.

His poor bewildered father in Rome was subjected to much of this wrath in letters that hurt him badly, but there was nothing he could do except make soothing noises and try to persuade the little inner circle of Jacobites in France to calm his son. There was little chance of that since they could not get on with one another either and were divided into factions which were always trying to upstage each other.

As the idea of making an immediate invasion receded, the French turned their attention to fighting the British in Flanders and Charles saw hope in fighting with the French armies there. As this would give him a taste of the military action for which his marathon journey from Rome and the preparations at Gravelines had whetted his appetite, he asked to be permitted to join the army in Flanders. But, again, Louis fobbed him off with half promises that he might join the campaign later on condition that he kept his identity concealed and retired to the estate of his father's half brother, the Duke of Berwick, at Fitz-James in the meantime. This would keep him well away from Paris, out of the public eye, and out of the King's sight. Needless to say, gloomy old Marischal wanted the Prince to accept the King's terms but Charles was determined to live in Paris where he could lobby Louis and his ministers for renewed support. He was willing to go along with the incognito part of the deal, which suited his love for aliases and disguise, and when he did make his way back to Paris he went willingly under cover.

On his arrival in the capital on 5 April, he found Louis had gone off to the war without him and had no intention of sending for him. Enraged, Charles found himself 'a pretty little house with a garden' in Montmartre in defiance of the French King's wishes and, incognito or no, settled down to a wild life of 'the wine and the play'. Frustrated at not being able to appear in public as Prince of Wales he went masked or in disguise to balls, the theatre and opera. Sometimes he passed himself off as a German baron newly arrived in the city and at others he was a student of the Scots College named Douglas, but of course people saw through his disguises, which all added to the thrill of defying His Most Christian Majesty. Once Charles attended a ball given by the King's daughters and had a narrow escape when he was recognised by one of the most notorious gossips at court, the Englishwoman Madame de Mézières: fortunately she kept her mouth shut for once. At a masked ball at Versailles at the start of Lent 1745 he sat close to the Queen, who demanded to know who the elegant young man was. He was only saved by a quick-witted lady-in-waiting who assured Her Majesty that he was her brother. Social life in the capital was hectic: as he said himself, at this time he was 'much hurried between balls and business'.[4]

Apart from making audacious appearances at court he took up with some disreputable people, including the son of the Glengarry Chief, Alasdair Macdonnell, a despicable traitor who later spied for the British. Young Glengarry was obviously a reader of Tobias Smollett since he chose as an alias in his espionage correspondence with the London government, the name Pickle after the character Peregrine Pickle. Roderick Random was another name he used. Glengarry was the most notorious of all the traitors to the Cause in the history of the movement and, although we cannot be sure, he may have been gathering intelligence while he was leading this wild life with Charles in low taverns in Paris. It was only years later that his treachery was discovered and more than a century before his true identity was confirmed.

There is no evidence that the Prince was womanising at this time, although one must suspect that the vow of celibacy he was supposed to have taken went by the board. Some months later, in early 1745, he certainly met a woman who was to become the love of his life – and probably his most passionate love ever. Marie-Louise de la Tour was his cousin; she had been rejected by James as a bride for the Prince years earlier, but now he met her for the first time when he went to stay with his uncle, the powerful Duc de Bouillon. Louise and her husband, the Duc de Montbazon, became Charles's close friends but at the time the Prince first met them she was pregnant with her first child. In such circumstances it is doubtful whether he did more than admire her then. On his return to France after the '45 matters were different: her husband was away at the war, Charles needed comfort and the result was a passionate affair which resulted in her bearing him a son who died in infancy.

As weeks turned to months it became clear that Louis had no intention of inviting Charles to join him in Flanders and the incognito order had been nothing more than a ruse to keep him silent. To British intelligence agents the situation was laughable, to the French it was irritating and to the Jacobites themselves it was frustrating and infuriating. Dealing with the French king was not so much holding on to a tiger's tail as trying to hang on to a snake: Louis slithered this way and that, passing the Prince from one of his ministers to another, while he made and implemented his own policies – largely behind his ministers' backs – and his insistence that Charles should always deal through these powerless officials was simply another piece of nonsense designed to get rid of the awkward young man.

He appointed his Finance Minister, the Comte de Vignory, the man least sympathetic to the Stuarts, as intermediary, where it would have been better for Charles if the delegated minister had been Cardinal de Tencin, whom Charles's father had helped to be elevated to the College of Cardinals. As for the other ministers who mattered – the Marquis d'Argenson (Foreign Minister) backed the Cause after 1744, but the Duc de Noailles, the Comte de Maurepas (Navy Minister) and the Comte d'Argenson (War Minister) were its enemies. The Duc de Richelieu was well disposed towards the Cause, and it had powerful female supporters – the King's mistresses the Duchesse de Châteauroux and Madame de Pompadour, and Madame de Mézières, that indefatigable Jacobite plotter. Stupidly, he made an enemy of Pompadour later. It was not just a matter of King Louis's ministers being pro- or anti-Jacobite, however. They were rivals, even sworn enemies of each other, and their personal relationships got in the way of their support for the Prince and his Cause.

To his credit, even in this situation Charles never lost sight of his goal. On 10 April he told his father, 'Whether I am free from company or diversions, it's all alike to me for I can think of nothing, or taste nothing but your service, which is my Duty.'[5]

In the autumn of 1744 the French King fell dangerously ill while he was with the army at Metz and was so close to death that he confessed to his priest the Bishop of Soissons – a confession which included a promise to make amends if God spared him. One of the admissions Soissons wrung from the King was that he had been unfair to Prince Charles and as a result Tencin was appointed to handle the Prince's relations with Versailles; however, as expected, he proved powerless to help. Towards the end of the year this former friend was instructed to inform Charles that Louis wanted to have nothing more to do with him and that he had never been invited to France in the first place. So much for His Most Christian Majesty's 'death bed' confession, but then Louis XV never had any conscience about lying, even to God.

Poor, dull James in Rome could only watch this Paris pantomime in despair and bemoan that 'the Prince has manifestly been made a sacrifice of on this occasion'.[6] The Jacobites who surrounded Charles were equally powerless to help, for they became more divided among themselves.

Jacobites had been disunited ever since 1715 and now when the Cause came under pressure in 1744 these divisions blossomed into a full-scale dispute that did the movement great harm, not just while Charles was planning his expedition to Scotland, but also during the rising itself. Naturally, the bickering and and tittle-tattling back to Rome stirred up more trouble between the Prince and his father – discord already serious enough because Charles was convinced (with justification) that secrets he sent to Rome were being leaked immediately to spies and were soon on their way to London. It did not occur to Charles that the same was true of his own confidential intelligence, and with the added twist that the French had their own agents working against him too.

Old Tom Sheridan, his friend and tutor since childhood, joined him in Paris, and along with Father George Kelly, that old reprobate of many years' villainy, and the Prince's close friend, Thomas Lally, Baron Tollendal, he formed the core of the Prince's coterie. Ranged against them were Balhaldy, who had carried King Louis's message that brought Charles from Rome, James's two representatives in Paris, Sempill and Daniel O'Brien (the Earl of Lismore), and O'Brien's wife, who was suspected of being King Louis's mistress and a spy. There were others of varying shades of loyalty – Marischal, Lord Clancarty, who claimed to represent the English Jacobites, but who was described by the spy Oliver Macallester as 'a slovenly, drunken, blaspheming rogue, one of whose eyes had been knocked out with a bottle by General Braddock in a tavern brawl'.[7] No wonder the French Foreign Minister, the Marquis d'Argenson, complained of being 'pestered by women, priests, and ragged Irish adventurers'.[8] James sent Sir John Graeme to mediate – to absolutely no avail.

The 'ragged Irish adventurers' insinuated their way into control over the Prince, with Kelly as the villain who undermined his trust in most of the Scots around him. Sempill and Balhaldy were squeezed out, and before 1744 turned to 1745 Sheridan and Kelly had taken over power. This eclipse of the Scots was to dog the Prince all the way to Culloden and to drive out a number of Scots who would have made better leaders.

One Scot who resisted the machiavellian Irishmen was John Murray of Broughton, who had become a kind of unofficial agent for the Jacobite Association in Scotland. Broughton had acted as the Pretender's Scottish agent after the War of Jenkins' Ear with Spain broke out in 1739, and a year later was instrumental in forming the association of chiefs to prepare for a new rising. He met Charles in Rome in 1742 and became so ardent an admirer that the following year, when the French invasion plan was afoot, he dashed to Paris to promote interests among Scottish Jacobites there. He visited Paris again in July 1744 during all the Irish–Scottish, King's party–Prince's party bickering and with typical dour Scottish frankness put Charles right about the rosy prospects others were presenting to him about an immediate rising.

Broughton met Charles secretly at the house of the Paris banker, Aeneas MacDonald, a son of MacDonald of Kinlochmoidart, just behind the great stables at the back of the Louvre, but unfortunately the Prince brought Sempill and Balhaldy along with him. These two had been claiming grandiosely that if the French would send as few as 3,000 fighting men the Highland chiefs would field an army of 20,000, which Broughton dismissed as arrant nonsense – if the chiefs managed to rally 4,000 clansmen, he said, that was as many as the Prince should expect.[9]

Murray realised he could not possibly argue his case with Sempill and Balhaldy present, so he asked for another meeting which was granted the following day without them. At this he railed against all the false friends with whom the Prince had surrounded himself and the unattainable hopes they were raising in him. He even inveighed against the French, who were so tied up in their war in Flanders that there was scant hope of support from them in Scotland. Uncharacteristically, Charles did not explode at this destruction of his most longed-for hopes, but told Murray frankly he intended to come to Scotland next spring even if he were accompanied by only a single footman.[10]

Broughton has been accused of encouraging the Prince to come to Scotland, alone if necessary, and in spite of his denials the letter he sent to Charles from Senlis on 21 September 1744, after his visit to Paris, shows that even before he left France he was trawling among Scots leaders for support and money.[11] Broughton talked secretly with Sheridan before leaving in October to return to Scotland and prepare for the Prince's arrival the following year. Clan chiefs and certain loyal Lowland lairds were to be alerted, and caches of arms were to be hidden in remote Clanranald country.[12] He travelled home via Holland and there tried to recruit support for the projected rising.

Although Murray was dogged by both British and French spies throughout his time in Paris, nothing of importance appears to have leaked from all the secret meetings for two reasons: discussions were confined to the closest of the Prince's circle and agents were unable to believe that so soon after the collapse of the French invasion and with the French fully committed to their campaign in Flanders, there was any likelihood of the Jacobites finding support in Paris. The 'moles' working in France and Scotland probably also believed the Jacobites were too disunited to put together an invasion, and certainly not without foreign help. It was no secret that Broughton continued to undermine Sempill and Balhaldy in Scotland while they in turn were criticizing him in France and to the Pretender in Rome. As Andrew Lang commented, 'The party was playing a game of blind man's buff in which all were blinded.'[13]

Back in Scotland Murray set up an association called the Bucks' club in Edinburgh at which leading Jacobites met regularly to talk and drink loyal toasts, and it was here that he canvassed support. The chiefs were horrified to learn of the projected plan for the following spring, and responded sharply: in the words of Elcho, 'Most of the Gentlemen . . . looked upon it as a mad project and were utterly against it. Mr Murray and some others who were in desperate circumstances certainly encouraged the Prince underhand; others such as the Duke of Perth, out of Zeal.' But some agreed that if he did decide to come, 'they could not hinder themselves from joining his fortune'.[14] Thus, according to Elcho's account, Broughton saw a rising in Scotland as a means of restoring his own fortunes.

The Bucks' Club drafted a memorial to the Prince, which they handed secretly to Lord Traquair to take to London to find a courier to carry it on to Paris, but Traquair could not find a messenger 'cheap enough for his penuriousness', according to Elcho. Twenty-five pounds was the best price he could find, but that 'was not low enough for this indifferent nobleman, and, rather than expend more money, he kept the letter in his pocket. After four months he had the effrontery to return it to Murray.'[15] So much for the reliability of even the most trusted couriers.

Traquair's overall role in the '45 is not an attractive one: Andrew Lang described him as 'a Jacobite from vanity', who did nothing to help the Restoration,'[16] yet he made the grand gesture of locking the great gates to the avenue leading up to his house on the Borders and vowing that they would never be opened again until the Stuarts returned. The Stuarts never did return and the gates of Traquair have remained shut to this day.

The message the Edinburgh Jacobites sent demanded that Charles Edward should stay away unless he could bring with him 6,000 regular French troops, arms for 19,000 more and 30,000 louis d'or in cash. There was little chance of that since the Jacobites had served their purpose and, as far as Louis was concerned, had ceased to be a factor in European politics.

Back in Scotland Broughton met at least seven members of the Bucks' Club secretly, only to find all of the chiefs appalled at the idea of a rising – apart from James Drummond, Duke of Perth. MacLeod of MacLeod, who was drunk at the time, declared that the idea 'mad', and Cameron of Lochiel thought it 'a desperate undertaking', but both agreed to 'come out' if the Prince raised his standard in Scotland. Just to be sure, Murray asked Lochiel to call on MacLeod next morning to confirm that he meant what he had said: he found the Dunvegan chief still in bed but nevertheless he agreed to keep his word and join the Prince.

In Paris, Charles set about winning support from the French King and his father, neither of whom knew a thing about the idea – it can hardly be graced with the name plan as yet, for nothing had even begun to take shape. In his biography of the Prince, Frank McLynn recounts how Charles informed Louis that the English Jacobites were ready to field 30,000 men provided France would support them with 12,000 men plus arms. Should this not be possible, then an attack could be mounted in Scotland with only 3,000 Frenchmen. McLynn believes Charles was using a clever negotiating tactic, 'making an impossible primary demand in the hope that a compromise by the French king would secure the secondary one'.[17] Needless to say, King Louis did not take the bait and still did nothing to help. But that did not stop Charles Stuart: as he had told Broughton, he would go to Scotland alone if necessary and he would shame Louis into sending a force to back his rising.

Grudgingly, the Pretender in Rome gave his assent to the idea of a Scottish rising but only in the broadest outline and provided it had French support. By no means could that be interpreted as firm approval, but it was enough for Charles Stuart: from that moment on he dedicated himself singlemindedly to the project, saying he would put himself in a tub like Diogenes if necessary to achieve his goal.[18] Needless to say he could not resist breaking the terms of his incognito and made a visit to Paris, attending masked balls and the opera, and he kept his eye in with the gun by treating himself to occasional hunting expeditions.

All through the spring of 1745 he worked assiduously to complete his arrangements, telling no one – not even his father – about his scheme, but the Pretender was aware that something was happening and realised that his agents in Paris were not part of it. However, there was no chance of finding out what was afoot since the French end of the movement was now almost totally out of the hands of the Scots and under the control of Charles's Irish friends, especially Father Kelly, old Tom Sheridan and Colonel John O'Sullivan. The banker, Aeneas MacDonald, later remarked ruefully that 'the expedition to Scotland was entirely an Irish project'.[19]

James, still largely in the dark, gave permission for his son to borrow 40,000 livres from the banker, Waters, using his mother's Sobieski jewels as security and allowed him to use the money to buy a quantity of weapons and stores – around 11,000 guns, 2,000 broadswords, 20 small field guns, ammunition and a good supply of brandy.

Now Prince Charlie had his revenge on the treacherous French: Louis himself, never in close touch with his ministers, was still away at the war front with his mind on the campaign, so it was easy enough to hoodwink him. Lord Elcho claimed the ministers in Paris were kept in the dark, with the exception of the Navy Minister, Maurepas. With the help of the tight little clique of buccaneering Irish ship-owners and traders who operated out of the Brittany coast ports he set about finding a means of travelling to Scotland. Two Irishmen in particular, Antoine Walsh and Walter Ruttledge, were sympathetic to the Cause and not only helped him to store the equipment secretly but also enabled him to maintain contact with England and the Scots and, when the time came, to find ships for the expedition.

Every move remained shrouded in secrecy, but leaked half-truths helped to dupe the ministers in Paris. Using the same trick as he had tried with Louis when he asked for a large amount of assistance to invade England, Charles applied to Paris for permission to allow the privateers to act as intermediaries to Jacobites in Britain. When that was refused he asked leave for a single ship, the *Elisabeth*, to sail off the West coast of Scotland in order to keep in touch with Jacobites there. Maurepas agreed.[20]

The plan was working well: his father in Rome and all his circle of agents in Paris were still largely unaware of what was going on and were powerless to do anything about what little they did manage to uncover. Irritation and frustration born of this helplessness were evident in Sempill's letter to James on 5 July. He knew something was afoot and was upset that the Prince had not come to Paris as promised, but he had no idea that Charles had already left for Nantes. He was inclined to believe that Waters, the banker, was in on the scheme, since orders had been given for letters to be delivered via him, but the Irish were accused of being instigators of whatever was afoot. 'I plainly saw that Sir Thomas Sheridan and Kelly had taken advantage of the Prince's ardent and lively temper, and led him into a measure that might prove fatal to the Royal Family and your three kingdoms . . . Your Majesty's letters from the P. will certainly explain the whole scheme, which to me seems to be formed with no more than five or six young men, some of whom are much liked but have very little influence in their country,' wrote Sempill.[21] Even the Irish traders who were to play such a crucial role in the expedition had scarcely a glimmer of what they were about to be involved in until the very last minute, although it must be suspected that, as seasoned privateers, they would be able to read the signs as to what was afoot.[22]

Towards the end of May Charles sent Sir Hector MacLean of Duart in Mull to Scotland to warn Murray of Broughton, the Duke of Perth and other members of the Association that he would be with them soon. To Murray he wrote, 'I am now resolved to be as good as my word and to execute a resolution which has never been a moment out of my thoughts since I first took it in your presence.'[23]

That left two major tasks still to be undertaken – to make a final attempt to involve the French and to advise his father of what was about to happen. Charles felt that luck was running his way because at the beginning of June news reached him of a great French victory at Fontenoy on 11 May, won thanks to a brave charge by the Irish Brigade in King Louis's service. The British, under George II's son, the Duke of Cumberland, had only been saved from annihilation by the recently formed Highland regiment, the Black Watch. So many more British fighting men were required in Flanders now that England and Scotland were poorly defended, which was just the incentive Prince Charlie wanted.

Using the trick that had fooled King Louis, British spies and his own brother when he left for France in January 1744, he pretended to take a trip to Navarre, but instead dashed off to Nantes.[24] Before he did so he sent final letters to King Louis asking for help and to his father in Rome, but he instructed the Rome courier to take his time on the way so that his father would not receive the letter until it was too late.

To the French King he wrote: 'Monsieur Mon Oncle, After vainly trying all means of reaching Your Majesty in the Hope of obtaining from your generosity the necessary help to enable me to play a Rôle worthy of my birth, I have made up my mind to make myself known by my Actions, and undertake alone a project, which some small aid would make certain of success. I venture to hope that Your Majesty will not refuse me such aid.' A little flattery sweetened the request. 'I should never have come to France if the Expedition planned more than a year ago had not led me to recognize Your Majesty's good intentions on my behalf, and I trust that the unforeseen accidents, which rendered that expedition impracticable for the time being, have in no way changed these intentions of yours.' Charles remembered to congratulate the King fulsomely on his recent victory – or was he simply being scornfully sarcastic since regiments of British origin had played such an important part in the victory? 'May I not trust, at the same time, that the signal victory which Your Majesty has just won over your enemies and mine (for they are one and the same) has resulted in some change in Affairs; and that I may derive some advantage from this new blaze of Glory which Surrounds you?'[25] Louis was too busy savouring his Fontenoy triumph to take notice of yet another plea from that pestilential young man who was well out of sight, as he thought enjoying life with his Bouillon relatives in Navarre.

On the same day he wrote the long letter to his father, which was to be read only after he had sailed for Scotland. This not only informed James of his impending departure but delved deeply into the reasons for his decision to go, and his relations with his father. It began with the understatement that he had to tell his father 'a thing that will be a great surprise', and the untruth that he had 'been invited by our friends to go to Scotland . . . the only way of restoring the crown to you and them to their liberties.' He complained bitterly about his 'scandalous usage' by the French, which left him with the choice of remaining in France in miserable hope or giving up hope and returning to Rome. Here he slipped in an undeniable and uncomfortable truth:'You yourself did the like in the year '15,' he wrote, adding that the circumstances were now much more encouraging. He could have said also that his preparations had been much more thorough than those in 1715, which was an amateurish, ill-organised business. He set out all his preparations and urged his father to come to Avignon as soon as possible, without even asking French permission, so that he would be ready to come to Britain.

This letter showed that Charles was not the hothead that history has painted him: he faced up to the fact that nobody had helped the Cause during the past twenty years and more, and that King Louis, for all his bluster, could not be trusted. If it suited him he would make peace with Britain and forget Charles Stuart and the Jacobites.

His seven chosen companions – the four Irishmen, Kelly, Sheridan, O'Sullivan and Macdonnell, the Scots, Aeneas MacDonald and the Jacobite Duke of Atholl, and the solitary Englishman, Sir Francis Strickland – were instructed to make their way secretly to Nantes to join him. They formed a strange group, all getting on in years, and certainly not the men who would have been chosen by his father; Charles had been specifically warned against Strickland, who had been Prince Henry's tutor and was dismissed by the King in Rome. None had much in the way of experience and all lacked flair to lead an army into battle.

The Seven had been recruited in a most casual way, the Irish because they said what the Prince wanted to hear and MacDonald the banker because he carried the purse. The banker gave his own version of how he became enmeshed in the enterprise, telling how Charles invited him to dinner one evening, and when the meal was over, turned to him and said quite suddenly: 'I hear, MacDonald, that you are going to Scotland.' MacDonald in fact was due to leave for Scotland in connection with a lawsuit in which he was involved. 'I am going there too – we had better bear each other company,' Charles continued, and that was that. Aeneas MacDonald became one of the Seven. He played an undistinguished role in the rising and, when it was over, returned to Paris only to die in the Revolution.

At Nantes Charles and the Seven joined Walsh and sailed secretly down the Loire to St Nazaire, where they embarked next day on the frigate, *Duteillay*, and left Belle-Isle on 12 July accompanied by a much larger warship, the *Elisabeth*. The letters were sent off to Louis and James, and with that the two vessels sailed. Charles was on his way.

Preparation for the rising had been kept within a tight little circle so that not even the French with all their elaborate intelligence system rumbled what was happening until Charles sent his letter to King Louis. Count Maurepas's chief of police, de Marville, reported on 20 July that he had read in letters from England that three men had been arrested in London on charges of high treason, 'one named Robert Fleich, who was said to be the son of the Chevalier de Saint-Georges'. He asssured the Minister that his correspondents were well-informed people, who believed that concealing Charles Stuart's identity as Fleich was simply an English trick to avoid causing them embarrassment.[26] Two days later de Marville's agents were on to the real story, reporting that the Prince had made a descent on Scotland with a large force. Everything, he assured Maurepas, was in 'un grand mouvement' in London and Count Löwental was preparing to invade England with a fleet from Dunkirk. Over succeeding days he provided highly exaggerated details of the voyage of the Prince and his Seven Men.

England, too, remained almost totally in the dark thanks to the fact that de Bussy, the man who had betrayed the 1744 invasion preparations, had now left London and was of much less value to his friend the Duke of Newcastle. But the world was soon aware of the secret of Charles Stuart's year-long labours to organise a campaign in Scotland.

It had been a period of triumph which had given him much satisfaction. When he went in Gravelines early in 1744, he arrived in disguise under the name Chevalier Douglas, and few recognised him. False identities and stuck-on noses, blackened eyebrows and priest's clothing became part of everyday life while preparations for the '45 were under way and Charles loved the deceit of disguise. To his great delight, on the French coast in 1744 he heard himself discussed by strangers who did not recognise him. 'Everybody is wondering where the Prince is,' he wrote to his father gleefully, 'and sometimes he is told news of himself to his face, which is very diverting.' The man who acted the role of king in Rome doubtless saw little to amuse him in a prince of the royal blood playing a cheap game of hide-and-seek.

Charles was never happier than when he sailed for Scotland aboard the *Duteillay* in July 1745. It was the end of a period of his life that showed him at his best and his worst – he had lived outrageously, yet he organised a major expedition far beyond anything his father had been capable of. As was to be discovered later, he had also revealed himself to be a poor judge of men: for he had surrounded himself with unreliable, unskilled companions incapable of sustaining his campaign or his Cause. And he had revealed himself also as more devious and ingenious than any of the agents that Britain or France could field against him. For the best part of a year he had worked to organise this expedition under secrecy such as no other leader, Jacobite or Hanoverian, managed to achieve before or after. That it had been organised under the nose of the devious King of France and all his ministers and spies gave the Prince added satisfaction.

'What is proof against the money of Great Britain?' George Lockhart of Carnwath once wrote.[27] Charles Stuart had proved that all the money and ingenuity of France as well as of Britain could be subverted by a single man with his flair for the art of intelligence and counter-intelligence. Prince Charlie had proved himself no mean manipulator of men and secret intelligence.

CHAPTER SIX

Prince Regent of Scotland

Were our glasses turned into swords,
Or our actions half as great as our words,
Were our enemies turned into quarts,
How nobly we should play our parts.
The least that we would do, each man should kill his two,
Without the help of France or Spain,
The Whigs should run a tilt, and their dearest blood be spilt,
And the King should enjoy his own again!

From *A Collection of Loyal Songs*, printed in 1750. Quoted in Andrew Lang's *Companions of Pickle.*[1]

The Presbyterian Kirk's parish of Ardnamurchan is vast, remote and sliced by long sea lochs, which make travel difficult for its minister. The southern half stretches across the Ardnamurchan and Sunart districts of Argyllshire while Moidart, Arisaig and South Morar to the north lie in Inverness-shire. The Argyll portion is largely Protestant but the Inverness area is Catholic; consequently it was not an easy 'calling' for its minister in Jacobite times but the Reverend Lauchlan Campbell did his best to watch over all his parishioners of both faiths.

On Thursday 25 July 1745 people in North Ardnamurchan were astonished to see a large ship anchor just off the coast – something none of them had ever witnessed before. A few made it their business to investigate the mystery and on their return would say only that it was a smuggling vessel carrying brandy, which was so dear that none of them would buy it. Then, after the ship moved away, they denied it had ever been there.

Here was a mystery the minister felt it his duty to uncover and Lauchlan Campbell delved to the bottom of it. Catholics were cock-a-hoop and were whispering among themselves about it being 'time for them to assert their Liberty, and be rid of Usurpation and Presbytery'. Campbell was certain that a Jacobite rising was imminent, but bided his time until the following Sunday when he was due to hold a Communion service at Kilmory in the north coast of Ardnamurchan where many Catholics lived. He faced a restive congregation, with many absentees, but undaunted he preached a sermon on the evils of rebellion, which was not well received especially when he reminded them of the fate of Absalom. One of his parishioners approached him afterwards to warn him, 'Sir, do not preach in yon stile again, else beware of the consequences.'

That evening his suspicion that the Pretender's son had arrived was confirmed by Anna Cameron, a staunch Whig, whom he gently questioned outside the manse.

'What news did you have yesterday when you were visiting your brother and sisters in Kinbraes?' the minister asked as they walked together in the July evening.

'I have no news,' Anna answered.

'But you have,' Campbell persisted. 'I preached such a sermon today in Kilmory and the people were like to go mad. I can take my oath upon it that the Pretender is in my parish.'

Anna hesitated. 'Can you take your oath on it?'

'According to my present conviction I can,' the minister assured her.

'God be thanked,' said Anna, and admitted that she had been sworn to remain silent about the ship. The news was true, she told the minister, the Pretender was in Kinlochmoidart, although with only six men, she said, but he had sent word to the clan chiefs to meet him.

Thanks to the Ardnamurchan minister and Anna Cameron, the government received its first certain news of the arrival of Prince Charlie in Scotland.[2] The poor man did not have enough money to send this vital intelligence by an express, so he did the next best thing, hurrying to tell it to Donald Campbell of Achindown, who passed it on to the Duke of Argyll's factor, Campbell of Airds, who in turn wrote to the Duke's chamberlain, Campbell of Stonefield, at Inveraray. By this devious chain of word of mouth and letter the information reached Andrew Fletcher, Lord Milton, the Lord Justice Clerk, who forwarded it to the Scottish Secretary of State, the Marquis of Tweeddale, on 7 August. For once the government's intelligence system was not only unreliable, it was dilatory.

Although the British authorities were at sixes and sevens and Charles succeeded in outwitting French intelligence and his father's dreary little court in Rome, he did not really arrive in Scotland unexpected or unannounced as is so often claimed. British agents as usual had wind that something was afoot, although their masters in London could scarcely believe what they were hearing and did very little about it. They were also handicapped by the fact that the King was away in his beloved Hanover at the time and the army was fully committed overseas. However, intelligence filtering into London and Edinburgh suggested that the young Stuart prince was planning some kind of adventure, and the Royal Navy had been put on the alert.

By sheer bad luck the Prince lost one of his ships on the voyage when the *Elisabeth* was attacked by HMS *Lion* 100 miles west of the Lizard and was so badly damaged she had to limp back to France. That left the *Duteillay* to sail on to Scotland alone with few arms and little more than his seven close companions, the Seven Men of Moidart. Anna Cameron had not been far out when she told the minister the Prince had six men with him.

Duteillay made landfall at Barra Head, the southernmost tip of the Outer Hebrides, on 20 July. The plan had been to land on Mull, where the Duart chief, Sir Hector MacLean, the man sent from Paris in May to alert the chiefs, should have been waiting, but MacLean was in prison and Charles had to sail on to the island of Eriskay, which belonged to the strongly Catholic and Jacobite Clanranald MacDonald chief.

Sir Hector had been taken prisoner on 5 June, almost the moment he returned to Edinburgh, because, like most characters in the Jacobite story, he talked too much and according to Aeneas MacDonald, was overfond of the bottle.[3] In the capital he 'appeared too publickly' among eavesdropping government moles and professed anti-Jacobites; consequently he was arrested while still carrying letters to Broughton and other Scottish leaders in his pocket. He was taken to London, where he was examined by the Marquis of Tweeddale himself and charged with serving in the French army. He told Tweeddale that a Captain Barclay referred to in the letters, actually the code name for Charles Edward, was a Captain Stewart who had been obliged to leave Paris because of matrimonial difficulties, and this was accepted.[4] MacLean was put on trial on a capital charge of being in the French service and recruiting for it but was able to prove he had been born in Calais and consequently was a French citizen who should be treated as a prisoner of war. He was held until the amnesty in 1747 following the rising. As Murray said, with true Scottish understatement, 'I can safely say it was one of the greatest misfortunes that could have befallen the Prince at that time.'

Duart's arrest and the Navy's destruction of every boat that might have allowed the MacLeans on Barra to join a rising, threw the Scottish leaders into such confusion that they were uncertain as to whether the landing was to be made on Mull or Uist. Worse was the fact that no experienced leader had been appointed to organise the Prince's reception. 'I fear the Consequences, but I pray God it may turn out contrary to the present idea I have of it,' Donald Cameron of Lochiel wrote to Murray of Broughton. 'I shall endeavour to act in the best manner I can and in the most cautious and [illegible word here] what further Commands you may have occasion hereafter to honour me with.' Some indication of the security risk couriers ran in the Highlands at that time is demonstrated by his final plea: 'Pray send some other than the bearer as he has been so often here.'[5]

Broughton dashed north to discuss the situation with Lochiel, taking care to travel incognito. 'Afraid lest my going at that time should create suspicion in the country people, being alarmed at Sir Hector Macleane's being taken into custody, and as they are naturally an artful inquisitive people . . . I went under a borrowed name, and pretended to be come from England to buy wood,' Broughton wrote. He stopped off at an inn a mile or so from Cameron's house at Achnacarry, sent a message to the chief and the two talked secretly: Lochiel could not believe his ears – the Prince surely would not come without warning and in any case Traquair had taken a message to him advising him that the chiefs were against a rising without French help. But Traquair had not delivered the message and Murray assured Cameron that Charles was on his way. He also told Lochiel he had been assured that the English were willing to rise and in the circumstances did not see how Lochiel and the other Highlanders 'could in honour excuse themselves'.[6]

It is questionable whether Prince Charlie would have held back had he received the chiefs' messages and now on Eriskay he was committed – if he had lost the MacLeans there were other clans, especially the MacDonalds among whom he was now living happily and adventurously.

This was not the landing the Stuart heir could ever have dreamt of during all his preparations in France: there was no harbour on Eriskay where he could make even a symbolic landing to reclaim his family's ancient kingdom. In driving rain so bitter he must have felt this was the depth of winter rather than a Scottish summer, he was carried ashore on the shoulders of a clansman. As they reached the sandy shore, sails appeared on the horizon and the disembarkation descended into an undignified scramble to find a hiding place. Fortunately the ships passed without spotting the *Duteillay* but it was decided that the Prince should remain on the island overnight as a precaution. The Prince sent a message to the nearest leader, Clanranald's half-brother Alexander MacDonald of Boisdale in South Uist, and the very next day Boisdale arrived on Eriskay – but not to welcome the Prince with delight.

Clanranald was an old man full of rheumatics, so could not join the rising himself: more important than the pains of old age in persuading him to stay at home, though, was anxiety to avoid having his lands confiscated as had happened after the rising of 1715. As for the two great chiefs in Skye – Sir Alexander MacDonald of Sleat and Norman MacLeod of MacLeod – Boisdale could offer no hope of support from either. MacDonald, he said, had made it clear that he would not join a rising that had no French support, but MacLeod, who had been a member of the pro-Jacobite Bucks' Club in Edinburgh and agreed to support the rising, had simply gone back on his word. These two key chiefs were virtually blackmailed into declaring for the Hanoverians by Lord President Duncan Forbes of Culloden, the government's chief law officer in Edinburgh, to save themselves from prosecution over a scandal involving the kidnapping and deportation of their clansmen to the American colonies as bond servants. A loyal supporter of the Hanoverian monarchy, Forbes worked harder than any man to thwart the Jacobite rising and had spies working for him throughout the Highlands.

Although the compromising of those two great chiefs was his greatest triumph Forbes also succeeded in holding other chiefs for King George by authorising them to raise independent companies for the army under Sir John Cope, the King's commander-in-chief in Scotland. Among those dedicated Whigs, compromised chiefs and waverers were George Monro of Culcairn, the Laird of Grant and the Earl of Sutherland.

Spies and informers, manipulated by the Marquis of Tweeddale and Forbes, worked successfully all summer to infiltrate Jacobite and clan circles, so that by July when Charles landed, both Parliament Close in Edinburgh and Whitehall in London ought to have been aware that a rising was imminent, but they were not. Certainly MacLean's arrest and agents' reports from France suggesting that the French were preparing a new invasion (probably based on little more than Charles's letter to Louis asking for support immediately prior to his departure) had alerted the British to an imminent rising in Scotland, but Whitehall and Edinburgh still remained very much in the dark even after the Prince was actually on Scottish soil.

Charles had been in Scotland a week before Secretary of State Tweeddale was able to confirm on 30 July that the Prince was even on his way. Tweeddale wrote from London to Andrew Fletcher, Lord Milton, the Lord Justice Clerk in Edinburgh:

> This day have been communicated to the Lords Justices several informations, importing that the French Court was meditating an invasion of His Majesty's dominions, and that the Pretender's son had sailed on the 15th Inst. [New Style: Britain still went by the Old Style calendar which was 11–12 days behind the NS one used on the Continent] from Nantes, on Board a French man-of-war; and by some accounts it was said that he was actually landed in Scotland, which last part I can hardly believe, not having had the least account of it from any of his Majesty's servants in Scotland.
>
> Your Lordship will easily judge how necessary it is for all his Majesty's servants to keep a strict look out; and it has been recommended to me by the Lords Justice that I should give you an account of this intelligence, that you may consult with the rest of his Majesty's servants, and concert what is proper to be done in case of such an attempt taking place, You will likewise give the necessary orders for making the strictest inquiry into the subject matter of this intelligence (copies of which I have sent to the Lord Advocate), and transmit to me some constant accounts of any discovery you shall make.[7]

Two days later (on 1 August) the Duke of Newcastle advised the Duke of Argyll, the government's principal organiser for the implementation of its policies in Scotland, of the Prince's reported departure on 15 July 'on board a ship of about sixty guns', attended by a frigate loaded with arms for a considerable number of men. 'The King has undoubted intelligence that the resolution was taken at the Court of France to attempt an invasion of His Majesty's British Dominions; they have not the least doubt at Hanover of the truth of it,' he told Argyll.[8] On the same day a proclamation was issued from Whitehall offering a reward of £30,000 for the Prince's capture.

The news was received in Edinburgh with incredulity, but it sent Lord Milton off to Inveraray to warn Argyll[9] and it was on the way there that he received the Ardnamurchan minister's firm news that Charles Edward

Stuart had arrived. Other reports soon filtered in from various sources because the *Duteillay* was moving around the isles and the Morar coast: the MacLeod chief reported seeing a vessel 'hovering on parts of the coast between Ardnamurchan and Glenelg',[10] which was most likely when the minister's witness learned of the Prince's arrival and an informer sent a letter to Cope with the news on 3 August.[11]

Shortly after receiving the Ardnamurchan minister's report, Milton had independent confirmation from one of his agents in Glencoe and immediately sent another spy north to find out more.[12] Alarmingly, he had also heard gossip among the Highlanders that Earl Marischal's brother, General James Keith, was already in England 'or on that coast', and a rising would follow there. Obviously, the agent realised the danger he would be in if caught spying for the government, for he ended his report cagily: 'Let me understand if you want to keep the correspondence, per bearer.'[13]

On the day Lord Milton was travelling to Inveraray to alert the Duke of Argyll, Prince Charlie wrote from Lochailort to advise his father of his safe arrival. He was in good spirits he told his father, then spiced up the news by adding, 'but not with little trouble and danger, as you will hear by the bearer'. If he felt the slightest degree of pessimism he disguised it well: 'I am joined here by brave people, as I expected. As I have not yet set up the Standard, I cannot tell the number, but that will be in a few days as soon as the arms are distributed . . . I have not yet got the return of the message sent to the Lowlands, but expect it very soon. If they all join, or at least all those to whom I have sent commissions, everything will go on to a wish.' This was optimism worthy of his most sanguine Irish supporters.

There was bravery in his letter too:

> The worst that can happen to me, if France does not succour me, is to die at the head of such brave people as I find here, if I should not be able to make my way; and that I have promised to them, as you know to have been my resolution, before parting. The French Court must now necessarily take off the mask, or have an eternal shame on them; for at present there is no medium, and we, whatever happens, shall gain an immortal honour by doing what we can to deliver our country, in restoring our master, or perish with sword in hand.[14]

It was an exaggeration for Charles to tell the King in Rome that he had been joined by 'brave people'. Talk of joining him remained muted in both Highlands and Lowlands, not merely because he had come without French help, but in part at least because of a fear of remembered repression and retribution following the '15 rising. In the Lowlands, prosperity and Presbyterianism proved powerful motivators against joining the Jacobites and in the Highlands the three main reasons against 'coming out' were fear of confiscation of estates and property, the prompt action by British forces to quell doubtful clans and 'persuasion' by Duncan Forbes of Culloden, who proved himself the best friend King George had in the Highlands that summer.

The Argyll Campbells were aligned to the Hanoverians, of course, as they always had been, but other clan chiefs, who might have been expected to come forward, now hesitated or bluntly refused to 'come out'. Forbes had already 'blackmailed' Sleat and MacLeod into supporting the government and he now played on old Lord Lovat's greed and untrustworthiness so that the Fraser chief opted to lie low when the Prince landed. Forbes dashed north to keep many other clans out of the Stuarts' grasp, especially those in the far northern counties beyond Inverness, among them the Sutherlands, Munros and Seaforth Mackenzies. The Grant of Grant stayed at home too. Forbes spent £1,500 of his own money to achieve all this but managed to recoup only £500 from his ungrateful masters in Whitehall.[15]

It must have been with a sense of betrayal that Charles finally landed on the Scottish mainland at Loch nan Uamh (pronounced Oo-ah) and sent the *Duteillay* back to France, committing himself irrevocably to the campaign. If Calais was written on Mary Tudor's heart, Loch nan Uamh should have been carved into that of Charles Edward Stuart – it was here he first landed on the Scottish mainland and it was from this loch that he sailed back to France fourteen months later when the rising was over. In between, Loch nan Uamh provided a convenient posting point between Jacobite Europe and Jacobite Scotland; it was also the scene of the last battle of the '45 and the landing of French gold, which arrived too late to help the Prince's campaign, but became the Loch Arkaig Treasure, the curse of the final years of the Cause.

Unlike wild Lochs Nevis and Hourn, the great fiords which push far inland into the mountains of this part of the West Highlands, Loch nan Uamh has scarcely the appearance of a loch at all but simply suggests a bay set among gentle, wooded country. It could easily be mistaken for a landward extension of the Sound of Arisaig. The loch had the great good fortune, also, to provide a well-sheltered anchorage for ships against those storms, which can whip up unexpectedly in the West Highlands and blow for days on end at any season of the year. The loch is a remote place even today but in 1745 it was hard to reach except from the sea. Lying some thirty difficult miles west of Fort William, on a track that runs from Lochailart to Arisaig, it was relatively safe from government forces, yet conveniently set in staunch Jacobite Catholic country which made it an excellent centre from which emissaries could be sent out to warn the Jacobite world that its Prince had arrived.

While he waited in Borrodale for responses from the members of the Association, who had talked so expansively about just such an event but were holding back now, the Prince met a number of MacDonald chiefs, among them Glencoe, Keppoch, Scotus (representing Macdonnell of Glengarry), Morar's brother and Clanranald's son. Virtually none would agree to join him in spite of all his brave talk and moving appeals, so that the comment of Archibald Campbell of Stonefield rang true: 'This expedition looks extremely romantick,' he wrote, 'and to be sure no man in his senses would take up arms, unless there is some further support than yet we are in the knowledge of.' And yet Stonefield was sufficiently alarmed to be sitting up to write this report to his chief at three o'clock in the morning and to add 'but truly the inhabitants of those countrys are demented. From all hands I have it that they are quite ready to join [the Prince].'[16]

One who met Charles soon after his arrival and took up arms was young Ranald MacDonald, who became so carried away that he cried out he would follow his rightful Prince, even though no other man in the Highlands drew his sword. Highland honour forced his kinsman, Young Clanranald, to join with his father's men from the mainland. With Clanranald's acceptance, Keppoch and Glencoe followed, and finally Donald Cameron of Lochiel. The Cameron chief had sent his brother, Dr Archibald Cameron, to advise the Prince to return to France, but Charles demanded that a refusal from the Camerons should come from Lochiel himself, not from his representative.

Already compromised by having been told by Broughton that following the Prince was a question of honour, Cameron came to meet his Prince and Charles conquered – Lochiel uttered the magic words, which made the rising possible: 'I'll share the fate of my Prince, and so shall every man over whom nature or fortune has given me any power,' he said.

Murray of Broughton, another member of the Association, proved just as difficult to win over in spite of all his talk of honour to Lochiel and the part he himself had played in the time leading up to the rising. He also advised the Prince to return to France but when he realised Charles did not consider this option, committed himself and joined only the day before the standard was to be raised at Glenfinnan on 19 August.

In spite of the reluctance of chiefs to agree to bring out their men, Charles had every reason for optimism. The Highland grapevine was working well and, during one of his many meetings to persuade the chiefs, intelligence agents arrived with information that three companies of the Hanoverian army were on the march from Inverness to Fort William while another three were on their way with provisions for Fort Augustus. Ambushes were set up but the Fort William group never appeared. However, Keppoch, with fifty men, waylaid the other and after one smart burst of fire attacked them sword in hand, upon which the enemy surrendered. Among the prisoners was Captain Sweetenham, commander of the barracks at Ruthven, who was released on parole after the raising of the standard. He immediately went back on his word and reported all he could about the Prince's army.[17]

In spite of the initial small success, August was a difficult month for Charles, but it was awkward for the government too because the latter just could not believe what it was hearing from Scotland. Charles was still finding that many chiefs, whom he believed he could trust, were refusing to support him or hesitating. The sticking point was lack of French backing, which all considered essential. By 19 August, as he waited for the clans to arrive at Glenfinnan, he found himself surrounded by no more than his bodyguard of fifty of Clanranald's men, 150 MacDonalds of Morar, the same number of Gordons under old Gordon of Glenbucket, who had been out in the '15 and had acted as a double agent in the intervening years, and some MacGregors under James Mohr MacGregor, son the the notorious Rob Roy.

It was only in the late afternoon, as the day and hope were both fading, that the sound of the bagpipes in the mountains heralded the arrival of 800 of Lochiel's men and 300 MacDonalds of Keppoch. When the standard was raised by the elderly Jacobite Duke of Atholl and blessed by Roman Catholic bishop, Hugh MacDonald, the Prince had gathered around him an army of around 1,200 men, as well as his Seven Men of Moidart, Murray of Broughton, and one woman, Jenny Cameron of Glendessary, who brought him 300 clansmen. Jenny was a gift to the propaganda war that was to be part of the '45, as enemies of the Cause spread rumours that she was the Prince's mistress. There was not a word of truth in this, but it made an excellent story to discredit the Stuarts.

Even as Charles's standard was being raised at Glenfinnan, Whitehall still doubted that such an unbelievable event could have happened. In the light of all the government's own intelligence reports from the Highlands, officials were every bit as divided as the Jacobites had been earlier in France and now were in Scotland and could not hide their feelings. Lord Tweeddale disliked the Duke of Argyll intensely, but Duncan Forbes, Lord President of the Court of Session, and the Lord Justice Clerk, Lord Milton, were both Argyll men. From the security of London Tweeddale just could not believe what his own spies and the good minister of Ardnamurchan were telling him, so much so that Argyll felt driven to complain that 'nobody would believe him'.[18] The correspondence between Tweeddale and Milton turned bitter as days passed and London still could not accept what really was happening. As late as 24 August – five days after the standard had been raised – the Secretary of State wrote testily to the Lord Justice Clerk: 'I own I am surprised your Lordship is not more particular as to the Pretender himself, since there are several letters in town, absolutely contradicting the accounts sent to the government here from Scotland, of his ever having landed there. I think it is incumbent on all his Majesty's servants in that country, to use their utmost diligence to sift to the bottom the truth of this particular.'[19]

Lord Milton was stung, and replied in the most tart terms and at length:

> Your Lordship says you are surprised I am not more particular as to the young Pretender himself, since there were several letters in town absolutely contradicting the accounts of his ever having landed in

> Scotland. From whom the letter contradicting the accounts sent to the Government at London came, I do not know; nor can I conceive upon what foundation they proceeded; for my own part, I never saw any cause to doubt the truth I sent by my letter of the 7th, repeated in my letter of the 10th current, to your Lordship, that the Pretender's son was on board the French ship; and by the after letters I wrote, I took notice that my former intelligence was confirmed. I know the Pretender's friends for some time endeavoured to conceal his son's being in the Highlands and denied the fact. And I am willing to believe that such as sent intelligence grafted on their evidence, were imposed upon. I dare say, from the accounts I know your Lordship has now received from the Advocate, and in the channel of Sir John Cope by R. Roy's son, and a gentleman who came from the Pretender's son's camp on the 21st, there remains not the least doubt that the repeated intelligence I sent was true.

And just to underline his annoyance at Tweeddale's trivial criticism of the lack of a description of the Prince in his reports, Milton added: 'Nor was it worth while to mention his dress, which was said to be a white coat and a brocade vest; that he had the Star of George, and a broad-brimmed hat with a white feather, and other minutiae, not worthy to be noticed.'[20]

On 21 August the Duke of Newcastle woke up to the reality of the threat and the woeful inadequacy of preparations to counter it and sent a letter to the Duke of Argyll eating as large a slice of humble pie as a minister of the crown is ever likely to be able to stomach. 'I heartily lament for the sake of the publick that your Grace's advice has not been followed,' he wrote. 'It is a melancholy consideration that the Government has at present no friends and no force to defend it, but a small number of regular troops, when if your Grace's proposal had been pursued we might have had a much more considerable number in arms for the Government. The well-affected clans might be provided with arms from the Government from whom Sir John Cope has had orders to deliver them.'[21] At long last the loyal clans were to be recruited to fight the rebels.

Milton's angry letter to Tweeddale revealed that even at this early stage of the '45 campaign the government had 'gentlemen' reporting from within Charles's camp – call them gentlemen or moles, they were still undercover betrayers of the Cause. Among them was James Mohr MacGregor who had actually been spying for the government while his own men were rallying to the Cause. Double-dealing could not go much further than that. James Mohr's report to the Lord Advocate in Edinburgh was good news at least in part, since he was able to tell the government that the Jacobite army, although mostly 'good men', contained some young and raw ones as well as others old enough to have fought at Sheriffmuir thirty years previously. And they were ill armed – most of Lochiel's clansmen arrived with no weapons at all since they had been led to believe that arms would be provided. However, they went 'to Kinlochmoidart's house, or somewhere thereabouts and came back with arms'. MacGregor saw twenty-two field pieces about the size of one's leg together with a number of barrels of powder and ball and 'about 150 Pair of Pistolls'. The weapons were in poor order, 'some of them with the Locks broken and others with Broken stocks, and many of them wanted Ramrods, and the men were complaining that they were in great want of Smiths'.

Sir John Macdonnell, the ill-tempered drunkard, who had been one of the Seven Men, was found a job as instructor of cavalry during the '45 campaign – although, as James Mohr's report made clear, there were hardly any cavalry to instruct. O'Sullivan was appointed quartermaster and adjutant-general, and a few days after the standard was raised, Murray of Broughton was made the Prince's Secretary.

At the very time James Mohr MacGregor was 'moling' assiduously at Glenfinnan and Charles was telling his small army he had come to make his beloved Scottish subjects happy, other leaders, whom he might have expected to be at his side, were in Crieff, talking to King George's Scottish commander-in-chief, Sir John Cope. Self-interest was rife among Jacobites and they were trying to decide what would be to their best advantage. Among them were the Hanoverian Duke of Atholl, and the Glengarry chief, John Macdonnell, father of Pickle, who was sitting on the fence, just like Lord Lovat, waiting to see which way to jump. Lovat's clansmen were 'out' under Donald Macdonnell of Lochgarry, but he refused to commit himself – not that this saved him from being imprisoned at Fort Augustus towards the end of August 1746, charged with 'Treasonable Practices by People that were in Rebellion'. The Earl of Albemarle, who had taken over as government commander-in-chief by then, told the Duke of Newcastle soon after Glengarry's arrest: 'I am apt to believe (although he is a very stupid fellow) that in this particular he may be wrongfully accused as he showed a remarkable inclination to be useful to the King's Troops when they were at Fort Augustus, and when he was latterly employed by me.'[22] Because of a lack of evidence and this 'remarkable inclination to be useful' Old Glengarry was never brought to trial but he was held in Edinburgh Castle until October 1749.

From Albemarle's comment it seems evident that Old Glengarry, like his son, made his contribution to keeping the government informed. At Crieff Glengarry told Cope that Pickle was in France at that moment, where he had been sent by some of the chiefs to persuade Charles not to think of coming to Scotland without foreign help. Pickle missed the Prince in France and set out to return to Scotland in the autumn of 1745, but was captured at sea and spent the remainder of the rising in the Tower of London. He was only released in 1747, after which he became a government spy.

Also at Crieff was the Duke of Atholl's brother, Lord George Murray, a strong-willed veteran of many Jacobite campaigns, who came close to being persuaded to desert to Hanover. The fine hand of Forbes of Culloden can be seen here, almost succeeding in persuading Lord George Murray to change sides – *almost*, for Murray, who had fought for the Stuarts in 1715 and 1719 before the Prince was even born, eventually opted to join Charles and became his Lieutenant-General. Lord George was twenty-six years older than Charles Edward, but they were separated by much more than mere years: Lord George was a highly experienced soldier and his caution frustrated the impetuous young Prince more and more as the campaign progressed.

It was not just age and experience that drove them apart; Lord George's gloomy honesty and that link with the enemy at Crieff in August 1745 made Charles distrust his Lieutentant-General to the point that they were barely on speaking terms by the time they faced King George II's army at Culloden. There were faults on both sides, for the Duke of Liria wrote of Murray: 'Lord George Murray . . . has plenty of intelligence and bravery; but he is false to the last degree, and has a very good opinion of himself.'[23] Chevalier Johnstone's assessment was similar, but better disposed when he described Lord George as possessing 'a natural genius for military operations'. He said he had slight reservations about the Lieutenant-General's personality, although he had to admit that he was 'a man of surprising talents, which, had they been cultivated by the study of military tactics, would unquestionably have renderd him one of the greatest generals of the age'. The downside of the man was that he was 'proud, haughty, blunt, and imperious . . . and feeling his superiority, he would listen to no advice'. Not surprisingly,. the Lieutenant-General's difficult character and Charles Stuart's despotic manner fuelled a personal vendetta as fiery as the '45 campaign itself; it marred their brilliant joint achievement during those seven brief months together.

It seems poor Charles could not win: he was pilloried for not choosing the most competent man to lead his army in the crucial latter stages of the rising and he was criticised for appointing the most able one to be his secretary. John Murray of Broughton has gone down in history as the worst betrayer of the Cause, especially after the '45 was over, yet the irony is that Broughton remained faithful to Jacobitism throughout his life. Nothing was too bad to say about this man. Listen to Andrew Lang: 'Murray was poisonous; was shunned like a sick, venomed beast. His name was blotted out of the books of the Masons' lodge to which he belonged; even the records of baptisms in his Episcopal chapel attest the horror in which he was held for thirty years, for half his life.' Present-day historian Frank McLynn describes him as the evil genius of the Prince's Council of war during the '45 campaign, while Fitzroy Maclean called him 'Mr Evidence Murray, the Jacobite Judas'. But Lang admits that in spite of all his treachery, the man remained 'true in heart to the Cause . . . true to his affection for his Prince.'[24] And he was a far more competent secretary than the inefficient fool, Hay of Restalrig, who took his place after Broughton fell ill shortly before Culloden

John Murray, the son of a Peeblesshire laird, Sir David Murray of Broughton, admired Charles Edward enormously. In Rome as the Prince was growing up, the young Borderer stood out as loyal, true and full of enthusiasm for the Cause alongside all the self-seeking sycophants who crowded the Pretender's court. However, his devotion did not blind him to reality and it was probably Broughton who first sowed the seed in Charles's mind that if he were to abandon the Catholic faith he would remove the greatest obstacle to restoration. It was clear from his actions in Paris in 1744 that he was also the man who convinced the Prince that his best hope lay in Scotland rather than among English followers; he cannot be accused of encouraging Charles to come without French help in 1745, however – that was Charles's decision alone. All Broughton can be blamed for is dazzling the Prince into viewing Scotland as the Promised Land.

John Murray has been accused of betraying other followers and of trying to profit from his position as Secretary to the Prince, but that was all in the future: in 1745 the worst critisism that could be levelled against him was that he poisoned the Prince against O'Sullivan and Lord George Murray during the campaign. He certainly disliked the Irishman and found Lord George's arrogance hard to stomach so that when Charles formed his council of war it divided into a Prince's faction and Lord George Murray's almost immediately, with Broughton taking Charles's side. Broughton did foment the bickering that already existed between Charles and Lord George. Frank McLynn believed Broughton 'did most of his machiavellian work behind Lord George's back, insinuating to the Prince that his namesake was a traitor who had joined the Jacobite army with the sole purpose of betraying it. Alas, these absurd seeds fell on fertile soil.'[25] The relationship between the two Murrays was typical of the feuding and back-stabbing that became endemic within the Cause, but it did not affect the campaign during its early months.

With his small army Prince Charlie set out to face the finest fighting machine in Europe, but fortunately much of King George's power was concentrated on the European mainland at that moment and there were no more than 3,000 men – many untrained – in Scotland during the autumn of 1745. Although he had only recently taken over command of the army in Scotland, Sir John Cope was far better informed than his masters in the south during the summer of 1745 and had been warning them since before Charlie landed that the Jacobite clans were on the move; neither Tweeddale nor other ministers in London took much notice.

Cope tried hard to persuade Whitehall and Edinburgh to allow him to rearm the loyal clans, especially the Campbells, who had been disarmed along with all the others after the '15, but London was still too afraid to allow anyone in the Highlands to hold arms again. As a result Cope could only fret and complain. When he received intelligence that Charles had definitely landed he wrote to Tweeddale again: 'I submit it to consideration if the few Troops in Scotland can be thought sufficient to defend this country in case the enemy is supported from abroad; all I can say is, I will march with what I can draw together, wherever we can be of most service.'[26]

Cope was at long last instructed to take whatever action he thought necessary to stop the enemy and it was then that he decided to march north to Fort William and Fort Augustus. On his journey north he met Lord George Murray and Macdonnell of Glengarry at Crieff. At Dalnacardoch, north of Blair Atholl, he received his first eye-witness account of the raising of the Jacobite standard from Captain John Sweetenham, the British officer who had been captured by Keppoch's highlanders and released on parole. Sweetenham gave him the unwelcome news that the Prince had 3,000 men and intended to ambush Cope's inexperienced troops as they marched through the Corryarrack Pass, the highest and most remote point on Wade's road north. The general decided instead to make for Inverness in the hope of reinforcing his army from well-affected clans in the far northern counties of Ross, Sutherland and Caithness.

This allowed the Jacobite army to sweep south to Blair Atholl, then on to Perth, where it arrived on 4 September. By-passing the fortified castle at Stirling, Prince Charlie entered Edinburgh on the 17th and here too the castle defiantly held out. Under its decrepit 85-year-old commander, General Joshua Guest, the garrison never surrendered. That same day at the Mercat Cross in the High Street friends and enemies alike gathered to watch the Prince take Scotland back for the Stuarts.

Dour Presbyterian Patrick Crichton, author of the Woodhouselee Manuscript, gave an eye-witness account of the proclamation from the point of view of a non-Jacobite who dismissed it all as a 'commick fars or tragic commody'. The street and every window was crammed to watch the 'fars', as an ill-armed, rag-tag-and bobtail army of old men and boys gathered round the cross. 'I observed there armes, they were guns of different syses, and some of innormows length, some with butts turned up lick a heren, some tyed with puck threed to the stock some withowt locks and some matchlocks, some had swords over ther showlder, instead of guns, one or two had pitchforks, and some bits of sythes upon poles with a cleek, some old Lochaber axes.'

As bagpipes played, the elegant Mrs John Murray of Broughton, wearing a dress decorated with white rosettes and carrying a drawn sword, rode among the cheering crowd. Under the guns and swords of the soldiers the Herald and his Pursuivants reluctantly proclaimed James Stuart His Majesty King James VIII, King of Scotland, England, France and Ireland, and his son, Charles Edward Prince Regent. Proclamations were read promising political amnesty, security of the established religion and relaxation of unpopular taxes, pipers played, a trumpeter blew a blast, the clansmen flourished their broadswords as Mrs Murray had done and those with muskets fired them into the air. The crowd cheered the Prince and Scotland belonged to the Stuarts once more.[27]

Louis XIV welcomes the exiled James II at Saint Germain on 5 January 1689. (From the Romance of the White Rose *by Grant R. Francis)*

A beach landing by owlers on the Kent coast by Edmund Dowden. From Smuggling in Kent and Sussex 1700–1840 *by Mary Waugh. (Courtesy of Countryside Books)*

Daniel Defoe, author of Robinson Crusoe, *fell foul of the government for publishing a scurrilous pamphlet and was put in the pillory. He redeemed himself by going to Scotland and working clandestinely to promote the union of the parliaments. (Aberdeen University Library. MacBean Collection Cl.86)*

130 94 r 35 41 261 you haue obligd me in comandi

me to lay asyde the thoughts, 161 c q 10 38 z

f 46 48 76 n w u f 78 25 31 45 43 e 47 h b 201 146

neuer can come to any thinge 88 21 30 206 130 11

vnpleasents thinge in the world 141 9 5 31 46 2

92 71 d 91 25 37 21 33 71 107 43 1 e 33 f 47 r 174 I am su

I shall not dye for sorrow, though truly I ha

263 101 27 45 35 n f b 39 f 3 9 w 96 25 97 38 37 d 390

38 z 47 30 91 39 102 26 118 28 27 41 53 35 72 w 8 93 167

heartily 261 107 31 b 43 48 91 f 45 31 118 33 37 37 31 10

A secret Jacobite letter which no one has ever succeeded in decoding. (Courtesy of Traquair Charitable Trust)

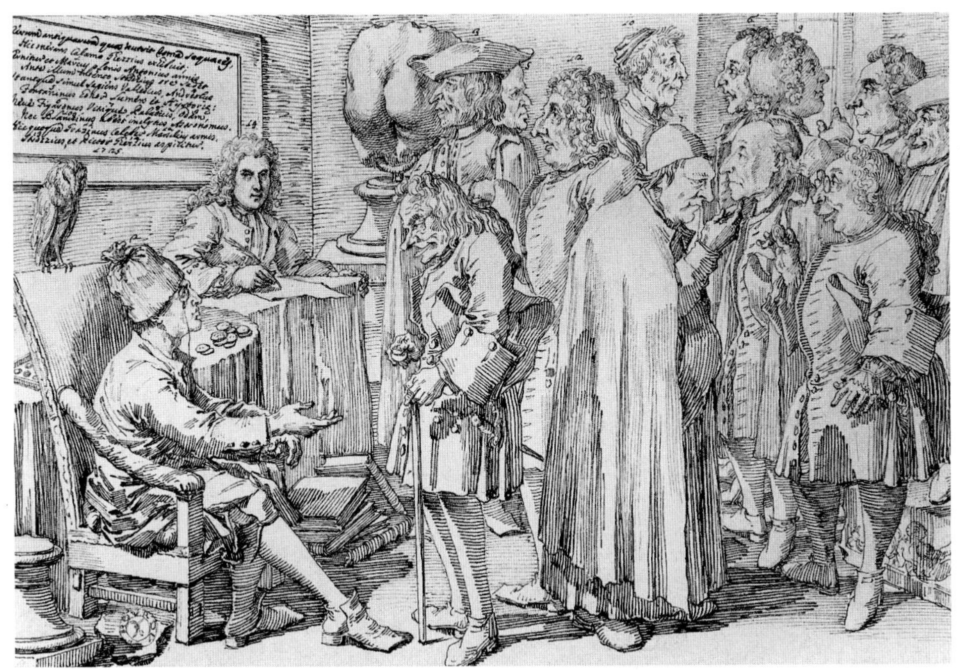

Roman art connoisseur and spy Philip von Stosch with a group of Roman antiquaries. (Albertina, Vienna: ALB. 45. 984 Res)

John Hay, Marquis of Tweeddale, Secretary of State for Scotland at the time of the '45. Portrait by William Aikman. (National Galleries of Scotland)

Prince Charles Edward Stuart from a poster offering a reward of £30,000 for his apprehension in 1745 – 'a likeness notwithstanding the disguise', it claimed. (National Galleries of Scotland)

Lord President Duncan Forbes of Culloden, the government's chief law officer in Edinburgh, persuaded many clan chiefs not to join the Prince. Portrait by David Allan. (National Galleries of Scotland)

Lord George Murray was the best leader Prince Charlie had, but the two quarrelled bitterly. Portrait by Robert Strange. (National Galleries of Scotland)

Major-General John Campbell of Mamore (later fourth Duke of Argyll) was in charge of the hunt for the Prince in the Hebrides. Portrait by Thomas Gainsborough. (National Galleries of Scotland)

Scotch female gallantry, *a Whig propaganda engraving showing women fawning over the Prince at Holyrood. (British Museum: print no. 138719)*

1745 23d Novr Mr Andrew McDougal says Lady Walass was not at the Aby visiting the [illegible] my Lord Justice Clerk says she was two bottles of Rum in punch certified GE

That Mr Grant says there shall be a Battle betwixt our army and the Rebels, on or before the 20th of December next, that the Reverend Mr Webster says no — 2 bottles of wine —

That the Reverend Mr Webster says the bridge at Warrington will not be broken down or defended, that Mr John Graham says yes — 2 bottles of Rum on the side of Mr Webster to one on the side of Mr Graham —

That Major Caulfield says the Highland army will not penetrate 20 miles into Wales, that Mr Stewart says yes — 2 bottles of Rum —

That Messieurs Cheape and Caffield say the Rebels will not march within a hundred miles of London that Mr Forrest and Lord Justice Clerk say yes, 4 bottles of Rum

That Dr Belhaven says they will be in Yorkshire before they be in Wales, that Mr Jno Grant says no. 2 bottles Rum

The authorities in Scotland may have been in a state of alarm during the '45, but members of Edinburgh society took wagers against one another on the Prince's fortunes. The usual stake was two bottles of rum or six of claret. (National Library of Scotland: Manuscript 17526 folios 33/34)

The March of the Guards to Finchley, *December 1745. How Hogarth saw the panic as London tried to mobilise against the invading Jacobite army. (The Coram Foundation/Bridgeman Art Library)*

The Battle of Loch nan Uamh *by Charles Brooking. In this last battle of the '45 HMS* Greyhound *leads HMS* Baltimore *and HMS* Terror *against the French privateer* Bellone. *(From* Ships of the Forty-five *by John S. Gibson)*

CHAPTER SEVEN

In London for Christmas – 1

> Bless the King, Thou knowest what King I mean; may the crown sit long and easy on his head, and for this man that is come amongst us to seek an earthly crown, we beseech Thee in mercy to take him to Thyself and give him a crown of glory.
>
> An Edinburgh minister's prayer in church on the Sunday following the Battle of Prestonpans.[1]

The two months between his arrival in Edinburgh in September 1745 and departure to invade England at the beginning of November were the high point of Prince Charlie's campaign – the apogee, the meridian of his whole life. For these brief weeks he was able to set aside deception and self-deception and be himself – Prince Regent of his father's kingdom, the throne that would soon be his. This was the moment when *Tearlach*, the Highland version of the name Charles, slid easily on to southern tongues as Prince Charlie.

As the envy-tinged, eye-witness account of John Home, no friend of the Jacobites, showed, even his enemies had to admit he looked every inch a Prince:

> The figure and presence of Charles Stuart was not ill suited to his lofty pretension. He was in the prime of youth, tall and handsome, of a fair complexion; he had a light coloured periwig with his own hair combed over the front; he wore the Highland dress, that is a tartan short coat without a plaid, and on his breast the star of the order of St Andrew. [He] mounted his horse either to render himself more conspicuous, or because he rode well and looked graceful on horseback. The Jacobites were charmed with his appearance.[2]

Prince Charlie arrived in Scotland disguised as a priest, but now ceased to be a man who had to travel under the false identity of visiting German baron, student or monk. He sloughed off all that cunning and was no longer the devious schemer he had been in France – although it might have been better for him to have retained something of the spy, because his new openness made it all too easy for the enemy to discover what his next move would be. But he was now too consumed with a sense of his own power to realise that he needed some kind of intelligence and counter-intelligence network to discover what the Hanoverians were up to and maintain secrecy about his own plans. His leaders tried hard to persuade him of the need, but he resisted and went his own way. By contrast government officials and commanders in the field remained obsessively diligent and as a result no Jacobite plan remained secret for long.

In the Highlands, the government was far better organised than the Jacobites, collecting information more resolutely and systematically almost everywhere, partly thanks to those clans that had remained loyal, but also because clansmen failed to appreciate the importance of secrecy. One of the wisest moves the government made was to order Major-General John Campbell of Mamore (later 4th Duke of Argyll) to raise eight independent companies, 'each of 100 men with the proper officers; and likewise to arm 16 companies more, without the charge of commissioned officers, who are to serve without pay and are to be raised from the Duke of Argyll's and the Earl of Breadalbane's Countrey'.[3] These men who wore the black cockade of Hanover, knew the Highlands intimately, and proved invaluable as harvesters of intelligence.

Mamore's information-gathering was highly successful because his clansmen spies were constantly on the move among the rebel clanspeople, picking up scraps of information wherever they went, which added up to firm knowledge of exactly what the Jacobites were up to. This secret espionage, allied to a brutally simple system of torturing those he caught, threatening their families and destroying property and livestock, kept him remarkably well informed. Yet it did not lead him to the £30,000 reward that had been offered for Prince Charlie's capture and remained available for the taking long after the '45 was over.

Charles gave no thought to intelligence during his first days in the capital – he was too busy accepting the admiration of the people, who gave the impression of being ardent Jacobites to a man, since all opponents had to leave the city or lie low. Only General Guest was still holding out in the castle and General Cope was valiantly trying to reach Edinburgh to make up for lost time and lost face.

Cope had suffered a triple humiliation within less than a month: first there was the ambush in which Captain Sweetenham was captured, then the general's refusal to fight at the Corryarrack Pass and his major tactical error of taking his troops north to Inverness, which left the Jacobites an open road to Edinburgh. By the time Cope marched his men off to Aberdeen to be shipped south to Dunbar, Charles was in Perth, and as the redcoats disembarked at Dunbar, the Prince was in Edinburgh.

There was no lack of information about Jacobite army movements, since everybody who was anybody was there to meet Cope and add to his humiliation – the Lord Advocate, the Lord Justice-Clerk, the Solicitor-General and a number of judges, who had all fled the capital, along with the few ill-trained volunteers who had failed to save the city. Cope had few friends now, so he must have been glad at least to learn from young John Home how small the army was that the Prince commanded. Home counted 2,000 men in all, and confirmed that they were as badly armed as Crawford of Woodhouselee had noted during the proclamation ceremony at the Mercat Cross. Cope had 2,500 officers and men, although most were inexperienced.

After much manoeuvring for position, the two armies met near Prestonpans with Lord George Murray's Highlanders holding the high ground of Falside Hill and Cope's men among cornfields below. This was just the kind of commanding position Highlanders preferred, but bogland lay between them and the enemy. Fortunately a local laird's son, Robert Anderson, knew a pathway across the marshland which he had used often while shooting, and he showed it to Lord George Murray, so that under darkness on the night of 20 September the Jacobites were able to cross by Anderson's route and at dawn they fell on the enemy like men possessed. They threw away their plaids with bloodcurdling cries, fired their muskets, then cast these aside too and drew dirks and broadswords. Cope's terrified, untried young men fled, and the battle was over before Prince Charles even arrived on the field. It was a massacre – murder in cold blood as clansmen cut down fleeing soldiers trapped by the walls of the park surrounding Pinkie House and the sight of it sickened Charles. His only other military experience, the siege of Gaeta, had been nothing like this and thus it was a somewhat subdued Prince who slept that night at Pinkie House, by one of those odd ironies of history the home of the Scottish Secretary Lord Tweeddale.

Charles had been so shocked by the slaughter he saw that he forbade public celebrations, and was angered when his men refused to bury the enemy dead. He wrote to his father of his disgust:

> Those who should bury the dead are run away, as if it were no business of theirs. My Highlanders think it beneath them to do it, and the country folk are fled away . . . I am determined to try if I can get people for money to undertake it for I cannot bear the thought of suffering of Englishmen to rot above the ground. I am in great difficulty how I shall dispose of my wounded prisoners . . . Come what will, I am resolved not to let the wounded men lye in the streets, and if I can do no better, I will make a hospital of the palace and leave it to them.[4]

Charles now believed his Highland army was invincible and was desperate to chase General Cope and his cavalry, already on their way to Berwick, across the Border into England. 'Wise' heads among his officers persuaded him that he had neither men nor supplies for this and in any case he had made no contact hitherto with English supporters nor built up an intelligence network to help organise an attack on the south. Reluctantly he agreed to return to the capital, but sent an agent, John Hickson, south to alert supporters. The man got no further than Newcastle before he was arrested five days later – no doubt a reflection on the small degree of sympathy for the Jacobite Cause in England as well as the lack of expertise among Jacobite and Hanoverian agents.

Back in Edinburgh on the 22nd, chiefs were sent north with the news of the victory, and this brought in a number of smallish clan groups to swell his ranks to around 5,000 men, but it had no effect on the big fish he needed to land: neither the great Sleat nor MacLeod chiefs responded even when they were told that the Prince now had assurances of assistance from both France and Spain.[5] The most important chief the Prince netted as a result of Prestonpans was that old renegade Lord Lovat, who ordered his son to lead the Frasers to follow Charlie – a fatal decision for the chief.

Help did arrive from France in the shape of four ships that landed half-a-dozen field guns and a dozen French gunners, but no great reinforcements of fighting men such as the English had demanded to persuade them to rise. More important from the point of view of princely prestige the Marquis d'Eguilles arrived from King Louis with news that a French landing could be expected any day. His reward was to be appointed His Most Christian Majesty's ambassador at King James's court in Scotland. Father Kelly was despatched to Paris with instructions to make the most of the victory when he saw the French King, and at the same time to underplay anything that might be detrimental to the Prince's cause.[6]

John Hay of Restalrig was sent to unsympathetic Presbyterian Glasgow to demand £15,000 (he got only about a third of that amount), arms were ordered and a council made up of chiefs and Charles's Irish friends was set up, a decison the Prince regretted almost immediately, for no sooner had the council begun its daily deliberations than it divided into two factions. It was the jealousies and backbiting of Paris all over again, except that now the protagonists were the Prince's party and Lord George Murray's. Unfortunately the Prince was outvoted on almost every issue and if there was one thing Charles Stuart could not abide it was to be thwarted by anyone – man or woman. Since the Scots did not have the guile to dissemble and humour him with the answers he wanted, they lost his trust.

The Council fanned feeling between the Prince and Lord George, which was to be a vital factor in the defeat at Culloden the following year, but in 1745 it was simply a case of Secretary Murray of Broughton stirring up trouble against the Lieutenant-General. Broughton has always been accused of being the evil genius of the Cause and certainly he did much to destabilise the constantly difficult relationship between the Prince and his Lieutenant-General in the Council. Already suspicious because of Lord George's meeting with Cope at Crieff, Charles listened to Broughton's whispered accusations of disloyalty and gradually relations worsened between the Prince and Lord George as they disagreed over the conduct of the campaign. In the end the Lieutenant-General could take no more, and he resigned leaving O'Sullivan to take command of the last desperate stages of the rising.

In spite of all these worries, Edinburgh had an up-side for Prince Charlie: at Holyroodhouse and as he moved among his troops he looked every inch a Prince and behaved like one, showing all the hauteur of a man who was aware that his family were monarchs by divine right and beings set apart even from the highest nobles and chieftains around them. Elcho worried that this might damage the Cause, but it had little effect: it was said, with a modicum of exaggeration no doubt, that two-thirds of the men in the capital were Hanoverians, but nearly every woman was for the Prince.

While Charles was acting out the role of sovereign at Holyrood and savouring the growing strength of his army, fear reigned throughout England, as indeed it had done since the moment Charlie's arrival in Scotland became widely known. Greatly exaggerated demonstrations of loyalty orchestrated by the Whigs to celebrate the return of King George from Hanover on 31 August did little to calm London. Initial panic following Prestonpans turned to defiance as newspapers, pamphlets and popular demonstrations whipped up hatred against Jacobitism and Roman Catholicism. In theatres in London an extra verse was sung to the national anthem:

From France and Pretender
Great Britain defend her,
Foes let them fall:
From foreign slavery,
Priests and their knavery,
And Popish reverie,
God save us all.[7]

Much that was written and sung during the initial phase of the '45 was carefully concerted Whig propaganda and it had its effect in persuading people not to support the Jacobites: towns, parishes and individuals everywhere were moved to contribute money or join loyal associations and some Whig nobility and local authorities raised armed forces to support the government. This Whig propaganda also silenced Jacobite sympathisers and made it next to impossible for Charles to obtain intelligence after he marched south into England during the first days of November.

After initial panic at the time of the landing and later when it was realised no immediate invasion of England was taking place following Prestonpans, there was relief among government ministers. At the time Charles landed, steps had been taken to recall troops from Flanders and Ireland, and the first of these arrived just before news of Prestonpans reached London. Among the army reinforcements were 6,000 Dutch troops as well as Swiss mercenaries – so much for Hanoverian accusations against the Jacobites bringing French or other foreign troops to fight for them. Field Marshal George Wade, a weary old man past seventy and suffering from gout, was sent north to Newcastle to defend the way into

England by Northumberland, where the invasion was expected, but he did not venture across the Tweed to risk a second Prestonpans while the Prince remained at Edinburgh. General Sir John Ligonier was posted to bar the western route through Roman Catholic Lancashire into Wales or on to London.

On the Scottish side of the Border Prince Charlie found few friends in the dour Lowlands of either east or west Scotland and activity against him was just as strong there as in northern England. Rupert C. Jarvis, editor of *Collected Papers on the Jacobite Risings*, made a study of information and intelligence in the south-western counties of Scotland and north-western counties of England during the weeks leading up to Prince Charlie's march south – and in doing so pointed to the difference between mere information (of which there was plenty) and intelligence, which was a much less readily available commodity. 'The essentials of gathering information are to collect quickly, and to transmit promptly, accurate statements regarding particular significant occurrences or facts,' Jarvis writes. 'Intelligence, however, requires something more: it requires a prompt mental apprehension of a current intention or a future probability, as distinct from a mere awareness of a report of a past or present fact – plus the quick realization of where exactly this must be communicated in order that timely action may be taken; that is to say, intelligence in this sense requires a quick grasp of the essential likelihood inherent in an immediate situation.'

To demonstrate this difference he cites a piece of news from a countryman travelling up Upper Tweeddale on 2 November at the time the march south began. The Provost of Peebles had been ordered to prepare 'Meat, Drink and Lodging that Evening for 1800 Men'. That was information, but it gave no indication of the Prince's intention – were his troops to march from Dalkeith to Kelso and then on by Wooler into Northumberland, or did they intend to turn off at Peebles or Selkirk for the western route to the border and Carlisle from where they could move east across Brough Moor to outflank Wade or head south into North Wales to be joined by a French invasion or simply push south to London? If the intention was to take the western route, then forward troops of the Prince's army would have to turn off at Kelso for Carlisle by way of Jedburgh and Langholm. 'This,' says Jarvis, 'is intelligence.'[8]

Jarvis also demonstrates the danger of careless talk in his account. He quotes a letter from a minister's wife describing Jacobite troop movements, which added that the Duke of Perth asked the magistrates at Selkirk whether the west or south road was best for Carlisle. They replied that the west one was best for carriages. This blew the secret – the Jacobites were bound for Carlisle.[9]

Charles left Edinburgh on 31 October and, after spending another night at Pinkie House as Tweeddale's uninvited guest, joined his army at Dalkeith. The forces then marched south in two columns, one by Kelso towards Wooler to give the impression that Newcastle was the Prince's destination, while the second passed through Jedburgh and on down the Rule valley to the English border. On 8 November the main army reached Carlisle.

Intelligence filtering in from the east suggested that Wade was on the march, so Charles marched his men to Brampton, where the country was hilly and well suited to his Highland fighting men – he even chose a suitable field but Wade failed to appear, probably because snow had been falling between Newcastle and Brampton, making the march impossible. Half of the Prince's army was returned to Carlisle to continue the siege while he himself stayed on at Brampton until the 17th. Although Carlisle Castle fell easily, this was the point at which Lord George Murray's temper snapped: his uncompromising dourness clashed once again with the Prince's arrogant refusal to accept advice and as a result the Lieutenant-General resigned. He remained with the Jacobite army, but no longer as its commander – that position was left in the hands of the incompetent O'Sullivan, which proved fatal to the campaign.

While at Brampton the Prince tried to warn English Jacobite leaders that he was on his way, but was singularly inept in his choice of courier. A letter to Lord Barrymore in Cheshire, leader of the movement in England and an old hand at Jacobite intrigue, was entrusted by Sheridan to none other than a Cockermouth grocer named Peter Pattinson, who had arrived without warning and glibly talked his way into the Prince's headquarters one morning.[10] Pattinson and a companion managed to hand the letter over to Barrymore's son, Lord Buttevent, who was anti-Jacobite and burned it.[11]

By the time the rebel army marched into Penrith on 21 November and Kendal the following day, the government and authorities in most northern towns were well supplied with information about the strength and disposition of the Prince's men, mostly gathered from local people, but this was information rather than intelligence that would point towards the Jacobites' next move. The government remained totally baffled as to where Charles intended to go – would it be York, directly south towards London, or to north Wales, where people still feared a French landing? This last destination seemed the most likely but London could not be sure, which is hardly surprising since the Jacobites had not made up their minds either. The one significant move London made at this time was to order the King's son, the Duke of Cumberland, home from Flanders to take command of all the forces in Britain but with special charge of the army that would meet the advancing rebels in the west.

Charles spent Sunday 23 November in Kendal so that his officers and men could all attend church services, Protestant or Catholic, according to their faith. Charles was showing toleration, but he himself had to forego attending, 'there being no churchman of higher rank than the curate then in the place'.[12] This has been interpreted as a diplomatic decision to avoid offending either denominaton.[13]

Two days later he reached Preston, the furthest point south that the Highland army had penetrated during the '15 rising and it was ready to go further now in spite of the fact that Lancashire was proving a disappointment: the county contained many Catholics but while the invaders met with no opposition and were wished well everywhere, few new recruits joined them. By the time Manchester was reached on 28 November it was clear that the English nobility, however sympathetic they had sounded in the past, however much they had sported tartan and dressed their maypoles and election hustings with Stuart favours, were not prepared to fight. When they were needed to fire a gun or lift a sword for the King over the Water, they failed him.

Worse than a lack of recruits was the fact that Charles's soldiers were now beginning to desert to drift back to Scotland and his leaders were at loggerheads more than ever over what their next move should be. In fact the only good news Jacobite agents brought in was that the government commanders were still disorganised and had no hope of catching up with the swift-moving Highlanders in the immediate future.

Manchester was the one place where they were given a welcome: the town was strongly Jacobite and was easily taken – by a drummer and a whore, it was said. Certainly 23-year-old Elizabeth Byrom, known as Beppy by her family, saw it all and recorded it in her diary: 'About three o'clock today came into town two men in Highland dress, and a woman behind one of them with a drum on her knee, and for all the loyal work that our Presbyterians have made, they took possession of the town.'[14] Innocent young Beppy saw the female drummer as a mere camp follower – Whig propaganda cast her as a whore.

Here the Prince received the warmest reception he was to encounter anywhere in England and a regiment was raised under the command of Francis Townley, almost the only gentleman in Lancashire to throw in his lot with the Prince. The Reverend John Clayton, who ran a grammar school in Salford, took his boys to watch the Prince ride in and when Charles passed he fell on his knees in the street and invoked a divine blessing on him.[15] Nobody gave more to the Cause than Dr Thomas Deacon, a Non-Juror, known as bishop of a small religious body calling itself the True British Catholic Church, whose extreme views on the divine right of kings led him to give unswerving support to the Stuarts. Three of his sons, Charles, Robert and Thomas Theodore, all enlisted in the Manchester Regiment – and paid dearly for it.[16]

St Andrew's Day was celebrated in the city with a proud display of St Andrew's crosses made by Beppy and her friends:

> I dressed me up in my white gown and went up to my aunt Brearcliffe's, and an officer called on us to go see the Prince. We went to Mr Fletcher's [Reverend John Fletcher of the Collegiate Church] and saw him go a-horseback, and a noble sight it is . . . his horse had stood an hour in the court without stirring, and as soon as he got on he began a-dancing and capering as if he was proud of the burden, and when he rid out of the court he was received with as

> much joy and shouting almost as if he had been king without any dispute . . . As soon as he was gone the officer and us went to prayers at the old church . . . Mr Shrigley [Chaplain of the Collegiate Church] read prayers, he prayed for the King and the Prince of Wales and named no names.[17]

England was a depressing experience: after unfriendly Cumbria, hollow cheers in Lancashire and a deceptively warm welcome in Manchester, which brought only a few hundred recruits, Charles was looking into the eyes of failure but refused to recognise it thanks to his own ability for self-delusion. For some days he had been whistling to hide the starkness of the situation, buoying his spirits by listening to suggestions from d'Eguilles that the French were not just on the way but had actually landed – and he even deluded himself with claims that the English Jacobites had at last agreed to rise.

Yet Cumberland had reached Lichfield and was fast closing in while Wade plodded around less purposefully and by now was encamped somewhere in the vicinity of Doncaster. For all their superior intelligence-gathering, neither had yet fathomed the Jacobite plan. After the St Andrew's Day parading in front of the good folk of Manchester, Charles held a council meeting at which the atmosphere was far from festive. A considerable body of opinion suggested returning to Scotland to await the long-promised French assistance and it was only after lengthy discussion that a compromise was agreed – on Lord George Murray's suggestion they decided to defer a decision on retreat until they reached Derby.

Since scouts were bringing in news that Cumberland was raring for a fight and was closing in, the same tactic was used as had succeeded in Scotland – a feint was made towards Chester to suggest they were bound for north Wales, but the main army continued to Macclesfield. On the way they scored a great intelligence coup when a patrol out in search of information captured Roger Vere, one of Cumberland's best spies, hiding under a bed at the Red Lion ale house near Stone. Vere, who had been supplying the British commander with a considerable amount of accurate information about Jacobite movements for some time, was sentenced to death but was reprieved thanks to another spy who pointed out that if Vere were harmed, Jacobite prisoners held in government gaols might be executed. As a result, he was eventually freed, which was a terrible mistake since the spy later continued his espionage work and at the end of the rising gave testimony that sent many Jacobites to the gallows.[18]

Cumberland was totally taken in by the Jacobite ruse and moved to Stone where he was so determined to fight that he even went out and chose his battlefield, but once again he had been outwitted and was marching his troops around the countryside to no avail other than to leave them weary and hungry. All his manoeuvring left the road to Derby clear and the Jacobite army marched along it to enter the town on the afternoon of Wednesday 4 December.

It was not as unwelcome as it had been further north, probably at least partly because reports from the places they had passed through had said nothing of the pillage and rape English people had been warned to expect when the Highlanders came, and in any case the town had a reputation of being ill-disposed towards the House of Hanover. The description of the Highlanders from here was no more flattering than that from some people in Edinburgh: 'Most of their main body are a parcel of shabby, lousy, pitiful looking fellows, mixed up with old men and boys; dressed in dirty plaids, and as dirty shirts, without breeches and wore their stockings made of plaid, not much above half-way up their legs, and some without shoes or next to none, and numbers of them so fatigued with their long march that they commanded our pity rather than our fear.'[19] Morale was high among the men, whose single aim was to write to tell their families they were well, to sharpen their swords and be on their way south as soon as they could. Prince Charlie agreed and, as he settled into comfortable headquarters at Lord Exeter's house in Full Street, his thoughts were turning towards the grand entrance he would make into London. His leaders, also comfortably billeted around the town, were less happy: the farther south they pushed the farther they were from home and they realised they were in great danger of being cut off by Cumberland's or Wade's armies. As they talked together they became more discontented.

There was much coming and going by local nobility, landowners, and sightseers, but virtually no one – aristrocrat or common man – volunteered to join the Prince's army and one spy, Eliezer Birch, who had been sent by Cumberland, was recognised by men of the Manchester Regiment and arrested. Among the 'gentlemen' who turned up at Exeter House was one Dudley Bradstreet, one of the most notorious spies of the entire Jacobite century – but thereby hangs a tale, a number of tales in fact, and each taller than the last.

The story of the authentication of Bradstreet's own credentials is a spy drama in itself, which Rupert Jarvis related in the preface to his *Collected Papers of the Jacobite Risings.*[20] It all began with the publication in Dublin in 1755 of a book entitled *The Life and Uncommon Adventures of Captain Dudley Bradstreet,* which Jarvis described as 'a piece of picaresque reminiscence fairly characteristic of the genre of that day . . . full of pimps and prostitutes, low life and high'. Wedged between an account of Bradstreet as a pimp in a regular 'Place of Pleasure' and a pimp working freelance was a claim that it was he who persuaded the Jacobites to retreat from Derby on 5 December 1745. Hardly surprisingly, little notice was taken of such a claim from a known rogue until someone searching in the British Museum in 1929 came upon catalogue references to Captain Bradstreet. Alas, most related to a Captain Bradstreet in the British army in North America, but a few did in fact refer to Dudley Bradstreet, a government spy during the '45. These turned out to be correspondence that had been included in the 1755 volume. So Bradstreet's claim was true – he had been a spy, he had played a part in that momentous Jacobite decision at Derby and he was singularly shabbily treated by his masters (so mean that one cannot call them paymasters) afterwards.

Dudley's background deserves an airing: by his own account he was born in Ireland, in County Tipperary, in 1711, the son of an army officer, who abandoned him to foster parents, and when he was sent to school all he learnt was to play cards, at which he took 8*d* off the other scholars and spent it on gaming dice. His career as a gambler had begun. From there it was a short step to conquering women, who fell before him. He was soon master of the art of love: 'Her rhapsodies in my Praise were so great, as to make her forget all those low, base, and formal Arts of Prudery, whose System is to gratify Inclination in secret, but disavow every Attribute of Love when the least Ray of Light appears,' he boasted.[21]

He tried honest trading in the linen business and brewing (being presented with the freedom of Dublin and made Warden of the Corporation of Brewers on the way) and from then took to selling illicit gin in London and working as ponce to a doctor, a man of about sixty-five years old who 'had commonly about twenty-five Women in keeping, some of whom are often conspiring against him, so as to endanger his Life; in short, never had *Arcadian* Shepherd so ungovernable a Flock'.[22] Bradstreet saved the doctor from a member of his harem who was trying to accuse him of rape, and was rewarded generously both financially and with a position of further trust: 'He soon after advanced me to be first Eunuch of his Seraglio, a Place of Trust and Pleasure,' claimed the Captain.[23] The British government was to prove far less generous.

In panic-stricken London Bradstreet saw his opportunity. The news of the Jacobites' continued march south spread terror through the capital. Business came to a halt, shops closed and there was such a run on the Bank of England that the only way to stop the panic was to pay out in sixpences. Newspapers were hysterical, screaming about rebellion and popery, and the Archbishop of Canterbury issued a special prayer seeking God's protection from the advancing Jacobites and the French invasion which was expected hourly. The King was ready to flee and the Duke of Newcastle, the Southern Department Secretary of State with responsibility for home security, sat so silently in Whitehall that many waited for him to desert to the other side.

That was the moment when Bradstreet offered his services and after an interview with Newcastle's secretary, Andrew Stone, was assigned to go to Hackney, Highgate and Hampstead, where many itinerant Irish harvesters worked, to sound out their loyalty. Following this successful first foray into the dark underworld of espionage Dudley was ordered to spy on the disaffected in another part of the capital. He uncovered a plot to seize the Tower, which won him the confidence of Stone, who then set up a plot for a false trial that would result in sending Bradstreet to prison so that he could eavesdrop on the talk among his fellow convicts and pass what he heard back to Newcastle's secretary. Among those he encountered in gaol was the girl who had been his first *amour*, now imprisoned for stealing a watch out of a man's pocket.

By the time the Jacobites reached Manchester, Bradstreet was full of ideas to move north and work as a mole among rebel troops and incite them to mutiny. 'Another Scheme was that I would take one of the finest Women in London with me', he wrote, and, 'as the young Chevalier was reported to be a Man of Gallantry, she might perhaps get into his Confidence'. This tempted the Duke of Newcastle himself to meet Bradstreet at the Cockpit and order him to slip into the rebels' camp and 'delay them by some Stratagem'.[24] The Duke's secretary called him 'Captain', a title which he used ever after.

Given £100 to dress the part of gentleman or spy, whichever suited him best, and a false identity, 'Oliver Williams', he went to Monmouth Street the following day and bought 'a Suit of fine brown Cloth, very richly laced with Gold, and every other Part of my Dress suitable'. Having made his will and paraded in his finery in front of astonished and envious friends at a public house, the gentleman Oliver Williams set out by post chaise from the Swan in Holborn at ten o'clock on the night of 2 December. After five hours' rest at Dunstable he was on his way to Northampton the following morning in the company of a man who claimed to be one of Cumberland's officers, but whom Bradstreet did not trust because of his odd behaviour and his keen interest in every detail of the road. The pair, Bradstreet and the suspicious stranger, hired horses for the next part of the journey, but their guide, a lad of no more than nine years old, lost his way and they spent five hours 'upon a Moor and Heath that lies between Northampton and Creek', where they decided to stay overnight. Next morning they continued to Coventry but when the officer announced that he intended to remain there for two or three days, Bradstreet called the mayor and alderman and, announcing that he was 'authorized by the Government as an Inquisitor', had the man arrested. Emboldened by this brave act he sent a letter to the Duke of Newcastle declaring that he had heard the rebels were not in Chester so he would insinuate himself among them wherever they were. 'I have a Heart and Hand ready to attempt any Thing that Man can do in this Cause,' he ended the letter.[25]

The farther north he rode the more rumours he heard of war until he arrived at Coleshill where he stayed on the night of 4 December. 'Here we had Alarms every Hour, that the Duke's Army and the Rebels were engaged', he wrote. 'Those Dealers in News sometimes giving Victory to one, sometimes to another . . . all other Subjects were disregarded, but what related to Battles, Victories, or Defeats, and their Consequences.'[26] The following day he arrived in Lichfield where he saw the Duke of Richmond, who told him the Duke of Cumberland was expected there shortly, so Bradstreet waited. Immediately the commander rode into the camp the spy sent word that 'Oliver Williams' had arrived and he was called at once to meet the Duke.

It was a moving meeting, recalled to mind as clearly ten years later when the Captain wrote his memoir as the day it happened. If Bradstreet left London 'all in an Uproar', he found the King's commander frustrated to have been cheated of a fight at Stone and in dread of the rebels reaching Derby. 'There are certain Seasons of Distress in the Lives of the greatest Heroes, that will incline them to deign to hear Advice from the humblest Mortals,' he wrote. The Duke was delighted to have Oliver Williams's help: 'The first Words he said, were that he longed prodigiously to see me, that he had heard a great Character of me, and that now was my Time to fulfil it,' wrote the Captain. 'I then desired his Royal H—ness to order me to do something that might be useful, which I assured him I would execute, or perish in the Attempt.'

Bradstreet's advice was that the Duke should destroy the road from Derby to Northampton and render all provisions and forage in towns and villages in between useless, thus forcing Charles Edward to take other routes south that would enable the government army to intercept him. 'He heard me with great Attention,' Bradstreet continued, 'and then told me, that I must go to them directly, and if I could contrive any Means to delay them but twelve Hours, I might make my own Conditions.'[27]

He interrupted his narrative at this point to explain the etiquette of how to behave on being received by princes. 'Here I will inform my Reader, that he must be a little more exact in kissing the Hand of a Prince than a Lady; he holds it up, and you take it in your Right Hand and kiss the Back of it; as to a Lady's, if you like her, 'tis to be supposed you are indifferent which part of her Hand you kiss.'[28] The retired London ponce was well qualified to discourse on the correct convention for hand-kissing although he must have had little practice hitherto in being greeted by princes.

Having kissed hands with the Duke in the most gallant manner, Bradstreet set out after four in the afternoon on the 16-mile ride to Derby, passing rebels and King's messengers on the way – he gave any Jacobites he met a shilling apiece in the hope that they would get so drunk they would be captured and he picked up what information he could from the King's messengers. As he neared Derby he destroyed all incriminating papers he carried, threw away his black cockade that identified him as a Hanoverian supporter and entered the town showing all the fine lace he could on his coat and coaxing his horse to champ and dance a little to draw attention to himself. His mind ranged through history from the Romans to the thought 'that Queen Elizabeth's deliverance from the Invincible Armada was not greater than ours from the Rebels'. No doubt he cast himself in the role of Sir Francis Drake.

The rebels whispered among themselves that an English lord had come to join them and took him to Exeter House, where he was shown into the room next to the one in which the Prince's Council was meeting at that moment. There he met Colonel Stewart, Lord Kilmarnock, the Duke of Perth and O'Sullivan, who all accepted his story that he was travelling under the name 'Macdonald' to protect his family, and not four hours ago he had seen Cumberland whose army was waiting at Lichfield to cut off the Prince's retreat as soon as he left Derby, while the Duke of Richmond planned an attack on the right flank. Warming to his tale he invented a non-existent army of 8,000 or 9,000 men waiting to intercept them at Northampton. The worried Jacobite leaders asked Bradstreet to wait while they disappeared into the inner room where the Council was in session, but soon returned and ordered him into the room. The spy, Dudley Bradstreet, had penetrated the Prince's highest deliberations and stood before Charles Stuart's leaders.

This was the second meeting of the Prince's War Council that day. Earlier there had been a long and hard debate during which Lord George Murray argued for a retreat to Scotland, but Prince Charlie disagreed violently. Murray spelt out their danger – they faced three armies, Cumberland's, Wade's and another beginning to be gathered on Hampstead Heath to the north of London, making an army of 30,000 against their own 5,000. They might defeat Cumberland, but, taking casualties into account, they then would be left with a totally outnumbered army to face the other two. And should they lose to Cumberland, the remnant of their army would be massacred before it could return to Scotland. Lord George spoke bitterly against the English and the French: the Scots had played their part to support an English rising or a French invasion, but neither had come to the aid of the Cause. It was time to go back to Scotland and wait for such support.

Charles heard him out and listened to other members of his Council, almost all of whom supported Murray, then he flew into a rage and accused all who had spoken in favour of retreat of betraying him. Lord George Murray wrote afterwards: 'His Royal Highness had no regard for his own danger, but pressed with all the force of argument to go forward. He did not doubt but the justness of his cause would prevail, and he could not think of retreating after coming so far; and he was hopeful there might be a defection in the enemy's army, and that several would declare for him.'[29]

A march into Wales was suggested and rejected, and the meeting broke up without a decision. For the rest of the day Charles lobbied all the leaders to back him, but without success. Only Clanranald, Perth and O'Sullivan supported him and that was the situation when the Council gathered again in the evening.

The Prince's problem was that a number of those senior officers who would have supported him were not members of the Council, and therefore had no say,[30] and others such as Lochiel, who had stayed silent, now came out against him. The ultimate machiavellianism came from Broughton who argued for retreat in the morning, but when he saw that this was inevitable anyway, he told the Prince that he favoured a march to London and had only argued against it earlier in the day because he thought it pointless to expect an army to fight if the morale of its officers was low.[31]

By the time Bradstreet was summoned into the meeting it was clear that the Prince had lost the argument. But that was not how the Captain saw it. He wrote that he told his story, but 'when I came to that Part concerning an Army being at Northampton, the Rebel Prince, who was in a Closet just by, opened the Door, and pointed at me, saying, "That Fellow will do me more Harm than all the Elector's Army." Turning on the Council Charles added, "You ruin, abandon, and betray me if you don't march on", then shut the Door in a Passion.'[32]

Bradstreet was ordered to leave and a vote was taken. It cannot be claimed (as the spy himself did later) that his was the death thrust, for too many of the leaders were already on Lord George's side, but now not a single one of his Prince's leaders – not even his Irish friends – supported him. He had to accept defeat; they would turn back. But before his officers left he told them bitterly, 'In future I shall summon no more councils, since I am accountable to nobody for my actions but to God and my father, and therefore shall no longer either ask or accept advice.'[33]

Bradstreet had no doubts about the value of his part in the decision to retreat, and summed up his triumph without modesty. 'I thought they would have sent some body to Northampton, but was so indifferent as to my own Fate, that I regarded not the Consequences if this mighty Business was accomplished, which was to delay them twelve Hours; but this delayed them for ever.'[34]

He drank with the Duke of Perth that evening until, towards midnight, Lord Kilmarnock found him a bed to share with a Highland major. At the major's side the spy dreamed of the doomed Stuart royal family, although his grasp of their tragic history was none too sure:

> When in Bed, I began to muse a while on the Stuart Family . . . if history be true, so unfortunate a Sovereign Race was never equalled; James Stuart the 1st was murder'd on the 12th of February 1437; James the 2d. kill'd before Roxborough Castle, by the bursting of a Cannon; James the 3d. slain at Bannockburn by his rebellious Subjects; James the 4th. slain by the English near Linlithgow; James the 5th died of a broken heart; Mary Stuart, married to Henry Stuart, was murdered, and his wife, Mary Queen of Scotland, after an imprisonment of sixteen Years, beheaded in England; James the 6th. his Reign uneasy in England; Charles the 1st beheaded. Charles the 2d. long exiled; James the 7th of Scotland abdicated.'[35]

It was a travesty of the Stuart story and he had confused Bannockburn with Sauchieburn, where James III was murdered as he fled from the battlefield, while James IV died at Flodden not Linlithgow, Mary Stuart, the tragic Mary Queen of Scots, and her husband, Henry (Lord Darnley) died without violent deaths, and their heirs knew misfortune and calamity. The Captain, in his reverie, had got one fact right – the Stuart tragedy was never equalled in any royal family.

With that Captain Bradstreet fell into a sound sleep, soothed by the satisfaction of a job well done.

CHAPTER EIGHT

In London for Christmas – 2

'Tis certain I was a Prisoner, but appeared to be in some State, for they allowed me to wear my Sword. I conversed most part of the time we marched this Day with Lord Kilmarnock, who promised me, that in less than two Days I should be under as little Restraint as himself, and in the mean time should live as he did.

The spy Dudley Bradstreet's description of his departure from Derby with the retreating Jacobite army on Friday 6 December 1745.[1]

They called 6 December 1745 Black Friday because that was the day the Jacobite army pulled out of Derby to start the long, dreary trek back to Scotland, a sombre moment in Jacobite history. Whether it was the right decision has been argued over ever since. A case can be made for withdrawal to Scotland, but an equally strong one may be put forward for pushing on to London, which lay within a few days' march.

The Prince's argument that London was in chaos and that the government's armies would have no hope of catching up with him, was a strong one. It is perfectly easy to believe, too, that his arrival in the capital, where the Stuarts still had many friends, might have heralded another revolution as glorious as that of 1688. People of influence were already fleeing with their money and valuables, and Charles never abandoned the belief that if his leaders had kept their nerve the Stuarts could have been restored. But the chiefs and other leaders had a good point too. The English had done nothing and long-promised French support had not materialised, so there was no guarantee that if they continued to London they would find any more men ready to fight for them. And to march farther south left them more vulnerable, with their lines of communication back to Scotland lengthened so that they would be trapped in the event of losing the battle that must inevitably take place. Cumberland was close, although no one in Derby (except perhaps Dudley Bradstreet) realised how confused he was about the Jacobites' plans, and tired old Wade had only managed to make it to Doncaster. But there was that third army at Northampton of which Bradstreet warned them – how could the leaders know that it was still nothing more than a phantom, a few regular soldiers and volunteers being assembled hurriedly at Finchley to the north of London? The Black Watch, which had saved the day at Fontenoy, had arrived back from Flanders, too, and was on its way to join the defenders of London but for whom would it fight if Prince Charlie was leading its opponents? Government ministers were aware that, as well as distinguishing themselves at Fontenoy, these Highlanders had mutinied in 1743 and been savagely punished so no one could be certain that they would not defect now.

Bradstreet slept well in the major's bed that night in Derby and in the morning was told by Lord Kilmarnock that the Prince was not pleased with the news he had brought and had given orders for him to be detained. His horse and arms were to be taken from him, but Kilmarnock, clearly taken in by the gallant Irish captain, promised him the use of one of his own geldings.

Riding the Scottish leader's gelding, hemmed in among a company of Life Guards in the charge of an officer he named as Macnaghten, Bradstreet left Derby under cover of darkness on Black Friday morning. The first of the Prince's army followed at seven o'clock, Charles himself rode out about nine, and the last of his men were clear of the town by eleven. To confuse the townspeople and any government agents who might be watching, they did not take the direct road north but went by a circuitous route before doubling back on to the Ashbourne road. It was the trick Prince Charlie had used leaving Rome in 1743 but, in the black mood that enveloped him that morning, one thing is certain – the idea was not his.

The Highlanders believed they were on the road to London and it was only after dawn broke that they realised they were heading north-west. This was the first anyone except the tiny innermost circle of the Prince's most senior officers knew of the decision to return to Scotland, and there was much anger among the officers and much wailing in the ranks of the clansmen. All felt betrayed except the bold Captain who chatted nonchalantly with those he had been drinking with the night before. The officers questioned him about what had been happening in London and as he answered he felt proud to be riding in such state, and allowed to wear his sword in spite of the Prince's instructions: 'I spoke freely to every body, having three great Advantages, being best dressed, best mounted, and seemed to have more ready Money than any Gentleman among them.'[2]

At Ashbourne Bradstreet was given good quarters and allowed to join the Prince's senior officers, which nearly cost him dearly. Old Tom Sheridan recognised the Captain from his Dublin days, and actually addressed him as 'Mr Bradstreet', but fortunately Lord Kilmarnock was standing near and after whispered words between the two, Sheridan was told to call him Macdonald.

At Ashbourne, too, Bradstreet met Captain Vere, the spy who had been captured on the march to Derby and was now lying bound and starving, and under sentence of death. Perth was angry that Vere had not been executed already, and demanded he should be hanged next day, but Bradstreet warned against this: 'I told his Grace . . . that as the Elector had all the Gaols in England almost full of our Friends, one Example would be enough for him to hang an hundred.' Kilmarnock agreed to put this argument to the Council and Vere was reprieved next day. He was eventually freed after Carlisle was retaken and he returned to London.

By his own account Bradstreet was the hero of the march north. He drank with every Jacobite leader, he rode in a carriage with Lady Ogilvy and Mrs Murray of Broughton, and he even saved a poor man who stupidly drank to King George in the presence of some Jacobites. He also managed to fit in a little espionage at Macclesfield when they were quartered at a house where the housekeeper did not hide her dislike of the rebels. Bradstreet took her aside and asked what she thought of her visitors and their rebellion. She answered, 'Pray God may direct us all right.'

'I plainly see, Dame,' replied Bradstreet, 'you are of my Way of Thinking, that is, you wish King George well.' When she looked astonished he said, 'Be not surprised, good Woman, if you love the King and government, shew it by doing what I bid you when we march out of this.'

'Dear Sir,' the woman replied, 'I will do anything in my power to serve the King, let me know what it is.'

It was perfectly simple. As soon as the Scottish army departed she was to hurry to a justice of the peace who could be trusted to be loyal and tell him that Oliver Williams had told her the rebels were marching to Carlisle and would divide there. This information must be forwarded immediately to the Duke of Cumberland and the Duke of Newcastle. The woman did as ordered, and so the government army learned of the Young Pretender's retreat.

Captain Dudley Bradstreet, alias Macdonald, alias Oliver Williams, remained with the Jacobite army as far as Preston, where he was called to meet Mr Secretary Murray one evening while 'deeply engaged at Cards' – old habits died hard with Dudley Bradstreet. Broughton told him he now had the chance to serve the Prince:

> I . . . was to take my Horse and made the best Enquiry I could, to learn where the Duke of Cumberland's and Wade's Armies were, likewise those of Hawley and Ligonier, or if they had joined the Duke; that when I returned I should have the Honour to kiss the Prince's Hand, and hear of something greatly to my Advantage. This Commission I chearfully accepted . . . Next Morning early I was prepared, and shook Hands with Lord Kilmarnock, whom I never saw after till he was going to the Scaffold, upon which I was, to Execution, and I rode to Wigan that Morning.[3]

Bradstreet had acheived the distinction of becoming a double agent, although he had no intention of spying for the rebels. His final gesture to the Jacobites was to offer the Prince the fine horse that had been taken from him at Derby and presumably he rode south on Kilmarnock's gelding.

From Preston the spy, who claimed to have done more than anyone to wreck Prince Charlie's hopes, rode out of the '45 but not out of the Jacobite story. The Cause had not heard the last of Captain Dudley

Bradstreet, nor had the Duke of Newcastle and King George. Bradstreet had such trouble wringing payment out of Newcastle that he had to write a letter to the King and bribe one of the palace pages at St James's deliver it. As a result, he said, His Majesty ordered the Secretary of State to pay £120 on account, which Newcastle did, but with great annoyance at the Captain's audacity. Exactly how that matter was resolved eventually is unknown as the only firm evidence so far found is the letter from Bradstreet to King George in the British Library asking for £20 for his pains.[4]

While the jubilant and successful agent rode south in hope of collecting his reward, a very different Prince sullenly headed north in a mood as bitter as the short icy December days. He no longer rode at the head of his army, but tagged on towards its end, not even riding now, but hidden away in a coach much of the time and looking dejected and glum. He seldom troubled to issue orders any more.

Angry local people and militia companies of Lancashire proved a greater nuisance during the retreat than the British army since Cumberland was still plodding behind without a hope of catching up. He ordered weary old Wade north to Hexham from where the Highlanders' retreat to Carlisle might possibly be cut off, but snow made this impossible so Major-General Oglethorpe was sent to Lancashire where he just missed the Jacobites at Wigan.

Disinformation, deliberate or not, helped to confuse the enemy. McLynn recounts some of the yarns that were spun to Oglethorpe by prisoners:

> Captain John Mackenzie of Glengarry's Regiment, a young man of twenty-one, swore that he had heard from Lochiel, Keppoch and Lochgarry that at Derby Lord George Murray had wanted to press on to London and that Perth had been in favour of retreat. Since Murray was then suspected of wanting to lead the Prince ino a trap by advancing, he was placed under open arrest, having his sword taken from him and two men set to watch him at all times. Even more ludicrous was the 'intelligence' received from a prisoner in Ogilvy's Regiment: under questioning the man claimed that Charles Edward was so panic-stricken that he had already left the army in disguise.[5]

It was true the Prince and his former Lieutenant-General were behaving irrationally and this got through to the common soldiers. Charles's petulant delays and prevarications amounted to a virtual death wish as bad weather and appalling road conditions over Shap Fell held them up further. He ordered that nothing, not so much as a cannon ball, was to be left behind and Lord George Murray responded bloody-mindedly by offering his men sixpence apiece to carry 200 balls over Shap when there was no other means of transporting them.

The enemy was on their heels by the time they reached Kendal. At the village of Clifton, near Penrith, Lord George Murray ignored the Prince's instructions to retire to Penrith and in a short skirmish John Roy Stewart's and Cluny Macpherson's men sent the Hanoverians packing. This allowed the Jacobites to reach Carlisle safely on Thursday 19 December.

That night another bitter confrontation took place between Charles and his leaders. The Prince wanted to hold Carlisle Castle for strategic reasons to delay Cumberland, he said: Lord George Murray – his most critical opponent as usual – was all for abandoning Carlisle, throwing every gun or piece of equipment they could not carry into the River Eden, and quitting England. Charles maintained that Cumberland did not have the artillery to take the castle and it could hold out until they returned – in reality the reason offered by his biographer, Margaret Forster, sounds more plausible. She wrote, 'The truth was, his pride would not allow him to leave England without something to show for it. Carlisle, his one English victory, was important for prestige reasons and nothing else.'[6] He could not bear to yield this last corner of English soil to the enemy.

In the end it was agreed to leave a number of French–Irish soldiers and the Manchester Regiment (who had no desire to quit England anyway) to defend the castle, and many of the women were also left behind because it was going to be too difficult to get them across the Esk river, which was running very high and fast. Only a handful of the female regimental followers were with the Highlanders when they set out on the 20th.

At the riverbank the Highlanders waded straight into the flood. 'The foot marched in, six abreast,' wrote Lord George Murray afterwards, 'in as good order, as if they were marching in a field, holding one another by the collars, every body and every thing passed, without any lossess but two women, yt belonged only to the publick, yt were drowned.' A couple of women hangers-on were of little account in a war! On the Scottish bank pipers played a reel and the Highlanders, delighted to be on home ground again, lit fires and danced themselves dry.

Ten days later, as the prince was reviewing his troops on Glasgow Green he was given the news that the impregnable Carlisle Castle had fallen to Cumberland just as easily as it had done to the Jacobites – the English general had simply brought up cannon from Whitehaven, battered the castle into submission and taken the Manchester men prisoner. Because they were English the London government considered the men worse traitors than any other participants in the '45, and large numbers of them were executed or transported.

Scotland was just as surly and unwelcoming to Prince Charlie as England had been and Scottish officialdom was better prepared for his arrival than they had been the last time he set foot in the country. Edinburgh had been retaken the moment the Jacobite army marched south and the government quickly re-established itself. Neither officialdom nor the common people panicked in the capital as had happened in London.

A small document in the National Library of Scotland[7] reveals that members of the aristocracy, the chattering classes and the clergy of the capital all remained remarkably sanguine over the rebels' progress, laying bets against one another, usually for bottles of claret or rum, or in one case 'half a Gallon of Arrack to be drunk at Edinburgh – gallons Scots'. The wagers were on many aspects of the rising – how far the rebels would march into England, where the next battle would take place and even on who had been disloyal enough to visit Holyrood to see the Prince. The Lord Justice Clerk was an ardent gambler, laying bets at various times that the Jacobites would invade England (he won two bottles of rum), that they would march to within a hundred miles of London (he lost four bottles) and that Lady Wallace went to Holyrood to visit 'the tartan prince' (he almost certainly won that, for Lady Wallace was an ardent supporter of the Cause).

While the Jacobites were in England Lord Elchus and others promised to forfeit two bottles of rum each if the Prince attacked Edinburgh. They lost their wager because Charles had to travel north by way of Dumfriesshire and Glasgow since Edinburgh was back in government hands. He did not have to fire a shot to take the city, but the welcome there was distinctly Presbyterian and cold, so that he soon realised that if he had any hope it lay further north – or in France.

France had as yet sent little support: there had been plenty of noise and action of a kind but practically nothing had materialised. As Andrew Lang put it, Jacobite affairs in Paris were still 'perplexed' by the divisions within it. Sempill, Balhaldy and Lismore were all intriguing and in September, by the time the Prince reached Edinburgh, Marischal and Clancarty travelled all the way to King Louis's headquarters in Flanders to lobby d'Argenson for help. Their efforts did the Cause little good for the Minister tartly changed the subject by asking why Marischal was not with the Prince in Scotland, and he was outraged by the slovenly appearance of the one-eyed Irishman. 'Sir, your wig is ill-combed. Would you like to see my perruquier? He manages wigs very well,' he asked Clancarty. The Irishman leapt to his feet and shouted in English, 'Damn the fellow! He is making his diversion of us,' and stormed out. This story came from the spy Oliver Macallester admittedly, but it certainly reflects the feeling that existed between the Jacobites and the French at the time.[8]

The Prince's success during the first weeks of the campaign achieved everything Louis wanted without his having to strike a blow or take a risk for the Jacobites. Large numbers of British troops were withdrawn from Flanders and George II was forced to parley with the Emperor to save his beloved Hanover. There was even hope of peace with Britain on terms to suit King Louis. None the less, the French King had not abandoned the Jacobites, although why we cannot be sure, since he still had serious doubts as to whether their English followers would pluck up the courage to fight even if France sent an army to England. James's powerful pleas helped and a plan was mooted for an expedition to be mounted at Calais and Dunkirk with some 6,000 men of the Irish Brigade and Fitzjames's cavalry, all to be moved secretly from Flanders and sent to London,

Ireland or wherever the King chose. Louis could not lose by this for even if the fleet never sailed, its very presence on the Channel coast would divert the British troops from fighting his army in Flanders and it would leave the Prince free to take Scotland. His Ministers were far less enthusiastic, which is why Louis sent the Marquis d'Eguilles to Scotland to assess the situation there and assess the degree of support the rising ought to be given.

Eguilles's arrival shortly before the Jacobite army's march south was well timed and the Prince took it as a sign that French help would soon be on its way. The real reason for his mission did not occur to Charles. The Pretender in Rome was taken in by the French invasion plan and sent Prince Henry, now a young man just turned twenty, to Avignon where he and the Duke of Ormonde were to wait to be summoned to Paris to join the expedition.

In the midst of all this turmoil of plotting, planning, talking and, in the case of the young Duke of York, interrupting a life of prayer with preparations for a first taste of war, there came glorious news. English smugglers arrived in Boulogne with word of the routing of King George's army at Prestonpans and said that the way was open for the Prince – now proclaimed Prince Regent in Edinburgh – to march into England. Eguilles and Father Kelly in due course confirmed this and forced the French to consider much more seriously the question of what action they ought to take to ensure Charles Edward's success.

Although a former enemy of the Cause, d'Argenson now became its enthusiastic advocate, and James's followers in France were less united than ever. Clancarty, Marischal and Lally Tollendal were working hard towards engineering an expedition, while Sempill, Balhaldy and Lismore intrigued and interfered. In desperation the Duke of Ormonde was driven to tell their master in Rome, 'too many people are meddling in your Majesty's affairs at this juncture'.[9]

In October, while Charles was pondering his next move at Holyrood in Edinburgh, the French made a firm decision at last to mount an invasion, but in England and not Scotland, which made sense since Charles already held Scotland apart from a few castles and forts that had been bypassed to save time. And this decision was embodied in the Treaty of Fontainebleau, the last military alliance ever to be signed under the Auld Alliance. This treaty, signed by O'Brien on behalf of the King in Rome and d'Argenson for the King of France, promised armed assistance to Charles Edward against their common enemy 'the Elector of Hanover'. It committed Louis XV to helping to restore the Stuarts to their throne – the only trouble was it did not make clear whether this meant that of Scotland or England, or both.

'In a secret article appended after the signatures,' writes Frank McLynn, 'it was stipulated that in return for the use made of the Scottish and Irish regiments in the service of the king of France, their officers should have a free hand in recruiting to the regiments in whatever territories came under the dominion of Charles Edward.'[10] Had the '45 succeeded, the Treaty of Fontainebleau would have given France access to all those Highlanders who helped Britain in subsequent years to win its colonial and trading empire – it is a sobering thought.

Lord John Drummond was sent to Scotland immediately with 800 men of the Royal Ecossais and the French Irish regiments, who landed at Montrose on 22 November, by which time Prince Charlie was in Penrith. Instead of heading south Drummond settled down at Perth to recruit more men. Prince Henry in the meantime arrived in Paris, where he was received by the King while he waited to sail with the invasion fleet. All were confident that the French would be in London by Christmas.

Britain's moles in Paris soon picked up rumours of the planned invasion, but the difficulty was to discover whether the attack would be aimed against Scotland or England and where precisely it would take place in either country – would it be the original target of Maldon, might it be the Channel coast, or further west? Or would it be the east coast of Scotland, perhaps near Edinburgh since the Jacobites held the Scottish capital. Ireland was another possibility. But nobody knew the planned location, which is hardly surprising since the French themselves were still arguing over the best target.

While the French pondered this the British seized the opportunity to sow seeds of doubt through disinformation from their many agents and counter-agents in both London and Paris, all cleverly done by surreptitiously playing on every obstacle the invasion might meet and subtly damaging the Stuart Cause at the same time. Bussy, who had wrecked the 1744 preparations, was back in Paris, but still in the pay of London and he now performed the British another great service by sending King Louis a long memoir which suggested that a landing in the London area even by as many as 10,000 Frenchmen would stand little chance of success. He proposed instead a ludicrous landing in northern England, which would trap Wade's army between the invading army and the Prince. This was followed by a second memorandum to the King, unsigned this time, but written by another agent or someone in the pocket of those ministers in the French government who were opposed to the Jacobites. This second report went even further, and warned that the Royal Navy would stop a Channel crossing but in the unlikely eventuality of reaching England, the invaders could never succeed against superior British numbers. On the surface all this advice appeared very patriotic and it took the French King in.[11]

On the up-side, however, there were plenty of emissaries from Charles who confirmed the Prestonpans success, the glory of the Prince's 'reign' in Edinburgh, and the decision to march into England. Even Eguilles became caught up in the Jacobite euphoria and sent back glowing reports that exaggerated the numbers of fighting men Charles commanded – in fact, virtually doubled the actual troops the Prince had at his disposal. This achieved the dual effect of persuading Louis to proceed with the invasion, while at the same time lulling him into believing there was no hurry: if the Prince was leading an army of 10,000 men he did not need French help urgently. The King began to scour Europe for support, while the Duc de Richelieu was appointed to command the expedition and that experienced privateer, Antoine Walsh, was given charge of organising the little armada.

In the meantime the Jacobite hero, Charles Wogan, the man who had rescued the Pretender's bride, Clementina Sobieska, from imprisonment at Innsbruck on her journey to Italy to marry James, was busy in Spain trying to persuade a reluctant King Philip to send money and reinforcements to the Prince and with much difficulty succeeded in wringing a promise of a small number of men and a little cash. As with the French enterprise it was to prove too little and too late.

The French believed that *le Prince Edouard* was succeeding triumphantly on his own, thus preparations for the expedition were allowed to proceed at snail's pace in the face of obstruction from ministers opposed to it and the need to support Saxe on the Flanders front. In the meantime tiny amounts of French aid were winning through to Scotland, but at great risk and cost in lost ships and men due to Royal Navy vigilance. A number of the ships were intercepted off the east coast of Scotland, and the men and arms they carried were captured. Among them was young Alasdair Ruadh Macdonnell, the man who became Pickle the Spy, then a captain in the Royal Ecossais, who was taken in December 1745 on his way to Scotland with a detachment from his regiment and the Irish Brigade. Macdonnell, who was held in the Tower of London until 1747, was destitute and had to write to the Stuart banker, Waters, asking for help. Although he may not have been a spy at this time, he probably made the contacts that brought him back to London to sell his services to the British government when he found himself again without funds in the years following the '45.

Christmas came, but the expedition promised by Lord John Drummond when he landed his 800 men at Montrose in November still was not ready, although both Richelieu and Prince Henry had moved to the coast at long last to prepare for their departure. By now the British were beginning to realise that the target would be the south rather than Scotland – although they still had no idea where the invasion would land. Neither did most of the French who were involved, even at this late stage. But that was another matter!

Then came another bombshell – news of the retreat from Derby, which is the explanation usually offered for the cancellation of Richelieu's invasion. Frank McLynn, who has produced the most detailed study of France's part in the rising to date, does not accept this as the only reason – or even the main one – although many, including the Duke of Newcastle and his spies on the English coast, accepted at the time that it was. 'Despite the numerous assertions made over the years that the news from Derby occasioned the French to abandon the invasion project, it is quite clear that Richelieu decided to press on despite this setback,' wrote McLynn. 'As he wrote to the War Minister [d'Argenson], he considered himself too good a citizen to be afflicted at the prospect of seeing his enterprise founder because of the news from Derby and he was still determined to sail as soon as the winds were favourable.'[12]

The cursed Protestant winds were not the only problem Richelieu was facing: the British Navy played a highly successful cat-and-mouse game with his fleet of transports, blocking the French ports and causing great devastation among any vessels that dared to show face in the Channel during the last weeks of December and early January. The worst problem, however, was the continuing inability of the French themselves to coordinate even the last stages of fitting out their expedition.

At the root of the trouble lay continuing disagreement among Jacobites and inside the ministries in Paris, which resulted not only in indecision but in every secret being leaked to London. Nobody was able to agree with anyone else – the Ministers for the Navy and Army were at loggerheads, Richelieu and Prince Henry disagreed, Saxe wanted his soldiers back in Flanders and Louis allowed all this dissent to continue unchecked, which made his annoyance with Richelieu after the final collapse of the exercise all the more unreasonable.

In the final analysis Louis must carry the blame: he played his usual double-dealing game, quite sincerely wanting to help Prince Charlie yet allowing his ministers and officials to wreck the assembling of the expedition. It was not enough for him to rage against the Duke when the invasion failed and demand that another should be sent. It was now too late.

As Richelieu set about organising other means of getting reinforcements and money to the Prince, events in Scotland moved on and Charles Stuart's campaign was almost beyond help from anyone in spite of yet another victory. By 2 January Charles had had enough of Glasgow's cold shouldering of him and his men, and the following day he moved to Stirling, still confident that 10,000 Frenchmen would soon be with him. In the north the clans were still recruiting for him too, among them Lady Anne Mackintosh, who gathered together the men of the clan while her husband was serving with King George's army.

But clan feuds still scarred the campaign. On the march north a Clanranald MacDonald accidentally shot Young Glengarry's brother, Aeneas, in the street at Falkirk and the Glengarry clansmen demanded that he should be punished. The Clanranald man was executed, but even that and the Prince's decision to accord Aeneas the honour of being buried in the grave of the hero, William Wallace's companion, Sir John Graeme, did not placate the Glangarry clansmen. Many deserted.

Charles spent most of the month at Bannockburn House, the home of Sir Hugh Paterson, glad to be among friends and to rest after the weeks of stress in England. His health always tended to break down in times of stress and early 1746 was no exception – the Prince fell ill with a feverish cold and was nursed by Paterson's niece, Clementine Walkinshaw. On

17 January he left Bannockburn House to begin the siege of Stirling Castle and to defeat Cope's successor, General Henry Hawley, at Falkirk. He returned to Bannockburn House on the 19th. Both Dr William King of Oxford and Lord Elcho, who turned against Charles later, claimed Chementine became his mistress then, but there is no proof, only surmise based on a legend of an illegitimate child buried at Finsthwaite in the English Lake District and the fact that Clementine never married during the intervening years until he brought her to live with him in 1752.

As relations with his leaders crumbled life became more difficult. Lord George Murray's temper finally snapped and the former Lieutenant-General sent Charles a letter demanding that he should call a Council of War made up of the actual army commanders. He threw in Charles's face the delay the Prince insisted on at Lancaster, and sacrifice of the men left behind at Carlisle. Murray pulled no punches: 'It is to be considered that this Army is an Army of Volunteers, and not Mercenarys, many of them being resolved not to continue in the Army, were affairs once settled.'[13]

In a cold fury, Charles began his long letter of reply: 'When I came into Scotland I knew well enough what I was to expect from my Ennemies, but I little foresaw what I meet with from my friends.' He would not accept Lord George's plan for a committee of the army's commanders, and resented the imputation that he had to treat his officers differently because they were volunteers:

> Every one knew before he engaged in the cause, what he was to expect in case it miscarried, and shoud have staid at home if he coud not face Death in any shape: but can I myself hope for better usage? At least I am the only Person upon whose head a Price had been already set, and therefore I cannot indeed threaten at every other Word to throw down my Arms and make my Peace with the Government. I think I shew every day that I do not pretend to act without taking advice, and yours oftener than any body's else, which I shall still continue to do, and you know that upon more occasions than one, I have given up my own opinion to that of others.

After defending the delay at Lancaster and the abandonment of the Carlisle garrison, he ended by telling Murray he would not yield to anyone's authority. 'I have insensibly made this answer much longer than I intended, and might yet add much more, but I choose to cut it short, and shall only tell you that my Authority may be taken from me by violence, but I shall never resign it like an Idiot.'[14]

After the Battle of Falkirk Charles had retired to his sickbed at Bannockburn House and possibly to Clementine, leaving his leaders without direction and their men with nothing to do while booty from the battle was crying out to be taken home. They deserted in droves. By the end of the month Lord George and seven of the chiefs wrote to Charles, pointing out that clansmen were disappearing in such numbers that they risked having to fight Cumberland, who had now arrived in Scotland with a greatly weakened army. They suggested a retreat into the Highlands where they could capture those forts the Hanoverians held there and when the French arrived, they promised they would rise again immediately, bringing with them their clansmen who had recently deserted. Charles was beside himself with rage and beat his head against the wall. 'Good God. Have I lived to see this?' he cried. But in the end he had to agree to their demand.

In his covering letter sent with the chiefs' petition, Lord George made a significant remark: 'One thing we think of the greatest Consequence, whatever His Royal Highness determine, let the thing be kept as secret as the nature of it will allow; and only those consulted who may be depended upon for their Prudence and probity.'[15]

Lord George Murray had a far greater sense of security than the Prince, who went through the entire campaign unaware of the value of intelligence – obtaining it or preventing his enemies from acquiring it. His sole use of agents was as couriers to carry news of his exploits to France to encourage Louis XV to send him reinforcements, and even now, with Cumberland closing in, he appears to have made no effort, other than the day-to-day sending out of scouts, to keep ahead of his enemies.

As arrests made at the end of the rising show, Cumberland's leaders not only made deliberate attempts to find information, but waged a bitter espionage war against supporters of the Prince. Many were arrested on the slenderest grounds, and a man could land in gaol for a long period simply 'on suspicion'. Hugh Ross was arrested at Montrose simply on the grounds that he was 'suspected of being a spy', and Charles Petry, son of a soldier serving in Stirling Castle, was 'held on suspicion of discovering what was doing in the Castle'. Both were discharged without trial, but not before they had spent a considerable time in gaol – Petry was still in Edinburgh Castle eleven months after his arrest. Robert Scott, a salmon fisher from Angus, was seized 'for carrying a letter from Major Bagot, a rebell, directed to Provost Skinner of Montrose', and was held for a year, but never tried.[16]

Ever on the alert the Hanoverians nearly caught the Prince in mid-February when he stayed overnight at Moy Hall, the home of the beautiful 'Colonel Anne' Mackintosh who raised her husband's clansmen to fight for him.[17] Charles had spent Saturday night 15 February as an unwelcome guest of the staunch Whig, Grant of Dalrachny, at Inverlaidnan, near Carrbridge, and – as usual careless about security – let slip the fact that he planned to move on to Moy the following day. Grant or one of his men saw his chance to earn the £30,000 reward and the everlasting gratitude of the government by tipping off the Earl of Loudoun, who had command of the force stationed at Inverness, and Loudoun laid a plan to ambush Prince Charlie with 1,500 men during the night.

Fortunately for the Prince, Hanoverian security on this occasion was no better than his own: the fourteen-year-old daughter of the innkeeper at one of the inns in Inverness overheard Loudoun's officers discussing the planned raid on Moy and, without waiting even to put on her shoes, she ran with the news to the house of the dowager Lady Mackintosh, who lived in the town. Old Lady Mackintosh immediately sent a young lad, Lachlan Mackintosh, to raise the alarm and the lad evaded the government soldiers to reach Moy ahead of the enemy. Charles was asleep in bed when the alarm was raised and, thinking enemy troops were in the house, leapt up, threw on a dressing gown and a bonnet over his nightcap, thrust his feet into his shoes and, without taking time to buckle them, escaped. His hostess by this time was running through the house in her shift 'like a madwoman, imagining the enemy was already within the house'.[18] Lochiel and a detachment of his men, the only guard the Prince had, took Charles to a hiding place beside Loch Moy and waited.

In the meantime the Moy blacksmith, Donald Fraser, and four men, who had been keeping watch on the Inverness road, raced towards Loudoun's approaching men, and by shouting imaginary orders, naming various regiments of the Prince's army and firing at random, so convinced the attackers that a whole Jacobite army was about to fall on them that they turned and ran. The single victim of the Rout of Moy, as the incident became known, was the MacLeod piper, Donald MacCrimmon, who was shot dead.

Prince Charlie was a victim of the Rout indirectly: in the cold February night he caught another cold, which turned to a severe fever – probably scarlet fever. This put the Prince out of action for much of March, but it did not hinder (in fact his absence may have helped) his leaders in consolidating the great psychological victory of Moy. During that month Loudoun fled north of the Beauly Firth and Inverness was retaken, then Fort George and Fort Augustus, although Fort William, the biggest strong point in the north, managed to hold out. A large number of small forts in Perthshire fell to the Jacobites as well and to crown an excellent month for the Cause Cumberland was given a bloody nose in a skirmish at Keith.

Then luck ran out. The Jacobites were so desperately short of money by now that they were paying their troops in meal, and when that ran short, they ordered the engraver Robert Strange to engrave copper plates from which paper money could be printed. The plates were completed only two days before Culloden so were never used. They were found in a bog near the battlefield in about 1860.[19]

More important than printing money was to receive cash in hand from European friends and Charles still hoped that something miraculous like that might happen. He had received nothing since £2,500 arrived from Spain in January, but still hoped France would honour all her promises. Jacobites in France were still pushing for an expedition following Richelieu's failure but enthusiasm had distinctly taken a downward turn at Versailles and in the end all that got within sight of the Scottish coast was the appropriately named ship *Le Prince Charles*, with some men – and even more welcome – a supply of money. Because the Scottish east coast was so well guarded it was decided to sail north through the Pentland Firth and land the cargo somewhere on the Moray Firth but even there she was unable to avoid the ever-alert Royal Navy. Four English cruisers intercepted her in the Firth and chased her for five hours until she ran aground near Tongue in Caithness. Lord Reay seized the money and arms and took 200 men prisoner and the Earl of Cromartie, who was sent to recover the *Le Prince Charles*'s cargo, not only failed but ended up a prisoner himself.

Prince Charlie's luck had really run out – he was without money, without his secretary since Murray of Broughton also fell ill with the fever, and all that was left was to face Cumberland – sooner than he or any of his army wanted, for the Hanoverian prince was closing in.

To the last Prince Charlie made wrong decisions, listening to O'Sullivan on the choice of battlefield when he ought to have heeded Lord George Murray. After sending the Lieutenant-General out to reconnoitre a favourable position, he rejected Murray's choice of an easily defensible position near Dalcross Castle and asked O'Sullivan's opinion. O'Sullivan recommended Drummossie Moor, an uneven piece of land close to Culloden House, moorland pitted with bogs and little lochans, a position hard to defend. As Lord George complained afterwards, 'Not a single souldier but would have been against such a ffeeld had their advice been askt.'[20] But then O'Sullivan was not a trained soldier and Charles Stuart was too arrogant to seek the advice of experts likely to contradict him.

Having chosen the wrong 'ffeeld', the Prince proceeded to send his army on an ill-advised, ill-organised and futile surprise attack on the enemy on the night of 15 April – ill-advised because he believed he could catch Cumberland's men off-guard while they were celebrating their leader's twenty-fifth birthday and ill-organised because the Jacobite commanders left it so late to begin their march that reveille sounded in the Hanoverian camp before they reached it. All the unfortunate Jacobite soldiers could do was return to their own camp, where they arrived about six o'clock, starving, dog tired and dejected beyond belief. As Lord Elcho reported, a great many then set out towards Inverness in search of food, while the remainder lay down to sleep where they were, many so exhausted that Cumberland's guns failed to wake them and they were bayoneted where they lay.

The Duke of Cumberland may not have been a brilliant soldier, but he was astute enough to realise that now was the time to strike. Quickly he brought his army into position, soldiers having to wade up to the waist at times as they dragged cannon through the muddy waterholes of Drummossie Moor until, by one o'clock on 16 April 1746, they stood face to face with the enemy. Cumberland had 9,000 well-disciplined men at the ready, facing a Jacobite army only half as large because many of Prince Charlie's men were still asleep or away foraging for food. Those on the field, already tired and hungry, were now cold as well because

O'Sullivan had positioned them facing into the freezing rain and sleet that was blowing across the moor. Part of the army was also hemmed in by the walls of Culloden estate. In contrast, Cumberland's men were well set out with their backs to the bad weather and raring to fight.

The Prince's first line of battle was mainly Highland, but his second comprised largely Lowland regiments and Scottish and Irish units from the French army, behind whom stood the few cavalry he possessed. The Prince sat on horseback on Balvaid hill where he could look over the whole field.

Before two o'clock it was all over: Cumberland's murdering guns cut a swathe through the Highland line and his deadly bayonets followed through. That afternoon 1,200 of Prince Charlie's men lay dead, surrounded by as many more wounded or dying; the Duke had lost only 364. In tattered disarray the Jacobite army was fleeing in all directions pursued by redcoats, while the Prince sat immobile, disorientated, distraught, demented and too dazed to do anything until Cameron of Lochiel's uncle, Major Kennedy, led him away, with 'loud huzzas of victory' from Cumberland's army ringing in the distance.[21]

Lord George Murray had the final word on Culloden. Before the first shot was fired on Drumossie Moor Lord Elcho asked him how he thought the day would go. The Lieutenant-General turned to him and answered simply, 'We are putting an end to a bad affair.'

CHAPTER NINE

The Very Last Battle

> When the vessel of the English commandant began to fire, the Captain of the Marines called on him to throw himself on his face. Mr Hales answered that he was not in the habit of doing that, and was killed.
>
> Lord Elcho's description of an incident at the Battle of Loch nan Uamh[1]

With as much dignity as his overweight belly allowed, His Hanoverian Royal Highness the Duke of Cumberland settled his buckskin-clad buttocks on a large flat stone, known to this present day as the Cumberland Stone, to watch his men complete their morning's work. The scale of their victory was gratifying, even humbling, to this man already aware of his own importance, and one account describes how he simply sat there for a while and stared ahead in silence. 'After some minutes of deep meditation he rose and walked among the dead. He laid his hand upon his breast and lifted his face up to the sky, and said, "Lord, what am I, that I should be spared when so many brave men lie dead upon this spot?"'[2]

Having accepted the Lord's generosity he ordered surgeons to take care of the wounded, then ate his midday meal still seated on the stone, surrounded by the dead and dying. His men, rewarded with rum, brandy and an extra ration of biscuit, threw their bonnets in the air and cheered. 'Billy for Flanders', they shouted time and again, and at that moment were prepared to follow him back to Flanders, or anywhere, for they had tasted glory.

Cumberland was too mesmerised by the scale of his victory and his men too busy killing, burning houses and rounding up prisoners in the vicinity of Drumossie Moor to think of ordering an immediate search for the Prince. Thus Charles was able to ride south unmolested, guarded by Captain Robert O'Shea of Fitzjames's Horse and O'Shea's men. At his side for comfort rode his old friend and mentor, Tom Sheridan, who had accompanied him all the way from Rome – all through his life in fact – and now felt heartbroken. These Irishmen were Charles's only consolation; John Hay of Restalrig and a few Scottish officers also in the party were merely tolerated. Scotsmen were no longer to be trusted.

At the ford of Faillie on the River Nairn they encountered O'Sullivan and Lord Elcho, and paused to discuss what should be done next. Elcho wrote afterwards that the Prince was 'in a deplorable state' and so convinced the Scots were going to betray him that when he saw a group of them riding towards him he 'ordered them to go away to a village a mile's distance from where he was, and he should send his orders thither'.[3] He 'neither Spoke to any of the Scots officers present, or inquired after any of the Absent, (nor at any of the preceding battles he never had inquired after any of the wounded officers),'[4] said Elcho, who never was able to forgive this disgraceful treatment of his countrymen who had made so great a sacrifice for the Cause.

Having talked matters over with the favoured Irish clique, Charles decided to push on down the valley of the Nairn accompanied only by Sheridan, O'Sullivan, Captain Felix O'Neill and no more Scots than were absolutely necessary for his safety and to show him the way. Those Scots he retained were Elcho, aide-de-camp Alexander MacLeod the Younger of Muiravonside (usually known as 'Sawnie'), 'Sawnie's' servant Ned Burke, a North Uist man who had carried one end of a sedan chair in Edinburgh in more peaceful times, and a Roman Catholic priest, Father Allan MacDonald.

It is amazing that neither side had given proper thought prior to Culloden to what immediate action should be taken in the event of defeat – or victory for that matter. Charles had deliberately shirked the issue and had not even agreed a specific order for a mustering point in the event of defeat, despite Lord George Murray's pleas for a rendezvous. Ruthven was suggested as being remote and safe but nothing was decided, for the simple reason that Charles Stuart was unable to contemplate losing a battle. More than a month earlier, when Murray begged Charles to start gathering stores and meal in the Badenoch mountains for a guerrilla campaign should the need arise, he was ignored.

As a result, in the wake of Culloden the remnant of the Jacobite army, already hungry and short of weapons, simply scattered towards their homes and relatively few stayed together to reorganise and fight on. In normal circumstances clansmen could hide among the mountains and live off the land with little difficulty, but after Culloden they were pursued by Cumberland's unrelenting, systematic vengeance without the support of leaders or chiefs.

As for organised intelligence gathering, that was forgotten by both sides in the wake of the battle. The Jacobites were in headlong flight, while Cumberland stood by and watched his men murder wantonly and as he rode to Inverness later that afternoon he passed evidence of carnage every step of the way, where his redcoats had slashed and stabbed at the fleeing and the wounded, at the guilty and the innocent. The killing was vicious and unrestrained – escaping rebel soldiers, men and women drawn to Culloden by nothing more than ghoulish curiosity, women seeking to help their menfolk and beggars lurking to rob the dead – all were cut down indiscriminately. Few escaped and a redcoat wrote that by nightfall on the day of the battle both Drummossie Moor and the road to Inverness were 'covered with blood, and our men, what with killing the enemy, dabbling their feet in the blood, and splashing it about one another, looked like so many butchers'.[5]

Cumberland obviously was not the only butcher on Culloden field that day, but he was the one who had to live with the name. When a grateful London proposed to make him a freeman of one of the city livery companies, an aldermen was heard to growl, 'Then let it be of the Butchers.'[6] The name stuck, and Duke Billy, hero of Culloden, became 'Butcher Cumberland'.

At Inverness prisoners were herded together until every secure space was filled and they had to be transferred to ships lying offshore for transport to prisons in the south. To begin with the search was concentrated on the area running westward from the Great Glen to the sea, forcing raiding redcoat parties into remote glens where even the silence frightened them. 'These were mighty and dreadful mountains', whose eeriness affected the soldiers with 'hypochondriacal melancholy'[7] and fear of ambush by clansmen who knew the territory better they they ever would.

With the help of the clan militia over the ensuing weeks the Duke made systematic sweeps of this vast wild region, his men leaving behind total devastation wherever they went. Anyone concealing arms was shot out of hand, women were raped and families murdered or driven into the bleak hills without shelter. Homes were burnt to the ground, belongings and implements destroyed and cattle driven away. Hundreds of men, women and children, some guilty, but the majority innocent, suffered the living hell of what Professor Allan Macinnes goes so far as to call a policy of 'state terrorism . . . that verged on ethnic cleansing.'[8]

Unaware of what was happening around Inverness and with nothing decided about the future, the Prince and his companions struck southwards through Strathnairn as far as Aberarder, from where they crossed into Stratherrick and continued to Gorthlick, near Loch Ness, a few miles short of Foyers. They were now 20 miles or so from Culloden, in Clan Fraser country. The further the Prince distanced himself from Culloden and the day's disaster the more his spirits rallied. Lord Lovat's 'doer', or land factor, lived at Gorthlick and here the Prince met that old villain, the Fraser chief, Lovat himself – the one and only time the two came together. Lovat now treated Charles to a fine example of his ability to face in two directions: at seventy-nine years of age he was as treacherous as ever – he had given his support to the King over the Water in the '45 only after the Prince's first major victory at Prestonpans made a Stuart restoration look probable and, although he himself was too old to fight and his heir also managed to miss Culloden, he left it to a 20-year-old lad, Charles Fraser of Inverallochie, to lead his clansmen. Poor Inverallochie was shot in cold blood by one of 'Hangman' Hawley's men as he lay wounded on the battlefield. At Gorthlick Lovat gave the hungry Prince some food and wine and with this very welcome meal – the first

Charles had eaten all day – more of his dubious advice, supporting Elcho's strongly expressed view that to begin with the clansmen ought to take to the hills and continue a cat-and-mouse campaign until they were ready to fight again. Lovat dramatically exhorted the Prince to remember how his ancestor, Robert the Bruce, had been defeated eleven times before he finally won the Scottish crown at Bannockburn,[9] but then Fraser changed tack and cast doubts on whether a campaign could be sustained in the mountains. Much to Elcho's disgust Sheridan and his Irish cronies tended to agree and Charles himself, obviously in much better spirits, suggested he should go to MacDonald country in the west until it was clear whether a guerrilla campaign could be mounted. If this proved feasible, then he himself would sail to France to obtain money and arms from King Louis.

While he rested at Gorthlick Charles ordered 'Sawnie' MacLeod to send Cluny Macpherson a letter beginning, 'You have [heard] no doubt ere now of the ruffle we met with this forenoon. We have suffered a good deal; but hope we shall soon pay Cumberland in his own Coin.'[10] The terrible defeat had become no more than a 'ruffle', reflecting the reviving resilience of the man who had been in the lowest depths of despair only hours earlier. It is hard to believe, as the Fraser chief claimed, that during the deliberations, Charles broke down in tears. 'My good lord,' he wept, 'we are all ruined; I am heart-broken for the misfortunes that beset the poor land of Scotland', then fell into a faint.[11]

'Sawnie' was ordered to tell Cluny MacPherson they would rally at Fort Augustus, not Ruthven in Badenoch as had been mooted but never confirmed before Culloden. His order is absolutely clear: 'We are to review to-morrow [Thursday April 17] at Fort Augustus, the Frasers, Camerons, Stuarts, Clanranalds, and Keppoch's people. His R.H. expects your people will be with us at furthest Friday morning [the 18th]. Dispatch is the more necessary that his Highness has something in view which will make ample amends for this day's ruffle.'[12]

For a second time, Culloden was reduced to a 'ruffle', and Charles expressed the intention of making amends by launching a plan to re-engage the enemy. It has been suggested that 'His R.H.' had no such idea in mind: he had decided at Gorthlick to return to France and, well aware that the enemy spy network would learn of his plans very soon, ordered 'Sawnie' MacLeod to send off that 'ruffle' letter to Cluny Macpherson, simply as a blind because he knew that one of the many government spies around would soon report it back to Cumberland. The Duke would not know whether to send his redcoats to Ruthven or to Fort Augustus, thus giving Charles time to escape to the west coast and make contact with a French ship.[13] Such disinformation would have been a clever tactic.

Although already well distanced from Culloden, Gorthlick was too unsafe a place to linger that night, so the party pressed on down the Great Glen to Invergarry Castle, where the resourceful Ned Burke found and cooked a couple of salmon, which made another excellent meal. The

Prince did go to Fort Augustus, but gave his clansmen no time to muster: as they had not turned up there by midday he either lost patience or panicked, and headed westward without waiting for them. By nightfall he reached Donald Cameron's cottage at Glen Pean, but was on his way again first thing the following morning and reached Arisaig on the 20th.

O'Sullivan told of this decision to make for Arisaig:

> 'Well,' sayd the Prince, 'I see as well as yu yt my scituation is desperate; I'l make the best of my way to Arisaig. Il be there in Clenranolds Contry & near Locheil, far from Forte William, altogether out of the way of the enemy at least for some time. Il soon know if my friends can undertake any thing at least to guarde their Contry. If they are, Il joyn them, & as there is no mony, without wch it is impossible to keep together or subsist, if they promise to keep out, Il go my self to France to see & bring them Succor of money and men, I hope my presence will do morre with the King then any body I can send.'[14]

These are not the words of a man who is running away as his enemies have suggested – Charles intended to go to Arisaig, it is true, but the plan was to wait there to discover whether his supporters could 'guarde their Contry' before sailing to France. This confirms the statement made in a letter written by 'Sawnie' MacLeod, saying that provided the chiefs gave their promise to remain 'out' for the Cause, he would go to King Louis and bring 'Succor of mony & men'. That all seems perfectly reasonable but what is harder to understand is why he did not hold to the original mustering place of Ruthven. This may be explained by his confused state of mind at the time perhaps, or simply his impetuous nature and ignorance of the country. The advice he was given by O'Sullivan and Lovat did nothing to help either, so it seems hardly fair to accuse Charles of cold-heartedly abandoning the Highlanders to save his own skin. Yet at the time and afterwards that is what many felt. Another important factor easily overlooked is Charles's inherent Stuart belief that he had a God-given divine duty to preserve his royal line, so his personal safety as heir to the House of Stuart transcended every other factor.

Cluny showed the Prince's letter to Lord George Murray, who had already learned from the clan grapevine that Charles was on his way to Clan Donald country, and understood at once what was afoot. Beside himself with anger, he turned the letter over and scrawled savagely on the back:

> Dear Sir, Mr McLeod's letter seems to be a state of politiks I do not comprehend, tho' I can guess it is wrote the day of the Battle; and, instead of sending any word to us, every body are ordered from Lochaber to Badenoch to cover H.R.H. from being pursued, which I wish it had taken effect. Adieu. I wish we may soon see better times.
>
> Your's, G.M.

The words *'to cover H.R.H. from being pursued'* demonstrate how obsessed Murray was by the thought that the Prince was deserting them: he emphasised the point even more by adding a bitter little postscript in which he observed that Charles, having proposed a muster at Fort Augustus, did not wait there long enough to meet the clansmen who obeyed his instruction to come there: 'I observe the rendezvous was to be as yesterday at Fort Augustus, but those who came from that last night, say H.R.H. was gone for Clanronald's country.'[15]

To add insult to the deep hurt Murray felt at that moment, Michael Sheridan, old Sir Thomas's nephew, had been ordered by the Prince to return and collect the money Charles had given to Aeneas MacDonald at the Ford of Faillie for distribution among his needy followers. 'It is a very hard case that the Prince carries away the money while so many gentlemen who have sacrificed their fortunes for him are starving,' he exclaimed. 'Damn it! If I had ten guineas in the world I'd with all my heart and soul share it with them.'[16]

Lord George reached Ruthven in Badenoch on 17 April, where he was joined by the Duke of Perth, Lord John Drummond, a few other chiefs and some 1,500 Highlanders. They were a ragged, disorganised, dispirited, leaderless band, apart from the Macpherson and Ogilvy regiments that had escaped with light casualties. Elcho had expected the campaign to continue among the mountains until the Jacobite army was ready to face Cumberland again and so had Lord George Murray, but both now realised they were without supplies, officers or their prince.

Bitterly angry at the terrible casualties his kinsmen of the Atholl Brigade had suffered at Culloden because of O'Sullivan's disposition of the Jacobite forces and now white-hot with rage at the Prince's betrayal, Murray sat down and dashed off a long letter to Charles, pouring out his rage first against the foolhardiness and incompetence that had characterised the rising from beginning to end, then about his choice of leaders. He berated the Prince for sailing to Scotland without French help: 'It was surely wrong to sett up the Royal Standard without having posetive assurance from his most Christian Majesty that he would assist you with all his might,' he raged but saved his most vicious censure for the organisation of the campaign, damning Charles for choosing O'Sullivan as adjutant-general and for putting Hay of Restalrig in charge of supplies. 'Happy had it been for us that Mr O'Sullivan had never got any other charge or office in our Army than the care of the Bagage & equipages, which I'm told he had been brought up to & understood'. As for Hay, 'he served yr R.H. most egregious ill' with the result that the army was starving and short of equipment when it faced Cumberland. 'Had our feeld of Batle been right choise, & if we had got plenty of provisions, in all Human probability we would have done by the Enemy as they have unhappily done by us.' Nothing more was left to the Lieutenant-General after such plain speaking, but to resign his commission and that he did.[17]

The Jacobite historian Henrietta Tayler called this letter inopportune and Lord George's biographer, Winifred Duke, described it as 'an angered, outspoken, somewhat injudicious letter' and she believed that if the Prince ever received it, it was at least partially responsible for the venom with with Charles Stuart tried to hunt down his former Lieutenant-General in exile.[18] Certainly from that moment there was no chance of a reconciliation between the two.

According to Chevalier de Johnstone, those who mustered at Ruthven arrived in good spirits, anxious to reorganise and retaliate – highly improbable so soon after the battle for an army that had been so badly mauled, scattered and left broken and disorganised. No prince appeared in Badenoch to lead them – only his ADC with a curt message, which made matters worse: 'Let every man seek his safety in the best way he can,'[19] they were told by 'Sawnie' MacLeod. Two days later a second letter from the Prince confirmed that it was now every man for himself:

> When I came to this Country it was my only view to do all in my power for your good and safety. . . . Alas! I see with grief, I can at present do little for you on this side of the water, for the only thing that can now be done, is to defend your selves till the French assist you. To effectuate this, the only way is to assemble in a body as soon as possible, and then take measures for the best, which you that know the Country are only Judges of. This makes me be of little use here, whereas by my going into France instantly, however dangerous it be, I will certainly engage the French Court either to assist us effectually, and powerfully, or at least to procure you such terms as you would not obtain otherways. My presence there, I flatter myself, will have more effect to bring this sooner to a determination than anybody else.[20]

The letter was read out by Lord George Murray before the clansmen were dismissed to return – as best they could – to their homes. Chevalier de Johnstone described the moment:

> Our separation at Ruthven was truly affecting. We bade one another an eternal adieu. No one could tell whether the scaffold would not be his fate. The Highlanders gave vent to their grief in wild howlings and lamentations; the tears flowed down their cheeks when they thought that their country was now at the discretion of the Duke of Cumberland, and on the point of being plundered; whilst they and their children would be reduced to slavery, and plunged, without resource into a state of remediless distress.[21]

'Bring it to a determination!' the Prince had written. News their comrades brought of Cumberland's cruelties as they arrived at Ruthven confirmed to the clansmen what *determination* Cumberland envisaged and they believed their Prince was abandoning them to that fate. The common men had nowhere to go but home to await their fate, but there was a choice for the chiefs: some returned to their clan lands, but many chose exile.

Lord George Murray made his way south to Atholl where he hid in the vastness of the great woodlands of Glen Lyon, but the Duke of Perth was too ill to skulk in the hills, so he and his brother, Lord John Drummond, made their way to the coast in the hope of finding a boat to take them to France. Lord Elcho, angry and disillusioned over the Prince's conduct and his treatment of the Scots at the Ford of Faillie, headed for the coast too.

Had Charles Stuart wanted to fight he could have found a nucleus of leaders to wage a guerrilla campaign in the mountains beyond the Great Glen – they were already gathering in the very part of the West Highlands where he himself was now seeking refuge. But Prince Charlie had already made his decision to leave and was hidden by the MacDonalds in Arisaig while he waited for a French ship. Unwittingly, Charles Edward Stuart had struck a crucial blow against his own Cause, although there were still men among his leaders who continued to hold out hopes of renewing the fight even without him. Some of his most faithful were gathering only a few miles away at the head of Loch Arkaig, among them Donald Cameron of Lochiel, whose family believed he had fallen at Culloden until he arrived home at Achnacarry, carried by his clansmen who had snatched him from the battlefield. With both ankles broken, Lochiel made the painful journey from Culloden slung across the back of a horse, yet he arrived at Loch Arkaig with neither spirit nor enthusiasm for the Cause diminished. In hiding with him now were his brother, Dr Archibald Cameron, and John Murray of Broughton, who had been too ill to fight at Culloden, but had come to Cameron country in search of Lochiel and others likely to help him to revive the campaign. In their hideout close to Loch Arkaig, Lochiel and Broughton discussed how they might bring the chiefs together to plan a new campaign.

Arisaig was no random choice of refuge on the part of the Prince or the chiefs: it belonged to the Clanranald MacDonalds, which made it safe in one sense but also meant it was highly probable that the area would soon be searched by redcoats or militia, so Charles's MacDonald guardians decided to spirit him away to the Outer Hebrides. From there escape to France could be arranged just as easily since Long Island was another landfall favoured by his French friends. With this in mind, on the night of 26/27 April the Prince was rowed to Uist – and of course the voyage began from the convenient Loch nan Uamh.

On the Long Island, the MacDonalds evolved an elaborate new plan: instead of waiting for a French ship, they would take Charles to Stornoway on the island of Lewis, pass him off as a shipwrecked sailor and hire a small boat to take him to Orkney, then across the North Sea to Norway and thence back to France.

What neither Prince Charlie nor his guardians realised was that as he was being rowed to Benbecula, two French ships were approaching

Scotland and only two days later they dropped anchor in Loch nan Uamh. What is more, they had come with orders to bring the Prince back should he be in need of rescue – an odd instruction in the light of the fact that news of the disaster of Culloden did not reach Paris until nearly the middle of May.

The man with the 'second sight' to arrange this was the faithful Antoine Walsh, the privateer and slave trader who had brought the Prince to Scotland the previous year and had been involved in the abortive French invasion plan of December 1745. Walsh was an astute man as one would expect someone so successful in the precarious privateering business to be, and all through the campaign he had kept a close watch on the progress of the rising.

Alarm bells rang in Walsh's mind the moment he learned of the Jacobite withdrawal to the north in February, and realising the rising was in deep, deep trouble, he submitted a memorandum to Maurepas, the Navy Minister in Paris, suggesting that no more men should be sent to Scotland until there was better news of the campaign. With an acute awareness of the Prince's danger, Walsh proposed that two privateers should be despatched to Scotland quickly with money and arms, but also with instructions to bring *le Prince Edouard* back to France if he could no longer hold out in Scotland. Walsh tried to sound optimistic by saying, 'It could well be that, before the ships reach him, the Prince's cause will have revived.'[22] But this carries the ring of an unconvinced man.

Louis XV granted permission and two vessels, the *Mars* and *Bellone,* were fitted out and despatched to Scotland. They anchored in Loch nan Uamh on the second last day of April to be greeted by a ragged group of clansmen, who broke the news that the Prince had been defeated and was in hiding among the mountains. The French captains decided to unload their cargo of arms and money – and several hundred casks of brandy – to sustain a summer guerrilla campaign by the clansmen in the hills until the Prince had time to regroup the remnants of his army.

Good fortune mattered as much as good leadership in the aftermath of Culloden and by a stroke of luck the ships were less than 20 miles from the hiding place of Lochiel and Broughton, who had by now been joined by the Prince's aide-de-camp, 'Sawnie' MacLeod, and old Tom Sheridan, who had to be left behind when the Prince sailed to the Outer Hebrides. These two confirmed that Charles was now in the Outer Isles and had made up his mind to return to France to seek King Louis's help. Lochiel was greatly upset by such a betrayal of the Cause, and sent his brother in search of the Prince to persuade him to stay. Flight, said Lochiel, would be 'so dishonourable to himself and so harmful to the whole Scottish nation.'[23]

After the initial shock of Culloden, news travelled fast along both the Jacobite and Hanoverian grapevines that summer and by 1 May Captain Thomas Noel in HMS *Greyhound,* lying at anchor off Isleornsay in Skye, had word of the Frenchmen's arrival. He raised anchor and set off in pursuit next morning, accompanied by the sloop, HMS *Baltimore*, and a second sloop, HMS *Terror*, which he was lucky enough to meet up with off the island of Eigg, so at dawn on the morning of the 3rd this little flotilla of three Royal Navy vessels sailed into Loch nan Uamh as the Frenchmen were busy unloading their cargo.

John S. Gibson, who has written much about the role ships played in the '45, captured the viciousness of the fight that followed from eye-witness accounts left by a young French lieutenant, Guillaume Frogier, and Lord Elcho:

> The *Greyhound* was now able to come in close, haul across her forefoot, rake her [the *Mars*'s] with her broadside, and then put about and give another broadside. Against this onslaught *Le Mars* could only bring to bear the two guns in her forecastle . . . There the guns were smashed from their mountings. Muskets were shattered. Seventeen were dead or wounded. Blood was everywhere. Panic seized over a score of the survivors who fled to shelter under the quarter deck, only seven remaining at their duty. Fearing that his ship was in imminent danger of being boarded, Captain Rouillée sent a reinforcement of forty men to the stricken forecastle; and the bolder spirits among the ship's gunners, not being able to bring their guns to bear on the British ships, seized pistols and muskets, and rushed in a crowd to the point of danger, shouting, 'Vive le Roi'.[24]

Dozens of clansmen on shore also had a ringside view of this last battle of the '45. 'We saw the combat as well as if it had been a combat prepared expressly for our benefit, and the vessels were sometimes so near the shore that we heard the words of command on board of each,' wrote Elcho afterwards. He saw one of the Jacobite escapees, Major Hales of the French Royal Ecossais Regiment, die on the quarterdeck of the *Mars.* All of which suggests that even those on the loch shore were too close to the action for comfort: in fact at one point the *Greyhound* fired directly on the clansmen as they rushed to and fro, 'carrying the arms, money, and powder off from the seashore; which service they performed with amazing resolution, many a cannon ball being fired in order to hinder them by the largest of the English ships', wrote Captain John Daniel.[25]

The battle was fought in the customary manner followed by the French and British navies at this time, the French firing at the enemy masts while the British blasted cannonballs straight into the Frenchmen's hulls. Both sides were highly successful; after six hours Noel's little fleet was forced to withdraw to the Sound of Mull to repair the damage to its sails, but the *Mars,* having foolishly remained at anchor when the action began, was left with sixty-five hits above and seven below the water line, and carried 3 feet of water in her hold. With so much damage and twenty-nine of her crewmen dead and eighty-five wounded, the best she and the *Bellone* could do was limp off home.

The final blast of the Battle of Loch nan Uamh – and of Prince Charlie's '45 campaign – came from neither the Royal Navy nor the privateers, but from a lone Highlander busying himself on the shore of Loch nan Uamh to make sure that the brandy would find a good home. He let some lighted embers from his pipe drop into a barrel of gunpowder, blew himself to kingdom come and sent his fellow clansmen racing for cover.

The Battle of Loch nan Uamh could be described as an honourable draw, but the French boasted afterwards that they had had the best of the encounter and the British Navy had behaved shamefully – *honteusement* is the word they used – which was a lie. Noel's little fleet had fought bravely: he may have had three ships, but they were smaller and mustered considerably less fire power. They would have returned after repairing their sails to resume the fight had the Frenchmen not taken a number of fugitive chiefs on board and slipped away out of sight within a few hours.[26]

Aboard the privateers when they sailed were the Duke of Perth, who died on the voyage, Lord John Drummond, glad to abandon the Cause and resume his career as an officer in King Louis's army, Elcho, who could not wait to put as great a distance as possible between himself and Charles Stuart, and old Tom Sheridan, now too old for the rebel life. Lockhart of Carnwath and John Hay of Restalrig were also in the party.

To their credit, Murray of Broughton and honest, high principled Lochiel, remained behind in spite of Broughton's illness and Lochiel's wounds, determined to stay with the clansmen in the hope of organising a campaign among the mountains, although their disillusionment with the Prince's conduct was growing. Murray admired the Cameron chief's resolve not to desert his clansmen: 'Mr Cameron of Locheil retired into a little hutt with Mr Murray where he expressed his unwillingness to desert his Clan in the unhappy Situation they were then in, as Inconsistant with his honour and their Interest; and observing that as them two had gone along hand in hand during the whole affair, he hoped he would not now leave them, but begd they might share his same fate together.'[27]

In addition to arms and the brandy, which had made so many Highlanders tipsy by the loch shore, the *Mars* and *Bellone* landed several casks filled with bags of gold louis d'or. This money, which became known as the Loch Arkaig Treasure, was to tear the clans in Scotland and Jacobites abroad apart all through the remainder of the movement's existence, and long into history. It was to cause anger, envy, mistrust, lying, greed, suspicion, backbiting and betrayal as its consequences reverberated all the way from Lochaber to Rome and back over the years.

The Loch Arkaig Treasure brought the honesty and loyalty of trustworthy men like Dr Archibald Cameron and Ewen Macpherson of Cluny into question, whilst at the same time it revealed the villainy of Pickle the Spy, whose treachery led to the execution of Dr Archie Cameron, the last victim of the '45. The fate of the Loch Arkaig Treasure also added a charge of theft to the accusations of betrayal made against John Murray of Broughton, who was suspected of helping himself to some of it.

Andrew Lang likened this hoard to the cursed Rhinegold in the legend of the Nibelungen,[28] and undoubtedly it became a canker of Wagnerian magnitude within the Jacobite movement, contributing in no small measure to the destruction of the Cause. Although both Lang[29] and Marion F. Hamilton[30] have made admirable studies of the Treasure there are still unanswered questions, so that to this day it remains one of the great and continuing mysteries of Prince Charlie's story.

The captains of the *Mars* and *Bellone* had been unwilling to land the money at Loch nan Uamh when they learned of the Prince's flight. They informed the chiefs that since there was nobody with sufficient authority to receive the money, they intended to take it back to France. Lochiel and the other clan leaders realised that the gold was vital to finance the campaign they still hoped to wage in the mountains, so Murray of Broughton was sent to talk the Frenchmen round. After all he had been the Prince's Secretary during the rising and consequently was the most important-sounding man of their group.

Murray was still a sick man so he did not travel directly across the mountains, but took an easier, though longer, route through Glendessary to the coast and then south to Loch nan Uamh. Even that proved too taxing for the sickly Broughton and he had to stop off overnight at Glendessary, perhaps taking the opportunity to visit his wife who was in hiding in that part of the country at this time, and was 'Bigg with child'. It took a further two days to reach Keppoch just north of Loch nan Uamh and he arrived there just as the sea fight was beginning.

When he was taken ill at Glendessary, Murray sent Archie Cameron and Lochiel's uncle, Major Kennedy, an officer in the French service, ahead to persuade the Frenchmen to release the money. Kennedy later operated as one of the Prince's principal agents under the pseudonym Thomas Newton to try to recover the treasure. At Loch nan Uamh, Cameron and Kennedy succeeded in persuading the French captains to hand over the money, partly by smooth talking and partly because the Frenchmen panicked at the sight of the British warships bearing down on them, and hurriedly landed six casks containing bags of gold louis d'or – handing the money over to the representative of the Prince's former Secretary was preferable to having it seized by the British Navy if they should be boarded.

The casks were hidden in a wood until the action was over, but when the time came to recover them one was found to be missing. No one has ever named the suspects but that evening two men were brought before a kind of drumhead court martial. However, before the 'trial' got under way a Roman Catholic priest, Father Harrison, turned up with news that he had recovered the missing cask, which was returned the following morning, intact except for a single bag of 700 or 800 louis d'or. The priest, who learned of the theft in the confessional, named no names and even Murray said only that 'the Authors [were] by description guessed at'.[31] Lang claims the thief was an Irishman, but perhaps a clue lies in a statement that after the Battle of Loch nan Uamh, the MacLeans disappeared back to Mull with 'one of the French long boats loaded with brandy and some cash'.[32] Could that have been the missing 700 or 800 louis d'or?

No sooner had the *Mars* and *Bellone* departed than MacDonald of Barisdale and young Clanranald turned up, demanding that the money should be shared out among them to recompense them and their friends for their losses. Broughton had to admit they had received no regular pay since March and had suffered much, so he not only paid their arrears but also allowed half a louis d'or for every wounded man and a little money for clan widows as well. He said he handed over 4,200 louis in all to the clansmen at that time.

For safety Murray decided to send the remainder of the money back to Loch Arkaig in the care of Archie Cameron so that it would be well out of the reach of those Royal Navy captains who knew supplies had been landed and were expected to return in search of them. At the same time Broughton made his own painfully slow way back to Lochiel but was horrified to learn on reaching Loch Morar that Dr Cameron had been stopped again by young Clanranald's men, who objected to the money being carried from Clan Donald to Cameron jurisdiction. By a mixture of threats and flattery Cameron prevailed on Clanranald to allow the money to pass.

Clanranald's demand was just a taster for the greed and treachery that was to follow over this treasure which the two Frenchmen had brought too late to benefit Prince Charlie's campaign.

CHAPTER TEN

The Great Rebel of the Isles

Cumberland: Is this the great rebel of the Isles?

MacDonald of Sleat: No, my Lord Duke, had I been the Rebel of the Isles, your Royal Highness would never have crossed the Spey.

First words exchanged between the Duke of Cumberland and Sir Alexander MacDonald of Sleat on meeting.[1]

As the euphoria of victory faded the Duke of Cumberland found himself miserable and isolated, even from his immediate circle of loyal Scots. He complained bitterly that he could get no intelligence and reckoned himself 'more in an enemys country' than when he was warring against the French in Flanders.[2] His officers and men felt no more contented with their lot.

Spring continued so slowly to show its face that bitter winds carried sleet and rain across the mountains every day, and nights remained freezing cold right into May, leaving the redcoat hunters as miserable, cold and hungry in their makeshift shelters as their quarry were, lying in hideouts, often within sight of their homes, yet unable to be seen there. Major-General John Campbell of Mamore complained early in May that he was running short of supplies as his pursuit of rebels was hampered by a violent storm of wind and rain that had raged for three days without let-up[3] and as late as the third week of May, Lord Loudoun sat down to write a report on the hunt for the Camerons to the west of Loch Lochy, but had to hand the task over to one of his officers after writing only a few words. His fingers were too numb to hold the pen.[4]

The hunt among the hills took as great a toll among the searchers as among their quarry. In the middle of July Campbell of Mamore complained bitterly to his masters in London, but received little sympathy. Henry Maule wrote: 'Sorry to hear you have a return of your rheumatick pains. The Duke [of Newcastle] bids me offer you his compliments and desires that whatever is done that is not agreeable to you that you don't complain of it. Patience is your only cure at present.'[5]

The rebels did not rush to surrender willingly, so on 1 May Cumberland issued a new proclamation, ordering civil officials, ministers of the Established Church of Scotland and other dutiful subjects to report the 'lurking places' of rebels, but even this had little effect. Again, clanspeople were being encouraged to spy on their own kinspeople, which gave some the opportunity to settle old scores, but the greatest danger to rebels in hiding was betrayal by captured clansmen under torture or by an accidental slip during questioning. For their part, the majority of the ministers of the Kirk, while pleased that the rebellion had been crushed, were less happy to report the names of young men who had been away from their parishes too long without explanation.

Only the Macphersons surrendered their weapons as a clan. Many chiefs were lying low in the mountains or making for the coast in the hope of being picked up by a French ship, while individuals or small groups of clansmen simply headed as far away from Culloden as fast as they could – anywhere out of reach of their pursuers. Fleeing Jacobites turned up in the oddest places: two Campbeltown sailors came on 'a Number of people in arms whom they conjectured to be Rebells' on the island of Ailsa Craig in the Firth of Clyde on 23 May. Customs officials at Campbeltown reported that the men 'saw severalls who be the Richness of their Dress appeared to be persones of Distinction. That having attempted to Land on the said Rock of Elze (Ailsa) the Sentrys Threatened to fire on them.' The sailors prudently withdrew.[6]

Even chiefs who had remained loyal feared for their lives and property, since Cumberland's orders even before Culloden were to 'distress the country' in order to ensure that the rising was crushed. A month before the battle Dougal Stewart of Appin and others wrote to General Campbell seeking a letter of protection against such depredations, but the answer he sent them on 27 March merely said, 'You can show this letter to any of the King's officers which may save your house until you get an opportunity to apply to the Duke for protection.'[7] Yet Campbell was a humane man, and Stewart's plea prompted him to issue an order to navy captains patrolling the seas around the Western Isles to 'take the utmost precaution to distinguish lands and houses of rebels from those of loyal subjects'.[8] Alas, they did not always heed him.

The Stuart Prince remained the main prize, however, and government spies were badly frustrated in their search for him. The single great post-Culloden intelligence triumph of the Jacobites was that the Prince always managed to remain a step ahead of his pursuers in spite of the questioning and torturing of prisoners, hunting by the army and navy and the £30,000 reward that still remained on offer. It is to the Highlanders' eternal honour that no one betrayed him for that money, which would be equal to £1 million or more today. Like the maquisards of the Second World War, they handed him on from one group to another, secretly, silently and always ensuring that only his immediate guardians knew his whereabouts. As a result, at any given time, many loyal supporters (even those closest to him ever since he arrived in Scotland) were seeking the Prince as desperately as his enemies. It was thoroughly confusing for everybody, although Charles Edward himself never appreciated how much these friends helped him.

While Cumberland concentrated on the area around Inverness in the weeks following Culloden, Campbell was left to fret at home in Argyll, raring to get his men across Loch Linnhe and into the heart of Ardgour, Morar and Moidart where he was certain the Prince and rebel leaders would be hiding. 'I propose my self to go to Fort William where I shall expect the honour of your Royal Highness's commands,' he wrote to Cumberland the moment he received the news of Culloden. 'I propose to scour the western islands, from which I think the rebells (as being the most rational rout) will attempt getting out of Britain.'[9] He asked for men to reinforce his militia, but the Duke was too busy in Inverness to send any help.

As a Highlander Campbell of Mamore was in the best position to glean information on movements of clansmen and over the early weeks of May he passed on much news of rebel activity. He learned that Cameron of Lochiel and Coll MacDonald of Barisdale had met with a few others in Badenoch and had discussed plans to rise again, and that Alexander MacDonald of Glencoe was back home, which at least gave him the chance to take some positive action relatively close by. He did not find the chief, but in the long term his efforts paid off for within a month, Glencoe, now a sick man, realised he could hold out no longer and that if he had to surrender, it would be better to give himself up to Campbell than to Cumberland. He was right, for Campbell allowed him to go to Inveraray on parole and he was not sent to Edinburgh Castle as a prisoner until the following March.

Mamore's intelligence gathering was highly successful because he constantly had his militia and clansmen spies on the move among local people, picking up every scrap of information they could about movements of fugitives. His agents could easily pass themselves off as sympathetic fellow clansmen so his methods did not need to be as brutal as those of the redcoats. The overall gathering of intelligence by the army and navy was hampered not merely by the difficulty of recognising who were the government's friends and who were enemies, but by the problem of communicating with one another in order to coordinate their movements along this empty and desolate coast. The atrocious storms of wind and rain remained their worst opponent, however.

Gradually the hunt shifted to the western seaboard as General Campbell had suggested, with reports from the glens indicating that the Prince and a number of his leaders were in the Morar/Moidart area looking for a ship to take them to France. Both sides misled their enemies by spreading lies or half truths, which added up to a triumph of disinformation – a term not known to the Highlander of 1746 but an art in which all were highly skilled. Half truths were always better than lies since a pinch of honest information lent plausibility to any lie.

One *mémoire* in the French Foreign Ministry archives[10] claims that Cumberland offered Lochiel 'very favourable terms' at this time and promised to use his good offices with the King in favour of other chiefs.

Whether this was a genuine gesture born of humanity, or mere disinformation to persuade the clan leaders to surrender, is not known (indeed it is uncertain whether any such approach was made at all), but if the Duke did make an overture to the chiefs it was rejected. Many still believed a new campaign was viable.

As the search for the Prince widened during early May, the navy intensified its patrols among the Hebridean islands while on land the southern and far western fringes of the Highlands were being scoured by the Independent Companies. The value of some of these companies of clansmen is questionable, however: the black cockade of Hanover in their bonnets meant little as the bond of clanship proved stronger at times than Hanoverian money. The government was aware of this and never really trusted the clan militiamen or their leaders, however loyal they appeared to be.

For a time after the Battle of Loch nan Uamh government commanders believed the Prince had escaped aboard one of the French ships, but eventually they found out he was still in Scotland and probably in the Outer Isles, so the search was resumed with renewed energy. Campbell of Mamore was delighted to be let loose at last on Lochiel's lands west of the Great Glen, while other troops scoured the glens around Fort Augustus. At the same time the navy was reinforced off the west coast to block further French help from reaching the Highlands.

Those chiefs who remained behind after the *Mars* and *Bellone* left held a council at which Lovat was present and proposed a guerrilla campaign in the mountains, for which the Fraser chief promised 400 of his clansmen. Suspicious of the old fox, Murray of Broughton drew up a detailed bond of good faith that all were asked to sign, but, significantly, Lovat would not be persuaded to put his name to it. Nor did the Master of Lovat appear with the promised reinforcements. Murray, still not recovered from his illness, realised that he and Lochiel were almost the only leaders prepared to continue the campaign in the hills and felt betrayed by their fellow leaders and their Prince, who could not trust his Scottish followers any more – except perhaps the MacDonalds. By his flight to the far isles and his clear statement that he intended to flee to France, they realised the extent to which they really had been abandoned.

Against this background, backbiting and enmity flourished among the chiefs as they tried to come to terms with defeat and look out for themselves. Murray complained that Aeneas MacDonald, the banker, sent a letter accusing him of mismanaging the Prince's money, while Lovat answered every question 'in his own evasive manner'.[11] Lovat was deeply immersed in treachery and Lochgarry and others were accused of thieving from other clans, many of which were already riven with enmity as their leaders tried to come to terms with their defeat.

The two loyal men, one Highlander and the other Lowlander, were worn out and without hope: Lochiel was still suffering much pain and Murray of Broughton remained weak, recovering only very slowly. In

Murray's words both were living in a 'skulking, starveing way, lyeing on the side of Hills all the day, and travelling, or rather wandering, all the night, with scouts at a mile or half a mile's distance, never dareing to stay two nights in one place'.[12] They could achieve nothing in Scotland for now, so it was agreed that they too would flee to the Continent and with that in mind, Broughton set out for the east coast to find a boat to take them to Holland.

Cumberland's manhunt may not have brought him the prize of the Prince yet, but it did earn him the satisfaction of netting old Lord Lovat on an island on Loch Morar. Some said he was caught hiding in a hollow tree but others claimed he was taken as he lay comfortably on the two feather beds which it took to hold his fat carcase.[13] A detachment from Fort William, commanded by a Captain Millar, claimed to have captured him but the man reputed actually to have made the arrest was Captain Dougal Campbell of the Argyllshire Militia.

Cumberland wrote with relish to the Duke of Newcastle: 'I imagine that the taking of Lord Lovat is a greater Humiliation and vexation to the Highlanders than anything that could have happened, as he is dignified with great Titles, and Ranks high in command . . . they thought it impossible for any one to be taken . . . especially as they had a high opinion of his skill to make the best use of these Advantages.'[14] Title, rank and skill proved useless to wily old Simon Fraser now: he was taken off to London for trial.

During the third week of May the Duke moved his headquarters to Fort Augustus – within easy reach of the heart of the Jacobite clan fastnesses, where he could wreak havoc as he had already done farther north. Many rebels still had not surrendered their arms, or if they had done, they brought in only a few ancient rusted firearms and swords. They remained as well armed as ever, he told Newcastle: 'I hope his Majesty will not imagine that by these people's laying down their arms the country is a jot surer from any fresh rising, for at this time almost every Highlander is possessed of two or three sets of arms.'[15]

While the scorched earth policy continued there was one great bonus for the Hanoverian army in the plunder of cattle to line the pockets of officers and men. Cattle were brought into Fort Augustus in such numbers that the grasslands beside the River Oich resembled a great Highland cattle tryst rather than an army headquarters. An army that smells blood is dangerous; but one that smells blood and money is lethal. Redcoats were allowed to sell the cattle they seized and in no time scores of Lowland and north of England cattle dealers began to flock north until the glens were virtually emptied of animals. John Prebble summed it up vividly – as he summed up so much that resulted from the '45:

> Neither fire nor sword, bayonet nor hangman's hemp, was to have so terrible an effect on the clan system as this vast robbery. His shaggy, timid animals were to the Highlandman what the buffalo was to the

North American Indian. He lived on them and by them, they were his wealth and his livelihood, and without them he had nothing. Cumberland knew, as General Sherman was to learn in the American West a century later, that a warlike people may be more easily starved than fought. So every day the cattle came lowing from Glen Tarff, Glen Garry and Glen Dow until the camp, said Michael Hughes, was 'like a country fair'.[16]

And as this rape of the clan country continued Prince Charlie remained safely hidden in the western islands among his MacDonald friends. The role of the 'Great Clan' as they were known, is one of the great enigmas of the '45. Clan Donald was the most numerous and most powerful clan in the whole of Scotland, with lands that extended across a vast stretch of the West Highland mainland and to the far islands of the Outer Hebrides. It had always been strongly pro-Jacobite, so Charles Stuart had every reason to expect its support when he called Clan Donald 'out' in 1745.

Instead, the response ranged from the bravery of putting Cope's army to flight at Prestonpans to the ignominy of their sulking refusal to charge when ordered to at Culloden because they had not been assigned the position on the right wing of the battleline that was traditionally theirs. Shamed by this petulance of his clansmen, the Keppoch chief bravely charged straight into the enemy and died. At the other extreme from Keppoch's bravery were Young Glengarry acting as a double-agent and Coll MacDonald of Barisdale helping himself to a large amount of the Loch Arkaig Treasure. Glory and shame coexisted in the 'Great Clan' .

Hardest to explain away was how the two most powerful MacDonald chiefs, well known to have Jacobite sympathies, stayed at home when the Prince sought their support. Sir Alexander MacDonald of Sleat and Ranald MacDonald of Clanranald had both refused to join him, although Clanranald sent his son and Sleat did not stand in the way of many of his Skye clansmen who joined the Prince's army of their own free will. Sleat raised a militia regiment for the government and this force helped to track down rebels after Culloden and destroy the livelihood of a great many of their fellow Highlanders; however, Cumberland never really trusted him. Tension between the two was ill-concealed.

Despite accusations of treachery or faintheartedness which have been made against these two Clan Donald chiefs, within a week of Culloden Prince Charlie found himself in the care of their clansmen and remained so until July, after which his hiding places were in close proximity to them until his escape to France the following September. Although the Skye chief's personal role remains something of a mystery, as long as Prince Charlie needed protection, Sleat's clansmen and women – and even the chief's wife – were there to help him evade capture. But for the MacDonalds of Sleat and Clanranald Charles Stuart was unlikely to have escaped.

By the time the Duke of Cumberland's Fort Augustus cattle fairs were in full flourish the Prince's Clan Donald protectors had found him a very comfortable lair in the Outer Isles, where he was able to enjoy peace of mind such as he had not known since his arrival in Scotland a year earlier. After the unsuccessful attempt to help him to escape by way of Orkney and Norway, Clanranald's men took him to a safe hideout at Corodale, a remote uninhabited glen set between the mountains of Hecla and Ben More. At a hut without so much as a road leading to it and impossible to reach from the sea he spent three idyllic weeks, watching Royal Navy ships patrolling the Minch, and enjoying the companionship of clansmen who trudged across the hills to visit him.

His principal companion was Neil MacEachain, one of the most underestimated characters in the Jacobite story, a quiet, self-effacing man who never talked grandly about his achievements – in fact spoke little about them at all. Neil spoke English, French and Gaelic, so was the perfect intermediary at this time when Charles was among Gaelic speakers and was trying to make contact with the French. It has been suggested that Neil kept silent like the well-trained spy some believe him to have been, and after the '45 was over he settled in France, where he adopted the name MacDonald. His son became one of Napoleon's generals and a Marshal of France.

In Corodale Charles Edward lived royally, enjoying peace of mind, a good supply of food, drink and company, and a fine bed of heather and green rushes to sleep on.[17] His health, both mental and physical, was poor, however, since he continued to suffer from dysentery and mood swings that swept him from wild manic highs to depression. Sometimes he would just sit in silence for long periods. For three weeks he remained in this safe place, shooting game by day and carousing by night with his MacDonald friends, Clanranald, Boisdale, Hugh MacDonald of Baleshare (captain of a militia company hunting him!) and other islanders, who might well have included Hugh MacDonald (another militia officer) and Angus MacDonald, step-father and brother of Flora MacDonald, who was soon to play an important part in his escape.

It has been said that it was during his flight that summer that Charles Stuart began the slide towards alcoholism that destroyed him in later life, and certainly there must have been a temptation to drink brandy to keep out the cold of that Highland summer, but his father had worried about his son's drinking even before he left Rome. By the time of his stay at Corodale the Prince had a good head for alcohol and one MacDonald carousal became legendary: Charles drank everybody else under the table, including Boisdale, reputedly one of the hardest drinkers in Scotland. Charles reverentially covered the casualties with plaids and sang 'De Profundis' over them before leaving them to sleep it off. One remarked afterwards, 'Never have I seen a punch bowl attacked more freely or frankly.'[18]

While the men hunted and drank with the fugitive, their wives contributed to his comfort: Lady Clanranald sent him shirts and a silver cup, and Lady Boisdale food and clothing. Even Sleat's wife, Lady Margaret MacDonald, whose husband was safely away at Fort Augustus serving with Cumberland, managed to send a present of fifty guineas, clothing and newspapers – delivered by one of her husband's militia officers. Once again a uniform was no badge of loyalty and the name MacDonald no indicator of loyalty. As the hunt for the Prince intensified, this became even more apparent.

Paradoxically, there were many secrets and there were no secrets in the Highlands that summer, thus Cumberland learned before the middle of June that his quarry had not sailed with the *Mars* and *Bellone*, but was still in the Hebrides. Gossip claims he had the news from ministers in Uist and Stornoway by way of MacLeod of Skye but it is more probable that it came from the Paris banker, Aeneas MacDonald, who had surrendered to General Campbell and admitted that Charles Stuart had been at Stornoway. Lord Lovat pinpointed the Prince's whereabouts more precisely when he blabbed that Charles was hiding on Uist. It is easy to condemn prisoners – even those known to be unreliable anyway – for breaking under interrogation but it seems that these two talked just too readily. It has to be admitted though that MacDonald believed he was telling his captors nothing more than they already knew. However, Lovat's revelation about Uist as the hideout was another matter. When he gave government searchers that information he must have been aware that they would realise Charles would be among friends there and attention would soon focus on Clanranald and Boisdale. This is precisely what happened.

Some MacDonald clansman must also have been passing false information to the authorities at the same time, however, for General Campbell suddenly rushed off to Tobermory, from where he searched Mull and the southern islands of the Outer Hebrides, then took several hundred men to St Kilda, that handful of tiny lonely islands more than 30 miles out in the Atlantic beyond Uist. Bewildered islanders there were frightened out of their wits at the arrival of these warships and soldiers asking about Prince Charles Edward Stuart. 'The poor creatures were quite amazed,' Bishop Forbes was told, 'and declared they knew nothing of that man, for they had never heard of him before. They said they had heard a report that their Laird, MacLeod, had lately been at war with a great woman abroad, but that he had got the better of her and that was all they knew of the disturbances in the world.'[19] The islanders probably *were* unaware of what was going on, but it was a masterstroke of disinformation on the part of whoever sowed the St Kilda seeds in General Campbell'a mind.

The St Kilda diversion wasted valuable time and was a triumph for the MacDonalds' friends, but it could only delay the Hanoverian bloodhounds temporarily and the searchers soon closed in inexorably. The MacLeod and MacDonald militia were ordered to the Outer Isles and Sir Alexander MacDonald, who still managed to remain well away at

Fort Augustus, admitted he was frightened they might capture the Prince and thus bring terrible shame on his clan. While the Prince's friends knew MacLeod could never be trusted, Sleat's dual loyalty allowed MacDonald militia officers to hunt the Prince by day and carouse with him by night, and made it possible for Sleat's staunchly Jacobite wife to send presents to him at Corodale. Cumberland's sense of distrust towards the great chief of Sleat was well justified.

Since the government now knew that Charles was in Uist, it was certain that Clanranald and Boisdale must be involved in protecting him. Boisdale was arrested, and his wife held prisoner in her own home, and, while the chief was questioned aboard HMS *Furnace* by Captain John Fergusson, one of the most brutal of the government's searchers, the hunt on shore concentrated on North Uist, Benbecula and South Uist. Two great sweeps of the islands were begun simultaneously from the north and the south – systematic searches, which were bound to penetrate to the Corodale hideout.

Accompanied by only a few friends, the Prince headed for Loch Boisdale at the southern end of South Uist, but there found himself cornered by the militia, and the party had to separate and take cover. With only Neil MacEachain and Captain Felix O'Neil, a Frenchman of Irish descent, left to guard him, the Prince struck north again into the empty hills to the east of Milton, within easy reach of the homes of both Boisdale and Clanranald. And this was where the Prince met Flora MacDonald for the first time.

Flora was a young woman of twenty-two, possibly just turned twenty-three, the daughter of Ranald MacDonald, a tacksman (a leaseholder of land from the chief) and thus a man of some importance in the clan hierarchy. Ranald had died when Flora was a child, but her mother, Marion, was soon swept off her feet by a MacDonald from the Skye branch of the clan. Marion's new husband, Hugh of Armadale, had led an adventurous life that included service with the French army in which he lost an eye and gained a nickname, 'Uisdean Cam' ('One-eyed' Hugh). In the '45 'One-eyed' Hugh served in MacDonald of Sleat's militia, but his sympathies leant towards the Stuarts. In June 1746, while Flora was living with her brother at Milton in South Uist, Hugh came to the island as a captain of one of those militia companies now combing the islands. On 20 June while Charles was hiding in the hills above Milton, Flora was sent alone to mind the cattle overnight at her brother's shieling, a hut on the summer pastures at Alisary on Sheaval hill, and it was here she met Charles Stuart for the first time. The meeting was carefully arranged although no one ever admitted as much: how else would a young woman have been allowed by her family to spend a night alone at a remote hut while the island was swarming with militiamen?

MacEachain and O'Neil, who were probably jealous of one other, gave different versions of the meeting, each claiming the honour of introducing the Prince to Flora. Felix O'Neil wrote that he went to the hut and asked Flora about militia movements in the area, then told her he had brought a friend to see her. 'She with some emotion asked if it was the Prince,' he recounted. 'I answered in the affirmative and instantly brought him in.'[20] MacEachain claimed it was he who woke Flora, but she had 'got scarcely on half of her close, when the prince, with his baggage upon his back was at the door, and saluted her very kindly'.[21] As for Flora, she contradicted herself. Soon after the event, when she may still have felt it necessary to protect MacEachain, she wrote, 'Captain O'Neil brought Miss MacDonald to the place where the Prince was.'[22] Later she said Felix O'Neil 'sent in a cousine of her own, who had been along with him and the Prince, to awake her.'[23]

MacEachain's version sounds the most believable since he, a kinsman, would be the man most likely to alert her and the impetuous entry of the stranger carrying a pack on his back bears all the hallmarks of the Prince. It took much coaxing before Flora agreed to the plan to escort Prince Charlie to Skye dressed as her maidservant, but having made the decision, she set out the following morning for Clanranald's house at Nunton on Benbecula to make arrangements for the journey. Unfortunately that meant crossing from South Uist to Benbecula by the ford, and as she had no permit to travel she was detained by militiamen there who happened to be MacLeods. She was held overnight but fortunately her step-father, 'One-eyed' Hugh, arrived in the morning and ordered her to be set free.

To Flora's horror, as she breakfasted with her step-father, O'Neil, who was still supposed to be hiding with the Prince on Mount Hecla, was brought in. He too had been caught at the ford because Charles's impetuosity had nearly ruined another plan. The Prince had become anxious because Flora was taking too long to return, so he forced poor, weary O'Neil to set off in search of her and he was captured. 'One-eyed' Hugh was able to vouch for him at the ford, and both he and Flora were freed.

Flora, Lady Clanranald, and other women at the Clanranald chief's house, then began to sew furiously to make a quilted petticoat, a gown of patterned calico, and a white apron over which he was to wear a dun cloak with a large hood 'after the Irish fashion'. A cap designed to hide as much of his face as possible completed the disguise as Flora's maid, Betty Burke. At last on the morning of Friday 27 June, two young MacDonald officers of the militia arrived to tell the Prince all was ready and they were to sail that night.

In due course Flora, her brother Angus, Lady Clanranald and Lady Clan's young daughter, Margaret, arrived from Nunton, and sat down with Charles and his boat crew to a meal, at which he took care to show great courtliness towards the ladies, setting Flora on his right and Lady Clanranald on his left. There was much conversation and laughter as the meal began, yet the Prince could not hide his nervousness as he veered from deep thoughtfulness to brittle high spirits. Then a messenger arrived with news that General Campbell himself had landed near Clanranald's house with 1,500 men. The merry-making turned to panic, which MacEachain described vividly: 'All run to their boat in the greatest confusion, every one carrying with him whatever part of the baggage came first to his hand, without either regard to sex or quality, they crossed to Lochisguiway [Loch Uiskevagh], and about five in the morning, landed on the other side, where they had supper.'[24]

As those who had any appetite left by then ate, news arrived that not only had the feared Captain Fergusson accompanied Campbell but he had actually arrived at Clanranald's house and had the audacity to sleep in Lady Clan's bed. Caroline Scott, another dangerous enemy of the Stuarts, was on his way too, they were told. The net had nearly closed. O'Neil estimated that around 2,000 government soldiers must be on Benbecula at that moment for the final sweep.

Campbell was either very lucky or singularly well informed to arrive at this juncture – probably the former – and could easily have taken the Prince that night but for the MacDonalds. As Lady Clan hurried home, 'One-eyed' Hugh sent Flora a letter to guarantee her safe conduct in case she should be stopped by the military.

Charles insisted on keeping his pistols under his petticoat but Flora would have none of it. If they were searched, the firearms would give him away she told him. 'Indeed, Miss,' he answered, 'if we shall happen to meet with any that will go so narrowly to work in searching as what you mean, they will certainly discover me at any rate.'[25]

At eight o'clock on the evening of Saturday 28 June, Flora, her 'maid' Betty Burke, and Neil MacEachain set out on the journey which was to become the linchpin of the Prince Charlie legend – the voyage over the sea to Skye in a small boat crewed by at least three Clan Donald militiamen on unofficial 'leave' from their companies, which were searching the islands. Next morning they landed close to Sleat's home at Monkstadt, where Lady Margaret, who had bravely been sending Charles presents while he was in Uist, was in a great state of panic in case he might be captured in her house. For his safety and her own she had to get rid of him. Charles was taken first to Kingsburgh, home of the Sleat factor, Alexander MacDonald, and then south to Portree, where Flora left him for the last time in the early hours of Tuesday 1 July. She made for her mother's house at Armadale, while Charles set out for Raasay, only to find the island so devastated that he had to move to the mainland instead. A few days later Donald Roy MacDonald, who had been their guide on Skye, received a brief note, which read simply:

> Sir, – I have parted (I thank God) as intended. Make my compliments to all those to whom I have given trouble.
>
> – I am, Sir, your humble servant
>
> James Thomson[26]

Donald Roy hurried to Armadale to show the letter to Flora. It was the last word of thanks she, or anyone else who had helped in the escape, received from Charles Stuart.

The first week of July was a good week for the militia and navy: although the navy wasted time unsuccessfully hunting a French ship, *Le Hardi Mendiant*, the soldiers picked up Flora's boat crew who had been sent back to Uist and one of them told of the Prince's escape in the disguise of Flora MacDonald's maid.

Clanranald and his wife were arrested; so too were the old boatman, Donald MacDonald of Galtergill and Felix O'Neil. Campbell now knew every detail of the voyage over the sea to Skye, down to the last sprig of lilac in the pattern on Betty Burke's dress, and he now had enough information to sail to Skye, where his first call was the Sleat chief's house to interview Lady Margaret, who feigned innocence: 'Lady Margaret was surprised when she knew of our errand, told us most frankly upon our inquiry that Miss MacDonald had dined at her house on Sunday the 29th, that though she pressed her to stay all night, yet she could not prevail and that she had a man, and a maidservant with her. I think her ladyship did not know the maid's quality,'[27] Campbell said of the interview.

Her ladyship proved a very plausible liar – unless the general was tactfully trying to avoid the embarrassment of having to arrest the wife of a very important chief who was actually out fighting for King George. The latter seems the more likely explanation but in any case Lady Margaret was only a bit player in the drama: there were other more guilty people to be questioned.

From Monkstadt, Campbell and Captain Fergusson moved on to Kingsburgh, where Fergusson cunningly had one of the dairymaids brought on board the *Furnace* and questioned before he went to the factor's house. Needless to say the girl told everything she knew, and she knew plenty – even that the Prince had given her mistress a lock of his hair! Armed with this information, Fergusson went ashore and cross-examined Kingsburgh and his wife about Flora's visit, then asked archly in which room 'the person along with her in woman's clothes' slept.

'I know in what room Miss MacDonald herself lay,' Kingsburgh told him, 'but where servants are laid when in my house, I never enquire anything about it. My wife is the properest person to inform you about that.'

Fergusson turned to Mrs MacDonald and asked whether she had 'laid the young Pretender and Miss MacDonald in one bed.' 'Sir,' she answered angrily, 'whom you mean by the young Pretender I shall not pretend to guess; but I can assure you it is not the fashion in the Isle of Skye to lay the mistress and the maid in the same bed together.' Kingsburgh eventually admitted Flora's involvement in the escape but unwisely told more than he need have done about Charles's move to Raasay and then to the mainland.[28]

It was now time to confront Flora. On 11 July Fergussson anchored off Armadale and sent a message to her, asking her to come to Castleton, near Armadale, to answer some questions a lawyer, Roderick MacDonald, wanted to put to her on behalf of MacLeod of Talisker. Donald Roy tried to warn Flora that this was a trap but she insisted on going, so Donald Roy took the precaution of destroying her step-father's letter of safe passage, the 'James Thomson' note and another from Lady Margaret to Charles which he had been unable to deliver. As she walked to Castleton on 12 July, Flora was arrested and taken on board HMS *Furnace*, but the wily Donald Roy took to the hills and was never caught.

Virtually all the participants in the escape from the Long Island were now in custody and only the Prince remained free. When questioned Flora was so discreet she misled her inquisitors: she incriminated neither her step-father nor the MacDonalds in Uist and gave away no information that might lead to the Prince. Campbell knew perfectly well that Clanranald and 'One-eyed' Hugh had masterminded the plot but could prove nothing against either – which made him very angry indeed. As early as 24 July he complained to the Earl of Cromartie about Hugh: 'This villain met me in South Uist and had the impudence to advise me against making so close a search and that if I should for some days a little desist he made no doubt of my success,' he said. 'I suspected him at the time and have given it in charge to the officers in Skye to apprehend him.'[29] But like David Roy, Hugh had already escaped into the hills.

Life for Flora aboard HMS *Furnace* was as uncomfortable as it was frightening, for the vessel was a single-decked sloop, converted from a bomb-ketch that had once explored the North-West Passage, and consequently was very primitive. Prisoners, whose numbers increased daily, were kept in the hold with only a short spell allowed on deck each day for air: they had to sleep on coils of rope, on boards or on the ship's ballast without blankets, and for food were allowed only half a seaman's ration. Flora was kept apart until she reached Applecross in Wester Ross on 21 July to be questioned by General Campbell. Unfortunately her evidence differed from what Kingsburgh had admitted – each named some names, but withheld others.

Campbell was impressed with Flora's courage and apparent honesty: she would have made an excellent spy, for she told her tale well, beguiling him into believing what she wanted him to believe, and history has shown her deposition to be more interesting for what it omits than for what it reveals. She was careful to avoid incriminating Lady Margaret or Lady Clanranald and made a valiant effort to save Kingsburgh but the basic facts of her story were accurate enough – she was simply being economical in naming names and supplying detail that would have gone against her.

Campbell of Mamore was greatly taken with the young woman's openness and believed she was an innocent girl who had been drawn into the plot. He ordered that she should still be held, but that her guards should treat her with respect. At Applecross Flora met Felix O'Neil again and admitted her fear of being sent to London for trial but he reassured her: 'If you are carried to London I can venture to assure you it will be for your interest and happiness; and instead of being afraid of this you ought to wish for it. There you will meet with much respect and very good and great friends for what you have done.' He warned her not to be frightened into saying anything that might turn her judges against her. 'Never once pretend . . . to repent or be ashamed of what you have done,' he told her. 'I do not think that the Government can be so very barbarous and cruel as to bring you to trial for your life.'[30]

Flora's fears were well founded: about the middle of August she was put aboard HMS *Eltham*, where she was in the care of Commodore Thomas Smith, a much more humane man than Fergusson, for the long voyage round the north of Scotland and all the way down the east coast to London, where she finally arrived in November.

Cumberland reached London long before her. As summer advanced he became increasingly frustrated because he felt he and his troops, now committed in this godforsaken land, would be better employed fighting the French in Flanders. He could not wait to leave the Highlands where he realised both land and people had been subdued but not pacified. Yet, in the three months since his day of glory at Culloden, Duke Billy *had* achieved much. King George's rule had been imposed all the way to the farthest islands of the west, the rebels were in flight, clan lands devasted and the chiefs lay in gaol, skulked in the glens or were on their way to exile. If he had not yet captured Charles Stuart, there were few left with any heart to fight for the Prince. And yet he knew how far he was distanced from final success. 'I am sorry to leave this country in the condition it is in,' he told the Duke of Newcastle, 'for all the good we have done is a little blood letting which has only weakened the madness, but not at all cured it, and I tremble for fear that this vile spot may still be the ruin of this Island and of our Family.'[31]

On 18 July the commander-in-chief handed over the taming of the Highlands to William Ann Keppell, Earl of Albemarle, son of one of William of Orange's pages, who had commanded the front line at Culloden and hated the Scots as heartily as his predecessor in command.

'Butcher' Cumberland's last act epitomised his vindictiveness towards all clansmen, whether on his side or the enemy's. Having made his deposition in Skye, MacDonald of Kingsburgh was given the choice of remaining with Campbell or being sent to Fort Augustus accompanied by his chief to plead his cause with the Duke of Cumberland. He chose the latter course, which was a mistake – Cumberland was so enraged to learn that the Sleat factor had not arrived at Fort Augustus in irons that he sent a sharp reprimand to General Campbell, one of the last letters he drafted before he left Fort Augustus, and then had the poor factor manacled and carted off to Edinburgh Castle with a cavalry escort. Kingsburgh was never brought to trial, but he spent a whole year in prison.

Cumberland left but the hunt continued, switched now to the mainland, and with the Argyll militia aware that the Prince was in the Knoydart/Morar area. Campbell and Caroline Scott rushed to cut off escape by sea while a cordon was thrown across the hills from Loch Hourn to the head of Loch Eil. The fugitive Prince's only hope was to break through this cordon and head for the coast farther north. Accompanied only by MacDonald of Glenaladale, his brother John, and John MacDonald of Borrodale, Charles set out towards Glenfinnan. They had to change course when informants brought news that the enemy was at the head of Loch Arkaig and might cut them off, and worse still, 100 militiamen were at that moment at the foot of the hill on which they were actually hiding. By chance they met Donald Cameron of Glen Pean who knew sufficient about enemy troop movements to lead them to a neighbouring hill that had already been searched and from where they could not only see Loch Arkaig but also had a view of a militia camp not a mile away. There they lay all day, with nothing to eat but a little oatmeal and butter, and unable to light a fire to cook a meal.

At night the little group crept cautiously northwards, skirting Loch Quoich, coming closer to the enemy line, so that when dawn broke they had to lie low and spend another whole day skulking on the hill, which was scoured thoroughly without their being discovered. As darkness fell they set out again, so close to one of the enemy encampments now that they could hear the soldiers' voices, and in the darkest part of the night Prince Charlie was guided between the lights of the guards' campfires. Before dawn they were safely out of the net.

Throughout the period from then until September 1746 Charles Edward remained secure in the care of his trusted clansmen – mainly MacDonalds, Camerons and Macphersons. First Patrick Grant, with a couple of MacDonalds, three Chisholms and a MacGregor – the legendary Seven Men of Glenmoriston – guided him among the hills always just beyond the reach of government searchers as they scouted to find a French ship without success. It was a hard slog, but his spirits rose steadily until by mid-August, when Archie Cameron found him, he looked – and probably felt – every inch a Highlander. He was even thinking about a new rising, but Lochiel and Macpherson of Cluny were not encouraging.

Charles made his way to Badenoch where Cluny found him a refuge on Ben Alder, his last hiding place in Scotland. Known as Cluny's Cage, this was little more than a 'house' formed from trees in a recess on the mountain face. It was well hidden and had been turned into 'a very romantic comical habitation', thatched over and with a fire for cooking and warmth. 'The Cage was no larger than to contain six or seven persons, four of which number were frequently employed in playing at cards, one idle looking on, one backin [baking], and another firing bread and cooking.'[32]

The hunt for the Pretender began to be scaled down after Cumberland left and, although army patrols continued to scour the mountains, navy strength was reduced, so much so that it has been suggested the government no longer had any desire to capture Charles and bring him to trial. The Prince himself did not believe that: he said that if he were captured, he would be put to death immediately, perhaps by poisoning or in some way that would look accidental. Certainly a great public trial and execution would be the death knell of the Stuart Cause but it would also horrify the most ardent Whig – Mary Queen of Scots, Charles I and now the Stuart Pretender on the execution block would be too much for the British people to stomach.

There were a few who believed it would be worth making another Stuart martyr, however. Horace Mann, the Hanoverian spymaster in Italy, for one, wrote to Walpole in October 1746: 'He should be made a sacrifice of. It would cure them from making any more attempts, and would discredit France to the greatest degree. The Pope would make a martyr, and in time, a saint of him, but I had rather he should be prayed to by these fools in heaven than adored in Scotland or England, where in time he would make martyrs of us all.'[33]

CHAPTER ELEVEN

The Victims of Mr 'Evidence' Murray

'Men are like Watches, some of a finer and more delicate make than others; the one goes justly, the other not. I rather like the description of Murray [of Broughton]: A well-doing little man of a fair complexion, in a scarlet dress and a white cockade.'

'Yes,' said Kitty, 'I daresay he wasn't all bad, poor Mr Secretary Murray.'

'No,' said Isobel, going back to her book. 'It says here that certain things must be put "to the credit side of his strangely involved account with honour". I expect it was a case of a weak man tried too high. A friend wrote of him that he had such a fear of death that he might be brought to do anything to save a wretched life. . . .'

One Borderer on another: O. Douglas writing about John Murray of Broughton in *The House that is Our Own.*[1]

Prince Charlie was making his escape over the sea to Skye and back to the mainland when his two most loyal supporters, Cameron of Lochiel and Murray of Broughton, finally gave up hope of keeping the campaign alive and decided the only course was to make their own escape. After trying unsuccessfully to join the Prince, Murray set out for the east coast, by now safer than the west, to find a ship that would take Lochiel and himself to Holland, from where they could move on to Paris to join the chiefs already in France.

He was still so weak from the illness he suffered at the time of Culloden that he was able to cover no more than four or five painful miles a night, then lie low during the day. He travelled by way of Strontian, where he was reunited briefly with his still heavily pregnant wife, then moved through Glenlyon, Breadalbane and Balquhidder to Carnwath in Lanarkshire and into his Borders home country. Here he could feel safe among family and friends, but ironically it was in his sister's house at Polmood in Tweeddale that he was arrested by a troop of dragoons in the middle of the night of 29 June. He had been betrayed by a herdboy.

Broughton was a splendid prize and King George was so 'very sensible' of the achievement that the Duke of Newcastle sent special instructions on the manner in which he was to be treated. Cumberland, still at Fort Augustus, expressed delight through his secretary, Sir Everard Fawkener: 'This is a Prisoner of Consequence, and from whose capture it is to be hoped many advantages may result,' Fawkener wrote.[2]

Murray arrived at Edinburgh in no fit state to be questioned immediately. 'What with Fatigue or Drink, he was in such disorder that it required some hours sleep before he recovered,'[3] Lord Justice Clerk Milton reported to Newcastle. But after a few hours' rest Murray related as much as he knew about events following Culloden. He was allowed to see no one at this time except his young children and was closely guarded as a very special prisoner.

Newcastle ordered Broughton to be escorted to London forthwith but, before leaving Edinburgh, Milton was to question him closely: 'You will talk to him in such a manner (without however giving him any promise of His Majesty's Pardon) as may dispose him to make a full and ample Discovery of all he knows, which must be very material for His Majesty's Service, and your Lordship will send me a particular Account, before the Prisoner can arrive in Town, of the Temper you find him in, and of everything that shall have passed between you, that we may the better judge in what manner to talk to him here.'[4]

Early on the very day this letter arrived, Broughton had been sent off to London under guard on the instructions of Cumberland, travelling in a coach because he was too weak to ride. Milton, aware of the King's interest in this prisoner, was in such a state of consternation in case he should fail to follow His Majesty's instructions, that he was on the road himself within the hour, travelling at top speed to catch up with the prisoner. 'I followed Mr Murray in a post chase, and overtook him that night at Dunbar,' he reported to Newcastle, 'and nixt morning took a proper oppurtunity of seeing Mr Murray and told him yt as I had occasion to be at Dunbar, I thought it the properest place to see him, and to take that opportunity of knowing how his journey agreed with him, and if he wanted anything.' The Lord Justice Clerk made it all sound as if he had carefully arranged the Dunbar meeting, then warmed to the task of softening the prisoner up:

> I endeavoured to conciliate his Favour by telling him, that on account of his indisposition, a Coach was ordered for him, that I had particularly recommended it to Captain Gore [the officer of the guard detachment] to be civil to him, and to use him well, that he was to be carried to the Tower and not to the common Gaol. That tho' I had not permitted any of his Friends to see him in the Castle, that was not doing him any real Hardship; on the contrair, it was rather putting respect on him and showing the world of what importance I thought him, but that I had allowed his infant children at his request (who are but 4 or 5 years old), in presence of the Captain of the Guard, to see him; because I accompted them as

> nobody, which was all yt I considered to be in my Power, but that if he now had any message to his Freinds I would deliver it.

Milton then began to question Murray, gently at first, about his part in the rising, about when he had last seen the Prince, and what had happened to his papers (they had been burned at Carlisle, Broughton told him), and duly brought the interrogation round to the matter of giving evidence against other participants in the rising.

After protesting that he could not betray anyone, Broughton began to crack. 'He then said that if he could have any Hopes given him he would discover all he knew,' and later, 'if they would make him safe of anything he would discover all.' Milton warned the prisoner that he could give him no such assurance but advised him that 'the only Reparation that he could now make to the King and Countrey' was to repent – and of course to tell everything he knew. The interview ended with the sick and weary prisoner repeating that he would tell all, and attempt to strike no bargain: he was in the King's hands.

Why did Murray betray the Cause he had loved so dearly (and went on loving) throughout his life? The reasons are clear: at that moment he was a sick and exhausted man, who had made superhuman efforts to rally the chiefs to launch a guerrilla campaign in the mountains only to be let down by almost every one of them. At the same time he was worried sick because his wife, also in hiding, was 'bigg with Child' and he desperately wanted her to return to the south. As an ardent Jacobite she resisted begging Lord Albemarle to provide her with a pass to make the journey and eventually travelled disguised as a soldier's wife, 'induring hardships hardly to be bore by one in health, much less by a person with a big belly, till lately accustom'd to all the care and Conveniences of Life'.[5] Her child was born soon after.

With so much on his mind, Broughton was vulnerable to the intimidation of ruthless questioners; but more important, he was disillusioned with the Cause, the Prince, the chiefs and even the ordinary clansmen. With Charles's distrust of his Scottish supporters and his determination to return to France, there was no hope of a revival of the campaign as he and Lochiel had planned. The chiefs, especially that treacherous old weasel, Lovat, had gone back on promises to supply men and arms, and as for the common clansmen, their rapacity in dealing with supplies, especially the money and brandy landed at Loch an Uamh, had disgusted him. At that precise moment there seemed little to defend, so Broughton talked to his captors. He remained devoted to the Stuart Cause but this way he might live to fight another day.

Over the following months he was questioned at length and in the words of Andrew Lang, 'He did not tell *all* he knew, but on August 13, being examined in the Tower, he told a great deal.'[6] He named some of the English leaders: Dr Peter Barry, a London physician and known Jacobite, Lord Barrymore, Sir John Hinde Cotton, and the Welsh leader, Sir Watkin

Williams Wynne. Barry, who had been involved in pre-'45 negotiations, was imprisoned for a considerable time as a result of Broughton's information, although never charged. He also betrayed the secret of the Loch Arkaig Treasure and even offered to take government representatives to the spot and help them to find it but this offer was refused.

While Broughton waited in the Tower of London to be called to testify against former fellow rebels, the government was determined that there should never be another '45. Vengeance began long before the Battle of Culloden or Broughton was taken: by New Year's Day 1746, the Hanoverians held upwards of 400 prisoners captured when they retook Carlisle Castle, all of whom were sent to Lancaster, Chester and York 'to await the King's pleasure'. Before January was out 56 women and girls were held at these three places, as well as at least 15 young children, some 28 of whom are known to have been transported to the colonies. The remainder presumably died or were released and sent home. Three escaped from Whitehaven during August 1746, and twenty others, as well as several children, were freed after the transport ship, *Veteran*, was captured by a French privateer on its way to Antigua the following year.[7]

Among the Carlisle women were two females named Shaw: Mary described as aged forty and from Inverness, and Margaret, only fifteen, from Perthshire. They were probably mother and daughter but all we know for sure about them is that Margaret was able to spin and both were transported – one can only hope aboard the *Veteran*. Too often the record of the Carlisle women was like that of Jane Stratton and Anne and Margaret Straw, all held in Lancaster Castle at the same time, who were simply noted as 'taken in actual rebellion – fate unknown'.[8] Fate unknown all too often meant simply that they had died of disease in prison.

The unfortunate Carlisle prisoners lay in filthy, disease-filled gaols for seven months before their trials began at the court-house on St Margaret's Hill, Southwark, on 15 July 1746, the day Broughton was on his way to London and Prince Charlie was hiding in a cave in the woods of Borrodale. First to appear before the judge were the officers of the Manchester Regiment, among them Francis Townley, commander at Carlisle, and David Morgan, a Monmouthshire barrister who had acted as 'the Pretender's Counseller' while he was in England. He had been arrested on his way to London to spy for the Prince. Seventeen officers of the Regiment were tried in only three days.

The Manchester men were a pathetic little group, lads most of them, who had been carried away by family loyalty to the Cause, or simply by their own youthful enthusiasm, to follow Charlie. Thomas Syddall's father had been 'out' in the '15, was caught, executed and his head hung on Manchester market cross for years as young Tom grew up; Tom junior, a barber, joined the Jacobites at Manchester and suffered the same fate. His head was displayed at the Exchange.[9] James Dawson, a Cambridge student, ran away to enlist in the Jacobite army and Christopher Taylor, a lad from Wigan, signed up on his return from France where he had been educated. Both gave everything up to join the Manchester Regiment, as did John Berwick and George Fletcher, who were both in the linen trade, James Wilding, a dyer, apprenticed to his father, and Wigan tallow chandler, Thomas Chadwick. John Sanderson was a Lancashire labourer, but nothing is known about the backgrounds of John Betts or John Holker, both of whom escaped either just before or during the trials. The last of the group were a Yorkshireman, Andrew Blood, a captain in the regiment, and a Northumbrian, John Hunter.

From the attitude of judges, gaolers and the baying mob who jeered them into court, all who appeared at Southwark must have known they had little chance of justice. They were right: the government had plenty of witnesses to denounce these young men as traitors. It was easy to prove they had fought for Prince Charlie and worn his white ribbon: and, crime of crimes, as well as 'levying war' Thomas Chadwick had played 'The King shall enjoy his own again' on the church organ at Derby.

Peter Moss and Samuel Maddox, two fellow ensigns, saved their own skins by turning King's Evidence. Maddox told the jury at Tom Deacon's trial that Tom had 'sat at the table at the Bull Head, Manchester, took down the names of such as enlisted in the Pretender's service, and received a shilling for each. Between times as he awaited recruits he employed himself turning blue and white ribbons into favours, which he gave to the men who enlisted'.[10] That was more than enough to prove treason.

Roger Macdonald, a deserter from Strathallan's Horse in the Prince's army, was the main witness against Townley and he later testified against Lord Balmerino as well, receiving a pardon for his treachery. Most bitter of all against poor Townley, however, was James Bradshaw, an old army comrade and implacable enemy, who seized the opportunity to take revenge. The two had never liked one another but sending Townley to a gruesome death was vengeance far beyond mere settling of a few old scores.

Soldiers often betrayed comrades in the Jacobite trials that year and helped the government to put forward enough witnesses to obtain a conviction in key trials such as those of the Manchester Regiment men and the Scottish peers. The same people testified at several trials, and Sir Bruce Seton and Jean Arnot, authors of *Prisoners of the '45*, have shown that no fewer than eighty-four military Jacobite prisoners and twenty civilians testified for the Crown at Southwark. In spite of these large numbers of betrayers, Seton and Arnot believe that Prince Charlie's men on the whole remained remarkably loyal to their prince and to their comrades. 'If the Southwark figures be taken as representing the proportion of military to civilian witnesses as about four to one, it is fair to infer that the rank and file of the Prince's shattered army only produced some 240 men who were prepared to buy their lives, or at least their escape from transportation, by giving evidence against their comrades in arms,' they conclude.[11] The small figure bears testimony to the depth of loyalty existing within the movement even at this late stage, when all appeared lost, a point Prince Charlie probably never paused to consider. As far as he was concerned absolute loyalty and total sacrifice from his followers were his due by divine right.

Of the Manchester Regiment officers only Hunter managed to convince the jury that he had joined under duress and was acquitted. The others were found guilty and sentenced to death – and a grisly end it was. 'Let the several prisoners return to the gaol from whence they came,' the judge pronounced, 'and from thence they must be drawn to the place of execution; and when they come there they must be severally hanged by the neck, but not till they be dead, for they must be cut down alive; then their bowels must be taken out and burned before their faces; then their heads must be severed from their bodies, and their bodies severally divided into four quarters; and these must be at the King's disposal.'

And that was the sentence carried out on Townley, Berwick, Blood, Chadwick, Dawson, Thomas Deacon, Fletcher, Syddall and David Morgan on Kennington Common on 30 July. The only mercy is that victims usually died by hanging before that second grisly ritual of the sentence began. The head of Tom Deacon was placed on the Manchester Exchange alongside that of Tom Syddall – the town constables' accounts for carrying out this service read: 'Sept. 18th, 1746. Expenses tending the Sheriff this morn. Sydall's and Deacon's heads put up. £00. 01. 06.' One shilling and sixpence was cost to Manchester of this final vengeance.

Sentences on Charles Deacon, Furnival, Taylor and Wilding were commuted to transportation to the colonies, and two years later, the Lancashire labourer, Sanderson, was given a pardon on condition that he enlisted in the army.

Trials of the non-commissioned officers and men followed soon afterwards and in the words of the editors of *Prisoners of the '45*, 'This unit . . . was treated with a ferocity which indicated that its degree of culpability was held to be higher than that of any other in the Jacobite army.'[12] Treachery was expected of the Scots but the London government just could not forgive its English subjects who joined the revolt.

The brutal Manchester Regiment trials were a curtain raiser for the trials of Scottish Jacobites which lay ahead. And to obtain the verdicts it wanted, the government went to great lengths to find witnesses to testify. On 5 July Cumberland issued precise instructions to the army Judge Advocate in Scotland: he was to examine the evidence against each prisoner held but even where he could find none, that prisoner should not be freed. Cumberland was rubbing his hands over the recent capture of Lord Lovat, and was determined not to lose his prize witnesses, two of the Fraser chief's servants. They were to be questioned with great care, and when that was completed, the Judge Advocate was to ride straight to London to present his findings to the Duke of Newcastle personally.[13] 'Butcher Bill' was determined to make an unshakable case against every rebel sent for trial from the lowest camp follower to the little coterie who had surrounded the Prince.

When the time came for Cumberland to return south he showed impatience to get back to 'civilisation' as quickly as possible – his journey from Fort Augustus took only seven days because he paused barely long enough anywhere to accept the adulation, thanks, gifts and addresses presented in gold boxes at towns he passed through on the way. In London he was a hero, jostled and cheered by the people still basking in euphoria that had lasted since the news of Culloden broke in the city.

'All the bells in the City of London and Westminster rung, and at evening were illuminations and bonfires, with continual firing of guns for several hours, and all other demonstrations of the greatest joy from people of all ranks', said *The Gentleman's Magazine*,[14] and it published a half-length portrait of the hero over an illustration of Hercules killing the many-headed hydra. Around the figure of the Duke were the words 'WILLIAM DUKE OF CUMBERLAND ECCE HOMO'. To all of London, and even in the bosom of his ever-quarrelling family, this was indeed THE MAN. Poems, propaganda pamphlets and plays eulogised him, and for those who wanted to sense the clamour of the battle there was a ballet called *Culloden* at Sadler's Wells which featured 'an exact view of the battle accompanied by a prodigious cannonade'.

The royal family basked in Duke William's glory and, unusually for them, were briefly at peace with one another. For once they actually became popular with their people, something of a first for the House of Hanover. The King appointed Duke William Ranger of Windsor Forest and we have him to thank for creating Virginia Water out of swampland there. Tyburn Gate in London, where criminals were hanged, was renamed Cumberland Gate – an appropriate honour for 'The Butcher'. Parliament voted Cumberland a pension of £25,000 a year to add to the £15,000 he was already receiving from the civil list and at a magnificent victory thanksgiving service in St Paul's Cathedral Handel's 'Hail the Conquering Hero' was played for the first time.

The victor of Culloden and tamer of the Highlands timed his arrival in London well since the trials of Lords Balmerino, Kilmarnock and Cromartie, three peers involved in the rising, were due to be held only three days after his return, when his glory was at its height. London was delirious at the prospect. An excited Horace Walpole wrote to a friend, 'You will be in town for the eight-and-twentieth. London will be as full as at a Coronation. The whole form is settled for the trials, and they are actually building scaffolds in Westminster Hall' – not scaffolds to hang the peers but to hold seats for the hundreds who were demanding tickets of admittance.

The great hall had not witnessed such a scene since King George's coronation banquet in 1727, when it was crammed to the doors with the great and the good of the kingdom and their friends and relations who packed the galleries and let down hooks and pieces of string to catch morsels from the 130 courses that were served.[15] Without the 2,000 candles that illuminated the hall on Coronation Day the scene looked appropriately forbidding on Monday 28 July 1746, but the spirits of the onlookers who filled it were buoyant.

Every man and woman who mattered was there – Cumberland, in his commander-in-chief's finery, was smugly seated in a special box, alongside Frederick, Prince of Wales, who was jealous that his father had denied him brother William's glory by forbidding him ever to become a soldier, and the Princess of Wales who disliked brother-in-law Bill and was resentful of all this adulation of him. Members of the House of Commons sat in high, tiered ranks to the left of the accused with the Archbishops of Canterbury and York in front of them and foreign ambassadors were accorded a special box to themselves. There were four tiers set aside for peeresses and their daughters, and the remainder of society had been assigned to the galleries. The 136 dukes, marquesses, earls, viscounts and barons who were to try the prisoners sat in crimson and ermine rows around the dock.

The nobles to be tried that day were the Earls of Kilmarnock and Cromartie and Lord Balmerino, three of the five peers captured during or after the rising. Cromartie had been taken at Dornoch a couple of days before Culloden, while the other two were captured soon after the battle – Kilmarnock by sheer bad luck according to Jacobite legend. It was said that in the confusion at the end of the battle he had ridden up to a troop of Cumberland's cavalry, mistaking them for men of his own regiment, and was duly taken prisoner. As he rode into captivity he passed his own son, Lord Boyd, who had fought with the Royal Scots Fusiliers on the Hanoverian side, for the Boyds were another divided family. Kilmarnock's own version however, suggests that he deliberately surrendered himself to Lord Mark Kerr's dragoons.[16]

Balmerino, who had given 30 years' service to the exiled Stuarts, escaped after the battle, but surrendered voluntarily the following day, and was taken with Kilmarnock and Cromartie to the Tower of London, where a fourth noble, the English Earl of Derwentwater had already been held for many months. Derwentwater had been captured at sea aboard the French ship *Esperance* on his way to Scotland in November 1745, but there was no need to bring him to trial since he had already been condemned to death for his part in the '15 rising and that sentence still stood. Lord Lovat could not be tried that day because the government still awaited the arrival of Murray of Broughton and the Fraser traitors.

Each of the accused presented a very different face to his peers – Cromartie showed fright, Kilmarnock's dreary face betrayed no emotion at all and Balmerino hid his feelings behind a beguiling humour, which was quite lost on the unsympathetic Lord Hardwicke, Lord High Steward, who was presiding. Hardwicke was a Hanoverian through and through without sympathy for the Cause or the accused, so it made little difference whether the three wept, kept their thoughts to themselves, or laughed.

Kilmarnock and Cromartie both pleaded guilty and were led away but Balmerino was determined to enjoy his day before his peers – more than might have been expected of a man who knew what the verdict and sentence would be. He baited the ardent Hanoverian Hardwicke about the peers' right to try him, and at one point broke off to invite a small boy who could not see to join him in the dock beside him to get a better view. He won sympathy among onlookers, but not from his peers, whose verdict was a unanimous 'Guilty'.

Two days later, as the first of the Manchester men were going to the gallows on Kennington Common, the three were brought back for sentence and again Balmerino won sympathy with his humour and calm acceptance of his fate. The executioner's axe was to acompany them to Westminster – grisly advance warning of what their fate would be – and when there was some discussion as to which coach it should be carried in, the elderly Balmerino solved the problem by volunteering to take it in his. 'Come, come, put it in here with me,' he said. At another point he told the executioner who accompanied them, 'Take care, or you'll break my damned shins with that thing.'

All three were sentenced to be beheaded and each made a little speech, which affected Horace Walpole greatly. No longer was the scene in Westminster Hall a spectacle not to be missed, it was 'the greatest and most melancholy scene I ever yet saw! . . . this sight at once feasted one's eyes and engaged all one's passions . . . their behaviour melted me!'[17]

After sentence was passed the three were taken into a room off the great hall for refreshments, and even now Balmerino was able to joke, suggesting that as they would not be together when they were returned to the Tower they might as well enjoy another bottle of wine now. 'We shall not meet again,' he told the others, 'not until . . . ,' smiled and drew a hand across his throat. On the way back to the Tower the irrepressible Balmerino stopped the coach at Charing Cross to buy some honey blobs, the Scots name for gooseberries.

Thanks to his wife's pleas to the King – they said she almost swooned at his feet – Cromartie's life was spared, and he was eventually pardoned conditionally in the autumn of 1749. But the other two were executed on 18 August.

At the last, Kilmarnock acknowledged allegiance to King George and admitted that he 'cared not a farthing' for the two kings or their rights. It was hunger that made him join the Prince, he said: 'If Mohammed had set up his standard in the Highlands I had . . . stuck close to the party, for I must eat.' Balmerino was a convinced Jacobite, who on the eve of his execution, wrote to the King over the Water, saying, 'Sir, when his Royal Highness the Prince your son came to Edinburgh, as it was my bounden and indispensable duty, I joyn'd him for which I am tomorrow to lose my head on the scaffold whereat I am so far from being dismayed that it gives me great satisfaction and peace of mind that I die in so righteous a cause.'[18] On the execution block he cried, 'God save King James.'

With attention now focused on London and punishing the rebels, the commander in Scotland was able to lift the strict naval blockade of the west coast and open the Highlands up to food ships for both starving clansmen and hungry redcoats. For two years, crops had failed due to storms, but starvation became deliberate government policy, even before Culloden. The Lord Lieutenant of Ireland, Lord Chesterfield, refused to allow meal to be exported from Ireland to Scotland. 'Starve the loyal with the disloyal,' he advocated. 'The loyalest Highlanders shall not have an oatcake from hence.'[19]

By autumn there was scarcely an ounce of oatmeal to be found for civilians or soldiers, but now ships began to get through again, one of them the little mealship, the *May*, which sailed from Glasgow towards the end of August. It was a long voyage to the Highlands: her master, Lachlan MacLean, had to sail the length of the Firth of Clyde, round the Mull of Kintyre, then northward between the Hebridean islands and the West Highland mainland. As Captain MacLean pushed north, past Islay, Jura and his own clan island of Mull, he was struck by storms so fierce that by the time the *May* reached Ardnamurchan Point, MacLean was glad to turn her into the Sound of Arisaig and Loch nan Uamh for shelter.

The *May* rode out the gale until two well-armed frigates, flying the British ensign, sailed into the loch on Friday 6 September, and dropped anchor. MacLean watched the newcomers warily because navy vessels were no friends to west of Scotland ships' masters, and he became greatly alarmed when one of the ships lowered a small boat, which was rowed over to his little mealship. He told the authorities later what followed: 'After they came to anchor they sent their boat with 16 men, boarded our vessell, told us we were prisoners of war in the French King's name, carried us all on board their largest ship, called the *Happy* frigate, commanded by Captain Boullue.'[20]

The new arrivals were indeed French. The privateer, *Heureux*, carrying 36 guns and 275 men, and her slightly smaller companion, *Prince de Conti*, with 30 guns and 225 men, had come to Scotland in search of Prince Charles Edward Stuart. The British colours were a blind to deceive any Royal Navy vessel among the islands or Hanoverian sympathiser on shore who might happen to sight them.

The unlucky captain was taken before the commander, Richard Augustus Warren, a bragging Irishman, who began the '45 a bankrupt merchant in France, but managed to make his way to Scotland and talked the Prince into appointing him one of his aides-de-camp. Warren had been sent back to Paris shortly before Culloden with news of Jacobite success in the Rout of Moy and the account he presented to King Louis was so impressively exaggerated that when the time came for Prince Charlie to need rescue, Warren was chosen to lead this expedition in search of him. Aboard *Heureux* in Loch nan Uamh Warren still acted and talked extravagantly, overawing the poor meal ship master with expansive boasting. 'They took an inventory of our ship and cargo and money, put six of their men on board our vessel and one officer,' MacLean said. And for the next fortnight every man aboard the *May* remained a prisoner.

Although the hunt for the Prince had been scaled down, government informers were as busy as ever among the islands, so that the instant the *Heureux* and *Conti* touched land at Barra, word of their presence was on its way to Lord Loudoun, the Hanoverian commander at Fort William. Fortunately the government spies did not discover that the Frenchmen had then sailed to South Uist and on to Loch nan Uamh, so that Loudoun – less than 30 miles away at Fort William – had no idea how close he was to being able to catch his quarry.

The Frenchmen thus were able to lie in Loch nan Uamh unmolested from 6 to 19 September with the foul weather their best ally. Day after day, according to the logs of the *Heureux* and *Conti*, friendly winds carrying squally showers kept other ships away, but these storms died back briefly one day, allowing the Frenchmen to make a quick foray into the open sea to spy out for other shipping. They saw none, so returned to the calmer waters of the loch where the master of the *May* sat miserably idle. 'We hourly looked in vain for deliverance from our ships of war, but to our grief none appeared,' Lachlan wailed.[21]

John MacDonald of Borrodale, who had been hiding at the lochside when the big 'British' frigates sailed in, had taken to the hills, but cannily kept a close watch on every move they made. The clansmen remained in a high state of nervousness, passing every scrap of information about naval, redcoat or militia movements along the clan grapevine as a matter of course. After a day or two of inactivity aboard the vessels, Borrodale summoned up courage to find out what the vessels were up to and hit on a clever ruse to put a spy on board them.

Donald MacDonald, an Edinburgh tailor visiting this part of the country to collect money owed by local lairds, was with him at the time – a man in whom Borrodale said 'we hade great confidence'[22] – so he sent the tailor out to the *Heureux*, accompanied by the Clanranald chief's son, under the pretext of offering his tailoring services to the ships' officers. They were invited to stay and dine with some of the men who had accompanied the expedition and found they included Captain Michael Sheridan, nephew of the Prince's friend, old Tom Sheridan.

Young Clanranald and the tailor returned with the joyous news that the vessels were French and had come in search of the Prince. As Borrodale later related to Bishop Forbes:

> After nightfall twelve french, with two officers at their hade [head] came to a smal hut we repaired sometime before that for our own reception, as all our houses before that were all burned; the names of the officers were jung Sheridan and Capn O'Neil, who at their arrival, enquired for us all, as they knew us weel formerly, and wished much to have some discourse of consequence with us. Upon our being informed of this, we appeared, and after a long conversation were convinced of their sincerity, and oblidged them

> to produce their credentials from France, before we revealed any parte of our secrets to them.[23]

In that environment of duplicity and double dealing one could never be too careful.

It was inevitable that news of the presence of the *Heureux* and *Prince de Conti* at Loch nan Uamh soon leaked out and the whole of Lochaber was in a frenzy to find the Prince. The Hanoverians learned of the visiting ships too because the little Edinburgh tailor, in spite of Borrodale's 'great confidence', passed on every morsel garnered among his Highland clients to the government when he came to be questioned a week or two later. Lord Loudoun learned of the vessels' presence in Loch nan Uamh on 13 September, but did nothing. The thought must come to mind that, like MacDonald of Sleat, Loudoun was not anxious to go down in history as the man who captured the Stuart Prince.

The tailor gave a full account to Lord Albemarle in Edinburgh before the month was out, telling the commander-in-chief that discussion of the rescue plan on board ship had been open and frank when he and Young Clanranald visited the *Heureux*. The French had been in great fear up to that moment, he said, lest they might fail to make contact with the Prince and were actually contemplating leaving the west coast to sail through the Pentland Firth to ask about him at a friendly house near Stonehaven, which of course was strong Jacobite territory. The tailor was prepared to name names and added that the French were contemplating sailing as far south as Edinburgh in order to enquire about Prince Charlie at the houses of Norwell Hume near Bathgate, Lady Bruce in Leith, and Lady Cunningham at Priestfield. Fortunately all those useful scraps came too late.[24]

Alarmed at how nervous the leader of the *Heureux/Prince de Conti* expedition was becoming, the clansmen began feverishly to track the fugitive down, which was just as well since news was spreading quickly and other followers were arriving at Loch nan Uamh out of curiosity or in the hope of being taken back to France. John MacDonald of Scotus, a member of the Glengarry family, known as Spanish John because he had served in the Spanish army, visited the ships, but decided to return to his clansmen although he had served the Cause well and deserved to escape.

Less deserving, but more anxious than anyone to seize this chance of freedom, was another member of the Glengarry family, Coll Macdonnell of Barisdale. He rushed to Moidart and, satisfied that there would be a place for him on board the Frenchmen, hurried home to set his affairs in order. Coll did sail to France, but not in the manner he planned – Warren took him aboard the *Prince de Conti* in manacles. Barisdale, a giant of a man, known as Coll Ban because of his blond hair, remains an embarrassment to Clan Donald to this day. Some writers on the Jacobites have glossed over Barisdale's treachery, but Bishop Forbes, when collecting accounts of the Prince's escape for his *Lyon in Mourning*, was told that, when captured after Culloden, Barisdale made a deal with the

Duke of Cumberland to give information about the Prince in return for his own safety. Barisdale thus had 'touched Hanoverian money',[25] an unforgivable breach of Highland honour, a crime that could not be expiated even by the fact that during the weeks leading up to Culloden this giant rogue had 'brought to the Jacobite cause the same energy and enthusiasm which he normally devoted to raiding his neighbours and stealing their cattle . . . harassing the local Whigs and looting or burning their property'.[26] Not even that lordly government supporter the Earl of Sutherland was safe from Coll Ban.

Military historian, John Selby, credits Barisdale with being 'notable as one of the leading cattle stealers in the Highlands, and also the foremost exponent of the practice which added a new word to the language . . . black-meal, or blackmail, a forced levy in meal which, if paid by chiefs, ensured that their cattle would be protected by Barisdale's men from lesser thieves'.[27] Sixty of Barisdale's men were put ashore from the *Conti*, but Coll himself was taken to France where he rotted in jail until 1749, then was returned to Scotland, only to be thrown into Edinburgh Castle's dungeons. He died there the following year. Andrew Lang described Scotland's farewell to this legendary Highland giant, who crowned a career of cruel swaggering and theft with deliberate treachery: 'Six soldiers, with no mourners, carried his bulky and corpulent carcase to a grave at the foot of the *talus* of the Castle.'[28]

Having visited the ships personally to satisfy himself that they were genuine, Borrodale sent his brother, accompanied by two French officers, to tell Major John MacDonald of Glenaladale of the ships' mission. 'After a night's rest they were desired by Glenadil to return to their ships, and that he would go in search of the person they wanted,' he told Forbes.[29] The spirit of secrecy remained so much alive that even as Barisdale told his story to Bishop Forbes later he referred to going in search of 'the person they wanted'. Prince Charles Edward could not be named even then.

'Glenadil' had a fair inkling as to where the fugitive might be found: his cousin had helped to pick the Prince's path between the enemy campfires in the mountains and left him in the care of the Seven Men of Glenmoriston, who in turn handed him over the Camerons. But there the trail went cold. In only three weeks Charles Stuart had vanished once again – the 'need-to-know' policy was functioning admirably. By good luck Glenaladale encountered an old woman who was able to direct him to Lochiel's tacksman, Cameron of Clunes and, having instructed Clunes to go in search of the fugitives, Glenaladale rushed back to Loch nan Uamh to make sure the ships would not leave.

Again chance intervened: another of Lochiel's tenants, John McColvain, met Lochiel's brother and Cluny MacPherson, who were able to lead him to Cluny's Cage, where he arrived on 13 September. Within an hour the Prince and his guides had set out on their way westward to Moidart, a difficult and dangerous journey, which took them until the

19th to reach Loch nan Uamh, where the Prince was rowed out to the *Prince de Conti,* but later transferred to the larger *Heureux.*

Although Lachlan MacLean of the *May* did not actually witness the Prince's arrival, he realised something important was afoot. 'About six in the evening, after sitting to supper, a message came from the *Prince de Conti,*' he said, 'upon which Colonel Warren and the captain of the frigate got up in a great hurry, got on their best clothes, ordered us on board our vessell with our chests, where we remained guarded by their men and an officer until two next morning, the 20th, when Colonel Warren and one of his officers came on board of us . . . he was in top spirits, telling us plainly that he had now got the Prince on board with Lochiel.'[30]

An elated Charles Stuart watched the ships prepare to sail – he was on his way to France at last: even more important he was still surrounded by those good friends who had looked after him so well – Lochiel, Dr Archibald Cameron and John Roy Stewart. Before sailing he sent a note to Cluny MacPherson who decided to remain behind with Breakachie to ensure that the movement's interests would continue to be nurtured. 'Thanks to God I am arrived safely aboard the vessell, which is a verry clever one, and has another alonst with her as good,'[31] he told Cluny.

Anchors were raised in the early hours of the morning of 20 September, and the *Heureux* and *Conti* moved slowly out of the loch into the Sound of Arisaig, their passage illuminated only by the harvest moon in a clear sky. As the sun rose behind them next morning they passed Eigg and Muck on the starboard beam and Coll to port, then set course westward into the relative safety of the Atlantic. The storm had died down at last to make a peaceful end to the bloody adventure.

Charles Edward Stuart left behind in Britain hundreds of prisoners, whom the Hanoverian government was in no mood to treat lightly. All through the autumn transports continued to carry prisoners from Scotland to London, where they were to be dealt with – King George did not trust Scottish judges to deal severely enough with Scots prisoners. At first it was planned to house the prisoners in the Savoy Barracks, but as these were not ready, the Duke of Newcastle directed the Admiralty to land 300 at Tilbury, which was as many as the fort there could hold. The remainder would have to remain on board ship, but he asked the Commissioners for Sick and Wounded to 'provide the said Prisoners with Necessaries during their Imprisonment there',[32] and that those aboard ship should be allowed ashore daily 'for air'. None of this was done, so disease raged in the dank holds of the ships, until a month later Newcastle was forced to admit that it would be unsafe even to land those still in the transports. So there they remained, crammed into comfortless, unsanitary, typhus-infected holds, where their death sentence was pronounced and executed by disease and malnutrition before the slow process of 'the King's pleasure' could be carried through. The names of 684 prisoners simply disappeared from the records – 'Fate Unrecorded' – but they were mostly victims of wounds in battle, or typhus and other diseases. John Wilson, servant to one of the army doctors, vanished in this way. He had sailed south in the *Dolphin* and was last heard of at Tilbury Fort in June 1746. He was only fourteen years of age.

The government realised it could not make 'a speedy example' of the rebels by attempting to put close on 3,500 men and women on trial – not even 3,500 less the 700 who had died while waiting for justice. A simple solution, effective after the '15 rising, existed: the prisoners would draw lots to select one man in twenty to be sent for trial.

Alexander Stewart, who had been captured in Perthshire a fortnight after Culloden and sent to Carlisle, described the lotting: prisoners were divided into groups of twenty and a hatful of tickets pushed in front of them with orders to draw one. On asking what it was for, Stewart was told it was to draw for their lives. He drew number fourteen, which saved him from trial, but not from punishment, for he was transported from Liverpool to Wecomica, Maryland, in May 1747. He was one of the few who managed to escape from America and returned to Scotland the following year.[33]

Many Scots prisoners had already been sent to Carlisle and London, and those still held north of the Border were excluded from the lottery as were women, important members of the Prince's circle and some chosen specially by the Duke of Newcastle himself, probably on the basis of information from his spies.

The Jacobite Cause became a series of sideshows in London that autumn when sightseers crowded to watch the army practise the bayonet menoeuvre that had won victory at Culloden, or to spectate at executions at Cumberland Gate or hangings of army deserters at Hyde Park. And for a Sunday outing there was always a trip down the Thames to stare at the Jacobite prison ships, *Pamela* and *Royal Sovereign*. On 8 December the mob enjoyed a flash of the previous summer's entertainment when Lord Derwentwater was beheaded at the Tower.

More prisoners kept arriving, including the most famous of them all, Flora MacDonald, who was brought south aboard HMS *Eltham*. Even Cumberland's successor, Albemarle, had put in a good word for Flora, so she was well looked after on the voyage and after her arrival in the Thames in November 1746. She spent only a few days aboard the *Royal Sovereign* before being transferred to one of the messengers' houses in London.

Messengers were government officials who accompanied prisoners as they were moved around the country and some of them were allowed to lodge the more important prisoners in their houses, for which the prisoners paid out of their own pockets. It was an excellent 'little earner' for these erstwhile gaolers, who could charge as much as 6*s* 8*d*. a day, and sometimes offered their 'guests' very little in return for their money. Flora was lucky: she was in the house of Messenger Dick, with a number of her own friends and friends of the Prince around her – the Clanranald and Boisdale chiefs among them, as well as Malcolm MacLeod of Raasay, John MacKinnon of Elgol, MacNeill of Barra, and the old boatman,

Donald MacLeod of Galtergill. Even the Prince's wigmaker, Richard Morrison, was there waiting to be questioned.

Less welcome companions were government witnesses Lachlan McMhurrich and Kenneth MacDonald, both in London to give evidence against Clanranald and the Mackinnon chief, and Charles MacEachain, who had agreed to testify against MacDonald of Garrifleuch. It is thanks to another of Flora's companions in Messenger Dick's house, John Burton, that we know so much about the journey over the sea to Skye, for he later passed on all he had heard from Flora to Bishop Forbes for inclusion in his *Lyon in Mourning*.

Flora was detained in the messenger's house without being brought to trial until Saturday 4 July 1747, when an amnesty was declared and she was set free – she had been a prisoner for a year all but a day. By that time the government had taken nearly 3,470 men, women and children prisoner and executed 120 of them, but it is far from certain what happened to the others – nearly 1,000 were transported to the West Indies and America, a further 120 were simply banished 'outside our Dominions', a few were pardoned, and of course a great many just vanished from the records, probably claimed by death in gaols or prison ships.

King George's last flourish was the trial of his most prized prisoner, old Lord Lovat, whose duplicity had earned him the contempt of both sides. Simon Fraser was not brought before his peers until 7 March 1747, but the delay had proved well worthwhile for in the meantime both Hugh Fraser, Lovat's secretary and confidant, and Murray of Broughton, had been thoroughly questioned to assemble a case against him.

Westminster Hall was set out as it had been for the Kilmarnock, Balmerino and Cromartie trials with scaffolding to accommodate the hundreds who demanded admittance, but this time Lovat's notorious reputation added an edge to the proceedings. Although now over seventy and in failing health, he put up a strong defence, but stood little chance before a court presided over by the ever-unsympathetic Hardwicke.

When Murray of Broughton was called to give his testimony on the second day, the old man objected that, since Broughton himself was attainted, he could not give evidence for the King. The argument continued throughout the whole day, interrupted frequently by the old renegade, whose courageous persistence won him sympathy as Horace Walpole reported: 'It hurt everybody at old Lovat's tryal, all guilty as he was, to see an old wretch worried by the first lawyers in England, without any assistance but his own unpracticed defence.'[34] In the end Lovat lost the argument: Broughton was heard.

The following morning Broughton gave his testimony, earning himself the name Mr 'Evidence' Murray among those who were angered by his betrayal of the Cause rather than his betrayal of Lovat. Murray held Lovat in contempt and recounted in his *Memoirs* how the Fraser chief let the Cause down, 'at the same time taking Occasion to apologise for his Clans not having acted with that Vigour and unanimity the others had done;

but the excuses were in themselves frivolous, and consisted more in telling a parcel of Old Stories, and vaunting himself of a Loyalty which his Actions gave him no title to.'[35]

Lovat was a traitor to both King George and King James, and had let Broughton down by going back on his word to help to set up a guerrilla campaign among the mountains, so Broughton felt no need to protect him. In court he told the story of events leading up to the rising carefully, hiding little, but there is no doubt he could have revealed more and his testimony did not convict Lovat – there were plenty of Frasers to do that. But Broughton's testimony certainly helped to confirm the government's case and in due course Lovat was found guilty and sentenced to death.

Lovat expressed loyalty to the Stuart Cause at the last and accepted his fate with greater dignity than he had displayed in his life hitherto. When Hardwicke asked if he had anything further to say he replied, 'Nothing but to thank your lordships for your goodness to me. God bless you all, and I bid you an everlasting farewell. We shall not meet all in the same place again, I am sure of that.'[36] He reserved his acid tongue for the rabble as he left Westminster Hall when a woman screamed at him, 'You'll get that nasty head of yours chopped off, you ugly old Scotch dog.' 'I believe I shall, you ugly old English bitch,' he answered equably, and passed on.[37]

The following week he followed Kilmarnock, Balmerino and Derwentwater to the block at Tower Hill, and once again London made a festival of the event, so much so that one of the specially built stands collapsed, killing several spectators. On hearing this he remarked, 'The greater the mischief, the better the sport', and mounted the block, handed the executioner a purse containing 10 guineas, and told him, 'Pray do your work well; for if you should cut and hack my shoulders and I shall be able to rise again, I shall be very angry.' And so the chief, who had said so much yet done so little for his Prince, died.[38]

Nobody was executed as a result of Mr 'Evidence' Murray's denunciations, although some did spend a long time in gaol and a few must have passed some uncomfortable months wondering if they would be his next victims. He was especially careful to protect the Scottish leaders, disclosing a lot of information about them, but most of it nothing more than what the government already knew. This was disinformation of a kind and it certainly did not lead to any convictions. He was careful not to incriminate men like Lochiel, Macpherson of Cluny or MacDonald of Sleat, but took fewer pains to protect Lord Traquair, who had done nothing for the Cause, Sir John Douglas or MacLeod of Dunvegan, who helped the Hanoverians openly.

Was there some hidden agenda behind Murray of Broughton's behaviour? He had been exceedingly bitter about the English role in the campaign, and in the words of Robert Fitzroy Bell, editor of Murray's *Memorials*: 'Their failure to rise and join the Prince had, day after day, from Carlisle to Derby, caused the bitterest disappointment, and at last resulted in the disaster of the retreat: and this after all the plottings and promises of years. Again, Murray argued, through them his country was the scene of cruelties unexampled in civilised warfare, his Prince was a fugitive, his friends dead or exiled, and nothing was left but revenge on the false friends, for the open enemies were unassailable.'[39]

Murray claimed that before his execution Lord Lovat sent him a message, saying 'he was not the least hurt or offended by anything I had said'.[40] Prince Charlie was less forgiving; he wrote to his father: 'Poor L^{d}. Lovat is executed by ye Rascallity of J^{n} Murray, and it is much fierd many others will suffer in ye same manner.'[41]

The entire movement took its cue from the Prince and disowned Broughton for his betrayal of his comrades: he was shunned by Jacobites everywhere, and the freemasons' lodge in Edinburgh to which he belonged excised his name from their records. The government pardoned him in 1749, but he remained a Jacobite, though on the fringes of the movement ever after.

He consorted with that arch spy, Pickle, which further damaged his name, but it is unlikely that he had the faintest inkling of Young Glengarry's treachery. Andrew Lang suggests that Murray passed information about the Loch Arkaig Treasure to Pickle, and perhaps even 'a few crumbs of intelligence' which ended up with the London government as well.[42] He even arranged for a priest named Leslie to pawn Mrs Murray's watch to help Pickle at a time when Young Glengarry was starving.[43]

Broughton's wife, Margaret, who was one of those fanatical Jacobite spouses who followed the army all the way to Derby and back, left her husband, not because of the theft of her watch – she could forgive him for that – but for his treacherous behaviour in 1746–7. The beauty who rode a white horse and flourished a sword as Charles's father was proclaimed king in Edinburgh, could not stomach her husband's betrayal of the movement they had both loved so dearly.

History has been harsh on Prince Charlie's loyal and efficient secretary – if he quarrelled with the other leaders, he was doing nothing beyond the general run of behaviour among Prince Charlie's leaders; if he betrayed Lord Lovat he was turning on a man who subverted his and Lochiel's plan to keep the campaign alive in 1746; if he 'peached' against the English Jacobites, they had failed the Cause and in any case what he told was never sufficient to put them on trial; if he consorted with Pickle the Spy he did so in ignorance and out of pity for a man he did not know to be a spy; and if he took money from the cache at Loch Arkaig it did him little good for he ended his life in poverty.

Cowardice in the face of arrest and threat of trial for his life was Murray of Broughton's worst sin and it was a common enough one that summer of 1746. Andrew Lang pronounces a final, utterly believable verdict on the man. '"Lead us not into temptation",' he wrote. 'The view of death brought Murray face to face with a self in his breast, which, it is probable, he had never known to exist: that awful contradictory self to which each of us had yielded, though few in such extremity of surrender.'[44]

John Murray of Broughton stands out from other traitors to the Cause as not just a common betrayer, but as a man who had given everything to it yet was unfortunate enough to be asked to make an even greater sacrifice at a moment when he was at his most vulnerable – ill, weak and feeling betrayed himself. O. Douglas's verdict fits perfectly with that: he was a weak man tried too high.

CHAPTER TWELVE

One War – Three Campaigns

Our ancient crown's fa'n in the dust –
Deil blin' them wi the stoure* o't, * dust
An write their names in the black beuk* * book
Wha gae the Whigs the power o't!

Awa, Whigs, awa!
Awa, Whigs, awa!
Ye're but a pack o traitor louns,* * rogues
Ye'll do nae guid at a'.

Jacobite song by Robert Burns based on an earlier fragment in David Herd's manuscripts.[1]

During his last weeks in Scotland Prince Charlie was in better spirits than he had been at almost any time during the rising. The vivid description of him left by the Presbyterian minister at Fort William does not describe a beaten man: 'He was then barefooted, had an old black kilt coat on, a plaid, philabeg and waistcoat, a dirty shirt and a long red beard, a gun in his hand, a pistol and durk by his side. He was very cheerful and in good health, and in my opinion fatter than when he was in Inverness.'[2] In spite of the disappointment, deprivation and discomfort of the past four months, the Prince sailed for France in high spirits and with the additional spur of hope that he would soon be back. He may not have won, but he had not been disgraced either.

The '45 rising was three campaigns – military, espionage and propaganda – fought simultaneously, and although the Hanoverians came out victorious in all three in the end, it was a much more closely run contest than the result suggests. Scottish historian Bruce Lenman goes so far as to say that the '45 was 'never a big rising', and rightly acknowledges the influence of Lord President Duncan Forbes in ensuring that in the Highlands active Jacobites formed a distinct minority. 'It is worth stressing that no really great Scottish magnate ever committed himself to the '45,' he commented.[3]

The '45 caught the imagination of future generations, however, largely thanks to the charisma of Prince Charlie. It struck such fear into the British government that the administration took the most horrific revenge on the Highlands and destroyed the clan system for ever.

To achieve so much with an oddly-assorted, untrained, ill-armed following makes Charles Edward's achievement in 1745–6 all the more remarkable: almost to the end the outcome was never a foregone conclusion and it was achieved by a prince who was not a natural general, with leaders who, by and large, were even less competent or spent much of their time bickering among themselves. The outstanding exception was his Lieutenant-General, Lord George Murray, a military genius, but unfortunately a difficult man with whom the Prince could never work, and this was probably the single factor that led most surely to defeat at Culloden.

With his army he outmanoeuvred the British commander Sir John Cope to take Edinburgh within weeks and rout Cope's better-organised forces at Prestonpans within minutes. He was never defeated in England and on his return to Scotland won battles at Falkirk and minor victories in the Highlands during the spring of 1746. Culloden was his only defeat, but it may be argued that it was lost as much through Jacobite quarrelling and mismanagement prior to the battle as by the tactics of Cumberland's highly-trained redcoats on the field.

Perhaps Culloden might have been won, or not lost disastrously, had Charles kept his nerve and delayed the confrontation, or at least chosen a field to suit the Highlanders on which to fight as Lord George Murray had done at Prestonpans. The military campaign of the '45 was lost for many reasons: the Prince's personality contributed, as did his inability to work with the best general he had, and his abdication of leadership from the moment the decision to retreat was taken at Derby. And at no time during the campaign did he turn his army into an organised or trained fighting machine – his men were 'bonnie fechters' to a man, but they did not have the weapons, experience or spirit of a fighing unit.

Clansmen fought by the season and when spring or harvest-time came round they had more important work to do at home to ensure that their families would be fed, so home they went. They also fought a war battle by battle rather than as part of a campaign, and when victory was won the age-old instinct was to take their booty and go home. As a result desertion was endemic. Having said that, the Highlanders – and Lowlanders too – fought a good military campaign, but were let down by their English and French friends, whose support might have turned defeat into victory.

But the final defeat was what counted for Prince Charlie. Culloden was total, and he had made no preparation for it. As a result he found himself and his army hunted like animals with no chance of taking to the hills to reorganise and pursue a guerrilla campaign until help arrived from France. The tragedy for the Prince was that his army was not scattered to the four winds after Culloden as is so often assumed: a goodly proportion could have reassembled and reorganised to wage a winter campaign in the mountains, which Cumberland could hardly have won. By spring, who knows, help might have arrived from France. The military campaign of the '45 might have been so different but for these factors – however, 'buts' lose all wars.

The espionage campaign of the '45 was as badly organised as the military one. It was a time during which properly organised spy work could have been of enormous value to military and political leaders, yet it was a sadly neglected business on both sides.

The very fact that the clan chiefs were taken by surprise when Prince Charlie landed shows how badly prepared, poorly informed and ill-organised Stuart followers were in the lead-up to the rising. And the British were little better, with Secretary of State Tweeddale and Lord Justice Clerk Milton arguing about whether the Prince was even in Scotland after he had already taken first blood and raised his standard at Glenfinnan. Nobody had certain knowledge of what was about to occur until it actually happened.

With the start of the campaign proper, intelligence improved very little on either side. There was plenty of scouting and spying on enemy troop movements and passing of information, but most of this was on an *ad hoc* basis, largely news of troop movements acquired by chance rather than through deliberate planting of moles among the enemy. There was little real intelligence-gathering and information was rarely turned into useful military intelligence by examining and evaluating what had been brought in. The greatest drawback to the efficiency of both sides in keeping abreast of their opponents' activities was sheer lack of organisation.

The clans were at a great advantage in the Highlands, where they were among friends and spoke Gaelic, which the English and Lowlanders could not understand. Thus Prince Charlie's army learned quickly what moves the enemy was making. In the western Highlands, where Campbell of Mamore and his militia were operating, this advantage was cancelled out as Campbell was better organised, infiltrating the clans with his informers to glean news of where the rebels were hiding. This was how he managed to keep track of the Prince's movements while Charles was hiding in Morar and the Outer Hebrides, but fortunately Campbell's spies always remained far enough behind for Charles never to be captured.

Even after the rising was over and Cumberland handed over to Albemarle the spy war continued, and it was then that the Jacobites achieved their greatest success. For four months Prince Charlie was on the run in the Highlands and Western Isles, constantly on the move. A price of £30,000 waited for anyone who chose to betray him, but not only did no one do so, they managed to spirit him from hideout to hideout, from the mainland to the Outer Isles and back, and then through the redcoat cordon to the safety of Cluny's Cage. It was an achievement of which the clans are still proud.

Albemarle must have felt sick about this clan success. He hated Scotland and its people intensely, and never wanted to take over as commander-in-chief in the first place, but all his pleas to Cumberland and Newcastle, 'writ with a heart full of sorrow',[4] were to no avail. Once the appointment was foisted upon him, he had to make the best of it. Ever fond of *le mot juste,* in rather poor French he told Newcastle,

'En un mot, My Lord, L'Ecosse est ma bete.'[5] Surely he meant to say Scotland was his 'bête noire', his pet hate, but his French was not up to that.

He worked hard through the autumn and into the winter of 1746/7 to round up rebels and keep London informed of subversive activity, but by the end of November was compelled to send Newcastle a list of seventy important men against whom he held proof of having been involved in the rebellion, but still had not captured.[6]

His spies brought in information, which made depressing reading for the government; considering the vengeance to which the clans had been subjected, they remained in astonishingly good spirits and from everywhere the commander-in-chief kept receiving rumours of a new rising planned with France's support for the following spring. Report after report confirmed that the clansmen were in good heart, still armed because they had handed in only old rusty weapons and had managed to retain an amazing number of their cattle. They were looking forward to joining the expected spring rising with only one immediate problem, a shortage of meal.[7]

The spirit of Betty Burke was still alive and well in the Highlands and in January 1747 Albemarle forwarded a report to Newcastle from one of his spies, saying, 'There are several men going through Lovat's Grounds and Seaforth's in Women's Cloaths, conversing with and frequenting the Houses of those notoriously known to be disaffected, and it's thought they are distributing some papers brought from the South amongst the people who are professed Jacobites; Every one spiriting up another to a Rebellion in the Spring, as they have great assurances of a Landing, as they say, and seem all willing to join.'[8] These were the heady days soon after Charles's return to France, when he was trying to encourage King Louis to mount a new campaign, so although hopes may have been greatly exaggerated, they certainly alarmed the Whigs.

When 20 December (Prince Charlie's birthday by the Old Style calendar) came round, Albemarle was infuriated to discover a plan by Edinburgh dissidents to celebrate the occasion and went to great lengths to stop them. He was at the end of his tether now and begged Newcastle to allow him to join Cumberland in Flanders. Again resorting to his smattering of French, he wrote, 'Au Nom Du Dieu retire moy d'icy, & pray, Lett me have Leave from the King to come away.' Albemarle had tasted enough of Scotland and soon his wish was granted.[9]

The Hanoverians had won the greatest espionage prize of the '45, however, in the Jacobites' decision to retreat from Derby. Although no one was enthusiastic about marching on to London without French help, the leaders might just have resolved to continue the march south but for Dudley Bradstreet's gloomy news of an imaginary army advancing from Northampton. There can be no doubt this influenced the waverers. The Irish spy took an enormous risk to carry off this coup and deserved every penny of any reward he managed to wring out of the Duke of Newcastle.

Throughout the half century between the Glorious Revolution and the '45 rising both Jacobites and government were so acutely aware of the worth of propaganda that the art was developed into a weapon of value to both sides. Poems, songs, broadsheets, plays and novels proved far more effective than siege guns or broadswords.

The Whigs had many friends to turn out high-quality propaganda for them, among them some of the most important names of eighteenth-century literature – Defoe, Fielding, Locke and Sterne. These authors were a godsend to the politicians who, contrary to today's belief that Jacobitism was a passing nuisance rather than a dire threat, made good use of propaganda as a weapon to fight the Stuarts. From them and a host of anonymous writers and cartoonists poured a succession of pamphlets, poems and drawings lampooning the Jacobites, while the Jacobites responded similarly with screeds of anti-Whig material.

Fielding used the theatre as the medium for his satire; first he railed against Walpole's corruption and King George, but later he turned on the Jacobites with a pamphlet *A Dialogue between the Devil, the Pope and the Pretender* – a blatant display of religious intolerance, and later his *History of the Present Rebellion,* another piece of political propaganda rather than a history as its title suggests. The *True Patriot* was more anti-Stuart propaganda, which led eventually to his novel, *Tom Jones,* although that did not appear until three years after the rising. Fielding proved a master of propaganda and did the Cause much harm.

By the time Prince Charles landed in Scotland in 1745 the propaganda machine was thoroughly oiled with every cogwheel turning smoothly – if only the military campaign had been as well organised the outcome might bave been different. Propaganda material poured from both sides: long Gaelic poems circulated orally throughout the Highlands; popular ballads were hawked round the streets of Edinburgh; sermons were preached by Whig and Jacobite clergy and then distributed to a wider audience as broadsheets; cartoons mocked the Pretender; and Henry Fielding was in his stride as publisher of the *True Patriot.* Printed propaganda was a burgeoning industry, although its value must have been limited since only a small proportion of the population was able to read.

The Whigs were always jealous of the females who flocked to worship the Pretender wherever he went and seized every opportunity to lampoon women who supported the Cause, especially Flora MacDonald and Jenny Cameron – the latter was depicted in one satirical drawing saucily riding pillion behind him. Both Flora and Jenny appeared in another, flanking the Prince's portrait and captioned with a quotation from the *Beggar's Opera,* 'How happy could I be with Either, Were t'other dear Charmer away.' In another cartoon women swooned before him as he entered Edinburgh, and in an illustration of Holyrood they crowded round him in an ante-room, in which a bed stood in a corner. The half dozen verses of doggerel underneath ended:

But while those foolish Females take
And to their Bosoms clasp the Snake
Let English Nymphs the Pest beware
For Poison lurks in Secret there.

No base-born Wretch let William stand
The Pride and Darling of our land.
William on Earth the young Nassau
Born to defend the World below.

The bed spoke volumes, even if the verse added little to the Whigs' cause, but in 1745 it did not matter in the least that Charles's self-imposed celibacy was a fact known to all. Whig satirists seized every opportunity to insinuate sexual and unprincely undertones wherever they could. Oddly though, they missed Clementina Walkinshaw, the one woman who could have been the Prince's mistress during the '45 campaign.

The Jacobites had their propaganda revenge in one of the most famous of the many prints that circulated during the rising. Entitled *The Agreable Contrast*, this depicts Flora MacDonald turning her back on Cumberland who is standing alongside a young woman and an elephant, and gazing wistfully at the Prince who is leading a sleek greyhound. Speech balloons emerge from the mouths of each of the four – Young Woman: 'Let nobody like me be deceived with such a pittiful tail'; Cumberland: 'Bad Words'; Flora: 'Oh, the agreeable creature'; Charles: 'Mercy and Love, Peace. etc.'

Each move, each victory, was marked by a surge of verse, so that first part of the '45 may be chronicled through poems and songs, seldom factually accurate – but then neither was what purported to be straightforward news reports in the press of the day. On the Jacobite side it began with a host of songs in Gaelic and English expressing the longing of his followers for the King over the Water to return and their joy at having his son among them now.

When France had her assistance lent
Our darling prince to us she sent,
Towards the north his course he bent,
His name was Royal Charlie.
But, O, he was lang o' coming,
O, he was lang o' coming:–
Welcome Royal Charlie!

When he upon the shore did stand,
The friends he had within the land
Came down and shook him by the hand,
And welcom'd Royal Charlie.
Wi', 'O, ye've been lang o' coming,' etc.

The dress that our Prince Charlie had
Was bonnet blue and tartan plaid;
And O he was a handsome lad!
Few could compare wi' Charlie.
But O, he was lang o' coming.

The facts of the poem are a travesty of history and the most devoted Jacobite must have realised that France had neither lent assistance nor sent the Prince. Had she done so he would have arrived in 1744. No more did Charles's friends hurry to take him by the hand and welcome him ashore. On the contrary they urged him to leave at once, and he had to use all his charm and authority to win them over. Fact counted for nothing against the deep sense of longing expressed in the chorus. Charlie had been 'lang o' coming'.

Praise poured from Highland bards and Lowland ladies as Prince Charlie captured Edinburgh and won his first major victory at Prestonpans. And while there were glamourised descriptions of the rout and massacre, most of the Jacobite scorn was reserved for Cope, a good general, who had been made to look foolish, and is remembered for the song that lampoons him.

Cope sent a challenge frae Dunbar,
'Come, Charlie, meet me an ye dare,
And I'll teach you the art of war,
If you'll meet wi' me i' the morning.'
Hey, Johnnie Cope, are ye wauking* yet? * awake
Or are your drums a-beating yet?
If ye were wauking I would wait
To gang to the coals i' the morning.

When Johnnie Cope to Dunbar came,
They speer'd* at him, 'Where's a' your men?' * asked
'The deil confound me gin I ken*, * if I know
For I left them a' i' the morning.'
Hey, Johnnie Cope, etc.

Now, Johnnie, troth ye were na blate*, * shy
To come wi' the news o' your ain defeat,
And leave your men in sic a strait,
So early in the morning.
Hey, Johnnie Cope, etc.

'I' faith,' quo' Johnnie, 'I got a fleg*, * fright
Wi' their claymores and philabegs,
If I face them again, deil break my legs!
So I wish you a very gude morning.'
Hey, Johnnie Cope, etc.

Not a word of all that is true, except that Cope's army was defeated: none the less, it is the image of the general which existed in 1745 and which has been handed down from generation to generation ever since. It is what the world at large believes even today.

Not many on the Hanoverian side saw humour in the rout of Cope at Prestonpans, but Horace Walpole managed to extract a wry joke when he wrote that he might soon have to exchange his comfortable apartments in Arlington Street for a wretched attic in Herrenhausen and perhaps be reduced to giving Latin lessons to the young princes in Copenhagen: 'The dowager Stafford has already written cards for my Lady Nithsdale, my Lady Tullibardine, the Duchesses of Perth and Berwick, and twenty more revived peeresses, to invite them to play at whist Monday three months,' he added.[10] Whitehall did not share his amusement.

In England the press carried lurid reports of Highland barbarities which, far from strengthening the will to fight, struck terror into the heart of the rulers and the ruled. Here, sermons too were turned into popular broadsheets and pamphlets: one preached at Islington on 22 September was reprinted under the title, *The Young Chevalier. No God Speed to Him.* 'No, Sirs!' it thundered, 'pretend what he will this *mock Prince* brings his tenets of Religion from *Rome*, and his Taste for Government from *France*: He comes with a Pretence to lead us into a Field larger, and gayer with Flowers of Liberty than ever; but, *Britons*, venture not to Step into it, for fear of the Snake in the Grass.'

In Edinburgh you paid your money for the papers and took your choice. The pro-Charles *Caledonian Mercury* exposed as false those claims in the English press that women were being exposed naked on Edinburgh's Mercat Cross and then murdered. The *Edinburgh Courant*, held its tongue for the moment like all other folk with Whig sentiments in the capital and even those ministers of the Kirk, who heartily hated the exiled Stuarts, said little. On the Sunday following Prestonpans Charles invited them to hold services as usual, but all fled or stayed at home except one, Neil MacVicar of St Cuthbert's. From his pulpit MacVicar boldly prayed, 'Lord, bless the king, You know which king I want to say. As far as that one that has come among us to seek also a terrestial crown we beg you in *ta miséricorde* to bring him to you, and give him a celestial crown.'[11] It took nerve as well as commitment to mount the pulpit in Edinburgh that Sunday.

For those glorious weeks while Charles 'reigned' in his father's capital, his supporters made a great noise to drown the voices of their opponents. White ribbons were worn, medallions struck and pamphlets and poems circulated in the streets and drawing-rooms; some were simply expressions of sheer joy, but many were bitter attacks on the Whigs and pointed out to the English the miserable state of Scotland since the Union of 1707.

That hated Union featured in songs peddled in the street, which touched the hearts of the people much more than all the pamphlets or polemics. 'Come all brave Scotsman and rejoice With a Loud Acclamation', may not have been great poetry, but it expressed the feelings of the moment. Its final verse called out:

All beasts that go upon all Four,
Go leap and dance around;
Because that curst Union's broke,
And fallen to the ground.[12]

After Derby the Jacobite songsters were silenced for the time being and they only took up their singing again after Culloden – to a very different tune. Tobias Smollett's 1746 poem 'The Tears of Scotland', summed up Scottish feelings:

Mourn, hapless Caledonia, mourn
Thy burnish'd peace, thy laurels torn!
Thy sons, for valour long renown'd,
Lie slaughtered on their native ground.
Thy hospitable roofs no more
Invite the stranger to the door,
In smoky ruins sunk they lie,
The monuments of cruelty.

By then Prince Charlie was a legend, so it is hardly surprising that he became the central figure of Jacobite song. Followers may have had him in mind as they sang, 'When you came over first frae France/Bonny Laddie, Highland Laddie' in 1745, but William Donaldson, a historian of Jacobite song, has demonstrated that they were parodying something much older, an ancient and, incidentally, erotic song. A version of 'Highland Laddie' appeared in Allan Ramsay's *Tea-Table Miscellany* a couple of decades before the '45 and included a verse in which the Lowland lass singing of her Highland lover sang:

A Painted Room and Silken Bed,
May please a Lawland Laird and Lady;
But I can kiss and be as glad
Behind a Bush in's Highland Plaidy.

But Donaldson traces the song even further back, at least to the Glorious Revolution.[13] It was so familiar by 1746 that even 'Butcher' Cumberland knew it and sang it once to Edinburgh folk who had gathered to see him off to the south at the end of the rising. 'As he mounted his horse he turned and, in a rare moment of humour, cried "Shall we not have one song?" and then as he galloped off he broke into the old Scots melody, "Will you play me fair, Highland Laddie, Highland laddie?".'[14] It just proved what the Whigs already knew – the devil has all the best tunes.

In the propaganda campaign the Whigs won the war of words, but the Jacobites beat them every time in the war of songs. The very fact that at least four versions of 'Charlie he's my Darling' exist – by Robert Burns, James Hogg, Captain Charles Gray and Lady Nairne – demonstrates the power of the Jacobite theme during the century following Culloden. In this, the last of the three Jacobite campaigns – military, espionage and propaganda – that were waged in 1745–6, immediate victory may have gone to the Whigs, but the ultimate triumph was Prince Charlie's.

An Charlie he's my darling,
My darling, my darling,
Charlie, he's my darling –
The Young Chevalier!

CHAPTER THIRTEEN

'Dealing with this Bloody Government . . .'

> I find it and am absolutely convinced of it that ye only way of dealing with this bloody Government is to give as short and sharp an answer as one can, at the same time paying them in their own coin by loding them with civilities and compliments, setting apart business, for that kind of Vermin, the more you give them the more they'll take.
>
> Letter from Charles Edward to his father, complaining about French treatment of him, 6 November 1746.[1]

The safe arrival of the *Heureux* and *Prince de Conti* in France was a blow to the pride of British intelligence since its own spies and even Paris café gossip had warned it in good time that Warren's little expedition was on the way to rescue the Prince. Although reports had been garbled and suggested Sweden might also become involved, they were firm enough for the Admiralty to instruct its Scottish naval commander, Commodore Smith, in early August to expect the arrival of ships from France or Scandinavia, or both.[2] Thanks to good luck and bad weather Warren dodged the Royal Navy and arrived in Loch nan Uamh safely, where he picked up the Prince and sailed with him to Franch on 20 September 1746.

Warren's plan was to sail his ships well out into the Atlantic to avoid the Royal Navy and then double back to Nantes at the mouth of the Loire, but by sheer good fortune he changed his mind and made for Roscoff on the north Brittany coast instead. He could not have known that by doing so he avoided a British naval raid on the port of L'Orient on the Atlantic seaboard, which would almost certainly have led to his capture. Obviously, the privateering instincts so much in evidence in all the Prince's sea travels were favouring Prince Charlie, or maybe he just had some well-deserved good luck at last.

It was a heroic '*Prince Edouard*' who stepped ashore at Roscoff on the afternoon of 11 October (30 September by the Old Style calendar), exhausted, but in high spirits, and no doubt unaware of the sad significance of this port in Stuart family history – it was here that his great-great-great grandmother, Mary Queen of Scots, had arrived on 15 August 1548, when she was brought to France as a child at the start of her tragic reign. If Charles knew this, it could hardly have dampened his spirits, however, for he set foot back in France, confident that he would soon persuade King Louis to support a return to Scotland.

Although weary to the marrow of his bones he sat down at once and wrote letters to inform his father and brother of his safe return. The letter to the King was short, and was sent to Prince Henry for forwarding to Rome – 'I send here inclosed t[w]o lines to my master, just to show him I am alive and safe, being fatigued not a little, as you may imagine', he told his brother.[3] There was no time to be lost: he ordered Prince Henry to draft a letter to the French King, presenting Charles's excuses for not writing to him direct, but expressing Charles's hope of meeting him soon. Henry was to discuss this letter with nobody but their closest advisers in Paris and, to emphasise its urgency, he added a postscript: 'Nota bene – It is an absolute necessity I must see the French king as soon as possible, for to bring things to a write head.' Warren was ordered to deliver both letters to Henry and to arrange for the brothers to meet the moment Charles reached the capital.[4]

Without a word to any of those Jacobite followers who had been in France or arrived there ahead of him, Charles took command of plans to organise support for a new rising, quite unaware that, while he had been isolated from family and friends for so long, events in Europe had moved on. As the reality of change became apparent he could not accept it, especially the fact that the war, which had been the catalyst for King Louis's abortive 'Jacobite' invasion in 1744, had changed. The Austrian succession, about which the conflict had begun, had been settled long ago and hostilities had drifted into a military quadrille in which friendships and alliances changed as easily and as frequently as partnerships on the dance floor. For the French, the Jacobites had been a useful diversion, helping Marshal Saxe to some excellent victories and enabling Louis to gain power in Flanders at relatively little cost. French assistance to Prince Charlie has been estimated to have cost Louis XV less than 5 million francs,[5] a quarter of which he recouped in booty with the capture of Brussels. Add to that what Frank McLynn calls 'spin-off' from the gains by privateering and smuggling during the hostilities, and the net cost to France was considerably less and the return high.[6] The saddest fact of all is that, by Aeneas MacDonald's reckoning, only about £15,000 of all the French cash reached Charles, plus some artillery, other materials of war and 1,200 troops.

The Jacobite 'bargain' did not bring France the glory or territory she craved and war was bankrupting the country, so by the time Charles Edward returned, the French government was on its way to negotiating a peace treaty that was eventually signed at Aix-la-Chapelle in 1748, a peace destined to be short lived, however, for within a few years the Seven Years' War had broken out and that was to rob France of much of her colonial power.

Great Britain was ready for peace too, but throughout the autumn of 1746 she was too busy exacting revenge on the rebels to take much account of what Charles Edward was up to in France. Intelligence from

Paris remained useful, but was directed more towards finding a way to peace than to thwarting the Jacobite Prince. This did not mean the British were any less complacent about the Stuart threat: they were momentarily triumphant and it was only after the distraction of punishing rebels and Highland communities was over, that they realised how serious a threat the Cause remained. London became as nervous as ever and increased its espionage and intelligence-gathering. With so many clan chiefs now living under the wing of the Kings of France and Spain and other European princes, the Continent became a beehive from which a swarm was expected to descend on Scotland or England at any moment. King George could not regard Culloden as the end of the Stuart Cause and the only consolation his ministers had was that English Jacobites were still too disorganised to support a rising. But late 1746 provided a brief intelligence interlude for the Cause.

On his return to the Continent Charles knew nothing of France's altered attitude to the war. He was out of touch with the changes of influence among individual ministers in Paris and, worst of all, he did not realise that Louis was taking over the handling of his foreign policy himself without the help of those ministers who remained nominally in charge but were constantly ignored or outmanoeuvred. Unfortunately the Prince had no one at his side to alert him to these new circumstances. Even if advisers had been there, it is unlikely he would have taken heed, though, for Charles Stuart had but a single objective – to mount a new rising – and he could never see this in relation to other political factors around him.

The one man who might have been able to explain the French political sea change was old Tom Sheridan, but Tom had been summoned to Rome to be carpeted for encouraging the Prince to set out on his rash adventure of 1745 and for not remaining in Scotland with his master after the rising collapsed. James did not appreciate that Sheridan was now past seventy – so old a veteran of the movement that he had fought as a youth at the Battle of the Boyne in 1690 – and his health had failed badly, undermined by months of living rough among the heather. Yet he alone was singled out for the Pretender's wrath, which was prompted as much by James's own sense of guilt, because he had allowed this man to take over his role as father to the Prince, as by the facts of Sheridan's part in the rising. Tom Sheridan had been a parent-substitute to Charles since childhood and James knew in his heart of hearts that the old tutor's advice had always contained the bold encouragement that he himself had never given to his son.

Tom reached France a couple of months ahead of the Prince, and valiantly began to gather together all the support he could for the Cause. He had seen Cardinal Tencin and other French ministers, only to find little enthusiasm, and warned the Prince of this in a letter (which, of course, Charles did not receive until after his return): 'All the answer I got from them was that till they knew what was become of your Royal

Highness . . . they could come to no resolution; but the truth is they were so bent on the hopes of a Peace that they seemed to think little of taking any rigorous measures towards renewing the war.'[7]

Even Tencin, so close a friend to the Stuarts that the Duc de Luynes once said he lifted his hat every time King James's name was mentioned,[8] was critical of the Prince, and went so far as to suggest to Sheridan that Charles had made mistakes – he had sent too many agents to and fro between Scotland and France during the rising, but had still failed to keep King Louis personally informed. However, when Sheridan persuaded the Duc de Bouillon to ask the king directly whether he was offended, a clear answer came back: 'Far from it.'[9]

On his arrival at the Bouillon estate at Navarre in Normandy on 12 August 1746, after his return from Scotland, Sheridan was dumbfounded to be handed the summons to Rome, which was far from the cordial letter so faithful an old servant might have expected. 'This [is] to require you to come and joyn me here with all convenient speed,' James commanded. 'Your silence since your return from Scotland has been a matter of surprise to me, when you could not but have given me many satisfactory, tho' not agreeable informations.' After assuring Sheridan of the high regard in which he had been held in the past, the King turned on the old man: 'I think it of absolute necessity . . . that I should have some free discourse with you, and so give you occasion of explaining many things to me, for I am unwilling to think that you are altered toward me, and should be sorry to have reason to be it towards you.'[10] The Paris banker was commanded to provide 1,500 livres for the journey.

It took old Tom two days to gather his wits together to reply. Humiliation and hurt oozed from every word: 'I could not without the greatest mortification, observe something in your letter which looked as if you had conceived some umbrage against myself. Upon the severest recollection I can find nothing that could give occasion for it, but my having concealed the Prince's design of going to Scotland. I now think that tho' the event proved so fatal, our first successes were sufficient to shew that they might have been compleat had they been tolerably seconded from abroad.' He was sufficiently stung by the King's harsh judgment to fight back – and spread his arguments over four sheets of paper. 'As for my own person,' he told the King, 'I never shrank from any danger which might have put an end to my days, but could not find an opportunity of perishing unless I had either shot myself with my own hands or wilfully thrown myself into those of the Enemy, of neither of which expedients I believe Your Majesty would have approved.' He ended with a pathetic plea: 'That I may still have the happiness to enjoy your good opinion is, next to the prince's safety, the sincerest wish of, Sir, Your Majesty's most humble, most obedient, most dutiful subject and servant. Tho. Sheridan.'[11]

Five days later, on 19 August, a year to the day since Charles Edward raised his standard at Glenfinnan, the old man sat down and wrote to the

Prince at even greater length. Ostensibly bringing his master up to date on the situation he would find on his return, this letter was really a rehearsal of the answers he himself would give to the questions he knew James would throw at him when they met. It also gave advice on how to cope with the problems Charles would encounter on his return. He wrote: 'I took occasion to tell the Comte d'Argenson [French Minister for War] that, as there would probably be a good many of yr. friends that would be obliged to provide in some shape or other, I thought it could not be better done than by forming two new Scots Regiments, to which he answered that there would most certainly be some Provision made for such people, and that he would do all in his power to facilitate the matter.'[12]

Sheridan named a few trustworthy followers who could help the Prince and naturally his own Irish compatriots, from Charles's little coterie of pre-1745 days, featured prominently among them – Lally and Bulkeley, who had distinguished themselves at Fontenoy and consequently were highly regarded in court circles, and that old renegade, one-eyed Clancarty, who had informed the Prince wrongly that English Jacobites would rise and who now continued to serve the movement just as uselessly.

Having done what he saw as his duty, the faithful Sheridan embarked on the long, hard journey to Italy, although his health was so poor by now that he could barely withstand such an exhausting undertaking. He was in Rome when Warren's letter arrived with news of the prince's safe return.

While Charles was penning his 't[w]o lines' to his father on 10 October, Warren was also writing to King James, taking great care to ensure that everybody at the Muti Palace would be aware of own part in overcoming the 'crowd of dangers run thro' by sea and land' during the Prince's escape. 'I congratulate your Majesty on this happy event, and think this is the happiest day of my life to see our great Hero delivered so miraculously from his enemys,' he told James, and boasted how he found time at Loch nan Uamh 'to lay hold of Barastel who wanted to betray him [Charles], and have brought him and his sons prisoners here'.[13] Warren was congratulating himself as much as the King over the Water.

In Paris he also delivered the good news to the French court and arranged for Cardinal Tencin to forward his letters to Rome through diplomatic channels, which were the fastest means of getting the news to the Pretender.[14] By Sunday 16 October the Prince's safe return was common knowledge throughout Paris, and Warren had been accorded a long audience with King Louis.[15]

Charles himself had arrived in the French capital by the time Warren met the French King, and was reunited with his brother, who had been waiting since 1745, first hoping to join the campaign in Scotland and then to serve with the French army. Henry was living at Clichy, at this time a pretty village just outside the city, on the hillside below Montmartre, and paused only to collect Charles's beloved dog, Marquis, before rushing off to meet him; the reunion of the brothers was as joyful as that between Marquis and his master.

The Duc de Luynes, who had never set eyes on the Prince before, was deeply impressed when they met at Versailles, and followed the Prince's every move over succeeding weeks.[16] Alongside the aristocrats at court, the Stuart Prince of Wales stood out, tall, elegant, bronzed and, if anything, fitter after his summer among the Highland hills. His noble features and military bearing reminded de Luynes of the Swedish king, Charles XII – a truly princely warrior figure. Those who had known him before 1745 believed him to be thinner, but de Luynes was inclined to dismiss this as simply due to his having cut his hair short and the fact that he was suffering from some kind of skin rash at the time.

O'Sullivan, who had played such a disastrous part in the '45 but was still in favour with the Prince, said he kept himself 'privet' for some days because he 'had not a second shirt nor a stoken to his foot,'[17] but the travel-stained kilt to which he clung did nothing to spoil the adventuring *montagnard* image he cultivated in public.

This tousled appearance sent Parisians wild. They saw not a defeated Pretender, but a conquering hero, a king in all but name, and took him to their hearts, making him as adored in the French capital as Cumberland had been in London. At court ministers who had been so cool recently, now vied to meet him and ladies looked on him almost as a saint whose stained and worn clothes were so many holy relics. After the Highland garb was finally exchanged for fine breeches, a rose-coloured velvet coat embroidered with silver and a rich gold brocade waistcoat with a 'spangled fringe set on in scallops', they crowded round him as the ladies of Edinburgh had done a year before. 'In short,' one eye-witness commented, 'he glittered like the star which they tell you appeared at his nativity.'[18] Charles Stuart was the cynosure of the most elegant court in Europe.

Tales of the Scottish adventures blazed across the streets of Paris, through the salons of Versailles and Fontainebleau, and every story gained with each telling. The Duc de Luynes described how the fugitive had hidden for three days among the heather, surrounded by redcoats, and protected by 'deux chefs de montagnards' called 'Lockel' and 'Cameran' – Lochiel and his brother Dr Archie Cameron would hardly have recognised themselves. He had lived on a little cheese and oatmeal washed down with rainwater collected in his bonnet. The over-abundant Highland rain sounded like nectar as the misery of trudging across mountains drenched in it receded.

Hero worship spread all the way across Europe and it is no exaggeration to say that Prince Charlie had become an instant legend, the hero of kings, princes and nobles, and a demi-god to the common people. This turned him into an even more formidable adversary in Hanoverian eyes and Prince Charlie was astute enough to make the most of this propaganda coup for his Cause.

Return to France even united the pro-Charles and pro-James factions who had bickered so destructively during the planning of the '45 expedition. Sir John Graeme, sent from Rome at that time to act as a moderating influence, was delighted to confirm to James that the Prince was 'in perfect health and spirits', and the brothers were the best of friends: 'It was an unspeakable pleasure to me to see how much they love one another and I hope in God it will always continue so.'[19]

By the time Graeme wrote this, Daniel O'Brien, James's representative in Paris and no friend of the Prince, had set out for Fontainebleau to arrange an audience with the French king, unaware that Warren had already seen Louis. The Jacobites were still nervous about how warm King Louis's reception might be. 'We await his [O'Brien's] return with impatience to know the manner of it, tho' by some letters already writ from thence we have reason to fear that the Court will insist upon its being done privately, which will not be to the Prince's taste, and it is no wonder,' Graeme reported on 17 October.[20]

Louis's ministers found themselves in a political ambush, trapped between fear lest a meeting at Versailles might jeopardise the peace talks going on at Breda[21] and the knowledge that they dared not oppose the frenzy of popularity that raged in the capital. The King, too, might have felt that the Jacobites had served their purpose, but was wise enough to realise that, for all his immense power, it would stir the nation up against him to ditch them now. This was the time for everyone from the King to the most hostile minister to be nice to Charles and all those pestilential Jacobites who were crowding Paris. One or two members of Louis's government tried to resist, but were overruled and Prince Charles was summoned to Fontainebleau for an audience with the King.

The meeting took place on the evening of Wednesday 19 October, but Charles was not received alone as he wished: Henry was commanded to appear with him and they were greeted not as princes of the Royal House of Stuart, but by their minor titles of Count of Albany and Baron Renfrew. The welcome was warm enough, but to Charles's intense irritation he was given no opportunity to put his case for a new rising and had to be content with no more than seeing Louis for the time being.

On leaving the King's presence, the Prince was received by the Dauphin, who hung on every detail of his great adventure and invited Charles back the following evening to tell him more. The Queen, Maria Lesczynska, who was related to Charles's mother, even left the card table to spend a good quarter of an hour talking to Charles, bringing with her a gaggle of six princesses and other excited ladies, all of whom he saluted gallantly.

Spies passed on this news. Even Horace Mann in far away Florence was forced to write to his spy-masters in London: 'Everybody talks of the distinguished reception which the French king is said to have given the Pretender's eldest son, and with assurances never to abandon his interest. The Pretender's people and the partisans are grown extremely insolent upon it, and flatter themselves with the greatest advantages.'[22] London scarcely paused in its train of vengeance against the rebel prisoners to ponder what this might mean.

Prince Charlie played Prince Charming admirably before the royal family and could not be ignored by the ministers, who now toadied to him and invited him to dine with them, although they never felt quite sure, in the light of King Louis's hesitation to call them Princes, how they should address the brothers. In the end they settled for 'Monseigneur' or 'Your Royal Highness' for Charles and 'Monseigneur' or 'Your Highness' for Henry.

The pair always remained conscious of their royal status in spite of Charles's affectation to pretend to be a modest man. De Luynes saw through this transparent pose with no difficulty. 'Prince Edward would not have liked very much to maintain a complete incognito,' he wrote. 'He has a sense of who he really is, and although not in the least proud, he has dignity; he even shows a great desire to please and be approved of . . . He says he is only a Highlander, that he no longer knows the customs of this country, besides he speaks French badly, and an infection he picked up in the mountains prevents him from hearing as well as he usually does'.[23]

Invitations poured in, although it is interesting that when de Luynes's turn came round, he had great difficulty rounding up more than three ministers of state to join the Stuarts at table. One evening the pair treated their hosts to a little impromptu concert on cello and harpsichord – a gesture that produced only one discordant note, a comment from de Luynes that Henry was the better player. The Duc seemed to have forgotten that while the Duke of York had had little to occupy his time but practise his harpsichord over the past eighteen months, the Prince of Wales had been living the life of a soldier and a hunted man in the wilds of Scotland.[24]

The climax of this fortnight of glory came on Sunday 23 October, when Madame de Pompadour, the King's mistress, invited Charles to take supper with her. The King put in an unexpected appearance during the evening and stayed for over an hour, making this an accolade for the hero-prince. It was spoilt only by the unfortunate fact that 'le Prince Edouard' and Pompadour did not take to one another. The two were almost exact contemporaries, but totally different in character: he made no effort to hide his contempt of her low breeding, while she dismissed him as a cold fish because he failed to respond to the charms that had won the French King's heart. It was a stupid move on the Prince's part to behave arrogantly towards this all-powerful woman – the one person in France who might have persuaded the King to continue to support him and Charles Stuart paid dearly for this lapse of political judgement.

He had no trouble with the common people of Paris, although he thought himself well above them too. Wherever he went he was adored and cheered, and at the Opéra received an ovation greater than that accorded to the King.[25] Charles accepted this as his due and responded by setting up his own little royal court at Clichy.[26] Here he gathered an ill-assorted group of supporters around himself, drawn from those who had encouraged him to embark on the Scottish adventure and others who had accompanied him.

There were discussions with court officials and more meetings with the Queen and Dauphin, who continued to idolise this brave man who had just escaped from the lion's den: Charles played the lion-tamer to perfection. He was not quite as bold or skilled in the role of statesman, however, and was not always tactful when he had meetings with Louis to attempt to persuade 'His Most Christian Majesty' to mount a new expedition on his behalf. The royal audiences always remained arm's-length affairs, hardly surprising considering how tactless Charles could be, forgetting civilities and badgering Louis for help to begin a new rising, while at the same time blaming his lack of support for the failure of the last one.

Rebuffing Pompadour had been a mistake for which he now paid dearly, but that was only one of many errors that turned the glorious return into no more than a gilded fortnight. Peace looked within France's grasp during the autumn of 1746 and Louis's ministers were determined not to lose the opportunity through the rashness of this hot-headed young man who had already failed once. Of course the King did not tell Prince Charlie that; he strung him along, pampering and flattering, yet giving little or nothing, and always insisting on seeing the Stuart brothers together. Charles refused to discuss affairs of state in the presence of Henry, and told Louis so.[27]

He sent several memos to the French King, setting out his achievement during the Scottish campaign and claiming lack of money, troops and supplies had cost him victory. With 18,000 to 20,000 men now to 'employ usefully in the king's interest and in his own, things would be different,' he said.[28] Again, Louis sympathised, but did nothing, and the Prince turned more angry and frustrated.

Although Charles continued to press for secret man-to-man talks with the King, the request was always refused – at least that was what the world believed, yet there is evidence that the two did have some confidential negotiations unknown to other Jacobites or even to Louis's own ministers, which would be perfectly in keeping with the French King's devious manner.[29]

Incredible as it may seem, Louis was now running his own secret diplomacy, often in direct opposition to what his ministers were trying to achieve – and while a peace treaty at almost any cost was the aim of his ministers, Louis wanted one in which he would outwit Britain. They called Louis's ignoring of his ministers *le secret du roi*, and it was so successfully covert that few in France ever knew about it. As part of this personal policy Louis tried several times later in his reign to mount invasions against Britain and it is quite possible that, had he felt able to, he might have been persuaded to give support to Charles in late 1746.

The Prince's biographer, Frank McLynn, has suggested another reason for the French King's hesitancy: Charles was now insisting on an invasion of England rather than Scotland. McLynn writes: 'The prince had perceived the fallacy, as he saw it, of a conquest of Scotland. He had been there and he had found the main task still before him. Only a descent on England made sense. Probably at this stage the French would have backed another rising in the Highlands, but they drew back from the scale of commitment needed for successful conquest of England. Yet anything short of that merely aroused the prince's suspicions.'[30]

All that came of whatever open negotiation and underhand manoeuvrings took place between Louis and Prince Charlie was a suggestion around New Year 1747 of limited support to raise a new campaign in the Highlands and a personal offer to Charles of the use of one of one of the royal houses at Vincennes as a place to live. The Highland campaign offer was withdrawn almost as soon as it was made and the promise of the royal house at Vincennes conveniently forgotten: instead Charles was offered a place at Bercy belonging to Pompadour's god-father, Pâris de Monmartel, and 12,000 livres a month to be shared with his brother. Most insulting of all was the fact that the offer of money was not made by the King directly, but via one of his ministers. Charles was incensed and rejected it out of hand, although he had in fact been receiving 8,000 livres a month from Louis since October, plus a further 3,600 livres towards the cost of his entourage.[31]

In the midst of all this manipulation and dissembling the Prince, now at the end of his tether, sent his father a letter complaining about the difficulty of 'dealing with this bloody Government', which took the attitude that the more one gave them the more they took. They were vermin, he said, who deserved to be paid in their own coin.[32] Charles reacted to French procrastination with his customary arrogant impatience; he was determined that even if Louis would not receive him as a prince of Britain he would present himself at court in a manner fitting that position. In all the finery of state he could muster he drove in procession to the royal palace – three carriages. The first carried George Kelly and Lords Ogilvy and Elcho, and the second brought Charles himself, splendidly displaying the Orders of St George and St Andrew on his chest and the Jacobite white cockade on his hat. At his side were Lochiel and Lord Lewis Gordon. His four chamberlains followed in the third, while Young Lochiel and other gentlemen rode behind on horseback.

The intention was not so much to overawe King Louis as to snub him with a reminder that he was receiving the representative of another reigning monarch. Louis and his ministers were irritated by this arrogance, but Paris enjoyed it and it must have brought a smile of satisfaction to the lips of the Duke of Newcastle in London.

Spies were soon reporting that safe return had not brought the Stuart family closer together. Nor had it reunited Jacobites at large. James, always a worrier, never ceased to bombard his sons with good advice and, while Henry continued to pray and behave primly, Charles fumed at the wimpishness of his father and brother.

The harsh treatment of old Tom Sheridan also rankled and Charles, unaware of how ill his old tutor was, longed to have him at his side; with his letter of 6 November to his father – the one in which he admitted to failing to read his father's correspondence – he enclosed a note for James's secretary, saying:

> My kind compliments to Lord Dunbar and all my friends there. I say nothing to Sir Thomas because I am in hopes he is already set out for to join me. My wanting of him gives me a good deal of trouble for tho I have a very good opinion of Kelly and must do him the justice of saying that I am very well pleased with him; yet neither he or any body else much less I woud absolutely trust in my secrets as I woud in Sir Thomas, which occasions in me a great deal of toil and labour.[33]

Whether Edgar had the opportunity to pass this compliment on to the disgraced and disappointed old tutor is doubtful for Sheridan was suddenly taken with an apoplectic seizure and died on 23 November. James sent his son the news a couple of days later, a bare letter containing little sympathy for this man who had given fifty-six years of unfailing service and devotion to three generations of Stuarts. All that can be said in the Pretender's favour is that he had the humanity at least to add: 'I had him buried with all decency in our own parich of S.S. Apostoli.'[34] And on the 28th he ordered Edgar to tell Sheridan's sisters, then living in Paris in very straitened financial circumstances, that they would continue to receive the pension the King had been paying them.

Charles's feelings can only be guessed at, but he must have been devastated to lose his old mentor at this crucial moment when he needed him more than he had ever done. The worst consequence of Sheridan's death was that it pushed Charles Edward further towards dependency on George Kelly, whose advice and company had always proved disastrous. Kelly encouraged him to see betrayal among all the supporters around him with the result that the brief post-'45 truce between his own faction and his father's ended before it had really begun. Surrounded by his own little clique, Charles reigned at Clichy as he had done at Holyrood, receiving any French nobility who cared to call and Scots exiles who arrived to pay homage or beg money.

O'Brien and Graeme gathered men like William MacGregor of Balhaldy and Lord Sempill, now working together as King James's agents in Paris, into their clique, while the Prince had Lochiel, Archie Cameron, Macdonnell of Lochgarry, Strickland, Roy Stewart, Lally and Sir James Stewart among his supporters, although some of these soon wavered. As usual it was to the Irishmen – O'Sullivan and Kelly – that Prince Charlie turned, and Kelly remained by far the most devious, evil and untrustworthy confidant and advisor he ever had. Old pre-'45 animosities waxed day by day among all the friends and followers of the Cause. Spying was resumed, carping and backbiting too, and tittle-tattle flowed to and from the Pretender's court.

Not content with handling his case badly, Prince Charlie damaged it further by drinking more heavily and from time to time illness overwhelmed him as it always did in times of crisis. 'The nasty bottle,' which had been essential protection against the wet Highland Summer, remained a necessity to shield him from all those 'bloody' politicians and other 'enemies' he saw around him. At best his behaviour provided gossip among his friends: at worst it supplied valuable ammunition to his enemies. Moles on both sides worked relentlessly to pass every detail back to their masters, causing great damage to the movement.

In Rome and Paris the Hanoverian government had spies everywhere, so that almost every message or letter sent to or from the King over the Water was relayed straight to London by Horace Mann, von Stosch and their friends. Everybody was suspect, even those closest to the King, O'Brien and his wife in Paris and the Abbé Grant in Rome. Charles was aware of what was going on in Rome, but never seemed to understand that his own actions in Paris were being spied on just as effectively by Hanoverian agents and reported back. He told his father less and less, but that was probably due to lack of trust rather than an awareness that they were being spied on, and he became secretive even with his friends and followers. While he chose to ignore men like old Lochiel who talked sense, he hung on every word of the unreliable Kelly.

Egged on by Kelly, Charles began to turn against the French, his father and his brother, who all complained about the low company he was keeping – so low that even old Clancarty once said that 'if he searched all the jails in Britain or Ireland, he could not have found such a set of noted, infamous wretches as those H.R.H. had about him'.[35] And no man was better qualified to make that judgement.

Charles was the last person to realise that deep at the root of his troubles were his father and himself. The last three months of 1746 had proved them to be separated irreconcilably by temperament and circumstance. The King over the Water was a gloomy, dispirited man, old before his time, while his son was bursting with impetuous energy and desperate to strike at his enemies. So, while the father did nothing, the son ran in every direction in search of new backing while leading a debauched life at the same time. During those few weeks he inflicted as much damage to his Cause as Hanoverian guns had done in a year in Scotland and reasonable men began to turn away from him.

Brother Henry came in for the sharpest criticism: Charles convinced himself that the Duke of York had not done enough to persuade the French to send support during the '45 and now Henry was inclining towards their father's spineless view that the Culloden defeat was final. Friction increased because the deeply devout Henry made no effort to hide his disapproval of Charles's behaviour and blabbed about it to their father, who bombarded his wayward son with letters urging him to behave in a more princely manner.

Sheridan might have maintained a balance between the brothers, but Kelly did not even try. He was as openly scornful of Henry as Charles was, virtually calling him a coward,[36] and once actually suggested that the prim Duke of York should find himself a wife and use the services of a whoremaster.[37] It all came to a head when Charles decided to move from Clichy to the Hôtel d'Hollande in Paris and Henry took his own house next door in the Petit Hôtel de Bouillon.[38] Even at Christmas they went their separate ways and it was clear for all to see that as a family the Stuarts were wholly disunited.

Worse was to follow in 1747 when Louis not only refused one more attempt to mount a British campaign, but the one real ally the Stuarts had, the Marquis d'Argenson, was dismissed from the Foreign Ministry and replaced by the Marquis de Puysieux, who not only disliked the Stuarts but also pursued one unwavering goal – peace with Britain. If that meant abandoning Charles Edward, then so be it.

Even the myopic Young Pretender realised there was nothing more to be gained from France, so once again he set out on a devious hare-brained secret plans designed to win him his own way and at the same time embarrass those he considered to have let him down – he would go to Spain, persuade King Ferdinand VI to throw his weight behind an invasion and this joint enterprise would make Louis look foolish.

Brother Henry had planned to go to Spain, but without the vindictive touch of upstaging the French King, and Charles simply highjacked his idea. He left France without asking King Louis's permission or telling the Spanish King he was on his way as protocol demanded, and as usual travelled with such speed that he left the few companions who accompanied him behind long before he reached Barcelona.

By the time he set foot in Spain what had started as a secret mission was common knowledge, thanks to his own impetuosity, yet he managed to blame others. 'I arrived at Barcelona,' he wrote, 'and finding that by the indiscretion of some of our own people (which the town happened then to be full of), it was immediately spread I was there; this hindered me to wait here for the rest of my people coming up, as I intended, and made me take the resolution to leave even those that had come there with me, for the greater blind and expedition, and take along with me only Colonel Nagle.'[39] No wonder the British never had long to wait to discover what Prince Charlie was up to.

He simply turned up in Madrid at the beginning of March, unexpected and unannounced, and demanded to see the King, but was only taken to Ferdinand's minister, Caravajal, 'with a great many ridiculous precautions,' he complained, and was advised for 'several very nonsensical reasons' to go home. 'I found all here like the pheasants,' he sneered, 'that it is enough to hide their heads to cover the rest of the body.'

Charles refused to leave and Ferdinand, who must have been a man of infinite patience, received him at 11.30 one evening, and told him courteously but firmly that he could expect no help from Spain. All he took away with him was a gift of money to cover his travel costs and an assurance that his pension would continue – even that generous treatment brought a gibe that as the pension had been 'very ill paid' in the past, this was little reward. Beyond its cost in louis d'or, the price of the trip had been almost all of his personal prestige.

The next madcap scheme was a search for a wife. Splendid dynastic marriages to set the family alongside reigning royalty and bring plenty of money to fill his empty purse had always been James Stuart's dream. Before Charles's sixth birthday there had been plans for betrothal to the Emperor of Austria's daughter; next came the Princess of Mecklenburg, heiress to the Russian throne, but nothing came of either plan. His cousin, Louise de la Tour, daughter of Charles's maternal aunt and the powerful Duc de Bouillon, a regular drinking and gambling crony of King Louis XV, was proposed next, but James wanted someone better for his heir, a king's daughter perhaps. And of course Louise de la Tour had another disadvantage – she had Sobieski blood and James remembered all too clearly the drama and heartbreak of his own marriage to the mentally unstable Clementina Sobieska. When Charles met Louise at last in 1744 she was happily married to the Duke de Montbazon and expecting his child; Louise and her husband became close friends of the Prince.

Charles was still not in love though and certainly was not yet ready for the husband role – marriage was a dynastic tactic and it is arguable whether he was ever ready for it. He himself raised the question with his father little more than a month after his return from Scotland and, although he did not name possible brides, it was clear he had a princess of the French royal blood in mind. His father solemnly lectured him that if the Cause were to be going well, he and his brother might 'have the first Princesses of Europe, whereas perhaps now you could not have the last . . . When you explain your idea to me I shall be better able to judge of it, and it is useless till then to say any more on the subject.'[40]

Finding a wife for both Charles and Henry became a recurring theme all through the winter of 1746/7. Various candidates were put forward, including Princess Fortunata or Princess Matilde, daughters of the Duke of Modena – a surprising suggestion since James himself had been rejected by Princess Beatrice, his cousin, there a generation earlier.[41] Charles, of course, had his own grander ideas. First he would accept no bride but Louis XV's daughter, the Princess Anne-Henriette; then he suggested the Infanta of Spain and later an Austrian archduchess, but he scaled the heights of improbability with Czarina Elizabeth of Russia – on condition that she would bring him a dowry of 20,000 troops to invade Britain.[42] His despairing father tried to bring him back to earth in April 1747: 'As long as we are abroad, it would be a jest to think that you could have either a Daughter of France or Spain, and I should think that during our misfortunes we may be very well satisfyed if you can marry a princess of the same Family as my Mother, & I doubt if you could have even one of them, except you nick the time in which the Court of France may be willing to do all in their power to soften the turning you out of France.'[43]

James was certain his son would never 'nick the time' to win France over; indeed, with Culloden a year in the past, he felt sure Louis XV would never support the Cause again. Prince Henry agreed and, being a Stuart rather than a Sobieski, was prepared to resign himself to this. It was not in his nature any more than it was in his father's to fight the whole world for what he wanted.

Following Charles's return from Spain a strange tranquility settled over the brothers' relationship, as if it had become becalmed and each had become reconciled to the other. They seemed at last to have agreed to coexist and the Prince was happy to accept an invitation to take supper at his brother's house on 29 April. He arrived to find the house lit brightly as it would be for an expected guest. Servants were all waiting to receive him, supper had been prepared exactly as the Duke of York ordered – but there was no Duke there to receive Charles. His aides and staff could give no explanation other than that His Royal Highness had driven out several hours earlier and said nothing about where he was going or when he would return.

Charles was annoyed at first by this discourtesy, then angry, but by the time midnight came and Henry had not appeared, he was beside himself with fear that his brother had met with an accident, been kidnapped or perhaps had even been assassinated by British agents. For two days he waited, his mind in turmoil, then on the third day a letter arrived, a letter from Henry, in which he apologised for his absence and told his brother simply that he had gone to Rome. He gave no explanation other than annoyance at the general attitude of the French government and a strong desire to see his father.[44]

If his brother was fool enough to go back to that stifling hothouse of the Muti Palace then so be it, Charles decided: he would get on with his own life and his Cause. He wrote bad-temperedly to James and Henry and went off to the country. Henry reached Rome on 25 May and for the next couple of months life continued as normally as it ever did for Charles Stuart, with bland letters arriving from Rome which almost made James and Henry appear the injured parties.

Then the bombshell burst, a defeat more lasting than the rout of his army at Culloden and this time the Cause itself was routed. The calmness of the words in James Stuart's letter to his son served only to make its contents the more devastating :

> I know not whether you will be surprised, my dearest Carluccio, when I tell you that your brother will be made a Cardinal on the first days of next month. Naturally speaking, you should have been consulted about a resolution of that kind before it had been executed; but as the Duke and I were unalterably determined on the matter, and we foresaw that you might probably not approve of it, we

> thought it would be showing you more regard, and that it would even be more agreeable to you, that the thing should be done before your answer could come here, and to have it in your power to say it was done without your knowledge and approbation.

The mealy-mouthed betrayer of his heir went on to insist that it would be wrong to constrain anyone in the matter of religion, and this applied equally to his sons. Henry had made his decision of his own free will and it pleased the King.

> I will not conceal from you, my dearest Carluccio, that motives of conscience and equity have not alone determined me in this particular; and that, when I seriously consider all that has passed in relation to the Duke for some years bygone, had he not had the vocation he had, I should have used my best endeavours, and all arguments, to have induced him to embrace that state. If Providence has made you the elder brother, he is as much my son as you, and my paternal care and affection are equally to be extended to you and him, so that I should have thought I had greatly failed in both towards him, had I not endeavoured by all means to secure to him, as much as in me lay, that tranquillity and happiness which I was sensible it was impossible for him to enjoy in any other state.

He had the effrontery to finish this rambling dissertation by lecturing the Prince – gently, admittedly – forgiving him all the trouble he had given his family, and asking only for his love and affection in the future.[45]

Charles was devastated. Henry a cardinal: he knew this was the destuction of the Cause by his own kith and kin. And it had been achieved by a two-faced piece of double-dealing worse by far than anything his professed enemies had ever perpetrated. With Henry Stuart a prince of the Roman Catholic Church, neither his father nor he could ever be restored; the British people simply would not tolerate a Roman Catholic as second in line to the throne.

Gradually the sequence of events leading up to the flight to Rome became clear and revealed that the appointment as a prince of the Church had been carefully pre-arranged and involved not just the Pretender and the new Cardinal, but O'Brien, the French King, old friend Tencin, and Foreign Minister Puysieux. The Judas-kiss for the Jacobite Cause had come from 'friends' – apart of course from Puysieux, the only professed anti-Jacobite among them.

Henry's betrayal has been traced to his homosexuality and the catalyst to the train of events was the ball following the Dauphine's wedding.[46] Already under pressure to find a wife, Henry was mortified to find himself being asked to dance with a number of ladies of the court and, terrified lest it might be thought women attracted him, he sent his father a letter – 'outing' himself in modern parlance. James suggested becoming a cardinal as the solution to his younger son's problem and so the process was set in train in the utmost secrecy and with the help of Tencin and O'Brien.

O'Brien was ordered to return to Rome while James wrote to Henry that he was needed beside him: the real reason was not given, of course. In the meantime Pope Benedict XIV was approached and, although astonished at the request, agreed. James then explained the plan to Louis XV in great confidence and from the memoirs of the Marquis d'Argenson it is clear that a number of others were in on the secret, including the Prince's uncle by marriage, the Duc de Bouillon.[47]

Followers of the Cause were as greatly upset by the news as Charles, Roman Catholics as much as any. George Innes, Principal of the Scots College at Paris, wrote to the Pretender's secretary that from the Prince to the lowest of his subjects all were unanimously 'crying out against what is done'. Myles Macdonnell called it 'a mortal deadly stroke', and another said it was a worse blow than Culloden.

The people of Paris were equally stunned and common gossip had it that both the Vatican and French ministers were bribed by Britain to persuade the Duke to accept the cardinal's hat. Pope Benedict actually admitted that the British had offered him £150,000 to make just such an appointment,[48] but claimed that this overture was made before James approached him.

Although the Pope was singularly naive, although Louis was just plain duplicitous and although followers like Tencin and O'Brien should have known the effect the appointment would have on the Cause, the main weight of guilt must rest finally with James and Henry who put the purple robe above a distant throne. Frank McLynn claims:

> It is hard to escape the conclusion that both Henry and James were motivated by bad faith. With James it was the desire to, as it were, pull up the drawbridge on Jacobitism, to ensure that his elder son could not succeed where he had failed. With Henry, not only was there general sibling rivalry at play, but there was also the issue of his sexual personality. It is not too much to say, when all the threads have been unravelled, that the *coup de grace* to the Jacobite movement was delivered by Henry's deviant sexuality, which made the thought of marriage purely horrific. This of course always remained something impossible to say in Jacobite circles.[49]

Charles raged, he stormed, he tore his clothes, he swore he would never set foot in Rome again – ever. Then there followed a deep, black silence which sent the spies scurrying for pen and paper to report the 'grande disunion' back to London. The Prince refused to write to his father and Charles's name was not mentioned in the Muti Palace for a long time, but eventually the Pretender wrote to his elder son 'begging him in very pathetic terms' to resume corresponding with him.

At last during the autumn of 1748 a letter arrived from the Prince: the spies reported that it was 'full of respect for his father which makes one believe that a reconciliaton will soon follow'. But the affection was all on the old King's side – from then on all he received from his son was a few lines from time to time demanding money or reporting his whereabouts. James wrote constantly begging his son to return home; Charles refused.

He stayed on in Paris, keeping open-house for Jacobite supporters who called, drank and went to the Opéra, where he was lionised not only by Parisian women but by Englishwomen who travelled to the French capital especially to see him. As far as Charles was concerned his Cause was still alive and he was its rightful heir.

CHAPTER FOURTEEN

Who Stole the Cursed Gold?

> As to Money matters as I never medled or maked in it, I can have nothing to say on ye subject and in reality, as to me in particular these Matters at present are the least of my conserns . . . Charles P.
>
> Charles Edward Stuart in a letter to his father, 6 November 1746.[1]

When Charles received his father's long, rambling letter with the news that his brother was to become a cardinal his reply was short and to the point: 'Had I got a dagger through my heart, it would not have been more sensible to me than the contents.'[2] Within weeks the dagger was twisted further .

In July 1747, the very month Henry took his red hat, the British government declared an amnesty for rebel prisoners and the majority were released to make their way home and resume their lives as best they could in the new world that had been created by London's repressive laws to quell Jacobitism and create a new Highlands in which the Stuart movement could never flourish again. It was a very different place with a changing people. Andrew Lang once wrote of it: 'The story of the Forty-Five is the tale of Highland loyalty: the story of 1750–63 is the record of Highland treachery, or rather of the treachery of some Highlanders.'[3] The accusation was accurate, but of course only a small number of Highlanders were involved in the treachery, which had started in 1746 the moment the '45 ended, when the disbanding of the Jacobite army and the Prince's flight to France left the clan system in a state of upheaval from which it never recovered. Confusion in mainland Europe was matched only by the turmoil among adherents on mainland Scotland.

Even before Culloden, the Duke of Cumberland had turned his mind to the future of the Highlands and concluded that 'the only sure remedy for establishing Quiet' lay in 'the transporting of particular Clans, such as the entire Clan of the Camerons and almost all the Tribes of the McDonalds (except some of those of the Isles) and several other lesser Clans'.[4] Exclusion of some of the island MacDonalds, presumably Sleat's people, was the Lord of the Isles's reward for remaining loyal.

By what he no doubt considered an act of leniency, Cumberland proposed that clanspeople should not be transported as slaves, but as settlers to form colonies in the West Indies. The government drew in its breath at the boldness of this propoal and asked how the Duke thought this might be achieved – 'whether by Trial and Condemnation, or by an Act of Parliament to be made for that purpose?'[5] It would be simplicity itself, the 'Butcher' replied: every man belonging to a banished clan should be declared an outlaw or transplanted under specially passed legislation, just as the MacGregors had once been proscribed and forbidden to use their name.

The wholesale clearance idea was dropped – whether for humanitarian or simply logistical reasons is not clear – but there was little sympathy in the angry language used in correspondence on the subject of quelling the Jacobites: 'this unnatural rebellion', 'suppression', 'utmost rigour of the law', 'military executions', 'transplanting of particular clans to the colonies' – the list is as long as it is uncompromising. Yet those involved would not have considered their actions unreasonable, not even Major-General John Huske, who wanted to bring back the law that allowed him to offer £5 reward for every rebel head brought in.

Ironically, although Cumberland's plan was rejected, his efforts did lead to a large number of clansmen and other Jacobite sympathisers ending their days in slavery on the other side of the Atlantic. More than 1,000 men and women taken at the end of the rebellion were transported to the colonies in America and the West Indies.

Government espionage increased when the fighting was over as the search for rebels and the Prince intensified. Many of those captured, like Murray of Broughton, betrayed fellow clansmen out of sheer fright, while a few did so to settle old scores, making this a time when trust, so long a deeply held article of faith in the Highland character, was undermined. The new Highlands that emerged in the aftermath of Culloden became the place of distrust and betrayal that Robert Louis Stevenson brought to life 140 years later in his novels *Kidnapped* and *Catriona*.

What followed as official government policy had an even more enduring effect. Professor Allan Macinnes called it the 'final convulsion in which the pace of change can constructively be depicted as effecting a dramatic social revolution'.[6] This new order robbed clansmen of the right to their language, dress, manner of life and, worst of all, it brought in legislation for a new form of land tenure that turned chiefs into landlords as grasping as their counterparts in the south.

The treachery of many chiefs and their tacksmen, or land stewards, robbed Highlanders of something more basic than Cumberland's depredations – their sense of honour. The culmination of the '45 and the changes it brought about resulted in the clearances, depopulation and hardship of the following century, something from which the Highlands has never recovered and for which the powers in the south have never been forgiven.

In spite of the havoc wreaked by the London government in the years immediately after Culloden, the movement might just have been revived to fight another day but for the treachery of those betrayers to whom Lang referred and the tittle-tattling, back-biting followers on the Continent, who put their own self-interest before the Cause they claimed to hold so dear. Murray of Broughton has stood accused, but a worse traitor by far was

Pickle, the heir to the Glengarry Macdonnells, who had caroused with the Prince in France before the '45, had been captured trying to reach Scotland, was imprisoned in the Tower of London and emerged penniless and willing to become a full-blown spy for financial reward.

Thanks to Pickle, the Duke of Newcastle and his brother, Henry Pelham, whose espionage system was already far more efficient than that of the Jacobites, were able to infiltrate all the Prince's counsels and thwart every action he planned. And because of the greed of Pickle and others, many Highland clans were torn apart by quarrelling over the gold that had been put ashore from the *Mars* and *Bellone,* the Loch Arkaig Treasure.

The treasure had been a curse since the day it was brought ashore as HMS *Greyhound, Baltimore* and *Terror* attacked the *Mars* and *Bellone* during that last battle of the '45 in Loch nan Uamh. All through the fierce exchanges in the loch crewmen of both sides had watched Highlanders carrying large quantities of the cargo up from the shore to the safety of the woods beyond. Captain Robert Duff, aboard HMS *Terror,* wrote afterwards, 'We saw a number of chestes of arms, and caskes which we took for powder and ball, on the shore, which had been landed from these ships and the country people were carrying off.'[7] The Frenchmen were disgusted by what they witnessed – much of the brandy was getting no further that the loch shore, so that by the time fighting broke off, many of the clansmen helpers were paralytic with drink. It infuriated the French that, while they had been fighting and many of their companions dying, those for whom they were risking their lives could not wait to open the brandy casks and help themselves. Donald Campbell of Auchindoun remembered that 'the French captains would land no more of the cargoe after the action was over when they understood what for freinds they had ashoar, the people were all mad and drunk and would not be commanded.'[8] As far as the Frenchmen were concerned, the clansmen could fend for themselves and would have no more of the supplies.

The orgy on the shore of Loch nan Uamh disgusted Murray of Broughton too – just another small irritation that propelled him towards his confessions after he was arrested. He related the story to the Lord Chief Justice in Edinburgh soon after his arrest and Lord Milton thought it worth passing on to the Duke of Newcastle that 'the brandy disappeared in a few hours, and that it was impossible to express the rapaciousness of the Highland Theives'.[9]

Prince Charlie may have claimed from time to time that money was the least of his concerns, but he was as anxious as anyone to get his hands on the Loch Arkaig Treasure or any other money available. When he sailed for France aboard the *Heureux,* the Prince took with him in his purse no more than 8,000 louis d'or of the money the French King had sent for the Cause with the *Mars* and *Bellone,* and for the rest of his life he cast an envious eye on the remainder of the French gold. He also badgered and begged followers in England and Scotland, who had given him so much already, to provide more money and expected every friendly European monarch to support him financially too. A number were remarkably generous.

After the *Mars* and *Bellone* left, Broughton prudently arranged for Archie Cameron to secrete three casks of the treasure, 15,000 louis in all, at three different spots in a wood beside Loch Arkaig, one concealed under a rock and the other two buried in specially dug holes. To mislead jealous rival clans into believing he had not abandoned this large part of the hoard in Cameron country, he filled the three empty casks with stones and carried them around with him for a while before disposing of them by dropping them into Loch Arkaig. According to Murray's story he arranged for a further 12,000 louis to be buried in two batches at the lower end of Loch Arkaig, but retained 5,000 'for necessary expenses'. That done, he headed south on the journey that was to lead to his capture.

Soon the French gold began to seep into the Highland economy, so that Albemarle's spies, who were constantly moving among clan communities, were able to report that, while there was a general scarcity of food and fuel throughout the West Highlands, they found plenty of French gold on their travels, even on Mull – hardly surprising since the MacLeans from that island had stolen several hundred louis d'or. Albemarle's spies also gave him information on how Cluny dispensed the money and on the friction that flared up among clansmen, who complained of Cluny's meanness towards them.[10]

Murray of Broughton was remarkably open about the manner in which he disposed of the remainder of the gold – 1,520 louis, he said, were left with Lochiel to cover the Prince's immediate needs, another 40 for Cameron himself, and 3,868 were buried in the garden of Mrs Menzies of Culdare, probably part of the 5,000 louis Broughton took for his expenses and had to abandon on the journey south because the gold was too heavy to carry further. In the Tower of London Murray not only gave details of the treasure, but suggested the government might retrieve it. 'Last time I had the honour to see you, I offered to lay my hand upon the 15,000 louis d'or,' he told his questioners, 'and am still certain I can do so, but as the season is now advancing, and the parties will probably soon be called in, it is not in that event impossible but the money may be raised.'[11] As Lang adds, the money was 'raised', not by the government who never found it, but by Archie Cameron.

An anonymous undated report sent to Colonel Napier in London told how assiduously the area was combed by government forces in search of the treasure, but they missed it in spite of the fact that it had been inexpertly buried – 'hid by Gentlemen, not used to work, it was very unskilfully done, and the stamps and impression of their feet (were) visible about the place'.[12]

Murray told his story again in his *Memoirs* and never deviated from it afterwards, but of course there were many who forgot his efforts in Arisaig to save the treasure from being pillaged and added theft to their accusations of treachery. He had betrayed the movement, so it was easy to say he robbed it as well: that was unfair, but it further blackened Mr 'Evidence' Murray's character.

The treasure left others under a cloud, especially two of the most honest men who ever served Jacobite Cause – Dr Archibald Cameron and Lauchlan Macpherson of Cluny: both came under suspicion of stealing Loch Arkaig money and remained so for generations, thanks in part to Pickle the Spy.

When Prince Charlie sailed for France in September 1746, Cluny remained behind in Scotland, acting for the Prince for years afterwards, and he was nominally in charge of the hidden gold. Archie Cameron loyally moved between the Highlands and Europe in the post-'45 years to promote the Cause and prepare for another rising. Cameron knew all about the Treasure, since he had handled it from the moment it reached Scotland – it was he who persuaded the reluctant French captains to hand it over in the first place, he dealt with young Clanranald's attempts to get his hands on it, and he carried it to Loch Arkaig. He was also involved in burying the gold at secret sites close to the loch.

After the Prince left, Cluny Macpherson dug up the 12,000 louis and took them to Badenoch for safety: a month or so later he moved the remainder. According to the anonymous report sent to Colonel Napier, Cluny handed out money to several chiefs for distribution among their clansmen, and 100 louis to the widow of the Keppoch chief who was killed when he charged into the enemy at Culloden while the rest of the MacDonalds held back. Lady Keppoch and a number of others were paid at the special request of the Prince.[13] For once Charles Stuart remembered some who had made the supreme sacrifice for him.

Cluny's attempt to ameliorate the suffering of one set of clanspeople only stirred up others, so that the Napier report suggested that 'the other Rebells in the highlands grumble egregiously That he has not done them justice'.[14] Even among those who received part of the treasure there was disagreement: by January 1748 an anonymous note to the government said sadly, 'Nothing but stealing and plundering prevails in all quarters here', a statement that reflected the prevailing general insecurity in the post-'45 Highlands, but more likely was intended to refer specifically to the Arkaig gold.

Others had their eye on the treasure, not least Charles Stuart, who never let up on his search for cash to fund his extravagant lifestyle. He sent Major Kennedy across to retrieve as much of it as he could, but Kennedy believed it was unsafe to venture into the Highlands because of government patrols, so he went only as far as Newcastle from where he sent Donald Drummond, the son of Balhaldy, to contact Cluny Macpherson. Cluny told him he could do nothing because of the summer sheilings[15] – presumably the quarters for the summer pasturing of cattle were close to the hiding places. Eventually Macpherson of Breakachy brought 6,000 louis to Kennedy at Newcastle to be taken to the Prince. In the small, backbiting world of Jacobitism, Kennedy was accused by Aeneas MacDonald of losing £800 of the money at Newmarket races before he returned and in the light of the way in which race meetings seemed to attract Jacobite supporters during the years following the '45, this seems perfectly feasible.

The ubiquitous Pickle, not as yet actually revealed as the traitor but already under suspicion, also succeeded in dipping his fingers into the Arkaig honeypot. Pickle was following in the footsteps of his none too trustworthy line. His grandfather Alasdair Dubh, or Black Alastair, was a great hero of early Jacobite battles, yet it was said his 'shineing qualities' were always 'blended with a few vices':[16] his father had been gaoled in Edinburgh Castle after the '45 in spite of the fact that Albemarle said he had been 'useful to the King's troops when they were at Fort Augustus and when he was latterly employed by me'.[17]

After his release from the Tower of London in July 1747, Young Glengarry had returned to France. Desperately poor and owing money to the French government and possibly to others, he had written to Waters, the Paris banker, from the Tower, asking for help. Empty pockets were no new experience for Young Glengarry; he had always been hard up, but now the French were pressing for the return of what they had given him and he was in desperate straits. He begged from Charles and the King in Rome, but neither was forthcoming to compensate him for his twenty-two months of 'tedious confinement in the Tower of London'.[18]

Even when 34,000 livres were awarded to nearly 50 supporters who had suffered – including 1,800 to his father ('Glengary L'Ainé) Pickle was not included. James was so short of cash himself at this time that he replied to a request from Charles for help for other followers in need: 'I really want no gentlemen here now, and am not in a condition to load myself with new servants or pensions, which I am the more sorry for because I had a mighty good character of Mr Hepburn of Keith: but as for the other gentleman you mention I have not the same knowledge of him, and tho' I were otherwise able I should not be very fond of taking into my family one in his circumstances.'[19] We have no idea whether or not Young Glengarry was 'the other gentleman', but Alasdair himself sat down and penned a letter to the King only a couple of weeks later, assuring him of his loyalty and bemoaning the lack of encouragement he had received. Still no money was forthcoming from either Rome or the Prince.

As was customary for 'subjects' making journeys abroad, Glengarry informed the King at the end of September that he intended to visit England on private business, the exact nature of which was unspecified, but he wrote again at the beginning of October asking to be recommended to succeed Lochiel as colonel of the Scots-French Albany regiment, only to be informed that the King had already put Young Lochiel's name forward. And as for money, the King's response was equally bleak – and typical of James Stuart: there was no chance because he himself was more poverty-stricken and sorry for himself into the bargain. His secretary, James Edgar, penned the reply:[20] 'H.M. is sorry to find you so low in your circumstances, and reduced to such straits at present as you mention, and he is the more sorry that his own situation, as to money matters, never being so bad as it now is, he is not in a condition to relieve you as he would incline.' However, he did instruct Edgar to send Glengarry a duplicate of his grandfather's warrant as a Peer, which he assured Glengarry was genuine. 'You will see that it is signed by H.M., and I can assure you it is an exact duplicate copie out of the book of entrys of such like papers.'

Alasdair Ruadh, Young Glengarry, had asked for preferment, he had asked for money, and what did he receive? – a duplicate – 'an exact copie' – of his grandfather's warrant as a peer – a peer 'over the water' at that.[21] Andrew Lang suggests it was disgust at this that turned Young Glengarry into Pickle the Spy. It certainly sounds a plausible reason for turning traitor, but the Hanoverian trap was more probably baited at the time of Glengarry's imprisonment in London, and all that was needed to close it on the young chief was financial desperation allied to disgust at his treatment by Rome. But that innate, in-built treachery evinced in the Glengarry character over the generations played its part too.

So Young Glengarry was to be found in London by the end of 1749, secretly trying to obtain permission to settle in Britain again, but so desperate for funds that he had to sell his sword and shoe-buckles and arrange for his travelling companion to pawn Mrs Murray of Broughton's gold repeater watch to Clanranald – much to her fury.[22] Aeneas MacDonald the banker, too, was complaining that he could not squeeze £50 owed to him out of Glengarry. Yet only three months later the young Macdonnell was strutting around with plenty of cash in his pocket. How had Pickle achieved such solvency in between? He may have received help from his father, who had been released from prison about this time, but the answer was probably much simpler – he had found the road to Loch Arkaig and its secret hoard.

About the same time, on 23 September to be exact, Glengarry sent a letter written in French to O'Brien (now Lord Lismore),[23] in which he hinted that he had received overtures from the British government: friends in London told him he would have no difficulty falling in with the Hanoverians wishes – 'Je ne ferais point de difficulté de me conforme aux intentions du Gouvernment,' he wrote – but nobly assured O'Brien that he would never abandon his loyalty to his family and true sovereign, although financial embarrassment might compel him to flee France.

Andrew Lang suggests that Glengarry had already sold himself to King George by the time he was in Rome, playing the repentant loyal servant of the Stuarts, during the controversy over the Arkaig treasure. As early as August 1749 the Duke of Cumberland spoke to an English Jacobite leader, the Duke of Bedford, about 'the goodness of the intelligence' the government was now being offered. To Bedford he wrote, 'On my part, I bear it witness, for I never knew it to fail me in the least trifle, and have had very material and early notices from it. How far the price may agree with our present saving schemes I don't know, but good intelligence ought not to be lightly thrown away.'[24] It was to be three years later before the finger of spying was first pointed at Glengarry, but it is quite possible that Pickle the Spy was the person to whom Cumberland and Bedford were referring.

Around this time one of Glengarry's clansmen had been in Scotland and reported that the Highlands were ready to rise again. Other reports were suggesting that the north was awash with French gold, so this seemed an ideal time for Pickle to take a trip home. He and his cousin, Donald Macdonnell of Lochgarry, set off for Scotland towards the end of the year in search of whatever was to be had. First they found trouble, then money.

Quarrelling among the Macphersons, Camerons and Glengarry Macdonnells over the Loch Arkaig gold was nothing new, since an anonymous report dating from a year earlier had named all three families involved in a squabble over it. Using cyphers the author of the report stated: 'Scyphax [Cluny] is still in the country and there are disturbances between him and the Dorians [Camerons] and Ætolians [Glengarrys] over the goods left by the Young Mogul [Prince Charlie].'[25]

The report to Colonel Napier set out Cluny's problem with fellow clansmen fighting over the treasure and helping themselves to it:

> I know it is strongly suspected that Cameron of Gleneavis [Alexander Cameron of Glen Nevis], whose brother [Angus] was with Cluny at Carrying away the £12,000, has received a Large proportion by some means or other, and there is great reason to think so, as he was almost bankrupt before the rebellion and is now shewing away in a very different manner, particularly. This year about a month ago, there were 120 Louis d'ors sent from him to a man in Locharkeek [Loch Arkaig] to buy Cattle for him; and some of the Camerons having lately threatened to be resented of him for his behaviour about yt money, he met with them, and parted good friends, which is supposed to have been done by giving them considerably.[26]

Pickle joined in the game so successfully that Lord Elcho said he returned to France with 1,200 louis of the treasure. The figure was probably considerably larger in fact, although just how much can only be guessed at, but it could well have been the bulk of the 3,000 louis Murray of Broughton had deposited with his wine merchant brother-in-law, MacDougall, in Edinburgh. Certainly Lochgarry thought so.[27]

Pickle also carried back to France a considerable amount of ill-will against Dr Cameron, who had been incensed because Young Glengarry had forged the King's signature on a letter in order to get his hands on the money and wrote to Rome at once to tell James of this. In retaliation, Pickle sent letters to the Prince and the Pretender in Rome, accusing Cameron of having embezzled 6,000 louis for some business enterprise in Dunkirk. Pickle put his hand on his black heart as he assured the King that it was very disagreeable to him to have to pass on such information, then accused Dr Cameron of undermining the Cause in the Highlands as well as stealing the Prince's money. 'I have prevented the bad consequences that might ensue from such notions [of doing the Cause down],' he told the King, 'but one thing I could not prevent was his taking 6,000 louis d'ors of the money . . . which he did without my opposition as he was privy to where the money was laid, only Cluny Macpherson obliged him to give a receipt for it.'[28]

This brought everybody scurrying to Rome in the spring of 1750 to lay their version of what was happening to the treasure before the Pretender – Archie Cameron, Lochgarry, Sir Hector MacLean, and Pickle himself. Both Dr Cameron and Pickle gave their versions at this time, and these and later documents shed light on what actually happened to the money – and at the same time cleared Dr Cameron and Cluny Macpherson of accusations of embezzlement.[29]

Cameron's memorial bears neither date nor signature, but is certainly in his handwriting, so was most likely written in September 1749 and handed over by him to the King in Rome about February or March the following year.[30] Pickle's 'Confession' was made at Rome on 30 August 1750.[31] The account by Macpherson of Cluny was made when he was called to France by Prince Charlie in the spring of 1755,[32] and there exists another account drawn up in 1754 under the title 'State of the Effects which are presently in Scotland ye 27 Augt. 1754'.[33] This is based on Lochgarry's information, and is in the handwriting of Charlie's mistress, Clementine Walkinshaw, with annotations by the Prince himself.

Simplified, Cameron's memorial set out his account thus:

	louis
Taken in charge by Murray	35,000
Stolen at the time of landing	800
Arrears to Clanranald and others	4,200
'Carryd south by Mr Murray'	3,000
'H.R.Highness in Sepr. 1746 brought abroad'	3,000
	11,000
Remainder left	24,000
'To different setts of people' as directed in writing	750
Angus Cameron	3,000
John Cameron (for ties on Lochiel's estate)	350
To recompense people who had suffered	500
To Cameron of Fassifern	100
Sent to Prince Charlie via Major Kennedy	6,000
Macpherson of Breakachy (who carried the money to Kennedy)	600
Supporting himself and family over four years	1,200
Money never recovered	481
	12,891

Pickle responded by laying his long piteous letter of 'confession' before the King, wallowing in his own suffering, and ingratiating himself in the most sickening manner – 'Your Majesty's countenance and protection will always console me for any hardships I or my name may endure in promoting the royal cause,' he told James. 'God grant how soon, I may have occasion to give palpable proofs that none of your Majesty's subjects is readier nor would more cheerfully draw his sword and shed his blood for his King and Country than I would.'

He went on to explain away the tiny amount of the Arkaig gold that he admitted his hands had touched, assuring the Pretender that it was part of the money Murray had carried south and passed on at Broughton's capture to his brother-in-law, MacDougall, for safe keeping. 'I proposed that if he would deliver in my hands what remained, part of which I would distribute to such as had received no assistance since H.R.H. left the country,' wrote Pickle, playing the good Samaritan to the Cause brilliantly. He gave to poor widows of Glenmoriston, he helped his brother's widow who had been most cruelly treated, and he took a little to pay off the ministers' stipends due on his family lands. 'Yet I never would have meddled in any manner whatsoever with this money could there ever been the least expectation of recovering it for H.R.H,' he assured the King, adding a touch to remind his royal master of the villains such as Cluny who surrounded his royal person: 'Besides your Majesty will see by the enclosed list that it would have been at any rate imbezled.'[34] He listed all recipients of the money, a couple of dozen in all, ranging from £581 15*s* 6*d* to 'the Infirmary for the expences of the enemy wounded at Gladesmuir' to 2 guineas 'to a servant sent to Carlisle'.

The Glengarry 'confession' in the Stuart Papers is unsigned and is a copy made by Andrew Lumisden, but detective work by Marion Hamilton makes it clear that the document is genuinely Pickle's: the author had been in Rome for five months in August 1750; he belonged to a leading Roman Catholic clan; his father was ill and had been a prisoner in Edinburgh Castle; and he had a brother who died in the '45 and left a widow and young children. Only Pickle meets all of these criteria.

But could anyone believe such a man's oath? All that can be said in his favour is that the figures he quotes tally reasonably accurately with those quoted by other sources, down to a balance of £878 9*s* 8*d*, which comes very close to Lochgarry's estimate of £900.

With the two protagonists badgering him in Rome, limp-minded, weak-willed James did nothing as usual, except whine to his son about the forged signature alleged against 'a certain person': 'What there may be at the bottom of all this I know not, but I think it necessary you should know that since your return from Scotland I never either employed or authorized the person, or anybody else, to carry any commissions on politick affairs to any of the three kingdoms.'[35]

At this time, neither Charles nor James lifted a finger to clear either Archie Cameron or Cluny, both of whom were the most upright and devoted followers they ever had, and as a result the slander of stealing from the Loch Arkaig Treasure for their own use continued to hang over them. Andrew Lang did his best to exonerate both, but in her paper written for the Scottish Historical Society, Marion Hamilton raises doubts over some of Lang's informants, whose names he never revealed anyway. She further suggests that the testimony of Cameron, who 'undertook the long and dangerous journey to Rome solely to ask permission from James Francis Edward to use the French gold for the distressed Camerons',[36] should be more reliable than that of Lang's anonymous informers or Pickle.

Among the Royal Archives Hamilton discovered Cameron's own copy of Cluny's account of the expenditure of the gold during the period leading up to 1749, in which he states explicitly that he never touched the 6,000 louis except to take 300 louis to cover the costs of his journey to Rome. Yet he *did* give Cluny a receipt for that amount. Why?

Hamilton draws attention to a sentence in the Cameron document which states that in September 1749 Cluny was worried about the large amount of the Treasure he was holding: 'As he was torn to pieces by the Countrey about that money he would keep none of it, but what he would take for himself for the most of which he had the Princes allowance in writeing,' he said. Since that was the autumn in which Pickle and Lochgarry were active in the Highlands it is hardly surprising that poor Cluny felt so 'torn to pieces' by the greed and jealousy of clansmen that he no could no longer bear to carry all the responsibility for the Treasure. Archie Cameron, who was about to set out for Rome in any case to ask the King's permission to use some of the money to support Lochiel's family who had suffered especially severely after the '45, agreed to give him a letter stating that he had taken the 6,000.[37] But he only gave Cluny a receipt for the amount and never actually took it, apart from the small sum to cover the costs of his journey.

Having accepted the assertion that the accounts prove Cameron did not receive the money he signed for, one problem still remains: when Hamilton compared Cameron's 1750 account with that of Cluny's 1755 statement rendered to both the King and the Prince, she found a disturbing discrepancy. Cluny stated that, on his first return to Scotland after the rising, Dr Cameron took 6,000 louis to help Lochiel's family *on the Prince's authority*. The only 6,000 louis figure featured in Cameron's 1750 account is the sum taken to Charles by Kennedy, and several amounts, totalling around 4,650 louis, passed to clan members or used by himself and his immediate family.

Why should these two men – otherwise as honest as the day is long – give differing accounts? Hamilton suggests that, whereas Dr Archie had no reason for hiding the truth, Cluny did. In the Cameron version, Archie stated that Cluny brought his brother, (John Cameron of Fassifern), north to receive 5,700 louis, running the risk of enraging Charles for handing out money without his authority, even if he did so to support Lochiel's family. Cluny told what Hamilton describes as 'a white lie' by taking care to say Archie told him he had HRH's authority. Dr Cameron had agreed that the receipt for the money could be shown to the King if need be, but by the time Cluny sent James his account Dr Archie was dead anyway, so it did not really matter if he were to be found out.

According to Andrew Lang, Fassifern admitted to receiving 4,000 louis from Evan Cameron of Drumsallie for Lochiel's family, which he deposited with John Macfarlane, an Edinburgh advocate, who in turn lent it to Wedderburn of Gosford.[38] Cameron of Glen Nevis named the sum as 6,000 louis and the donor as Cluny. Further confirmation that it was Fassifern who received the money and not Dr Archie – and that the Prince knew about it – is to be found in the statement written out by Clementine Walkinshaw in 1754: this contained an item 'To Archibald Cameron & now in trust for Lochealls sons (which is to be recovered), 6,000'. Beside this Prince Charlie noted: 'Given to Camerons Brother Fassfern without orders.'

All these scraps of information add up to a strong case to identify Fassifern as recipient of the money and, while it has to be admitted that the 1754 statement is based largely on information from Lochgarry, there is no reason to doubt its accuracy, even if Charles Stuart's memory in money matters was, to say the least, unreliable – the Prince did after all accuse Kennedy of stealing the 6,000 Louis he was sent to England to collect, but had to admit later that he did receive it!

Taking both Cameron's and Cluny's versions together, Hamilton breaks down the disposal of the Loch Arkaig Treasure in brief as:

	louis
Stolen at the time of landing	800
Given away by Murray of Broughton	4,200
Stolen by Murray of Broughton	5,000
Taken away by Charles Edward to France, 18 Sept '46	3,000
Accounted for by Macpherson of Cluny, 1755	24,000
	37,000

The hidden gold was a curse at the time and it has haunted the Jacobite Cause ever since. The son of James's secretary, James Edgar, spoke for many when he wrote in May 1753:

> I wish with all my heart the Gov. had got it [the Loch Arkaig Treasure] in the beginning, for it has given the greatest strike to the cause that can be imagined, it has divided the different clans more than ever, and even those of the same clan and family; so that they are ready to destroy and betray one another. Altho I have not altered my opinion about Mr M[urray] yet as he may on an occasion be of

> great use to the cause with the Londoners – I thought it not amiss to write him a line to let him know the regard you had for him, for as I know him to be vastly vain and full of himself I thought this might be a spur to his zeale.[39]

And yet, the story of the treasure, with all the betrayal, bitterness, jealousy and double-dealing it fomented and the damage it did to the Cause, highlights the finest qualities of the clans as well as the worst. Pickle apart, many of those who touched French gold in the Highlands during the decade following Culloden did so simply that they and their families might survive, rather than from personal greed.

Marion Hamilton, who laboured so diligently to clear the reputations of the principal players in the drama, ought to be allowed the last word on the Loch Arkaig Treasure: 'We see in this story what all through is both the strength and the weakness of the Jacobite movement – family tradition, which kept loyalty alive but brought with it petty jealousy and suicidal rivalry. It is satisfactory, however, to know that the spending of the Treasure was for the most part by those who had lost all for the Cause and not by their ungrateful Prince.'

And as for the 'ungrateful prince' and his ineffectual father, it is to their shame that neither said a word to exonerate those who suffered so much because of the cursed gold. Charles was too busy chasing his own sad dreams and James remained as he had been for years, lost in his self-made hopelessness and misery.

CHAPTER FIFTEEN

To England via Fairyland

What can a bird do that has not found a right nest? He must flit from bough to bough – ainsi use les Irondel [just like the swallow].

Note written by Charles Edward Stuart on a scrap of paper in June 1749.[1]

Autumn of 1747 should have been a time for rejoicing since most Jacobites prisoners were released then under the general amnesty announced in July. Instead it proved a time of black despair for Prince Charles as the enormity of Henry's defection sank in. However, in spite of the apparent hopelessness of his situation Prince Charlie refused to give up.

He failed to appreciate the changes which had taken place in Britain just as he had misinterpreted those in France, and he ignored the new order in the Highlands and throughout England. Individual Jacobites, like Lady Primrose and her little circle in London, may have continued to drink toasts and talk treason, but they now appeared even less prepared to lift a gun or a sword for the Cause. The sea change in England stemmed mainly from an inbred dislike of foreign interference, and after the '45, as old loyal families began to identify the Cause with foreign warmongering, many became politically inactive or even moved over to the Hanoverians.

In his darker moments Charles felt deserted, and as unforgiving towards French and Spanish ministers as to his own followers, who in his eyes had let him down. He baited Louis by affirming his love for his people in Britain, but when Lord George Murray travelled to Paris to make his peace, refused to see him. Charles reacted, as always when thwarted, by becoming rebellious and wild, and encouraging his followers in wild drinking and whoring. Louis XV was deeply disturbed about his 'guest', but was reluctant to do anything because the mob still adored Charles.

The Prince found a bolt-hole from Paris and all his problems when the Rohan family lent him one of their houses at St Ouën, which kept him away from the court at Versailles, yet close enough to allow him to enjoy the social life of the capital whenever he wished. He began to see more of his cousin, Louise de la Tour, the bride whom he had rejected, and her husband the Duc de Montbazon. Then as autumn progressed it became noticeable that his mood had lightened, for Charles had fallen in love, the first of a succession of spectacular and boisterous affairs, liaisons that produced at least two illegitimate children and scandals that mystified and entertained Europe over the next decade. This wild private life could have provided the British government with a unending supply of anti-Jacobite propaganda had Charles not been such a brilliant master of deception that few spies were able to keep up with his moves and disguises.[2]

The fact that the affair that lit up his life in the autumn of 1747 was with cousin Louise, whose husband had gone off to the war in Flanders, meant that it had to be conducted in great secrecy and out of sight of her in-laws. Nevertheless, passion ran white-hot on both sides and the affair ended only when Louise's mother-in-law, the formidable Princesse de Guéméné, discovered what was happening and dropped heavy hints that Louise dared not ignore. Charles cruelly abandoned the distraught girl, and one night she arrived at the Opéra only to see him with a new mistress, the Queen's cousin, the Princesse de Talmont, a much older woman. Louise was pregnant and bore Charles Stuart's son on 28 July 1748. But the child died in infancy. The only trace of this bitter-sweet affair is a pathetic bundle of undated letters in the British Royal Archives at Windsor Castle, letters Louise had begged the Prince to destroy, but Charles was always a most untrustworthy lover.

Alongside his love problems ran a growing crisis over what would happen when the treaty to end the War of the Austrian Succession was signed, as it was bound to be soon. The treaty had been all but agreed by April 1748, but throughout the summer negotiations dragged on over British insistence that it must include a clause to expel the Stuart Prince from France. Although he still had affection for the Prince personally, Louis was prepared to sacrifice him to win the peace he badly needed. Charles, however, fought him every inch of the way.

There was no need for the Hanoverians to struggle to push Charles out of France; their work was done for them by Louis, his ministers, the Jacobites in France, the Pretender in Rome, and Charles himself. Persuasion, browbeating and wheedling appeals all failed as Prince Charlie fought to have the clause excluded. However, his resistance was to no avail: the treaty which was signed at Aix-la-Chapelle in October 1748, decreed that Charles Stuart must leave French territory.

Charles simply dug his heels in and stayed put, countering every cunning trick of Louis's ministers to persuade him to leave. He rejected an offer to move to Fribourg in the Swiss Confederation, refusing to receive the King's emissaries when they arrived to discuss the matter with him. When they persuaded his new lover, the Princesse de Talmont, to try to make him go he rejected that too. He even disobeyed a direct order from his father to leave. 'I see you on the edge of a precipice about to fall in, and I would be an unnatural father if I did not do my best to save you,' James told his son. 'I therefore here and now order you, both as your father and your king, to obey without delay Louis XV's order to you to leave his dominions.'[3]

The sequence of subsequent events was almost comic, yet it proved the Prince could still outwit the greatest political minds in France.[4] To ensure that Charles could not say he had never received his father's letter, Louis sent the governor of Paris, the Duc de Gesvres, to deliver a copy to the Prince, along with an order demanding that he was to be out of Paris in three days' time and out of France in nine.

Charles flatly refused to meet Gesvres, or to listen to the letter when his own followers tried to read it to him. On hearing the words 'I order you as your father and king', he simply walked out of the room. When the French countered by publishing the letter in newspapers so that the people of Paris would realise how intransigent the young prince was being, he countered by announcing that the letter had been written in French and no English king would ever choose to write to his son in French instead of English. He also complained that the letter Gesvres brought had not been delivered through the usual channels, and furthermore that his father would surely have withdrawn the powers of regency he had conferred in 1743 had he wished to order his son to leave France, which King James had not done. Charles concluded therefore that this letter was a forgery; however, he was a reasonable man, he said, and should it prove genuine, of course he would obey the command of the two kings.

Following that splendid piece of double-speak he twisted King Louis's tail further by demanding time to write to Rome to verify the authenticity of the letter. At the same time he made it known around Paris that he had letters in his possession from Louis guaranteeing him asylum in France for his lifetime.

Throughout this game of brinkmanship the court at Rome and Jacobite followers in France looked on appalled but powerless to bring the Prince to his senses. Some claimed Charles was chivalrously helping the Queen and Dauphin of France in their fight against the King's favourite mistress, Pompadour, but this seems improbable, even though he hated this woman so heartily that he tossed the letters she sent him into the fire unanswered.[5]

Louis by now was incandescent with fury: he had the treaty he needed so badly, yet could not rid himself of this wild – and wily – young man as he needed to in order to implement it. And Charles was still so adored by the whole of Paris that, if he were to be harmed, there was every chance the people would rise in protest. Throughout the summer and autumn of 1748 the Prince cultivated the common people of Paris by ensuring that they saw him walking in the Tuileries regularly with his Highlanders around him, and appearing at the Opéra, the Comedie-Française or balls. Attendance at mass was turned into a public appearance too. He was an elegant and familiar figure among them and they loved him. He could have left France at that point with dignity, having scored his victory and remained the hero of the people, but that was not in Charles Stuart's nature. He forced the exasperated King at last to sign an order for his arrest and, patient to the last, Louis was said to have muttered as the put his name to the paper: 'Poor Prince! How hard it is to be a true friend.'

The arrest was planned with meticulous care; detaining him at his own house was rejected because Charles threatened to kill himself if he were to be taken there – who knew how many other people he might shoot or run through in the process. He could not be seized in a public place for fear of the mob, which left no choice but to detain him quietly somewhere outside his home, but away from the general public. So a small cul-de-sac leading to the Opéra was chosen, the date was set for 10 December, and it was planned to be carried out with as little trouble as possible.

No government minister wanted to risk his popularity by being seen to be part of the trap, so a colonel of the Grenadiers, the Duc de Biron, was put in command of 1,200 soldiers dressed in civilian clothes, and a gang of locksmiths with scaling ladders was on hand in case Charles attempted to escape through one of the houses leading off the passage. Three surgeons and a physician also stood by in case the Prince tried to take his life.

All this organisation could not be kept secret and Paris soon buzzed with rumours that the arrest was imminent, but Charles ignored them, confident that the King would not dare to lay a hand on him. As he drove down the Rue St Honoré towards the Opéra that evening someone shouted: 'Go home, Prince, they are going to arrest you! The Palais Royal is surrounded.'[6] But Charles drove on, and was seized as he stepped out of his carriage at the Opéra.

His arms were pinioned by a group of the soldiers in civilian clothes and for a moment the Prince feared this was an assassination plot and yelled loudly until an officer named Vaudreuil stepped forward to say 'I arrest you in the name of the King, my master.' The brave Biron, in disguise in case he should be recognised, sat out of sight in his carriage until the job was done.

Charles screamed that no one but a senior officer of the musketeers had the right to arrest a prince of the royal blood, but he was marched summarily into a nearby house, where Vaudreuil ordered him to surrender his weapons. 'I shall not give them to you,' the Prince replied angrily, 'but you may take them,' and the officer removed his sword, knife and a pair of pistols.

Orders had been given to tie the Prince up and Biron – now considering it safe enough to emerge from his carriage – insisted on this in spite of an undertaking by Charles that he would not attempt to take his own life. As a compromise Vaudereuil bound his royal prisoner with crimson silk cords, apologising as he did so. Charles, who had calmed by now assured him: 'The shame is not yours but your master's.'[7]

From then on the Prince behaved with courage and dignity as he was driven to the Château of Vincennes and handed over to the governor, the Marquis de Châtelet, whom he knew well. The embarrassed Marquis ordered him to be untied, then led him into a small white-washed room where, to his great annoyance, he was unceremoniously stripped and every part of his body was searched again for weapons, even to his genitals. Nothing was found. Poor Châtelet became so upset at one point that he broke down and knelt at his prisoner's feet. 'Sir,' he blubbered, 'this is the most unfortunate day of my life.' Charles put a hand forward and raised him. 'I know your friendship for me,' he said. 'I shall never confuse the friend with the governor – do your duty.'[8]

Louis must have wondered whether he had made a gross error in arresting the Prince, for even the Dauphin wept and turned furiously on him. Paris, first stunned by disbelief, was enraged at this humiliation of its hero, perpetrated simply to please the English. Pompadour and Puysieux, both known to dislike Prince Charles, were cast as the villains of the arrest. The incident was one step along the road that led to the end of the French monarchy in 1789.

After cooling his heels in Vincennes for a few days Charles was forced to accept that he must leave France and Louis generously agreed that he need not be escorted all the way to Civitavecchia in Italy, but would be set free at the Pont de Beauvoisin at the border of Savoy, from where he could go wherever he pleased – so long at it was not back to France or to the papal city of Avignon. The plan envisaged by Louis, James and the Pope was for him to settle in one of the papal states in Italy.

Departure was set for the evening of 12 December, with an escort under the Marquis de Pérussis, but shortly before they were due to leave, Charles became ill with a fit of coughing and vomiting, the illness which always struck him in times of stress. They left Paris eventually on the 15th, but got only as far as Fontainebleau before he complained of feeling ill again and they had to stop. In his book, *The Love of a Prince,* Professor Laurence Bongie suggested that this may have been a feigned illness to allow his servants, who had also been set free, to catch up or a ruse to see Princesse de Talmont again. If the latter, it failed for the hated Puysieux would not permit Talmont to travel to Fontainebleau.

The nervous Pérussis was terrified his prisoner might escape or be assassinated, so he spent an uncomfortable night keeping watch over him. He had learned that two British travellers had arrived at the Cabaret de la Poste, where they were staying. The pair were General James St Clair, who had been involved in a small British landing in Brittany at the time of the Prince's return from Scotland, and his secretary, young David Hume, later to become a celebrated philosopher. The two were on their way home from Turin and had arrived at the Cabaret de la Poste purely by chance, and the landlord had put them in the room immediately above the one in which Charles Edward slept. St Clair had no idea at first who was in the room below, but reported on his return to Britain that 'his attendants said he was a Prince, but did not name him. However, as he wore a Star & Garter, he was soon known to every body.'[9] Pérussis was so worried that he roused Charles and had him on the road by three the following morning.

They reached the Pont de Beauvoisin on the 23rd, and having given his assurance of his respect for the French King and Queen and a promise neither to return to France nor to go to Avignon, Charles Stuart was freed.

At seven on the morning of the 27th, only four days later, the Earl of Dunbar, asleep in his bed in Avignon, was wakened and told that an Irish officer was demanding to see him immediately. The weary Earl recognised the man at his bedside as Charles Stuart dressed in the uniform of an Irish officer in the French service.

The four-day ride down the Rhône valley had done Prince Charlie's spirits no end of good. Royal blood coursed through him and he demanded to be treated as a prince, starting with an official welcome to the city. The papal Vice-Legate at Avignon agreed and went through an elaborate charade of sending the Prince and his retinue out one gate of the city and then receiving them at another with gun salutes, poems, and an official welcome in which 'les autorités locales vinrent le haranger copieusement' – they made many generous speeches in which he was described as 'a prodigy of valour', whose heroic deeds were the 'source of the peace we now enjoy'. Clearly the Vice-Legate and his officials were out of touch with events of the preceding year.[10]

Charles was installed in the Apostolic Palace where he held court, ate and drank prodigiously (at the Pope's expense), held balls regularly, enjoyed carnivals in the streets and attended boxing matches and bullfights. All that can be said in favour of the Prince is that the bullfights were not the cruel affairs in which the bull was killed, but a kind of bull-running, a *corrida,* in which the animal was infuriated but not harmed. But bullfighting, even of this milder variety, was forbidden by the papal authorities and the flaunting of such an edict made them distinctly uncomfortable.

When he learned that Charles Stuart was his 'guest' in Avignon, Pope Benedict had more to feel alarmed about than bullbaiting: he knew the French and British would be furious and demand that the Stuart Prince should be ordered out of the city. Benedict did not have to wait long for the first complaint. London blamed France for not escorting the Prince all the way back to Italy and made clear that it expected Louis to ensure that he was thrown out of Avignon forthwith. The British also put pressure on Pope Benedict to remove him from the papal city and even threatened to bombard Civitavecchia if he failed to do so.

Louis felt humiliated at this new threat to his precious peace treaty and at being made a laughing stock of his people, who still felt strongly about the shabby way in which Charles had been treated. Ever since the arrest at the Opéra, Paris had been swamped with pamphlets attacking the King's ministers and the press had taken up Charles's cause. In private people were poking fun at the King, while the mob still simmered, and poems and lampoons appeared mysteriously in the streets. Without a crown and in manacles, this prince was held in higher regard than Louis on the throne and Pompadour was blamed:

O Louis! Vos sujets de douleurs abattus
Respectent Edouard captif et sans couronne.
Il est roi dans les fers, qu'êtes-vous sur le Trône?
J'ai vu tomber le sceptre aux pieds de Pompadour
Mais fut-il relevé par les mains de l'Amour?

The Pope thought himself the injured party, and while he wanted rid of this ungrateful young man who had rewarded past kindnesses by lumbering him with threats from both France and Britain, there was little he could do immediately. He could only instruct his Vice-Legate in Avignon to persuade the Prince to leave the Apostolic Palace and to keep him under control until the business was settled. That was proving beyond the combined power of the Kings of France and Britain and the Pope, however, so what chance had a single poor Vice-Legate of curbing the excesses of his uninvited guest?

Charles was persuaded to move into a smaller house on the grounds that he would be more secure from assassination, but otherwise life continued as if he planned to settle in Avignon and to enjoy its social life to the full. Without regard to cost he set about organising a great festival before the start of Lent at which it was planned to have bullfighting, dancing, free food for all and a fountain of wine in the Place St Didier. The papal authorities managed to outmanoeuvre him on the bullfighting by ensuring no bulls were available and a storm did its best to wreck the occasion – another of those Protestant winds that had so often thwarted Stuart plans. The festival went ahead the following day, 12 February, with a huge parade round the city walls and, as its culmination, a great feast and a ball at which the Prince danced until eight next morning. Festivities continued until four that afternoon and to commemorate the occasion – as if anyone attending it (or the nearly bankrupted city fathers who paid for it) was likely to forget – the people of the city set up an equestrian statue of the Prince in the place St Didier where the fountain of wine had flowed.[11]

On the last day of the month it was announced that the Prince was indisposed and could see no one and all through the first weeks of March anyone who called at his house was told the same story. Even the Vice-Legate, who had been so generous and made the great festival possible, was turned away, while the doctor called daily and the Prince's household went about their work as usual. Then, as suddenly as his illness had been announced, the Vice-Legate was told that Prince Charles had left Avignon secretly, without a single servant and accompanied only by the faithful Henry Goring who had accompanied him on the jounrey to the city.

Why had he performed this vanishing trick? Everybody claimed credit:

> The Vatican congratulated itself on its 'security' disinformation campaign. The French felt that their unrelenting pressure had finally paid off. The British thought that the trick had been achieved by their threat to bombard Civitavecchia. None of this was the case. The truth was that the prince had all along wanted to cock a snook at France while humiliating the Pope at the same time. In this way the twin wounds of Henry's defection and the French expulsion could be assuaged. When the round of pleasure in Avignon became boring, the prince intended to move on to Phase Two of his defiance of Louis XV.[12]

And where had he gone? That was for the world to find out, and it proved a mystery that kept every spy in Europe occupied for the next ten years pursuing Prince Charlie through a misty world of rumour and speculation. At various times reports claimed he was in Sweden, Venice, Scotland, Ireland, Spain, Flanders, Austria, Germany, Poland and Russia: he was travelling as John Douglas, Dr Thompson, or Messrs Williams, Penn, Smith, Mildmay and Burton; he was planning marriage, he was plotting a new rising, he was on the brink of death, he was dead . . . and so it went on month by month, year by year.

Prince Charlie loved disguise and became a master of it during those years: he had had plenty of practice during his days at Gravelines while the 1744 expedition was being planned, in the Outer Isles as Betty Burke, and outsmarting a mother-in-law to reach the bedroom of Louise de Montbazon during the 1747 affair. Now he used disguise so often it became a way of life, and it is ironic in view of his contempt of the Church that his favourite persona was that of priest.

Pickle the Spy, now an active British mole in the Jacobite circle, saw this aspect of Prince Charlie at first hand, and reported on it to the Duke of Newcastle several years later:

> The Young Pretender had an admirable genius for skulking, and is provided with so many disguises that it is not so much to be wondered at that he has hitherto escaped unobserved. Sometimes he wears a long false nose which they all call *Nez à la Saxe* because Marshal Saxe used to give such to his spies whom he employed. At other times he blackens his eyebrows and beard and wears a black wig, by which alteration his most intimate acquaintances would scarce know him, and in these dresses he has mixed often in the company of English gentlemen travelling through Flanders without being suspected.[13]

Each government reacted in its own way, with Britain torn between exasperation and fear, France waiting like a cat at a mousehole to pounce on the Young Pretender should he ever appear, the Pretender in Rome pathetically anxious, Cardinal Henry just plain pathetic, but most others merely amused. Britain's ambassadors in Paris, Berlin, Vienna and every other capital spent large amounts of time and money gathering information to pass back to London, and there were rumours also of assassins waiting for orders from London to kill the Prince. All this was fuelled by false reports, many instigated by the Prince himself, and by Charles keeping constantly on the move. It was a marvellous story of intrigue and espionage, and Prince Charlie enjoyed the exhilaration of the chase just as he had done among the mountains and islands in 1746.

We now know where Charles was almost all of this time, but it is interesting first to examine where Europe thought he was during the year and a half from 28 February 1749.

A pamphlet published in 1750 under the title *A Letter from H[enry] G[oring], Esq* was an excellent piece of counter-espionage, a glorious red herring designed to confuse Charles's enemies and keep up the spirits of his followers in Britain.[14] The letter was said to have been left unclaimed in London by the addressee, and it stated that a mysterious stranger named the Chevalier de la Luze who spoke no English arrived at Avignon in February 1749, where the Prince received him with great honour. When a message arrived for him the stranger left as mysteriously as he had come. Charles and Goring departed the following morning, and French police traced them to Lyon, from where they travelled on to Strasbourg, where the Prince rescued a young woman in a fire and she fell in love with him on the spot. Leaving her, he then headed on to further adventures with would-be English and Scottish assassins in Prussia, a number of whom he killed as he defended himself. After carrying out some business with Frederick the Great the two rode on to the Baltic coast and from there sailed to Stockholm, narrowly escaping capture at Riga on the way. In the Swedish capital the Prince met Lochgarry, whom he believed had fallen at Culloden – anyone who knew anything about the Jacobites would have known that Lochgarry was with the Prince after Culloden, but the composer of the letter ignored that. In Stockholm Charles was entertained royally by the Swedish king, before he moved on to Lithuania where he fell in love with one of the Radzivils, old friends of his mother's family, although the girl in question was only eleven or twelve at the time.

The story was a splendid hoax, but it provided British spies with ample material to keep them busy.[15] Colonel Joseph Yorke in Paris reported that the Prince was back in Avignon by March, then was recognised again in Lyon on his way towards Metz. From others Yorke learned that the Prince was in either Poland or Sweden, but before March was out Yorke had a hint that he was in or near Paris. By May rumour had it that he was dead; but soon he was alive and well again and now in Poland.

Mann's Italian sources were hardly more reliable because they had him in Berlin visiting Frederick, then they caught a hint of the Radzivil marriage. To confuse London further the British envoy in Prussia, Sir Charles Hanbury Williams, suspected the Prince was one of several persons who had been seen passing through Leipzig on their way to Poland, so he put pressure on the Poles to have him ejected when he turned up there. On 12 May Hanbury Williams believed Charles not to be there after all, and less than a week later reported him in Paris. The following week the French ambassador told Williams he believed the Polish tale, but on 9 June he heard that Charles was in Venice. It was enough to send the brain of the most assiduous mole into a spin.

Williams felt so confident about his intelligence that he told his spymasters in London that the Radzivil marriage was being arranged by a priest named Lascaris, and offered to have the priest arrested as he passed through Austria on his way to Venice to meet the Prince. He

Prince Charlie dressed as Flora MacDonald's maid, Betty Burke, on the journey over the sea to Skye. Portrait by J. Williams. The Prince was a master of disguise, but this was one of his more unusual roles. (West Highland Museum, Fort William)

Sleat chief Sir Alexander MacDonald's militia hunted the Prince in the Hebrides after Culloden. (Private collection. Courtesy of West Highland Museum, Fort William)

Lady Margaret MacDonald, his wife, sent money and presents to the Prince, while the militia searched for him. (Private collection)

To
the Kings Most Excellent
Majesty beseeching the
King himself to read this
letter

May it please your Majesty / Feb^ry 24th 1745

I have been Employed for a year past by the Duke of NewCastle to Serve yr Majesty in wch time I discovered Several things against yr Majesty, that the first of Decr last I was ordered to put my self in the hands of the Rebels that before I went to them, I got a Horse from his Royall Highness the Duke of Cumberland (whom god for ever bless at Litchfield, that in three ~~houres~~ hours after I got the Horse I was among the Rebels in Derby and in their Councils for nine days after and sent yr brave and Royall Son Expresses from among them and to the Duke of NewCastle, while I was wth them I did yr Majesty what Service I cd
that in this time I Spent £204 in yr Majestys Service and am not yet paid that Expence
that I am every day attending at the Duke of NewCastle in hopes to be rewarded or paid my Expences, but to my great disapointment and to thee Comfort of those who hate yr Majesty and knows of my Surprizing danger and Success I am neither paid nor rewarded, and have not now a piece of Gold left, that my family and I are ruin:ed if not relived by yr Majesty that I will never hesitate at any danger to Serve your Majesty or your Royall family and am your Majestys Most humble obedient and devoted Servant and

Soldier Dudley Bradstreet

Letter from Dudley Bradstreet to King George II begging payment for the cost of his journey to Derby in December 1745 to warn Jacobite leaders of a 'phantom' Hanoverian army marching against them. (British Library Additional Manuscripts 32706, folio 209)

The Jiltmegant, *a scurrilous cartoon depicting Prince Charles Edward and Jennie Cameron. (National Galleries of Scotland)*

The cave at Glenmoriston where Prince Charlie hid during his flight after Culloden. Sketch by Alex Ross. (From The Itinerary of Prince Charles Edward Stuart *by W.B. Blaikie)*

A Sight of the Banging Bout in Litchfield. *Racing and election riots and Jacobite sabre-rattling went together in post-1745 England. This political print set at Lichfield races, refers to a 1747 election, and features people dressed in tartan and a fiddler playing 'The King shall enjoy his own again'. The riders racing in the background represent Prince Charlie and Cumberland. (British Museum PD 066 830)*

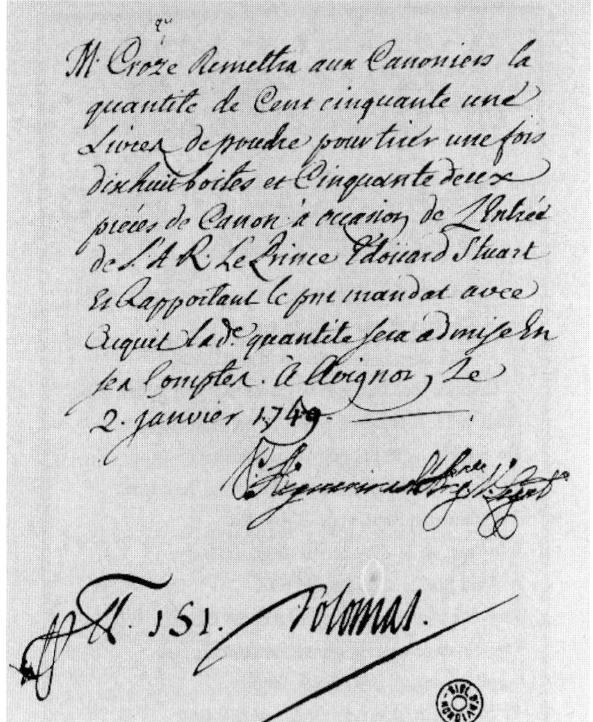

M. Croze Remettra aux Canoniers la quantité de Cent cinquante une Livres de poudre pour tirer une fois dixhuit boites et Cinquante deux pieces de Canon à occasion de l'Entrée de S.A.R. Le Prince Edouard Stuart En Rapportant le pnt mandat avec Acquit lad. quantité sera admise En ses Comptes. A Avignon Le 2. janvier 1749.

The order from the Vice-Legate of Avignon for a cannonade to be fired in honour of the arrival of Prince Charlie in the city in January 1749. (Bibliothèque Municipale, Avignon, Ms 2572 folio 27)

Clementine Walkinshaw, who became the Prince's mistress in 1752, and bore him a daughter. Portrait by an unknown artist. (National Galleries of Scotland)

Anne Drelincourt, Lady Primrose, by an unknown artist. Charles Edward walked into her drawing room in Essex Street, London, unannounced in September 1750. (National Galleries of Scotland)

Young Glengarry, the Highland chief and traitor, with his alter ego, Pickle the Spy, in the background. Painting by an unknown artist.

John Murray of Broughton's name was erased from the minutes of the Lodge Canongate Kilwinning No. 2 of the Freemasons. Inset: the eradicated signature. (From John Murray of Broughton's Memorials*)*

Lord Traquair shut the great Bear Gates at Traquair House, Innerleithen, when Prince Charlie left and vowed they would never be opened until the Stuarts were restored. They are still locked. (Courtesy of Traquair Charitable Trust)

Alexander Murray of Elibank, who gave his name to the Elibank Plot. (National Galleries of Scotland)

Prince Charles in about 1750 when he became the wild man of Europe. After Hussy. (Donald Nicholas Collection)

offered more: he would find a Pole who was willing to take the Prince to a seaport, presumably for shipment to England.

Lord Hyndford, ambassador in Moscow, was all for kidnapping the Prince too. On 19 June he wrote to London that the Prince had been at Potsdam, but had left, presumably for Poland. 'I am sorry that the Russian troops are not now in Poland,' he wrote, 'otherwise I believe it would have been an easy matter to prevail upon this Court to catch this young knight errant and send him to Siberia, where he would not have been any more heard of.'

Frederick the Great joined in the game when the Austrian ambassador to Berlin, Count Choteck, reported that his mistress believed she had seen the Prince at an inn near the home of the Earl Marischal and his brother Field Marshal Keith. Frederick knew quite well that Charles was in Venice at that moment, but he enjoyed baiting the Count: 'We have played a trick on Choteck,' he wrote on 29 June 1749, 'he spends much on spies and, to prove that he is well served, he had taken it into his head that young Edward, really at Venice, is at Berlin. He had been very busy over this.'[16]

So the chase went on from season to season with Mann in Italy usually trailing behind, although his information tended to be rather more accurate than that of other spies. On 30 May he reported Charles's arrival in Venice and knew the Prince was in sore straits for money, although he was trying to marry himself off to a daughter of the Duke of Modena. By the autumn von Stosch had him wooing Catherine the Great and rejected, but the truth was, nobody could be certain of Charles Stuart's whereabouts. Mann was 'quite at a loss', and James and the Pope were reduced to asking one another for information.

Among all that speculation lay fragments of truth, but these did little to reveal his true whereabouts. To unravel the truth it is necessary to go back to the beginning of March 1749 when he left Avignon.

First he and Goring went to Lunéville in Lorraine, where they parted, one for Paris and the other for Dijon, but after much swapping of carriages and a portmanteaux, both ended up in Paris. Charles entered the city in heavy disguise at the beginning of April and remained there for a couple of months, savouring the delicious adventure of living under the nose of King Louis and his police without being detected. It was probably revenge that brought him back to the capital in the first place, but Talmont kept him there and there can be little doubt it was she who found him the hide-out he used then and from time to time over the next two years, a place where his enemies – Louis, Puysieux and Pompadour – would never dream of looking.

Attached to the Convent of St Joseph in the rue Saint-Dominique was a retreat where society ladies could find respite from the stressful world of the court and society and two of Talmont's friends, Elisabeth Ferrand and the Comtesse de Vassé, were living there. They agreed to allow Charles to be installed in a small room, a little *garde-robe*, off their apartment, where he could hide during the day and listen to all the court gossip – much of it about himself – which their friends brought in. Then at night he descended by a secret stairway to the Princesse de Talmont's room below, and spent the night in his lover's bed.

It was an admirable arrangement and whenever he was in Paris from then on Charles spent his days savouring court gossip and his nights in his love nest. Unfortunately the renewed Talmont–Charles affair proved as stormy as it had been before he was expelled from Paris and the arrangement eventually foundered when the unfortunate Ferrand and Vassé could stand the noisy scenes between the two no longer.[17]

Mann and Frederick the Great had been right: Charles was in Venice around the end of May 1749, and the Prussian king no doubt learned that from the Earl Marischal, since the Prince had asked Marischal to accompany him, but the Earl had seen enough of Prince Charlie's tantrums and refused.

The Prince was not wanted by the Doge, and for an anxious moment the Pope feared he might move south and settle in one of the papal states, but Charles wanted nothing to do with the Church or his father, so he returned to Lorraine, where Talmont lived. There he took up with the Princesse again, but because of fear of spies they could not share a house, therefore Charles kept his own *ménage* and had to creep to his lover's bed under cover of darkness just as he had done when visiting his former mistress, Louise de Montbazon. It was not an arrangement Charles Stuart could endure willingly, especially if he were to be kept waiting at the door of Talmont's bedroom or turned away, so of course it led to new quarrels. If he had been content with his lot, Prince Charlie might have settled to a pleasant enough life in Lorraine, but he was never satisfied, never still.

His lifestyle during this time mirrored his flight in the Highlands at the end of the '45, when he was always on the move and had the scent of danger in his nostrils. It was not disagreeable to his impetuous temperament and became a way of life. He relished the hunt, turning up in unexpected places and disappearing just as quickly. He became yet more skilled at disguising himself and at laying more false trails. It was an admirable achievement to elude the armies, police, spies and court gossips of the whole of the Continent.

Inevitably, the British heard whispers that Charles was in Paris, but they could prove nothing because he had several hide-outs in the city and so used the convent only some of the time. Apart from visits to other countries he was also with his cousins in Navarre occasionally, so it was always hard for the police to track him down before he had moved on, although he did have some narrow escapes. Louis XV told the British, with every appearance of honesty, that he had been unable to trace the Stuart prince, but one suspects he did not try very hard. Indeed Charles himself confirms this, saying in one letter that the chief of Louis's police knew of one Paris visit, but 'the king winks at all this'.[18]

In public, however, the King promised that if Charles Stuart were to be caught in France he would be marched out of the country like a common criminal, and his chief of police threatened to throw Waters, the banker, into the Bastille if he lied about the Prince's whereabouts. Waters was able to answer truthfully that at that moment he had no knowledge of how to contact the fugitive.

The more time passed and Prince Charlie wanted to find some permanent home, the more he likened himself to that *irondel* that could find no branch on which to settle. No place wanted him, least of all Paris, to which he was drawn back time after time no matter how great the risk and how bitter a memory his arrest in December 1748 remained.

Prince Charlie turned himself into a master spy between 1749 to 1758, able to outwit Europe's espionage machine by the simple expedient of never confiding all details of any intended plan to any of his adherents. Each was told only as much as he needed to know, and Henry Goring, the only man privy to the overall project, co-ordinated their individual contributions. This worked brilliantly, but it made him more secretive and it detached him from reality. No wonder Andrew Lang called his account of this period 'The Prince in Fairyland'.[19]

Throughout his wanderings, his affair with Talmont and the battles of wits with spies, Prince Charlie never lost sight of his goal of ousting the Hanoverians. George II was now sixty-six and ailing, and was quarrelling with his heir, Frederick Prince of Wales – as indeed George and his whole family quarrelled constantly. King and Prince reached the stage where they had their own 'courts' in London and it was rumoured that Frederick was flirting with the Jacobites and the possibility of a coup. The waters of the succession were further muddied by the fact that it was feared Cumberland might try to seize the throne. The country was so divided that Charles now saw his opportunity in England rather than Scotland because support in the south was no longer confined to a few Catholics and Tories: many dissatisfied Whigs talked about Jacobitism as well.

In the aftermath of the '45 demonstrations and riots were commonplace, especially during elections and at sporting meetings when drink seemed to fire the rebellious spirit. Elections in those days were wild corrupt affairs spaced over days and, with riots, violence and bribery on such a scale, they could virtually ruin the winner. The Lichfield Races demonstration of 1747 combined both general election fever and riots and that year the Duke of Bedford received a horse-whipping from a country farmer on Lichfield racecourse.[20] Sir Thomas Gresley and Sir Charles Sedley appeared with about 150 of 'the Burton Mobb, most of 'em in Plaid Waistcoats, Plaid ribbons around their Hatts, and some with white Cocades'. The Duke of Bedford on that occasion was attacked, by 'an infamous person, a dancing master named Joul'. More trouble followed during elections in the 1750s.[21]

Alongside these political demonstrations, the common people also turned to the Jacobites as a means of displaying their grievances, as at

Newcastle, where strikers had the temerity to proclaim James King. In Oxford, always a centre of anti-government feeling, Dr William King made thinly veiled references to the King over the Water at the dedication of the Radcliffe Camera in 1749, and towards the end of that year King was reported to have collected 275 names of sympathisers at Lichfield races.[22]

The north-west remained strongly Jacobite, with argument and unrest between supporters of the government and Stuart followers. Leaflets continued to appear and at the start of 1749 Manchester was reminded of the tragedy of so many of its young men when a number of soldiers of the regiment that had fought for Charlie were finally transported on 11 January. In defiance, the heads of Deacon, Syddall and Chadwick were stolen from the Exchange where they had hung since their execution in the summer of 1746.[23]

Charles felt he had good reason to keep in closer touch with English Jacobites so he sent Goring to London to advise followers there of his plans. He also needed money badly and Goring managed to return with a welcome £15,000, but the price was high – Charles had to get rid of some of the staunchest Roman Catholics around him, including Kelly, the meddling priest who had caused him so much trouble before, during and after the '45. It was at this time that the Prince also tried to tap the Loch Arkaig Treasure by sending Major Kennedy to retrieve as much of it as possible.

In the spring of 1750 the Prince persuaded his father to renew his commission of regency, no easy task since the Pretender was still complaining bitterly that his son was 'a continual heartbreak' and was warning him not to expect friendship and favours from people whom he disgusted. Charles accepted the renewed powers of regency and ignored the lectures – events in England looked too propitious to waste time listening to a gloomy out-of-touch old man in Rome.

The quarrel between King George and his son had flared up again and prospects for a rising looked better than ever, so good in fact that he sent James Dormer, a son of Lord Dormer, to Antwerp to purchase 'with all ye expedition possible 26,000 Guns, Baionets, Ammunition proportioned with four thousand sords and pistols for forces in one ship which is to be ye first, and in ye second six thousand Brode sords.'[24] Charles had decided to go to England alone and for the expedition he ordered Goring to send a ship to Antwerp early in August.

On 12 August Lord Albemarle reported from Paris that Charles was lying dangerously ill, probably near the French capital – a deliberate leak to mislead. A fortnight later the English press announced Charles's death, Lang suggests as a countermove to try to draw the English Jacobites into issuing a denial. Albemarle was partly right: Charles was in the vicinity of Paris, but not ill, and he left there on 2 September, accompanied by Colonel Brett, to travel to Antwerp. Ten days later, on the 12th, he sailed for England 'in a hideous disguise' as plain Mr Smith and on the 14th he landed at Dover. By the 16th he was in London where he remained for nearly a week.

Charles had alerted no one of his impending arrival, not even Jacobite leaders in the capital, and when he turned up at the house of Lady Primrose in Essex Street, off the Strand, she was playing cards with friends as he walked into the room. She did not give the slightest hint of recognition, but simply carried on as if nothing had happened and later sent for Dr King, who was just as amazed to learn the news. 'If I was surprised to find him there, I was still more astonished when he acquainted me with the motives which had induced him to hazard a journey to England at this juncture,' wrote King. 'The impatience of his friends who were in exile had formed a scheme which was impracticable, but although it had been as feasible as they represented it to him, yet no preparation had been made, nor was anything ready to carry it into execution. He was soon convinced that he had been deceived; and, therefore, after a stay in London of only five days, he returned to the place from whence he came.'[25]

We have no details of what this 'scheme' was but it may well have been no more than the germ of an idea for a *coup d'état* that had been discussed in Paris earlier in the year. Andrew Lang did not believe the visit had any serious organised plan. 'The Prince probably crossed the water, partly to see how matters really stood, partly from restlessness and the weariness of a tedious solitude in hiding, broken only by daily quarrels and reconciliations with the Princess de Talmont and other ladies.'[26]

Charles attended a meeting at a house in Pall Mall at which fifty leading English Jacobites, including the Duke of Beaufort and the Earl of Westmoreland, discussed a plan to capture the King, probably the last time the Jacobites in England met to discuss the restoration of the Stuarts. Charles took Colonel Brett with him to the Tower of London to check how strong its defences were and was not in the least impressed. He decided that the gate could be beaten down with a petard. This was no doubt a reconnaissance for the projected *coup d'état.*

A letter to *The Times* a century later on 25 June 1865 claimed that the meeting took place at midnight when a guide brought the Prince to the house and left him locked in the room with the Jacobites to discuss a plot to capture the Hanoverian royal family, but Charles said he would not allow the King to be harmed: 'Dispose of me, gentlemen, as you please' he told them. My life is in your power, and I therefore can stipulate for nothing. Yet give me, I entreat you, one solemn promise that, if your design should succeed, the present family shall be sent safely and honourably home.' *The Times*'s correspondent blamed the French ambassador's lack of enthusiasm for the ultimate failure of this plot.

Aeneas MacDonald believed English Jacobites were equally guilty and told Sir Hector MacLean so. 'There are not in England three persons of distinction of the same sentiments as to the method of restoring the Royal family,' he wrote, complaining that they had neither the heart nor the money to carry out what they talked of doing for the Prince. Aeneas was scornful of the way they could squander enormous sums of money on elections, yet were unable to find any for the Cause.[27]

The most remarkable event of the visit was a last desperate attempt to win over the British people. The Prince had become so obsessed with the idea that Roman Catholicism was the chief obstacle between the Royal House of Stuart and the throne that he was received into the Church of England at the new church in the Strand – St Mary-le-Strand. He wrote about this himself nine years later: 'In order to make my renountiation of the Church of Rome the most authentick, and the less liable afterwards to malitious interpretations, I went to London in the year 1750; and in that capital did then make a solemn abjuration of the Romish religion, and did embrace that of the Church of England as by Law established in the 39 Articles in which I hope to live and die.'[28] He now had clearly drifted so far out of touch with feelings in Britain that he did not realise it no longer mattered whether he was Protestant, Catholic or atheist. In 1745 the gesture might have made all the difference, but by 1750 it was too late.

To mark the visit a medal was struck bearing a portrait of the Prince, a withered tree showing a healthy young shoot growing from it and the legend *Reviscerет.* Busts of the Prince were on open sale in London, and Dr King recalled that one day, after Charles had been drinking tea with him, a servant remarked that the doctor's visitor had looked very like the Prince.

'Why, have you ever seen Prince Charles?' asked King.

'No, sir,' the man answered, 'but this gentleman, whoever he may be, resembles the busts sold in Red Lion Street and are said to be busts of Prince Charles.'

With that Charles left London for Paris and was back in Lorraine by the last day of September, taking with him the germ of an idea that was to form the basis of yet another restoration scheme.

CHAPTER SIXTEEN

How Pickle was Trapped

> I was at Boulogne when Sir James Harrinton gave me directions to go to Gent . . . as I alighted of horseback at Furnes was tipt upon the shoulder by one Morison [Charles's valet] how [who] desir'd me to stop for a little at the Inn. I was not long there when the Young Pretender enter'd my room . . . The Young Chevalier was so positive of his schemes succeeding, that he told me he expected to be in London very soon himself, and that he was determin'd to give the present Government no quiet untill he succeeded or dyed in the attempt.
>
> Report from Pickle the Spy to his paymasters in London on the Elibank Plot, December 1752.[1]

If Dr King's servant was able to recognise Charles from the busts being sold openly in Red Lion Street, there were others who might see through his disguises and warn the Duke of Newcastle, so it was prudent not to linger in London. Charles left in the nick of time, for no sooner was he back in Talmont's bed at Lunéville than British spies were on his tail, although they failed to discover his exact whereabouts.

By the first week of October 1751 London had word that Charles was in the Paris area in the disguise of an *abbé*, no doubt on his way back to Lorraine, but it took nearly a fortnight longer for them to be told he had actually visited England. Their informant was Sir Charles Hanbury Williams in Berlin, who had it from one of his contacts at the French embassy, who had it from a lackey there, who had it from an unnamed Irishman. Williams's report claimed that Charles was in 'the heart of the kingdom, in the county of Stafford' and, although this was as inaccurate as third-hand information usually is, Newcastle sent troops rushing to Staffordshire in search of the Prince. A week later Hanbury Williams was claiming Charles was in Suffolk, but of course by then he was back at Lunéville in Lorraine.

Mann brought up the rear at the end of the month with a report from Rome that the Pretender had received a greatly disturbing letter from his son – Mann did not say whether this simply contained news of the visit, but more than likely it also informed him of the change of faith. Trumping his brother's ace on religion would be too juicy a morsel for Prince Charlie to keep to himself. For three months after this the Prince of Wales simply vanished and his father and brother were left in torment until Mann reported to London on 15 January 1751 that the Prince was on the Channel coast at Boulogne. He said Cardinal Albani had told him James and Cardinal Henry were ill with grief. 'Something extraordinary has happened to the Pretender's elder son,' Mann reported, and of course it had: although Mann was obviously not aware of Charles's conversion to Protestantism, the father and brother had been agonising over it for months.

Charles was too busy with his own problems to take notice of James's and Henry's distress, for he was consumed by the next move to oust the Hanoverians, while at the same time he was beset by financial problems, which could not be ignored, and his love life took a downward turn.

The relationship with Talmont had never run smoothly, but during 1749–50 it worsened as Marie-Louise became swept up in her own family tragedy, which Charles proved incapable of understanding. Her son died of smallpox in September 1749 and as a result of the strain of the boy's illness and death and the end of her marriage, which followed, she herself became ill, but received no sympathy from her lover. They continued to see one another and if anything became more passionate, but their quarrelling turned more vicious and frequent at the same time. Talmont was experienced enough to cope with her spoilt brat of a lover and refused to rush to him whenever he summoned her, and Charles found himself playing the Louise de Montbazon role in their affair. He was the one who was pleading with her to return to him. 'I am dying,' he told her, 'I love you too much and you love me too little'.[2]

Yet he could still wound her deeply, especially by excluding her from his plans, even from the details of the visit to London. This she could not forgive and matters came to a head when he summoned her to Lunéville on his return. She had to ask King Louis for permission to leave the capital to join Charles, but the King delayed until the very end of the year when he granted her five months' *congé* from January to May 1751. Even that was cut short because she took ill again and was unable to travel. Still she received not a scrap of sympathy from Charles, who not only refused to stay with her, but also vanished for two months, leaving her with no idea where he was.

In May he forced her to apply for an extension to her leave of absence, but on the very first night they should have been together she took ill again with the sickness and vomiting she suffered in times of stress, and he stormed out of her room and spent the night with one of her maids. In the morning he came to her and told her he was leaving, refusing even to allow her to send the servants out of the room while they made their final parting. He told her he would leave when he pleased and it was his intention to take another mistress. Poor Talmont, the humiliation in front of her staff was a terrible end to a long career as a courtesan.

Talmont's going did not affect Charles; he had other matters on his mind that spring. For one thing the little army of Scottish followers who had arrived in France after 1746 had now been augmented by many who were released under the 1747 amnesty. They and others, like Young

Glengarry, kept sending importuning letters, but Charles considered himself more deserving than mere followers.

Restoration was in his mind too because the political situation seemed to be turning in his favour. The death of a king or prince during eighteenth century Europe always brought a threat of war, and war provided a catalyst for Jacobite hopes: several deaths at the start of 1751 boosted Prince Charlie's dreams. Ever since his return from London he had been whispering with his closest confidants about the possibility of a *coup d'état* to remove the Hanoverians, but the matter became more urgent with news of two deaths – that of the King of Sweden and that of George II's heir, Frederick Prince of Wales. A third death was reported around the same time, that of the Duke of Cumberland, but it emerged soon after that it was a horse of the same name that had died and not the Butcher of Culloden![3]

Serious discussion of the coup began with clandestine meetings of the Prince's closest Scottish friends in Paris – the faithful Goring, Sir John Graeme, Lochgarry, and Alexander Murray of Elibank, the younger brother of Lord Elibank, laird of Elibank which lies on the River Tweed in the Scottish Borders. The Murrays came of an old and distinguished family, so staunchly Jacobite that Horace Walpole called the laird of Elibank 'a very prating, impertinent Jacobite,'[4] yet so canny that neither he nor his brother came out to join the Prince in 1745. Walpole recognised this too. 'Both were such active Jacobites that if the Pretender had succeeded they would have produced many witnesses to testify their great zeal for him; both so cautious that no witnesses of active treason could be produced by the Government against them.'[5] They generally managed to remain just far enough on the right side of the law to avoid arrest even in those ultra-sensitive times when to breathe the word Jacobite meant imprisonment. Murray may have been 'one of the Prince's less reputable associates',[6] but he had one great virtue in Prince Charlie's eyes – he had married into money and was able to lend Charles a few hundred pounds at a time when he was in desperate need. That was enough to recommend him as a warm friend of the Cause.

Alexander Murray became caught up in a particularly wild Westminster by-election during the summer of 1751 and ended up in Newgate prison charged with violence and intimidation. After he said he knelt only to God and refused to beg the pardon of the House of Commons on his knees, he was held in Newgate until the parliamentary session ended and emerged from gaol a hero of the London mob. He fled to France and joined the Prince with a warm recommendation from the London Jacobite leaders, Lady Primrose and Dr King, who assured Charles that Murray had it in his power to raise several hundred men for the Cause at Westminster. That, and ready cash to lend, cleared Murray's path into the Prince's closest circle and once there he stirred up the plot which had been simmering in Charles's mind all year. He was so closely associated with it that it became known as the Elibank Plot.

The idea was that Murray should return to London, accompanied by a few officers of Lord Ogilvy's regiment, and there gather together a large number of English Jacobite supporters. Charles would join them, and at a given signal, Elibank and his men would seize the royal family and murder them or spirit them away to France. The Elector's exit would follow the route Prince Charlie's grandfather had taken more than sixty years earlier. Charles would then be proclaimed regent as he had been in Edinburgh in 1745.

Pickle had well and truly insinuated himself into the Prince's trusted circle by the time of the conspiracy, and passed details of every movement the plotters made back to his paymasters, Secretary of State Henry Pelham and the Duke of Newcastle, in London. Unaware of this treachery, Charles continued to plan. He was astute enough to realise that he could not carry off such a huge enterprise without foreign help, but who was there to ask? Since 1748 and his expulsion he had become so neurotic about Louis XV that he flatly refused to have anything to do with the Paris government. In any case, he knew that for all his talk, the French King had never come up with support when it was needed. Nor had Spain, so the Prince refused ask there either.

Instead he turned northwards to Prussia and Sweden, in the hope that Frederick the Great would support the coup with a Scottish invasion by Swedish troops under the Marischal's brother. Since General Keith was one of the finest soldiers in Europe, and his family was highly respected in Jacobite circles in Scotland, he would make an ideal leader.

To win Frederick the Great's support the Prince knew he would need Earl Marischal's help – a difficult task since Prince Charlie and the Earl did not get on well. The crusty old veteran had disapproved of Charles's plans before and after the '45 and refused to help him. Ever hopeful, the Prince sent Goring to Berlin to make overtures, but to no avail: Marischal put forward all kinds of reasons why the Prussian king would not support such an adventure, especially his fear that such action might provoke the Russians into war. The Prince was therefore left to implement his coup solely with the help of English and Scottish Jacobites.

Then Frederick the Great suddenly made a strange move: he appointed Marischal his ambassador to Paris in August 1751, a decision that caused ripples in both France and Britain. George II was furious because the Earl still stood condemned for treason in London and to appoint him as envoy to an unfriendly court could only be seen as a very provocative – not to say belligerent – move. The Duke of Newcastle did not mince his words: 'One may easily see the views with which the King of Prussia has taken this step: first, for the sake of doing an impertinence to the King [George]; then to deter us from going on with our negotiations in the Empire, for the election of a King of the Romans, and to encourage the Jacobite party, that we may apprehend disturbances from them, if a rupture should ensue in consequence of the measures we are taking abroad.'[7]

Prince Charlie may be forgiven for thinking a warped sense of humour motivated the Prussian King as well as political malice, for the appointment was a tantalising yet annoying one in Jacobite eyes. Here was the King of Prussia offering what had every appearance of a helpful gesture, yet he had chosen someone who was far from well disposed towards the Prince personally or active in promoting the Cause. Charles realised, too, that Marischal, for all his talk, was another of those who put his personal career above the greater good of the movement, yet he was always crafty enough to manage to retain the confidence of followers in Britain and the King in Rome. Neurotic to the last about every move involving France, Charles also saw the appointment as some ploy by King Louis: 'Lord Marischal's coming to Paris is a piece of French politics,' he wrote, 'on the one side to bully the people of England; on the other hand to hinder our friends from doing the thing by themselves, bambousling them with hopes . . . They mean to sell us as usual.'[8]

Strong protests from Newcastle's envoy in France to Louis's minister, Puysieux, had no effect. In fact, the only person to show satisfaction over the appointment was the Pretender in Rome – it gave James another sympathetic ear in the French capital and a wise old man to keep his son under control.

The Prince sent Goring to Paris to persuade Marischal to throw his weight behind his plans, but as both envoy and Prince's intermediary were terrified of British agents and assassins, the encounter turned to pantomime.[9]

'My instructions are not to let myself be seen by anybody whatever but your Lordship,' Goring wrote to the Earl. 'There is a garden belonging to a Mousquetairs, famous for fruit,' replied Marischal. 'I could go there as out of curiosity to see the garden, and meet you tomorrow towards five o'clock . . . Remember, I must go with the footmen, and remain in the coach as usual, so that the garden is best, because I can say if it came possibly to be known, that it was by chance I met you.' If Goring knew a better rendezvous perhaps he would suggest it.

Charles's envoy complied and suggested the Tuileries, where he would come in disguise as an *abbé.* Marischal accepted and told Goring, 'I will go to the Tuileries when it begins to grow dark, if it does not rain, for it would seem too odd that I had choose to walk in rain, and my footman would suspect, and perhaps spye. I shall walk along the step or terrace before the house in the garden.'

Presumably that meeting did take place, although there is no record of it, and others followed, including one at the house of Waters, the banker, when Goring was to pretend to be a 'Hamborough Merchant' in search of lace and the ambassador was to be looking to buy lace. Charles himself may also have made a secret visit to Paris to talk to Marischal.[10]

Another letter talks of Waters's house or Princesse de Talmont's as meeting places, but Marischal was always frightened of being recognised even by his own footman, who 'would dogg' him there. Out of all these ghostly comings and goings – always after dark and in disguise – Charles received not so much as a promise of a good word on his behalf in the ear of Frederick the Great. Marischal was like the English Tory landowners, he was prepared to drink toasts on St Andrew's Day or James's birthday, but would do nothing to further restoration.

He told Pickle he thought poorly of these people who were trying to persuade him to betray his ambassadorial commission from Frederick in support of such a scheme as the kidnap of the British royal family, and Pickle passed on that news to the Pelhams. Frederick himself was equally devious, writing to Marischal in May 1753, 'It will be for my interest to encourage them in their design under hand, and without being observed. You will agree with me that the state of European affairs does not permit me to declare myself openly. If the English throne were vacant, a well-conceived scheme might succeed under a Regency.'[11]

Obediently, and tantalisingly, Marischal remained in contact with the London plot, keeping alive a sense of hope that he and his master might eventually change their minds and provide the Scottish campaign with the help the conspirators needed. Anticipation of Frederick's support also buoyed the Prince's friends as they continued to plot in secret.

Albemarle, now British envoy in Paris, was keeping Secretary of State Pelham informed and reported at one point during the autumn of 1751 that he believed the Prince had been in the city, but his disguises made it very difficult to identify him. Albemarle issued orders for a Dr Kincade to be stopped at Dover, and his papers seized. Kincade was duly 'culled like a flower' when he landed in England, but no compromising papers were found in his possession. Albemarle also sent a list of people known to be in correspondence with Britain, including Lochgarry who had been sent to Scotland by the Prince.

In a letter marked 'Secret', Albemarle wrote on 9 October: 'The Young Pretender has travelled through Spain and Italy in the habit of a Dominican Fryar. He is expected soon at Avignon. He was last at Berlin and Dantzich, and has nobody with him but Mr Goring.' Mann in Italy joined in the game with 'news' that the Prince was in Ireland and that he had given up his house in Avignon – but his reports did contain one significant morsel for London: 'Something is in agitation.' Rumours continued to abound in Europe – Charles was everywhere. Soon in truth he was to turn up in Ghent involved in a new love affair and with a desperate scrabble to find more cash on his mind as well as the Elibank Plot.

As Charles led his mysterious and nomadic life, Murray of Elibank and his friends on both sides of the English Channel were weaving together the intricate strands of their plan. In its final form, St James's Palace and the Tower of London were to be seized and the British royal family captured. At the same time the hoped for insurrection led by Swedish troops and General Keith would begin in Scotland. Plans for another proposed landing in Ireland came to nothing. The suggestion had first been to murder the British King, but Charles still would have none of that. Neither George nor his family must be harmed; the Prince insisted, therefore, that the Hanoverians were simply to be taken to France.

Throughout the summer of 1752 there was much coming and going between England and France and Flanders, with Goring making two forays to England and Murray of Elibank three. A number of supporters had been quietly organising themselves in London and Lady Primrose visited the Continent in the early part of the year to discuss plans but Charles showed himself at his most tactless by foolishly dismissing a French follower whom Lady Primrose trusted simply because he was French. And he did it while she was in France.

At last in the autumn of 1752 the conspirators felt ready to move, although they still had no commitment from Frederick the Great and another great worry had arisen – from the reaction of the government in London it was clear that much information was being leaked from the inner circle of conspirators. English followers searched diligently to discover the culprit, but could not uncover the Pelhams' mole.

Nobody suspected Pickle or his friends, although about the end of November 1751 an anonymous correspondent warned Waters, the Paris banker, that a priest named Leslie – the priest who pawned Mrs Murray of Broughton's watch to help Young Glengarry – was spying on the Prince's movements. Leslie, 'an arrant rogue', was 'going to discover if he can have any news of the Prince in a country which, it is strongly suspected, His Royal Highness had crossed or bordered on more than once.'[12] This referred to Charles's travels in search of a wife and his discussions with Frederick, Marischal, Goring and others in connection with the revolution he was planning in Britain.

Leslie and Glengarry were also in touch with Murray of Broughton (who most likely knew little or nothing of their treachery), and the pair were aided and abetted by another Scottish spy, Samuel Cameron, a lieutenant in the French service on half pay, who was eventually court martialled and ordered out of France. He was warned he would be shot if he set foot in the country again.[13]

Still Pickle remained above suspicion, even though John Holker, probably the young officer of the Manchester Regiment who escaped while he awaited trial in 1746, rumbled him, the only person to do so at this stage. Holker learnt something about Glengarry while he was in London with Charles in 1750, but when he suggested that Pickle was a traitor, nobody would believe that the heir to a great Highland chief could betray the Cause. In any case another spy had been discovered – Clementine Walkinshaw.

After he abandoned Talmont the Prince moved around Europe a great deal, partly organising the *coup d'état* and partly from fear of being discovered by assassins or spies who became extremely active as word of the kidnap plot leaked to London. One evening he had a narrow escape when three bandits set on him on the road near Metz, and the incident gave him the fright of his life, as did other rumours of plots, which showed the Hanoverians were determined to track him down.

He eventually left Lorraine to settle in Ghent, which was conveniently close to the Channel coast, from where he could continue with his plan for the London coup, while he remained hidden behind the alias Chevalier William Johnson. Having abandoned Talmont he had a number of casual sexual relationships with unnamed women, but such liaisons were considered too dangerous as they might lead kidnappers or murderers to him, so he decided to find someone permanent.

To that end he took a 'preti house and a room for a friend'.[14] But there was no friend to share his 'preti house'. Then he heard that Clementine Walkinshaw, the girl who had nursed him at Bannockburn House in 1746, was living in Flanders and she had made a promise that if he ever needed her she would come to him, so he ordered John William O'Sullivan, who had also been at Bannockburn at that time, to find her.

Utterly obsessed with the need for secrecy at all times, or perhaps aware that his followers would disapprove, Charles ordered O'Sullivan to burn the letter and mention his search to nobody. O'Sullivan answered immediately, denying knowledge of Clementine's whereabouts. 'I can assure your Hs upon my word of honor I dont know what directions to give to the bearer about her,' he told the Prince. 'Her lettre to me was from Dunkerque, where she gave me to understand, that if she had no account from yu, yt her intention was to go into a Convente.' He strongly advised against bringing Clementine to him, telling Charles, 'As to have her with you, I am afraid it wou'd be too dangerouse, as well for your Hs safety, as glory, in the present juncture.'[15]

Why should it be 'dangerous' to his safety or glory to take a new mistress, or, assuming they had been lovers at Bannockburn House in 1746, rekindle an old affair? O'Sullivan was clearly lying: he had certainly been in touch with Clementine, because within a couple of days of receiving the Prince's letter, he was able to pass on the information to her that Charles wanted her to join him. Clementine had recently told the Irishman she had decided against entering the Convent of the Poor Clares at Gravelines as she had intended, so he advised her that 'it is now a question of your going to him, as the Person in question absolutely desires'. In his long letter to her he emphasised the importance of not revealing to anyone any secrets she learned from the Prince, or letting slip to the Prince's messenger any information about her own life. He was adamant on these points. 'You must not under any pretext whatever, confide in him as to the past nor talk to him about the Person in question' wrote O'Sullivan. 'You know, moreover, of what consequence it is both for you and for the Person you are going to see to keep as an inviolate secret everything that he may tell you.'[16]

Only three days later, on 3 June, the Irishman was still denying knowledge of where Clementine was to be found, yet he knew enough to tell the Prince that he now believed she would abandon the convent for him even if she had already taken her first vows. O'Sullivan's story did not add up and only one reason makes sense – O'Sullivan himself had been having an affair with Clementine. There may be no firm evidence of such a relationship, but the clues point strongly towards it. Why did he warn Clementine, 'You must not under any pretext whatever, confide in him as to the past'? What past? Clementine Walkinshaw was a pretty, intelligent, eligible girl who could easily have made a good marriage, yet she told her family she proposed to enter a convent in France and from that moment right up to her mother's death, none of the family communicated with her.

Did they know she was going to France in the hope of taking up with Prince Charlie? Or did they fear she was intending to join O'Sullivan, who had been the man with whom she had the affair at Bannockburn. This is only surmise, but Charles was too ill at Bannockburn to have affairs with anyone, so the field was clear for O'Sullivan, his right-hand man, sitting there with time to kill.

It is interesting that when Charles had Clementine brought to him, the strait-laced Madame de Vassé and Henry Goring both refused to escort her. Such commissions, Goring told Charles contemptuously, 'are for the worst of men, but if you are determined to have her, let Mr Sullivan bring her to you'.[17] Later he went further and told the Prince 'the man who keeps a mistress is indeed not so much liable to censure, but surely he that procures her for him . . . is no better than a pimp'.[18]

There was something deep and dark behind the O'Sullivan–Walkinshaw relationship between 1746 and 1752, and the fact that the Prince dropped the Irishman ever after, suggests that Charles discovered what that secret was. Could it have been that the mysterious young woman, Clementina Douglass, who died and was buried in the remote churchyard at Finsthwaite at the southern end of Lake Windermere in 1771, was the child of Clementine Walkinshaw and O'Sullivan, and not Prince Charlie's child as legend claims? The Finsthwaite Princess's surname, Douglass, was an alias the Prince liked to use and Clementina was his mother's name, but Douglas was a common enough surname, and a devoted follower of the Cause could have chosen the name of the woman who had been the Pretender's Queen.

Whatever the truth of the Bannockburn incident and the strange silence that surrounds the years between 1746 and 1752, neither the Prince nor O'Sullivan ever referred to them, and Clementine always kept her thoughts too closely to herself to confide them to an outsider.

If Walkinshaw's relationship with O'Sullivan was mysterious, her position with regard to other Jacobites was crystal clear. Goring resigned rather than bring Clementine to Ghent and not just because of something in her past. Her sister, Catherine, was a member of the household of the Princess of Wales in London and all of Charles's supporters were convinced that she was the Hanoverian spy to whom Clementine was passing information about the current plot gleaned in Prince Charlie's bed.

The fact that every move was being transmitted to London almost as it happened was all the proof they needed, and as long as Pickle was clever enough to cover his tracks, Clementine was blamed for his treachery.

Lady Primrose and the English Jacobites became especially bitter about the Prince's new mistress and in time their hostility against Walkinshaw turned to personal hatred and disillusionment with Charles and the whole movement. One by one they began to abandon the Cause, but Prince Charlie still refused to submit to their meddling opinions. He had not changed: what he wanted he had to have – immediately – and now he wanted Clementine Walkinshaw without giving a thought to personal cost or price to the Cause.

Devious to the last, Charles ordered Clementine not to travel the 40 miles from Douai where she was living to Ghent direct, but to go to Paris, where a cold letter commanded her not only to join him forthwith, but never to say anything about their relationship – ever. In the unsigned letter he wrote: 'I hereby absolutely forbid you, from this instant forward, never to put pen to Paiper for anything whatsoever, and neither Sr John [O'Sullivan] or anybody whatsoever must know ye Least thing about you or what passes betwixt us, under pain of incurring for ever my displeasure.'[19]

In spite of this inauspicious start their liaison in Ghent brought happiness to both of them for a while, although there was no real enduring love between them. He showed kindness towards Clementine at times and Pickle the Spy, who was no friend of either, had to admit the following spring that 'the Pretender keeps her wll and seems very fond of her'[20]

In due course Clementine became pregnant and bore Charles a daughter, who was baptised Charlotte in the Church of Sainte Marie des Fonts in Liège in October 1753. They had moved to Liège to a house with more space in which to live as a family, but one insurmountable barrier always stood between them: Charles had abjured his faith in London and was violently anti-Catholic, while Walkinshaw remained a devout member of the Roman Church. One wonders whether he would have attended his daughter's baptism in a Catholic church and Compton Mackenzie has suggested that this was the cause of their first quarrel. That is improbable since the two had been arguing since the day they were reunited at Ghent.

As a result of the disagreement over Charlotte's baptism, the Prince ordered all his Catholic servants to be dismissed, then he issued an even more despicable order: 'My mistress has behaved so onworthely that she has put me quit[e] out of all patience, and as she is a Papist to, I discard her also.'[21] Needless to say, he did not send her away.

All this did nothing to calm Jacobites on either side of the Channel, who continued to badger him to get rid of his mistress because she was a spy; or if he would not accept that, surely he would let her go for his personal safety because they felt sure her presence might betray his whereabouts to assassins. Charles remained adamant: Walkinshaw stayed, and the only concession he made was to keep constantly on the move between Flanders, France and Germany, always in disguise and travelling under false names. And always plotting his London coup.

Clementine Walkinshaw's misfortune was to join the Prince just as the Elibank Plot approached the point of implementation, with 10 November 1752 set as the date for the seizure of the King. While London was being taken a new rising in Scotland would be led by the Camerons – Lochiel's brother, Dr Archie, Cameron of Fassifern and Cameron of Glen Nevis – and Young Glengarry, none other than Pickle himself.

The Highlands was an unhappy place in 1752 for great changes had occurred since Charlie left in 1746. As part of the government's determination to destroy the clan culture, fourteen estates of disloyal clans – among them those of Lovat, Lochiel and Keppoch – were forfeited to the crown. Now six years on under an Annexing Act provided for the management of these lands, commissioners were appointed to grant leases, appoint factors and use the rents and profits arising from the estates for improving conditions in the Highlands.

Clansmen on these forfeited estates would not accept the change: the clan system ran deep and they considered they still owed allegiance to the chiefs they had followed in the '45; so they continued to send their rents to them even if it meant paying twice – to the exiled chief and to the hated factor. Worse, the factor had the power to evict any tenant who failed to pay his rent, and it was while he was on his way to eject a number of tenants on the forfeited Stewart of Ardshiel estate in Appin, that the factor, Colin Campbell of Glenure, was shot dead on 15 May 1752.

The murder of the Red Fox, as Glenure was called, was never solved, but James Stewart, a half-brother of the Ardshiel chief, was arrested and tried as an accessory, and Allan Breck Stewart was accused of the crime but escaped to France. James Stewart was tried before the Duke of Argyll, chief of the victim's clan, and a jury packed with eleven Campbells, so the verdict was a foregone conclusion: Stewart was hanged.

The Appin Murder caused great anger among Jacobite clansmen and government ministers, but for different reasons. Highlanders believed an innocent man had died, but the Hanoverians were determined to make an example of James Stewart, a recalcitrant clansman. The murder sent a shiver down the spine of King George himself to think that the Highlanders still dared to perpetrate such a crime against one of his representatives and he took a close personal interest in the proceedings.

Much was written at the time, and afterwards, and the mystery of the Appin Murder entered Highland legend and Scottish literary history when Robert Louis Stevenson used the story for the plot of his novel, *Kidnapped.*

The fate of Allan Breck Stewart, who escaped, is as great a mystery as the murder itself. James Mohr Macgregor, who was spying for the British government in France at the time, attempted to kidnap him, but failed, and Allan Breck simply vanished – creating another legendary character in the post-'45 story.[22]

The killing of the Red Fox caused great turmoil in the Highlands during the spring and summer of 1752, so it was a wise move on the Prince's part for him to summon Macdonnell of Lochgarry (a relation of Pickle), and Dr Archie Cameron to Flanders, where he was now living under the name Chevalier William Johnstone to make sure the news of the Elibank Plot was relayed to sympathetic chiefs in Scotland. At a meeting at Menin, he briefed Lochgarry and Dr Cameron in great detail and ordered them to return to Scotland and pass the word on to chiefs who would be gathering for the great autumn black cattle market at Crieff. From Crieff the information was to be relayed to Cluny Macpherson and other chiefs in the Highlands to prepare them for the Swedish invasion organised by Frederick of Prussia.

Pickle was in on the entire plan, too, because he was so trusted that Charles sent for him also and related every detail to him personally. 'The discourse chiefly turn'd upon the Scheme in England, when he repeated the same assurances as to Lochgary, but in stronger terms,' Pickle told the Pelhams.[23] No wonder he was able to write from Boulogne on 2 November, 'You'l soon hear of a hurly burly, but I will see my friend or that can happen.'[24]

All through 1752, while the plot was being organised Pickle watched and reported in a series of letters signed 'Pickle', 'Alex^{r} Pickle', 'Jeanson' (his father's name was John), 'Alex^{r} Jeanson' and 'Roderick Random'. Names were crudely disguised in cyphers, sometimes with words substituted and sometimes with figures to represent the persons referred to. The Pretender was No. 8, Charles was 80, Earl Marishcal 2, Henry Goring 6, Sir John Graeme 72, Scotland 66 and the French ministry 0.

On the British side Henry Pelham was usually called his 'Great friend', and old Gwynne Vaughan was sometimes 'Grandpapa'. The Duke of Newcastle was referred to as 'Mr Kenady'. Leading Jacobites were given cyphers, with the Prince 'St Sebastien', and persons given placenames while places were referred to as people. Marischal was 'Venice', London was 'Mr Johnson' and the Highlanders 'Mrs Strange'.

Warned by Pickle, the Hanoverians monitored the secret comings and goings of Jacobites between France and England, and found among those who made the crossing, Eleanor de Mézières, the Englishwoman married to the Marquis de Mézières, who had long been notorious at the French court and in the Jacobite inner circle. Although now an old woman close on seventy, she was as ardent a Jacobite as ever and Pelham knew that wherever the Marquise was to be found, Jacobite trouble would be close by.

There is a local tradition in Surrey that Prince Charlie came to England at this time to await the coup and stayed at the house of Major-General James Oglethorpe, who had led some of Wade's men in the chase to intercept the Jacobite army on its retreat north from Derby in 1745. Oglethorpe was the brother of Madame de Mézières, who was also at the house near Godalming at the time, and a local legend has it that the ghost of Prince Charlie can be seen pacing the grounds, still waiting for the call from London!

Murray of Elibank was horrified to discover as the time to spring the plan approached that in spite of all Charles's talk and the secret conspiring of Eleanor de Mézières and others, nothing had been done to implement the plan – no Highland chiefs were ready, no help was on the way from Frederick, no Swedish troops were promised, no Irish invasion showed the slightest sign of materialising, Jacobites in Paris had done nothing to warm up the French to the scheme. Even the English had lost their nerve since they suspected details of the plan were being leaked to the government by Clementine Walkinshaw. English followers felt left out on a limb, so that if the royal kidnap were to go ahead on 10 November, it would fail.

Murray therefore postponed the attack on St James's and rushed back to advise Charles, who (if he had been at Godalming) had now returned to Paris. He realised by now that nothing was forthcoming from any of those friends he had been cultivating so assiduously for so long, and was reduced to trying to raise support in Paris – but still without going on his knees to beg it from Louis, whom he still had not forgiven for the humiliation of that arrest and expulsion four years earlier.

Charles had given Pickle express orders to travel to London in the meantime to see Lord Elibank, but on his arrival a shock awaited Young Glengarry. This was the moment when the plot was postponed. Elibank 'surprised me to the greatest degree, by telling me that all was put off for some time, and that his Brother [Murray of Elibank] had repassed the seas in order to aquent the Young Pretender of it, and from him he was to go streight for Paris to Lord Marishal'.

He was able to give the London government details of the plot and plotters. He named 'Sir John Douglas, Mr Charteris and Heparn of Keith' as all being in on the secret and said the Prince had been in correspondence with England 'for a year and a halph past', but the whole business had been organised 'by Whiggers' with no Roman Catholics involved. He named names quite willingly: 'Mr Carte, the Historian has carried frequent messages' and 'Elderman Hethcot [Alderman George Heathcote] is a principal manager. However, they never commit anything to writing,'

Pickle's full report of the Jacobites' activities ended by telling his paymasters that the Young Pretender had obliged him to give 'his word and honour' that he would write nothing to James Stuart in Rome concerning his discussions.[25] Pickle broke his 'word and honour' within a few months when he sent a letter to the Pretender's secretary, blabbing all the details of the plot. As Andrew Lang points out, 'He can have had no motive, except that of alarming James by the knowledge that his son had been on the eve of a secret and perilous enterprise, in which he was still engaged.'[26] He was aware that this would widen the rift between the old man and his son, and make further plots impossible.

Among the names of Scottish leaders that Pickle had given to the Pelhams were the Highland chiefs Lochgarry and Dr Cameron, who had set out for their tryst at the Crieff cattle market, unaware that they had been betrayed. Cluny was hopeful that he could raise an army to join the one promised from Frederick of Prussia and all seemed ready for a new rising. Then on 20 March 1753, the government struck – one of Major-General Bland's patrols trapped Dr Archie hiding in the hills above Inversnaid beside Loch Lomond. He was hurried off to Edinburgh and then to London where he was examined at the Cockpit in Whitehall on 17 April. Loyal to the last, Dr Archie betrayed neither the Prince nor his co-conspirators, and no new charges were brought against him. He was condemned to death on the attainder of being 'out' with the rebels in the '45 and was hanged and disembowelled at Tyburn on 8 June.

The execution of Cameron brought a very sharp response around Britain, even from those who had stood at the foot of the gallows and cheered most wildly as rebels were put to death in 1746. The man in the street was hardly even aware of the Elibank Plot and because Cameron had not been brought to trial they remained ignorant of the planned coup. The majority believed that 1745 was the Stuarts' last serious bid and accepted that Cameron's capture and execution were simply a case of another rebel Highlander who had escaped justice at the time being brought to account. They felt strongly that the government could have been magnanimous and spared the good doctor. Even the press, so loud in its cries for gibbet-justice in 1746, now thought it was time for clemency. The *Scots Magazine* in May 1753 pleaded for Dr Archie's life: 'In an age in which commiseration and beneficence is so very conspicuous among all ranks, and on every occasion, we have reason to hope that pity resides in that place where it has the highest opportunity of imitating the divine goodness in saving the distressed.'[27]

But the government had been more magnanimous than people realised. Through Pickle it knew the names of many of those in England as well as Scotland who had been involved in the plot. At the cost of the single life of the good man Archie Cameron, it had sent a message to every sympathiser who planned to participate in the coup. At a stroke the attempted revolution was over and all the plotters were sent scurrying for cover. In real terms this one execution not only ended the Elibank Plot, but finished Prince Charlie's Cause as a political possibility. Nobody but Charles Stuart now believed in an eventual restoration of his family.

The execution of Cameron on the 1745 charge also meant that Pelham never had to reveal the identity of the man who had supplied the information that led to the doctor's arrest, and Jacobites in Britain, already suspicious of Clementine Walkinshaw, were convinced that she was the traitor. Distrust of Clementine now turned to hatred, and the most loyal friends became openly bitter against her and against the Prince, but no one more so than Lady Primrose, who must have spent some uncomfortable months wondering whether she and her fellow conspirators might not follow Archie into the Tower and to the gallows.

The one member of the Prince's circle who came out of all this well was Pickle, who had always led a charmed life, and continued to operate undetected. Young Glengarry played a dangerous game of brinksmanship, supplying London with information while he continued to enjoy the trust of both Pretender and Prince. The reason was partly that neither the left hand in Rome nor the right hand in Paris (or wherever the Prince of Wales happened to be) knew what the other was doing, but it was also due to the care with which Pelham looked after his prize agent. Nothing, not even the downfall of Archie Cameron, was allowed to permit Pickle's cover to be blown. And even after Pickle and the Cause he betrayed were dead and buried, Glengarry remained a shadowy figure, a clan chief who, because he was a chief, must be above reproach.

During the nineteenth-century Pickle was identified as Rob Roy Macgregor's son, James Mohr Macgregor. It was Andrew Lang who eventually nailed Young Glengarry with a blindingly simple piece of detection worthy of MI6. Pickle's early letters were unsigned, but his later ones carried his name and many of both periods have been published, mainly by James Browne in his *History of the Highlands.* Lang ignored the previously published texts and went back to the originals in the Royal Archives at Windsor, and there he discovered one tiny damning detail – throughout Pickle's/Young Glengarry's correspondence the word *who* was always misspelt *how.* It was a tiny detail, but it was a convincing one.

John Holker had pointed the finger at Glengarry and Archie Cameron's widow later accused him of betraying her husband. Shortly after the doctor's death she passed on to the Pretender's secretary in Rome a piece of information she had just learned about the Macdonnell chief:

> Sir Duncan Campbell of Lochnell told me and others whom he could trust that in the year 1748 or 1749, I don't remember which, as he, Sir Duncan, was going out of the House of Commons, Mr Henry Pelham, brother to the Duke of Newcastle, and Secretary of state, called on him, and asked if he knew Glengarry? Sir Duncan answered he knew the old man, but not the young. Pelham replied, it was Young Glengarry he spoke of; for that he came to him offering his most faithful and loyal services to the government in any shape they thought proper, as he came from feeling the folly of any further concern with the ungrateful family of Stuart, to whom he and his family had been too long attached, to the absolute ruin of themselves and country.[28]

Pickle was thus exposed by the wife of his last victim, but too late to save the Elibank Plot, Prince Charlie's Cause or Archie Cameron's life. And he remained free to continue his work for the Stuarts' enemies until he succeeded to the chieftainship in 1754 and no longer needed to be in the pay of the Pelhams.

CHAPTER SEVENTEEN

Alone and Discarded by his Friends

To speke to ete
To think to Drink
To ete to think
To speke to drink

Lines written by Charles on the back of a letter following the failure of the Elibank Plot.[1]

The failure of the Elibank Plot had a grievous effect on Prince Charlie and the arrest and execution of Archie Cameron brought about a marked change in his character. This was the moment when he turned from the charismatic Prince who, for all his flaws, had carried the banner of Stuart aspirations nobly, into the wild and unpredictable drunkard who never quite gave up hope, yet knew in his heart of hearts that he had only the slenderest chance of success.

Cameron's fate changed his character in another way too, from 'bonnie fighter', afraid of no one, to a frightened man whose lifestyle was driven by fear that his life was under constant threat from Hanoverian assassins and spies whom he saw lurking in every shadow. From then on he rushed from hideout to hideout, much of the time 'so disguised as to make it extremely difficult to know him', with face painted red, eyebrows blackened and of course wearing those ridiculous false noses. He lived virtually permanently under a false identity too.

Prince Charlie was right about the agents, for the sinister Pickle, Oliver Macallester and other British 'moles' continued to work assiduously to keep Henry Pelham and King George informed of every move he made. His spy phobia became so overblown that he could no longer live in Liège with Clementine and their daughter, but dragged them round Europe or abandoned them while he went off heaven knows where in pursuit of his own solace and his crown.

The English Jacobites never gave up trying to persuade the Prince to rid himself of his mistress and in 1755 sent an Irishman named Macnamara to ask him once again, on the usual grounds that she was a spy and was harming his reputation among his friends. Macnamara was not the most tactful emissary for he referred to Walkinshaw as 'an harlot, whom, as he often declared, he neither loved nor esteemed'. When Charles flew into a rage as usual at such presumption, the Irishman was reported to have asked him, 'What has your family done, Sir, to draw down the vengeance of heaven on every branch of it through so many ages?' As James Lees-Milne, who quotes this rebuke, comments, 'Charles's grandfather and even his father would have had their ready answer, which was: "the sins of the flesh". It is unlikely that Prince Charles believed in the divine retribution for so innocuous a cause.'[2]

Over the years, spies searched diligently and reported him in Germany, in various parts of France, including Avignon and Lyon, and said he was about to become king of Corsica.

Those around him worried for his safety, even if they were able to bring him little comfort. When he proposed moving to Cologne in 1753, Goring warned him he must be careful because 'the Elibank game can be played by two or more, and princes have been kidnapped in our own day'. He advised Charles to take great care when he walked near the Rhine, 'for in your taking such walks it would be easy for five or six men to seise your person and put you in a boat, and Carry you to Holland'.[3]

Spies were not the only 'enemies' Charles Stuart saw round him during this nomadic period of his life – his staff and many friends of former days were found wanting and one by one they were to abandon him as each became disillusioned with his wild behaviour. Clementine and money were prime motivation for these quarrels with his followers, but there were others – especially the irrational discarding of perfectly good servants simply because they were Catholics.

English followers who had been involved in the Elibank Plot felt angry because they had been Charles's principal sources of finance for years, yet he continued to dun them for money. Worse, following the arrest of Dr Cameron and collapse of the plot, they lived in constant fear of Newcastle's knock on their door and arrest on a charge of treason. Although it never came, they turned as suspicious as Charles about spies, and about one 'spy' in particular – Clementine Walkinshaw, who, they were convinced, had been the source of the leaks that had led to Cameron's death. From the moment she joined Charles they nagged him to send her away, but he was adamant that she should stay.

Waters, the Paris banker, made matters worse by telling the King in Rome about Clementine. 'There is a woman with the Prince who is the author of all this mischief,' he warned, 'and unless she be got away from him without loss of time, it is only too apparent that HRH's reputation will be made very black over all Great Britain'.[4] James, who already had an inkling of the presence of Walkinshaw from young Edgar, his Secretary's son, demanded to know if this referred to Clementine. Was it true that they had a child? And where were they living? The Pretender seldom received a scratch of the pen from his son now, yet he persisted in trying to discover more about Charles's mistress and constantly demanded that she should be sent away. To his credit the Prince refused

– though probably for the wrong reasons – and he stopped writing to his father altogether.

As Frederick's ambassador in Paris, Earl Marischal continued to put his Prussian Majesty and his own interests first, perhaps in the reverse order for the Earl always saw himself right. He had done little for the Elibank Plot, yet no sooner did it begin to crumble than he set about warming Frederick to the scheme – because it happened to be in Prussia's interests at that moment to annoy Britain. He was too late; Archie Cameron was dead and the plot was history. But soon the merry-go-round of European politics made another turn and Frederick became King George's ally, making it unlikely that Marischal would be of further help to the Cause.

Marischal had been a disloyal friend to the Cause and the Prince through most of his life, yet to this day he comes out of the Jacobite story with great credit. If he had supported the proclamation of James at the death of Queen Anne, the Elector of Hanover might never have won the British crown – but he did not.[5] He fought in the '15 and '19 risings, it is true, but thereafter lived the life of 'a cheery, contented, philosophic exile, with no high opinion of kings',[6] Stuart or any others. And he and Charles proved oil and water, youth and age, never understanding one another and never trying to. Their relationship began badly in France prior to the '45, with Marischal belittling every notion that came into the Prince's head, not all of which were as madcap as the suggestion made in 1744 that they should sail to Scotland together in a herring boat! He refused to join the '45 even when Charles planned to sail to Scotland in a proper ship, but to his credit he did try to wring arms and men from the French during the rising. When the '45 failed, he deserted the Jacobites for a better master, Frederick the Great.

To say the least, Marischal was not a friend to be relied on. And yet, after the failure of the Elibank Plot this was the man the Jacobite party in England insisted on using as the intermediary between them and the Prince. As Marischal refused to have anything to do with Charles, or even to see him, this was a totally unsatisfactory situation for both, and it led to trouble.

As Charles slipped deeper into a world of his own, cut off from his friends by bouts of unreasonable rage and drunkenness, followers saw him no longer as the Charles Stuart of whom Lord Balmerino said on the execution block in 1746, 'I am not a fit hand to draw his character. But I must beg leave to tell you of the incomparable sweetness of his nature, his affability, his compassion, his justice, his temperance, his patience and his courage, which are virtues seldom to be found in one person. In short, he wants no qualifications requisite to make a great man.'[7]

Seven years later Dr Archie Cameron, who had spent time with him only months earlier, was able to stand at the gallows in 1753 and speak of Charles's princely virtues. Before his executioners, he declared 'as I have been his companion in the lowest degree of adversity ever Prince was reduced to, so I have beheld him too as it were on the highest pinnacle of glory amidst the continual applauses and I had almost said adoration of the most brilliant court in Europe, yet he was always the same, ever affable and courteous, giving constant proofs of his great humanity and of his love for his friends and country.'[8]

The Prince of the latter half of 1753 was a very different man, and the transformation had been swift as the assessment made by Sir James Harrington, one of the Cause's most loyal friends in England, showed. Writing only six months after Dr Cameron's death he felt it necessary to tell Charles: 'I have been hard put to it when I have been praising your good qualities to some of our friends, they have desired me to produce one single instance of any one man you have had the Compassion to relieve with the tenderness a King owes to a faithfull subject who has served him with the risk of his life and fortune.'[9]

The ever-faithful Henry Goring, who had spent years racing across Europe and making dangerous visits to England at the whim of the Prince, was now at the end of his tether too. He had bravely made his feelings about Walkinshaw clear by refusing to bring her to Ghent, but now he could remain silent no more. On 13 January 1754 he wrote an exceedingly long letter, spelling out to the Prince that his adherents in Britain were tired of being dunned for money, reminding him that his mistress was being 'loudly and publickly talked of', and complaining bitterly about the arbitrary sacking of loyal servants. Writing under his code name, 'Stouf', Goring warned of the danger of spies, clearly with Clementine Walkinshaw and her sister in mind. 'We have no opinion in England of female politicians, or of such women's secrecy in general', he told the Prince.

And if Clementine did not betray them, he knew another person who might be tempted. Charles had dismissed Dumont, one of his own agents, whom he had suspected of betraying Archie Cameron, a very dangerous move. Dumont knew key people like Young Glengarry (still not suspected of spying for London) and Jeremy Dawkins, and could betray them to the Pelhams. He might even denounce Goring himself to the French, so that the faithful servant would end up in the Bastille. 'What will our friends think of you, Sir, for taking so little care of their lives and fortunes by putting a man in dispair who has it in his power to ruin them, and who is not so ignorant as not to know the government will well reward him?' asked Goring. He knew that Henry Pelham and his brother Newcastle had bought many men, although he was not aware that Pickle was among them.

Goring then played his trump card: he said Dumont had sufficient knowledge of the Prince's own whereabouts to put enemies on to his track and in this he was soon proved right. At that exact moment Dormer, one of Charles's main sources of intelligence from England, warned Charles of British agents' discovery that he was living in Liège. In spite of Goring's arguments, however, the Prince refused to reinstate the unfortunate Dumont.

Goring had better luck in his plea for the reinstatement of all the Catholic servants who had been so unreasonably dismissed. He spread himself over several sheets to warn of the stupidity of such a move and could not resist a gibe against the Prince for retaining his more important Catholic servants, John Stafford and Michael Sheridan, while 'turning away three or four papist footmen, who can, by their low situation, have no manner of influence on your affairs. The wrong was compounded by the fact that one of the papist footmen was a relation of the poor man who was lately hanged [Archie Cameron]'. When that became public it would cause great harm to the Prince's character.

The Prince's display of religious intolerance annoyed Goring and he would not let it go. 'Do you think, Sir, your Protestants will believe you the better Protestant for it?' he demanded, and answered his own question. 'If you do, I am affraid you will find yourself mistaken; it will be a handle for your enemies to represent yu a hippocrite in your religion and Cruel in your nature, and show the world what those who serve you are to expect.'

Charles capitulated and agreed to reconsider the dismissals, although Dumont remained sacked.

Having spoken so frankly, there was nothing left for Goring but to do as Lord George Murray did in 1746 and offer his resignation. He did so gracefully and at length. 'Do as you think fitt, but let me beg of you to give such Conditions to somebody else; as I never could be the author of any such advice, so I am incapable of acting in an affair that will do you, Sir, infinite prejudice, and cover me with dishonour . . . I sware to the great God that what I write is truth, for God's sake Sir have compassion on yourself.'[10]

Spymasters continued to be bad paymasters and Pickle's cash flow remained little better than the Prince's, so that his correspondence was peppered with pleas for more money. Life became harder for him in the early part of 1754 with the death of his 'worthy great friend' Henry Pelham but his espionage activities continued as before.

There was plenty for Pickle to report since he was able to maintain contact with Lord Marischal and the Prince without arousing suspicion. Early in 1754 he was able to gather enough from Marischal about the new initiative by Prussia and Sweden to send to Scotland the invasion force they had first promised at the time of the Elibank Plot to inform London of it. Pickle had not got every detail of the scheme, yet he boasted confidently that he would soon be 'at the bottom of the most minute transactions'. He had plans to see Marischal and Charles to learn more, he told his masters.

Although he was busily employed gathering information through his agents in Europe, Pickle still had time to enjoy himself and share his pleasure with his London government contact, Gwynne Vaughan. Pickle had been trying out some paste, whose aphrodisiac qualities 'surprizingly answer Pompadour's intentions'. He found it so effective that he forwarded some to Vaughan at Bath, assuring him that 'it operates in the same lively manner upon the faire sex as it does on ours. (The Lord have mercy upon the Lassies at Bath!)' This time he signed himself 'Roderick Random'.[11]

On 8 April he wrote that he had not yet spoken to Marischal or the Prince about the Prussian-Swedish plan involving the Highlands but hoped to see both soon. After passing on the detail he had already garnered from Lochgarry and Aeneas MacDonald 'how [Pickle's usual spelling of *who*] luckly meet me here' he wrote to Vaughan demanding more cash as 'the whole accounts of our Tobacco and wine trade [Jacobite schemes] I am told, are to be laid before me by my friend at Venice [Lord Marischal].'[12] Never a man to underestimate his own ability, he assured his masters he could undermine the Prince's confidence in the plan. 'I think I can easily divert them from this, as I can convince St Sebastien [Charles] . . . that they would leave him in the lurch,' he wrote.[13]

Blissfully unaware of this treachery, Charles continued to worry about meeting Marischal and finding more money through Goring, none of it to pay the faithful poverty-stricken 'Stouf' for his loyal service. Goring still wanted to leave and said all he asked was 'a gracious demission, with which I will retire and try in some obscure corner of ye world to gain the favour of God, who will I hope be more just to me than you have been, though I despair of ever serving him so well as I have done you.'[14] Charles was infuriated by this audacious jibe. 'Will you serve me or not?' he demanded. 'Will you obey me? Have you any other Interest? Say yes or no, I shall be y^r^ friend iff you will serve me.'[15]

Six days later, on 16 May, Stouf/Goring wrote another letter to the Prince, pointing out many truths, which must have been unpalatable to the man whose divine right set him above all other men. He had served well, he told Charles, yet had been dismissed twice 'like a common footman with most opprobrious language without money or cloaths.' And as for friendship, 'No, Sir, princes are never friends.' That was Goring's last letter, and he travelled to Berlin with Earl Marischal at the end of June. There he joined the service of Frederick the Great.[16]

Marischal's prevarication had presented Charles with a terrible dilemma all through the Elibank plotting and he must have come to realise that Frederick and his ambassador in Paris were treating him exactly as the French had done between 1744 and 1746. That led to a final break between Charles and Marischal.

The breach came about at the time Goring left, and was linked to Goring's quarrel with the Prince. One of Charles's great grudges had been that Marischal agreed with Goring's criticisms and, while 'Stouf' had no difficulty in arranging meetings with the Earl, the latter always avoided Charles. But English followers thought highly of Marischal and sent money to Charles via him and Goring.

The climax came when Marischal accused the Prince of threatening to name those in England who had been involved in the Elibank Plot.[17] It was a ludicrous charge, for if Charles made any such threat he did so in a fit of drunkenness and certainly betraying any follower was something Charles Stuart would never have done. The Prince tried to make peace through Antoine Walsh, but Marischal would have none of it: he was finished with the Prince. Pickle disloyally reported all this to London.

By 1755 Prince Charlie was left without friends, without followers and without credibility. Even those Scots friends who had been so loyal protested about his behaviour and time did nothing to moderate the anger of the English. Five years after the Elibank Plot failed Murray wrote to the Prince: 'I learn that that infamous creature Lady Primrose has propagated over the whole kingdom that you are a drunkard. The only and most effectual way to convince your friends of the falsity and malice of her villainous lyes is to drink very little while these gentlemen are with you. In case any of them should propose drinking for God's sake evite it yourself because your character and success depend upon the report of these gentlemen upon their return to London.'[18]

Dr King, who had been so welcoming in London, went further, and accused him of meanness and lack of sympathy for those who had done so much for him. 'I never heard him express any noble or benevolent sentiments . . . or discover any sorrow or compassion for the misfortunes of so many worthy men who had suffered in his cause,' King wrote. 'But the most odius part of his character is his love of money, a vice which I do not remember to have been imputed by any historian to any of his ancestors, and it is the certain index of a base and little mind.'[19]

During the final stages of the Marischal rift in the spring of 1754, Jeremy Dormer, who had been his link with the English Jacobite party, warned Charles that Hanoverian agents had tracked him to Liège, so the Prince took Clementine and their baby to Paris. There he had numerous quarrels with the poor woman in front of friends in private and one especially fierce one in public in the Bois de Boulogne,[20] which drew attention to them. Oddly, British ambassador Albemarle failed to locate him in the French capital, but suspected he was there and told people he hoped to track him down through his tailor. He demanded that the French government should expel him from the city, but they pleaded ignorance.

It was time to move on again, however, and after talking of going to Spain, Charles settled for Basle, where he lived under cover as an English physician named Thompson in Switzerland for his health. Basle proved even more expensive than Paris or Liège so that money became the principal concern of the perennially poverty-stricken Charles and Clementine. To remedy this the Prince sent all the way to Scotland to demand that the ever-faithful Macpherson of Cluny, still in hiding in the 'Cage' where Charles had left him nearly a decade before, come to him in Basle. Cluny made the journey only to be faced on arrival with a demand for whatever part of the Loch Arkaig money he still had in his possession. But Cluny had none.

Unfortunately, he took the opportunity afterwards to give Charles some unpalatable advice on moderating his drinking, which was not a wise thing to do. Charles would not be hectored, and ordered his Secretary to tell Cluny, 'Some unworthy people have had the insolence to attack my character . . . conscious of my conduct I despise their low malice.'[21] And so he lost another long-faithful adherent.

There was nothing for it but to return to Liège, which was a cheaper place to live and there he resumed life very much as he had left it. He continued to treat Clementine cruelly, giving her as many as fifty beatings a day according to Elcho, a hostile witness prepared to see only the worst in his former idol. And out of jealousy he surrounded her bed with little bells so that no one else could come near. On the other hand he seems to have doted on his little Charlotte, whom he called 'Pouponne' and described as 'my only comfort in my misfortunes'.[22]

The couple lived miserable lives in a blurred world of alcoholism, but Clementine stayed on for the sake of her daughter, leading a life which was nearly as debauched as that of the Prince. She was humiliated by Charles, mocked by Europe and to the Jacobites remained a dangerous spy.

In England there were occasional flashes of support for the Cause, as at Oxford in 1754 when a great scandal blew up over an election which the Tories won, but their opponents staged a counterplot involving local Jacobites in this very Jacobite town. The government managed to unseat the victor, but in one of the ensuing plots a great furore arose when a grocer's wife in the city claimed to have found a set of verses in praise of Prince Charles hidden in a bundle of rags outside her husband's shop. The Oxford Rag Plot demonstrates the level to which the Cause had sunk by the mid-1750s.

And yet by 1756, when the Prince's prospects were at their lowest ebb, the tide turned again. The Seven Years War, which broke out between France and Britain and their allies, altered everything. And, for all his drunkenness, Charles set out immediately to turn the situation to his advantage.

He needed money, but had no one left to whom he could proffer his begging bowl, so he turned once again to Louis XV, the man against whom he had railed for a decade. At heart he loathed France more than ever, but he fought back his feelings and paid His Most Christian Majesty fulsome compliments, before pocketing his pride to admit that his sources of finance from loyal followers had dried up because of the war. There was still a spark of the old Charles Stuart in evidence when he told the King, 'I know not what destiny prepared for me, but I shall put it to the touch.'

He followed his request for money with a trip to Paris to lobby his old friend, the Duc de Richelieu, only to be told that France was too committed to her wars in India, Canada and on continental Europe for the moment to be ripe for an invasion of Britain,

Disappointed, he returned to Flanders, the bottle, Clementine, his Pouponne, and to a renewed incessant badgering from his father to mend his ways. It was a long dreary wait: two weary years, during which he never ceased to plague the French government to mount an expedition against Britain and to include him in it.

At last in 1759, with defeats in India and Canada and in Europe at the Battle of Minden behind them, the French realised that if they were to win this war they needed to cross the Channel and conquer the Hanoverians on British soil. And Charles Stuart could help them. Charles was suspicious of yet another French trick and took much persuading even to talk to Louis's Foreign Minister, the Duc de Choiseul, but in the end he agreed.

The plan was for a huge force of something like 100,000 men to invade England, using flat-bottomed boats, rather like the landing craft used in the D-Day landings during the Second World War, which would be difficult for the Royal Navy to intercept. This was no new idea – Dudley Bradstreet had told the Duke of Newcastle about it as long ago as 1747,[23] but there is no evidence that King George's minister took any notice. The British people were greatly alarmed by persistent threats of an invasion using flat-bottomed boats and in 1750 the actor David Garrick caught their mood when he wrote the words of the song 'Heart of Oak'. One verse went:

> They swear they'll invade us, these terrible foes;
> They frighten our women, our children and beaus;
> But, should their flat-bottoms in darkness get o'er,
> Still Britons they'll find to receive them on shore.

For all Garrick's brave words England was in panic as it waited for this strange, fearful fleet. When the real threat did come in 1759 there was alarm everywhere.

Oliver Macallester, who was hovering on the Channel coast in 1759 picking up all the information he could, found out about the plan and wrote to warn the government in London that the French were now gathering their men and the flat landing craft in preparation for an invasion involving the Jacobites but without the Prince.

To coincide with the English invasion there were to be landings in Scotland and Ireland. The French dearly wanted to exclude the Prince because they considered him unreliable and he remained sceptical of all things French. Charles could not bring himself to trust the French, even when one of his followers, probably Murray of Elibank, told him, 'I am perfectly convinced of the sincere intention of the King and ministers, and that nothing but the interposition of heaven can prevent your success.'[24] In the event they did manage to keep him away, although they did not stop him from preparing manifestos to be issued on landing in Britain, or from repeating his renunciation of his Roman Catholic religion which had been 'the ruin of the Royal Family'.

Thanks to the spy Oliver Macallester there were now plenty of rumours to alarm the London government.[25] Macallester had Charles in Paris at one point, living over a butcher's shop in the rue de la Boucherie, rarely leaving his house except to go to mass where he was recognised by one of Pouponne's former nurses. Then he was in Brest – where the troops were assembling – in disguise of course and O'Sullivan was there too, having been given a command in the French army. The only success the Jacobites had in this spy war was succeeding in having Macallester thrown into gaol at one point for calling Murray of Elibank a card-sharper. That must have been a pleasing little victory for those who were watching his prying into their affairs.

To the agents' delight old one-eyed Clancarty, drunk as usual, was going round the taverns in Dunkirk, 'bragging and lying, and showing the Prince's letters around. On the Scottish side Murray of Elibank dismissed the Prince's Irish followers scornfully – 'their bulls and stupidity one can forgive, but the villainy and falsity of their hearts is unpardonable.' The old Scots-Irish feud was happily reignited now that they had something new to argue about.

Andrew Lang suspects that Pickle was playing a double game during the preparations for the 1759 invasion, supplying information to London, yet watching to seize his chance if the French Admiral de Conflans managed to outmanoeuvre the British Navy, and escape from Brest to escort the invasion armada: 'If Conflans beat Hawke, and if Thurot [who had been appointed to invade Scotland] landed in the Western Highlands, then Pickle would have rallied to the old flag, *Tandem Triumphans*, and welcomed gloriously His Royal Highness the prince of Wales,' said Lang. 'Then the despised warrant of a peerage would have come forth, and Lord Glengarry, I conceive, would have hurried to seize the Duke of Newcastle's papers, which were of extreme personal interest to himself.' In other words he would not only have accepted the Jacobite peerage he had scorned previously, but would have destroyed all the incriminating evidence against him. Lang understood Young Glengarry's nature all too well.

The prying and day-dreaming spies and gossiping, card-playing followers knew more about what was happening on the French coast than Charles, who was privy to few details of the plan as late as the second half of October. Choiseul succeeded in keeping the Prince well out of the picture as his scheme matured and Charles became preoccupied with an argument with his father over whether James should abdicate and declare Charles king. James would have none of that, saying he would do so only when the family was restored. Endless arguments with both his father and the French wore Charles out.

The French planned to use two fleets to escort their great army, but one of these was severely mauled by the Royal Navy as it sailed from the Mediterranean to reinforce Conflans, whose ship lay trapped by the British under Admiral Sir Edward Hawke at Brest harbour. In November a Protestant wind for once blew favourably for the Jacobites' friends and Hawke's fleet was scattered, giving Conflans his chance to escape to join the troop transports.

On 25 November the British fleet reassembled and in spite of continuing storms, chased Conflans into Quiberon Bay where a fierce battle was fought until darkness forced both sides to break off. Morning revealed that half a dozen French ships had been wrecked, burned or captured, and the remnant of Conflans's fleet was racing for safety.

It was the end of this invasion, the greatest the French planned during the Jacobite century, and although no Jacobites were involved in it, Quiberon Bay was the last battle of the Cause. Hawke's victory left Charles Stuart worn out and no longer a man anyone looked up to, let alone the dashing Prince the world remembered. The strain of all the manoeuvring and arguing with the French left him physically and mentally ill, without love, without a home, without money, without hope – and soon he was to be without his mistress and daughter too.

At Bouillon, where he stayed on after Quiberon Bay, there was nothing left but to drink and argue and he and Clementine did plenty of both. Charlotte's education became a new battlefield when Clementine wanted to send the child to a convent in Paris to be educated while Charles insisted on keeping her with him.

If James thought this final defeat would persuade his son to abandon his mistress and return to Rome, he was mistaken. Now an old man and in declining health, he tried every argument to persuade his son to return to him, but Charles stayed on at Bouillon, hunting, drinking and quarrelling to excess with Clementine. It had long been crystal clear that he had no love for Walkinshaw, although he still adored his child, and would give up neither to please his father or his followers. He blamed Clementine for every slight, every wrong he suffered and continued to beat her until she feared for her life and decided she must escape. She remembered that the Pretender had suggested she might enter a convent and now contacted him through the devious Father Kelly. James was delighted to arrange for Clementine and Charlotte to enter 'one of the better convents in Paris'.

Towards the end of July, while Charles was away from Bouillon, Clementine secretly hired a coach and vanished, leaving behind a long rambling letter clearly written under great stress. It contained only one brief reference to their daughter and expressed no regret at taking his beloved Pouponne away from him. But at the end she did call him 'my dearest Prince'. Clementine told him she had lived for eight years with 'the dealy risque of loosing life', but could no longer bear the hardships that had affected her health, so she had been obliged 'to take this Desperate step of removing from your Royalle Highness with my child, which nothing but the fear of my life would ever have made me undertake . . . without your knowledge.' She continued, 'I put myself under the care of providence, which I hope wont abbandone me as my intentions are honest and that I never will doe a dirty action for the wholle world, I quite my dearest prince with the greatest regreat and shall allways be miserable if I don't hear of his welfair and happiness,' and she hoped for his future friendship for herself and her child. 'May God Almighty bless and preserve him and prospere all his undertakings which is the ernest wish of one how will be till Death, my dearest prince,' she ended.

She knew how furiously Charles would react, so in order to protect their staff at Bouillon she assured him than none of them – in fact no person he knew – had helped her. In view of Kelly's role that was not quite true, but Clementine felt she must do what she could to protect all those around the royal household.[26]

She was right: Charles did react with white-hot anger, and sulked and raged by turns at Bouillon, refusing to see anyone. He sent his valet, John Stewart, with a letter to the Jesuit Abbé John Gordon, head of the Scots College in Paris, threatening to burn down every convent in the city to find his daughter if he had to. He was too upset to write the letter himself, but added a postscript in his own hand: 'I take this affaire so much to heart that I was not able to write what is here above. Shall be in ye greatest affliction untill I greet back ye childe, which was my only comfort in my misforunes.'[27]

Not a word about his mistress: he only missed his Pouponne.

Abbé Gordon had seen the mother and daughter, found them a temporary place to live and had given her a heavy fatherly talk about her duty to return with the child, but he assured Charles he had given Clementine no money. She had asked for some, he told the Prince, but 'by the greatest good luck I had none in my pocket'. He refused to find them a permanent home in a convent on the grounds that he did not have 'the father's authorisation'.[28] That was nonsense: Charles may have been the child's father, but he was not the husband of Clementine and had never acknowledged either mother and child as his wife and daughter. He had no more right than Clementine to say where the child should go.

Clementine wisely realised that Gordon was not only mean and hectoring towards her, but would betray her as well – which he did, by writing to Charles the very same day. When he went to her lodgings the following morning she had gone.

Using Gordon as his intermediary, Charles sought the help of the Paris police and the War Minister, the Comte de Belle-Isle, but the minister was far too busy waging his conflict with Britain and her allies to break off to search for a mistress, however badly Charles Stuart wanted her back. Charles also issued a description of the mother and daughter, which provides a good idea of their appearance at the time, although it does seem odd that Charles did not know his child's exact age: 'The mother is about 40 years of age, fair, of normal height, freckled, her face thin. The child, aged 7 or 8, very fair, with round, full face, large eyes, a rather snub nose, plump and strong for her age. They took the road to Paris, but it is believed they may have gone on to Flanders.'

Stewart, Charles's valet, was sent to join the hunt and succeeded in finding her so quickly that one wonders if he was in on the escape from the first. Clementine told him she would kill herself and the child rather than return, so he allowed her to send for a coach in which he might accompany her on a journey to an unspecified destination. They drove for a while, but suddenly the coach stopped alongside another carriage and two men appeared. Clementine and Charlotte moved to the second vehicle and when Stewart tried to join them he was told, 'Go about your business if you have any.' With that they drove off, leaving the valet to return to his master to explain what had happened. The whole episode has a false, theatrical ring to it and again the suspicion is that Stewart understood the pressure Clementine was under and connived at the flight.

Charles refused to give up the search and drew up lists of every Jacobite follower he could think of who might be able to help. Even O'Sullivan was tracked down. Perhaps the Prince thought she might have returned to him, but O'Sullivan assured his former master she had not. Lord Elcho was asked but replied off-handedly: 'Why bother about the woman, take another.' The police could not help, even with posters displayed everywhere, so the search widened to Flanders, Nice and even Venice, still without success. And as the French police and government lost interest, Charles raged more, accusing everyone from Belle-Isle to Stewart, the valet, of apathy and incompetence.

Then Clementine reappeared as suddenly as she had vanished and it transpired she had never left Paris. After she abandoned Stewart on the road that night she had gone to the Convent of the Visitation de Sainte Marie in the rue du Bac. And there she was living, safely under the protection of Charles's father.

Prince Charlie now learned that James had worked to organise the flight for months before Clementine and Charlotte left, and the French government had been informed. King Louis had done nothing because Clementine had left on the orders of James and the reigning Stuart monarch's wish was supreme. On learning of this betrayal by his father and the French King, the Prince collapsed with a total physical and mental breakdown. He could not sleep or eat and even moderated his drinking for a while. Week after week he sat brooding at Bouillon, refusing to see any but his closest associates and answering no letters.

What hurt was not the loss of his mistress, but the humiliation of the manner in which she had left. He did care about his daughter, however, and would have given anything to have her back. Charlotte, his darling Pouponne, had gone, but unlike his Cause, she was not lost for ever.

Epilogue

> The Duchesse d'Aiguillon used to wear a miniature of Prince Charles in a bracelet. On the reverse was a head of Our Lord. People did not understand the connection, so Madame de Rochefort said, 'The same motto serves for both: My kingdom is not of this world.'
>
> Horace Walpole's comment on the Duchesse d'Aiguillon, a close friend of the Prince.[1]

At a quarter past nine on the evening of New Year's Day 1766 James Francis Edward Stuart, King James *de jure* III of England and VIII of Scotland, died peacefully at the Muti Palace in Rome, 'his usual mild serenity in his countenance'. On his deathbed the old king was surrounded by his household and officials of the Vatican, but neither of his sons was present. Henry could not bear to watch his father die, so waited in an adjoining room, and Charles, having decided at last to return to Rome after thirty-three years' absence, arrived too late.

It was the end of January before Charles reached Rome only to find no royal escort, no Church dignitaries, no Papal representative to greet him at the Porta del Popolo – just one well-padded and smug cardinal, brother Henry, and a small crowd the Cardinal of York had organised to raise a thin cheer. The Pope refused to address him as king or receive him, and had the royal arms removed from above the door of the Muti Palace under cover of darkness.

Charles wrote off to inform the kings of France and Spain and the princes of Italy of his accession, but all ignored him. Only in his own little palace was he saluted as King Charles III: elsewhere he was just old Mr Misfortune's son. If Europe and the Vatican would not recognise his royal status, Charles decided he would be known simply as John Douglas, an excellent face-saving compromise.

Although death had reduced the number of followers by now, there were some such as the Rectors of the English, Scots and Irish Colleges in Rome, prepared to kneel at his feet and address him as 'Your Majesty'. For their pains they were banished from the city. Charles retaliated by refusing to call on the Pope and shunning cardinals and Roman society.

Eventually, after nearly a year and a half, he was received in papal audience. The British had been lobbying with remarkable success all over Europe for the new King to be ignored, and the papal authorities knew that London would be very angry about the audience. They therefore instructed Cardinal Albani, a man suspected of indulging in a little espionage himself, to advise Mann of the proposal in advance. Mann reacted exactly as expected, so the Pope caved in and received Charles in secret and 'in plain dress and without ceremony'. He was kept cooling his heels in an ante-room while his brother, in accordance with his right as a cardinal, was shown into His Holiness's presence. When summoned eventually it was as 'brother of Cardinal York' and he was left to stand for the entire fifteen minutes of the interview.

Henry failed to notice the slight and was ecstatic that his brother now had not only returned to the true Church, but had been received by the Pope. 'God be praised,' he exulted, 'last Saturday evening after a good deal of Battleying upon very trifling circumstances, I carried my brother to the Pope's privately, as a private nobleman, by which means he certainly had derogated nothing of his just pretensions, and has at the same time fulfilled an indispensable duty owing to the Head of the Church.'[2]

Charles could not have given a damn about duty to the Head of the Church. The benefit for him was enormous, since it enabled him to emerge into Roman society and attend as many balls, concerts and plays as he wished. That, and hunting and shooting expeditions in the Albano hills such as he had enjoyed as a boy, filled his time.

Mann the diplomat had set the British government's imprint on the papal audience and now Mann the intelligence agent began work. He was pleased to inform the Hanoverians that the Pretender was still drinking and continued to fly into those unpredictable drunken rages which had been common gossip for so many years. And he could be just as unpleasant to his loyal staff as he was to others he thought had slighted him: 'Last week he committed some great outrage against some of his own people, in a drunken fit, by drawing his sword and pursuing them, so that they narrowly escaped being killed,' Mann told the Duke of Newcastle.[3]

In the Jacobite world in which Charles now passed his tragic and lonely life, there was little of his past glory. The world had moved on, but in Britain the government had been frightened by the spectre of Jacobitism for so many years that it could not really believe the Cause was dead – certainly as long as Charles Stuart lived. There was no longer a need for serious spying from Italy, however: a few gossipy reports from Mann to raise a smile in London were sufficient.

In the Scottish Highlands the new order imposed after Culloden had already changed people's lives. Chiefs had been turned into grasping landlords and many ordinary clansmen and women – good people like Flora MacDonald and her husband – were forced to find new lives in the colonies. Many clansmen joined the ranks of the British Army, the army they had fought against at Prestonpans, Falkirk and Culloden.

In the prosperous Lowlands the only real memory of the '45 and Prince Charlie's visit lay in the songs of Lady Nairne and Robert Burns, and in the Royal Oak Club, which met in Edinburgh on the first Monday of each month. There they talked a lot and drank many toasts, but there was no will to fight for Charlie.

Ireland too was sullenly silent for the present, but the island continued to simmer and was to explode before the century was out. However, like their Highland counterparts, at this time many Irishmen joined the British Army.

In England and Wales the movement continued to be used occasionally by rioting dissidents, and glasses were raised to drink the health of the King over the Water. The government monitored this closet Jacobitism closely, especially among the many clubs that flourished during the second half of the eighteenth century.[4]

In clubs such as the Cycle of the White Rose in North Wales, The Gloucestershire Society and the Oyster and Parched Pea Club in Preston, they talked a little treason coupled to empty toasts. The Oyster and Parched Pea Club may well have begun as a political organisation since no visitors were allowed in until 1784; though exclusively Tory, it had little serious political interest, however, and it continued to flourish long after the Cause was dead and gone. Other clubs became less political too, but the government kept a close watch on their activities. The Knights of St Francis of Wycombe became notorious and were suspected of being subversive, but members' notoriety did not lie in their Jacobitism. The government was wasting its time when it recruited that strange creature, the Chevalier d'Eon de Beaumont, to spy on the Jacobite activities of the Knights and other secret societies. Eon had been in French service in Russia and London, but fell out with his masters in Paris and was recruited by the British. He was one of the last spies to be recruited to hunt down Jacobite sympathisers, but he proved of little value in the dying world of Jacobitism.

By the time Prince Charlie was settled into the Muti Palace as King Charles III, most of his loyal followers were gone; so too were his enemies, and many of the agents who had spied on him all over Britain in the '45 and in Europe after that. Of his faithful core during the '45 rising none remained – Lochiel had survived only two years after Culloden before he died of brain-fever in exile in France. His brother, Archie Cameron, was executed as a result of Pickle's betrayal of the Elibank Plot, and Macpherson of Cluny died in exile after spending nine years in hiding in the cage on Ben Alder. All the others – Clanranald, Lochgarry and Lord John Drummond among them – made new lives for themselves in Europe, mainly in military service of a foreign king, but had little contact with Prince Charlie thereafter.

Lord Elcho spent his life after 1746 dunning Charles for the return of money the Prince had borrowed, but that was a hopeless mission since Charles Stuart never had enough to meet his own needs. The two were on such bad terms that once, when the Prince was on a visit to Paris, Elcho refused to call on him as courtesy demanded. When other Jacobites prevailed on him, he agreed at last, but when his name was sent up, Charles refused to see him because Elcho had written to London asking for a pardon, so was no partisan of the Cause. Elcho died in 1787.

Alongside all other adherents, Lord George Murray, the best general Prince Charlie had ever had, stands out nobly in poverty as he faced a lonely old age. Charles never had a good word to say about his Lieutenant-General and vindictively tried to hunt him down, but Murray accepted that philosophically. He said at the start of the '45 that he was prepared to risk everything for the Prince, and he did. He died with dignity in Holland, still loyal to the Cause, in 1760.

As for the other Murray – John Murray of Broughton – he has never been forgiven for 'talking' to his captors when he was taken in 1746. Rejected by every Jacobite, Mr 'Evidence' Murray led a troubled life throughout his remaining years. His wife abandoned him and once he foolishly picked a quarrel with Lord Traquair, who had him arrested for creating a breach of the peace. According to an account of his subsequent life sent to the Pretender's secretary in Rome, Broughton was in dire poverty by 1749 and was acting with 'not only the apprearance of a knave, but a madman'.[5] His home estate of Broughton was sold in 1764 and Murray was said to have lived in London thereafter and to have died in a madhouse on 6 December 1777. How much truth there is in all that, or in a tale that he visited Rome to present his son to King Charles III, is anyone's guess, but he certainly remained sane enough to write his *Memorials*, giving his side of the story. Whatever may be said against Broughton, he always remained loyal to the Jacobite Cause.

Like his friend Lord Elcho, Earl Marischal never had a good word to say for the Prince – or of Charles's brother for that matter. In his cups at Dunkirk one night while drinking with those two traitors, Clancarty and Oliver Macallester, he described Prince Henry as 'a Petit Maître' who tried to command everyone in matters of which he knew nothing. He called Charles a scoundrel and 'a coward and a poltroon' at heart. Although the Earl became governor of Neuchatel while Charles and Clementine were living in Switzerland, he would not see them. He was appointed Frederick's envoy to Paris and then to Madrid in 1759 and returned to Scotland after being given a pardon by George II, but disliked his home country so much he went back to Prussia and Frederick the Great. At his death in 1770, Frederick eulogised him as the only true friend he ever had. Neither Prince Charlie nor any follower of the Cause could say that of him.[6]

Of the Irish contingent, old Tom Sheridan was so worn out by rough living in the Highlands during the Prince's flight after Culloden that he did not live to see Charles after his return. O'Sullivan had a mysterious later career and was sacked by the Prince, possibly because of his connection with Clementine, and died around 1761.

As for the men Prince Charlie fought against in the '45, Cope, Hawley and Cumberland were all dead. Cumberland won only one battle,

Culloden, but that was enough to gain him immortality of a different kind from Charles Edward. He remains the 'Butcher' to this day.

Charles outlived the spies too. Stosch died in 1757, gossiping rather than spying to the last, and Mann lived on until 1786. But Pickle, the 'mole' who was never caught, disappeared from the espionage scene during the 1750s, shortly after Charles presented him with a gold snuff box – a memento of the man he had betrayed. He succeeded to the title of chief on his father's death in 1754, and thereafter was of little use to the Hanoverian government. He had lost his chief patron, Henry Pelham, in 1754, and it is a sad reflection on spies' paymasters that when he sent his last letter to the Duke of Newcastle in 1760 he had to remind him of who he was. The letter began: 'My Lord, As I am confident your Grace will be at a loss to find out your present Correspondent, it will, I believe, suffice to recall to mind Pickle, how [who] some time ago had a conference with the young Gentilman whom honest old Vaughan brought once to Clermont to waite of y^{r} Grace.'[7] Pickle was still unable to spell who! He had certain information to pass on, but could not commit it to paper, although it is perfectly clear he meant a new invasion in the Highlands. He offered to raise a regiment, provided he was given a commission as its colonel. Nothing came of the planned attack or of Pickle's offer to recruit for the government, which was the last that was heard of Pickle the Spy. He died among his clansmen on 23 December 1761.

Of Dudley Bradstreet, the most charismatic and successful of all spies of the Jacobite century, a lot and yet little is known. After successfully deceiving the Prince's Council at Derby over the phantom army that was blocking its way to London, he spent much time trying to obtain his well-deserved reward from the government. He had other ideas too and actually wrote in August 1747 to tell the government of the French plan to invade England 'without help of a ship, by a French army as numerous as she pleased and cannot with any avail be resisted with all the ships of War of England'. This was the plan to use flat-bottomed craft rather than naval transports, and he admitted it sounded 'as silly and ridiculous . . . as Christopher Columbus was thought of when going to search for the New World'.[8] He revealed nothing more of the scheme in his letter, and did not tell us whether the government listened to him or rewarded him for the information.

Bradstreet wrote the *Story of his Life and Uncommon Adventures* in 1755, of which 'all copies were sold except half a dozen which the publisher was desired to keep for subscribers' – a happy position for any author to find himself in. Nothing is known of the Captain's ultimate fate, but with his nose for spying and his ability to manipulate men and seduce women, it may be fairly assumed that the remainder of his life was adventurous.

Macallester, too, wrote his memoirs, which were published as a series of letters in 1767. These told a very anti-Stuart story of the Prince's life and the '45, and did no credit to the sneaking little spy, who spent his life forever tagging along at the lowest end of the Jacobite tail to eavesdrop and pass everything he learned back to London. Spies did not come much lower than Macallester.

While friends and enemies from his former life went their own way, Charles still hoped that if he could not have a kingdom he could at least have an heir and with that in mind he made a disastrous marriage. His bride, Louise of Stolberg, eloped with an Italian poet, leaving him a cuckolded, drunken old man. Ever unfathomable, he then wrote to the convent at Meaux where Clementine and Charlotte were living, offering, in return for Charlotte's company, to acknowledge her as his own daughter. He would treat her with every kindness, he told his former mistress, and would create her Duchess of Albany. She would also be heir to all that he possessed.

Charlotte was brought to him and Charles at once took on the mantle of the doting father. He gave balls in her honour, at which she wore the family jewels over magnificent dresses, and on St Andrew's Day he invested her with the Order of St Andrew.

In 1786, when Charles was sixty-five, he had a recurrence of a previous illness when his limbs became swollen and he had bouts of nausea, breathing difficulty and alarming heart attacks. He spent the summer recovering at Albano, and from there Mann collected the last pieces of gossip he was ever to pass on to London. Charles was indulging in 'the folly practised by his father and grandfather to touch people who are affected with scrofulous disorders. Many old men and women have been presented to him for the purpose, to whom, after the ceremony, he gives a small silver medal, which they wear about their necks.'[9]

In November, soon after Charles returned to Rome, Mann, the British envoy in Florence died. Without followers to badger him or agents digging into every detail of his life, Charles lived on, comforted by his beloved Charlotte. She became ill herself, yet continued to nurse him until a stroke struck him down on 7 January 1788, a week after his sixty-seventh birthday. Other attacks followed and on 31 January he died.

Even in death spies had the last word: Lord Hervey, who had succeeded Mann at Florence, reported home simply, 'This morning, between the hours of nine and ten, the Pretender departed this life.' However, an extra claim was added that Charles had actually died on the evening of 30 January, but his staff had not announced it then because that was the anniversary of the execution of King Charles I. Cardinal York's diary might have confirmed this, but the pages relating to this period have been torn out.

To the end, as Henry Stuart proclaimed himself King Henry IX, king of nowhere, the spies, gossips, rumour-mongers and rogues had the last word on the Stuart line.

Notes

AEMD — Archives Etrangères, Mémoires et Documents Angleterre, French Foreign Ministry Archives, Paris.
AN — Archives Nationales, Paris
Arsenal — Archives de la Bastille, Musée de l'Arsenal, Paris
BL — British Library
NLS — National Library of Scotland
PRO — Public Record Office, Kew
RA CP — Cumberland Papers in Royal Archives
RA SP — Stuart Papers in Royal Archives, Windsor Castle
SRO — Scottish Record Office, Edinburgh

1. A Cause to Spy For

1. Sir Charles Petrie, *The Jacobite Movement*, p. 77.
2. Bernard Newman, *Spy and Counter-Spy*, p. 53.
3. G.M. Trevelyan, *History of England*, (3rd edn, London, 1948) p. 473.
4. John Macky, *Memoirs of the Secret Services of John Macky, Esq. During the Reigns of King William, Queen Anne, and King George I. Printed in London in 1733* (Roxburghe Club, 1895), p. 8.
5. Ibid., pp. 12–13.
6. Ibid., p. 12.
7. Paul Kléber Monod, *Jacobitism and the English People, 1688–1788*, p. 155. See also William C. Braithwaite, *The Second Period of Quakerism* (London, 1919), pp. 151–2. Bryan Bevan, *Marlborough the Man*, p. 131 (his source is correspondence of George Clarke, Secretary at War, 1690–2. MS 749/1–13, Trinity College, Dublin).
8. Peggy Miller, *James*, p. 42.
9. Matthew Prior to Lord Portland, July 1698, quoted in Charles Kenneth Eves, *Matthew Prior: Poet and Diplomatist*, p. 115.
10. Paul Hopkins, *Sham Plots and Real Plots in the 1690s*, in Eveline Cruickshanks (ed.), *Ideology and Conspiracy: Aspects of Jacobitism, 1689–1759*, p. 92.
11. Edward Dicconson, *Life of James II, Collected out of Memoirs Writ in his own Hand*, ed. James Stanier Clarke (2 vols, London, 1816).
12. Ibid, quoted in Winston S. Churchill, *Marlborough: his Life and Times*, vol. i, pp. 369–71.
13. Frank McLynn, *The Jacobites*, p. 172.
14. W.S. Churchill, *Marlborough*, vol. i, p. 376.
15. Ibid., p. 366.
16. E. Cruickshanks (ed.), *Ideology and Conspiracy*, p. 92.
17. Magnus Linklater writing in *The Times*, 8 April 1999.
18. W.S. Churchill, *Marlborough*, vol. iii, p. 359.
19. George Lockhart of Carnwath, Lockhart Papers, vol. i, pp. 148 and 227.
20. Ibid.
21. Nathaniel Hooke, *Secret History of Colonel Hooke's Negociations in Scotland in 1707*, pp. 1–3.
22. C. Petrie, *The Jacobite Movement*, p. 170.

23. Duke of Berwick, *Mémoires*, vol. ii, p. 144.

2. In the Jacobite World and Underworld

1. Quoted as a chapter heading in W.A. Speck, *The Butcher*, p. 78.
2. C.K. Eves, *Matthew Prior: Poet and Diplomatist*, p. 347.
3. Sir Douglas Harkness, *Bolingbroke, The Man and his Career*, p. 134.
4. James Macknight, *Life of Bolingbroke*, p. 494.
5. Bruce Lenman, *The Jacobite Clans of the Great Glen: 1650–1784*, p. 132.
6. P.K. Monod, *Jacobitism and the English People, 1688–1788*, p. 100.
7. John Latimer, *Annals of Bristol in the Eighteenth Century* (Frome, 1893), pp. 107–8.
8. Ibid., p. 113.
9. L.T. Weaver, *The Harwich Story* (Harwich, 1975), p. 80.
10. F. McLynn, *The Jacobites*, p. 79.
11. G.H. Jones, *The Main Stream of Jacobitism*, p. 245.
12. *Culloden Papers*, p. 253.
13. Ibid., p. 426.

3. Secrets of the 'Secret Man'

1. P.S. Fritz, *English Ministers and Jacobitism between the Rebellions of 1715 and 1745*, pp. 123–4.
2. Lord Elcho, *Short Account of the Affairs of Scotland*, p. 29.
3. Dorothy Mackay Quynn, 'Philip von Stosch: Collector, Bibliophile, Spy, Thief', *Catholic Historical Review*, vol. xxvii (1941), 332.
4. Ibid., p. 339.
5. Basil Williams gives a concise picture of how foreign policy worked in the time of the first two Georges in *Blackwood's Magazine*, vol. clxxi (January, 1907), pp. 92–105.
6. Ibid., p. 99.
7. B. Newman, *Spy and Counter Spy*, p. 68.
8. Ibid., p. 68.
9. *Dictionary of National Biography*, vol. xx (1973 edition), p. 600.
10. B. Newman, *Spy and Counter Spy*, pp. 102–3.
11. Ibid., p.68.
12. Jonathan Swift, *Gulliver's Travels* (London, Random House Modern Library edition, 1958), pp. 153–4.
13. Kenneth Ellis, *The Post Office in the Eighteenth Century* (London, 1958), pp. 61–2.
14. Eveline Cruickshanks gives background to François de Bussy in *Political Untouchables*, pp. 57–60.
15. B. Williams, *Blackwood's Magazine*, vol. clxxxi (January, 1907), pp. 92–105.
16. AEMD, Paris vol. 76, f.79, quoted in P.S. Fritz, *English Ministers and Jacobitism between the Rebellions of 1715 and 1745*, pp. 123–4.
17. E. Cruickshanks, *Political Untouchables*, p. 21.
18. Romney Sedgwick (ed.), *The House of Commons 1715–1754*, vol. i, (London, 1970), pp. 68–9.

4. Travellers and Fellow Travellers

1. Mary Waugh, *Smuggling in Kent and Sussex 1700–1840*, p. 16.
2. *Memoirs of Thomas, Earl of Ailesbury, Written by Himself*, ed. W.E. Buckley, vol. i (London, 1890), pp. 316–9. I am indebted to P.K. Monod for this reference.
3. Ibid., vol. ii, p. 397.
4. Jeremy Black, *The British and the Grand Tour* (London, 1985), p. 2.
5. Lord Waldegrave to George Tilson, Under-Secretary at the Northern Department, 15 August, 1732, PRO 78/201.
6. J. Black, *British and the Grand Tour*, p. 22.
7. *The Craftsman*, 6 July 1728, quoted in J. Black, *British and the Grand Tour*, p. 170.
8. HMC Stuart Mss. vol. V, p. 239, quoted in C. Petrie, *The Jacobite Movement*, p. 286–7.
9. H. Douglas, *Charles Edward Stuart; The Man, the King, the Legend*, p. 28.

10. F. McLynn, *The Jacobites*, p. 174.
11. J.C. O'Callaghan, *History of the Irish Brigade* (Glasgow, 1870), p. 340, quoted by F. McLynn, *Charles Edward Stuart*, p. 73.
12. Andrew Lang, *Companions of Pickle*, p. 71.
13. Ibid., p. 72.
14. F. McLynn, *Charles Edward Stuart*, p. 80.
15. Ibid., p. 81.
16. Padre Giulio Cesare Cordara, *Commentary on the Expedition to Scotland*, Scottish History Society, third series, vol. ix (1926).
17. H. Walpole, *Correspondence*, vol. xi, p. 373
18. Sir Fitzroy Maclean, *Bonnie Prince Charlie*, p. 25.
19. H. Walpole, *Correspondence*, vol. xviii, pp. 373–9.
20. Ibid., pp. 378–9 and 396.
21. Custom House Library, Collier Mss, 613, quoted by C. Winslow in 'Sussex Smugglers', essay in Douglas Hay et al, *Albion's Fatal Tree: Crime and Society in Eighteenth-Century England* (London, 1976), pp. 156–7.
22. Ibid.
23. See E. Cruickshanks, *Ideology and Conspiracy*, p. 83.
24. Charles to Marshal Saxe, 11 March 1744, RA SP 256/121.
25. Jon Manchip White, *Marshal of France; Life and Times of Maurice de Saxe*, (London, 1962), p. 88.
26. Charles to Lord Sempill, 15 March 1744, RA SP 256/131.

5. With Such Friends, Who Needs Enemies

1. RA SP 265/294.
2. Frank McLynn gives a full account of the machinations of Louis and his ministers in *France and the Jacobite Rising of 1745*, chapter 2, pp. 35–74.
3. RA SP 256/121/124/125. I am grateful to F. McLynn for these references.
4. Charles to James, 28 February 1745, RA SP 263/24.
5. Ibid.
6. RA SP 258/13.31 258/122.
7. Oliver Macallester, *A series of Letters discovering the Scheme projected by France in MDCCLIX, etc*, p. 109.
8. A. Lang, *Pickle the Spy*, p. 31.
9. Murray of Broughton, *Memorials*, p. 90.
10. Ibid., p. 428, and Lord Elcho, *Short Account of the Affairs of Scotland*, p. 234.
11. Murray of Broughton to Charles Edward, 21 September 1744, quoted in H. Tayler, *Jacobite Epilogue*, pp. 204–5.
12. F. McLynn, *Charles Edward Stuart*, p. 112, quoting RA SP 1/199.
13. A. Lang, *Pickle the Spy*, p. 188.
14. Lord Elcho, *Short Account of the Affairs of Scotland*, pp. 235.
15. Ibid. p. 69.
16. A. Lang, *Companions of Pickle*, p. 71.
17. F. McLynn, *Charles Edward Stuart*, p. 112.
18. RA SP 261/109, quoted in Mahon, *Decline of the Last Stuarts*, vol. iii, p. x.
19. F. Maclean, *Bonnie Prince Charlie*, p. 31.
20. RA SP 263/18, 263/132. I am grateful to Frank McLynn for these references.
21. James Browne, *History of the Highlands and of the Highland Clans*, vol. iii, p. 430.
22. See F. McLynn, *France and the Jacobite Rising of 1745*, pp. 32–4.
23. Charles to Murray of Broughton, April 1745, RA SP 265/72.
24. J. Browne, *History of the Highlands and of the Highland Clans*, vol. iii, p. 429.
25. Charles to Louis XV, 12 June 1745, quoted in L. Dumont-Wilden, *The Wandering Prince*, pp. 49–50.
26. F. de Marville, *Lettres de Monsieur de Marville. Lieutenant-Général de Police au Ministre Comte de Maurepas*, ed. A. de Boislisle (Paris, 1896), vol. ii, p. 113.
27. Lockhart Papers, vol. ii, p. 400.

6. Prince Regent of Scotland

1. A. Lang, *Companions of Pickle*, p. 74.
2. W.B. Blaikie, 'The Landing of Prince Charles, 1745', *Scottish Historical Review*, vol III, 91 (April, 1926), 165–70.
3. A. Lang, *Pickle the Spy*, pp. 102–3.
4. Marquis of Tweeddale to Lord Advocate Duncan Forbes, 27 July 1745. Lord Elcho, *Short Account of the Affairs of Scotland*, p. 235, note 2.
5. John S. Gibson, *Lochiel of the '45*, p. 58.
6. Murray of Broughton, *Memorials*, p. 108.
7. Tweeddale to Lord Milton, 30 July 1745, NLS 3733/8.
8. Duke of Newcastle to Duke of Argyll, 1 August 1745, NLS 3733/2.
9. Sir James Fergusson describes Lord Milton's fairly leisurely journey from Edinburgh in *Argyll in the Forty-Five*, pp. 15–16.
10. W.B. Blaikie, *Itinerary of Prince Charles Edward Stuart*, p. 83.
11. Ibid.
12. John Home, *History of the Rebellion in Scotland*, p. 281.
13. Ibid.
14. RA SP 266/174, in Mahon, *Decline of the Last Stuarts*, vol. iii, p. xxiii.
15. C. de B. Murray, *Forbes of Culloden* (London, 1936), p. 183.
16. Archibald Campbell of Stonefield to Duke of Argyll, 13 August 1745, NLS 3733/4.
17. W.B. Blaikie, *Itinerary of Prince Charles Edward Stuart*, pp. 113–14.
18. Moray MacLaren, *Bonnie Prince Charlie* (London, 1972), p. 57.
19. F. Maclean, *Bonnie Prince Charlie*, p. 53.
20. Ibid., pp. 53–4.
21. Newcastle to Argyll, 21 August 1745, NLS 3733/6.
22. *Albemarle Papers*, vol. i, p. 212. Sir Bruce Gordon Seton and Jean G. Arnot, *Prisoners of the Forty-Five*, vol. iii, p. 65.
23. C. Petrie, *Jacobite Movement*, p. 257.
24. A. Lang, *Companions of Pickle*, p. 69.
25. F. McLynn, *Charles Edward Stuart*, p. 158.
26. Sir John Cope to Marquis of Tweeddale, 8 August 1745, quoted in F. Maclean, *Bonnie Prince Charlie*, p. 55.
27. Woodhouselee MS, pp. 24–9.

7. In London for Christmas – One

1. F. Maclean, *Bonnie Prince Charlie*, p. 94.
2. J. Home, *History of the Rebellion in Scotland*, p. 71.
3. Stuart Reid, *Like Hungry Wolves* (London, 1994), p. 19.
4. Margaret Forster, *The Rash Adventurer*, p. 112.
5. J. Home, *History of the Rebellion in Scotland in the Year 1745*, Appendix xviii. W.B. Blaikie, *Itinerary of Prince Charles Edward Stuart*, p. 18.
6. RA SP 11/88.
7. K. Tomasson & F. Buist, *Battles of the '45*, p. 80.
8. Rupert C. Jarvis, *Collected Papers on the Jacobite Risings*, pp. 39–40.
9. Ibid., p. 43.
10. F. McLynn, *The Jacobite Army in England*, p. 39. See also G.C. Mounsey, *Carlisle in the '45* (London and Carlisle, 1817), and H. Whitehead, *Brampton in the '45*, Carlisle Scientific Association Transactions, vol. 12 (1886–7).
11. R.C. Jarvis, *Collected Papers of the Jacobite Risings*, p. 86.
12. Murray of Broughton, *Memorials*, p. 138.
13. F. McLynn, *The Jacobite Army in England*, p. 67.
14. Beppy Byrom, *Bonnie Prince Charlie in Manchester. An Eye-Witness Account*, p. 29.
15. Ibid., p. 44.
16. Ibid., p. 44.
17. Ibid., p. 41.
18. Frank McLynn has compiled the story of Vere's capture and subsequent events from Lord Elcho's *Short Account* and

documents in the Public Record Office and British Library. It is related in his *Jacobite Army in England*, p. 114.

19. R. Simpson, *History and Antiquities of Derby*, vol i (Derby, 1826), p. 253.
20. R.C. Jarvis, *Collected Papers of the Jacobite Risings*, pp. ix–xii.
21. D. Bradstreet, *The Life and Uncommon Adventures of Captain Dudley Bradstreet*, p. 52.
22. Ibid., p. 106.
23. Ibid., p. 108.
24. Ibid., p. 116.
25. Ibid., p. 120.
26. Ibid., p. 121.
27. Ibid., pp. 122–3.
28. Ibid., pp. 125–7.
29. Lord George Murray, quoted in K. Tomasson and F. Buist, *Battles of the '45*, p. 91.
30. F. McLynn, *The Jacobite Army in England*, 127–8.
31. K. Tomasson, *Jacobite General*, pp. 110–14.
32. D. Bradstreet, *The Life and Uncommon Adventures of Captain Dudley Bradstreet*, p. 127.
33. K. Tomasson, *Jacobite General*, p. 114.
34. D. Bradstreet, *The Life and Uncommon Adventures of Captain Dudley Bradstreet*, p. 127.
35. Ibid., pp. 129–30

8. In London for Christmas – Two

1. D. Bradstreet, *The Life and Uncommon Adventures of Captain Dudley Bradstreet*, p. 131.
2. Ibid., p. 130.
3. Ibid., p. 134.
4. Ibid., p. 163. Captain Bradstreet to George II, 24 February 1746. BL Add. Mss. 32706, f.209.
5. John Stuart Atholl, 7th Duke of Atholl, *The Chronicles of the Families of Atholl and Tullibardine*, quoted in F. McLynn, *Jacobite Army in England*, p. 159.
6. M. Forster, *The Rash Adventurer*, p. 145.
7. NLS MS 17526 ff. 33/34.
8. O. Macallester, *Series of Letters*, vol. i, pp. 19–20.
9. A. Lang, *Pickle the Spy*, pp. 32–3.
10. F. McLynn, *France and the Jacobite Rising of 1745*, p. 87.
11 AEMD 82ff.166–70. 82f.173. AECP 420, f365/386/387/399/423. I am indebted to Frank McLynn for these references.
12. F. McLynn, *France and the Jacobite Rising of 1745*, p. 144.
13. Lord George Murray to Charles, 6 January 1746, quoted in W.B. Blaikie, *Itinerary of Prince Charles Edward Stuart*, pp. 73–4.
14. Charles to Lord George Murray, n.d., quoted in W.B. Blaikie, *Itinerary of Prince Charles Edward Stuart*, pp. 74–5.
15. Lord George Murray to Charles, 29 January 1746, quoted in W.B. Blaikie, *Itinerary of Prince Charles Edward Stuart*, pp. 75–6.
16. Lord Elcho, *Short Account of the Affairs of Scotland*, p. 436.
17. R. Forbes, *Lyon in Mourning*, vol. ii, p. 246.
18. A. and H. Tayler, *1745 and After*, O'Sullivan's narrative, p. 130.
19. Grant R. Francis, *Romance of the White Rose* (London, 1933), p. 5.
20. RA SP 273/96.
21. R. Forbes, *Lyon in Mourning*, vol. i, pp. 85–8.

9. The Very Last Battle

1. J.S. Gibson, *Ships of the Forty-Five*, p. 39.
2. J. Prebble, *Culloden* (London, 1961), p. 126.
3. R. Forbes, *Lyon in Mourning*, vol i, p. 190.
4. Lord Elcho, *A Short Account of the Affairs in Scotland*, p. 436.
5. K. Tomasson and F. Buist, *Battles of the '45*, p. 200.
6. H. Walpole, *Correspondence*, vol. iii, p. 288.
7. *A Journey Through Part of England and Scotland Along with the Army, etc . . . by a Volunteer* (London, 1747), pp. 109, 179.
8. Allan I. Macinnes, *Clanship,*

Commerce and the House of Stuart, 1603–1788, p. 211.
9. W.C. Mackenzie, *Lovat of the '45*, pp. 330–1.
10. Winifred Duke, *Lord George Murray and the Forty-Five*, pp. 190–1.
11. *Mémoires de la Vie du Lord Lovat* (1747), p. 102.
12. H. Douglas, *Charles Edward Stuart*, p. 165.
13. See F. McLynn, *Bonnie Prince Charlie*, pp. 262–4.
14. A. and H. Tayler, *1745 and After*, O'Sullivan's narrative
15. W. Duke, *Lord George Murray and the Forty-Five*, p. 191.
16. K. Tomasson and F. Buist, *Battles of the'45*, p. 207.
17. W. Duke, *Lord George Murray and the Forty-Five*, pp. 192–4. It has often been claimed that Charles Edward may never have seen this letter, but Susan Maclean Kybett discovered a copy among the Stuart Papers (vol. 273, f. 96), quoted in S.M. Kybett, *Bonnie Prince Charlie* (London, 1988), p. 211.
18. W. Duke, *Lord George Murray and the Forty-Five*, p. 192.
19. Chevalier de Johnstone, *A Memoir of the Forty-Five*, p. 148.
20. RA SP 213/117.
21. K. Tomasson and F. Buist, *Battles of the '45*, p. 208.
22. AEMD Memorandum Antoine Walsh to Comte de Maurepas, B4.58, fs.14,16.
23. *Scottish History Society Miscellany* third series (1941), p. 146.
24. J.S. Gibson, *Ships of the Forty-Five*, pp. 37–8.
25. Ibid.
26. Murray of Broughton, *Memorials*, p. 273.
27. Ibid., p. 271.
28. A. Lang, *Pickle the Spy*, p. 4.
29. A. Lang, *Companions of Pickle*, chapter vi, pp. 129–46.
30. Marion F. Hamilton, *The Loch Arkaig Treasure, Scottish History Society Miscellany*, third series, vol. xxxv (1941), pp. 133–68.
31. Murray of Broughton, *Memorials*, p. 273.
32. F. Maclean, *Bonnie Prince Charlie*, p. 231.

10. The Great Rebel of the Isles

1. H. Douglas, *Flora MacDonald: The Most Loyal Rebel*, pp. 52–3.
2. Duke of Cumberland, n.d., NLS 1696/29
3. Major-General John Campbell of Mamore to Duke of Argyll, 30 April 1746, NLS 3733/325.
4. Lord Loudoun to Alexander Campbell, Deputy-Governor of Fort William, 23 May 1746, NLS 3733/358.
5. John Maule to General Campbell, 17 July 1746, NLS 3733/439.
6. *Kintyre Antiquarian and Natural History Society Magazine*, no.41 (1998).
7. General Campbell to Dougal Stewart of Appin, 27 March 1746, NLS 3733/229.
8. General Campbell to Royal Navy captains, 28 March 1746, NLS 3733/231.
9. General Campbell to Duke of Cumberland, 30 April 1746, NLS 3733/314.
10. *Mémoire d'un Ecossais*, AEMD Angleterre, vol. 82 ff.216–21. I am indebted to John S. Gibson for this reference.
11. Murray of Broughton, *Memorials*, p. 277.
12. Ibid., Appendix, p. 412.
13. W.C. Mackenzie, *Lovat of the Forty-Five*, p. 332. The feather beds story appeared in *The Scots Magazine* (1747), p. 614.
14. W.C. Mackenzie, *Lovat of the Forty-Five*, p. 232.
15. RA CP 15/221.
16. J. Prebble, *Culloden*, pp. 192–3.
17. W.B. Blaikie, *Origins of the Forty-Five*, p. 239.
18. Ibid., p. 243.
19. R. Forbes, *Lyon in Mourning*, vol. i, p. 162–3.
20. Ibid., vol. i, pp. 106, 371.
21. W.B. Blaikie, *Origins of the Forty-Five*, p. 239.

22. R. Forbes, *Lyon in Mourning*, vol. i, p. 296.
23. Flora MacDonald to Sir John Macpherson, 21 October 1789, NLS 2618.
24. R. Forbes, *Lyon in Mourning*, vol. i, p. 297.
25. Ibid., vol. i, p. 111.
26. Ibid., vol. ii, p. 31.
27. David Campbell to John Maule, 21 July 1746, NLS, 3733/317.
28. David Campbell to General Campbell, 11 July 1746, NLS 3736/427.
29. General Campbell to Lord Albemarle, 24 July 1746, NLS 3733/447.
30. R. Forbes, *Lyon in Mourning*, vol. iii, p. 113.
31. BL Add. Mss 32,707. E. Charteris, *Augustus, Duke of Cumberland* (London, 1913), p. 288.
32. F. Maclean, *Bonnie Prince Charlie*, p. 278.
33. J. Doran, *Mann and Manners*, vol. i (London, 1876), p. 236. Walpole, *Correspondence*, vol. xix, p. 131.

11. The Victims of Mr 'Evidence' Murray

1. O. Douglas, *The House that is Our Own*, (London, 1940), p. 221.
2. Murray of Broughton, *Memorials*, p. 415.
3. Ibid., p. 412.
4. Ibid., p. 416.
5. Ibid., p. 306.
6. Milton to Duke of Newcastle, 10 July 1746, quoted in A. Lang, *Companions of Pickle*, p. 88.
7. B.G. Seton and J.G. Arnot (eds), *Prisoners of the '45*, vol. i, p. 214.
8. Ibid., vol. iii, pp. 356–7.
9. B. Byrom, *Bonnie Prince Charlie in Manchester*, p. 31.
10. B.G. Seton and J.G. Arnot (eds), *Prisoners of the '45*, vol. ii, pp. 151.
11. Ibid., vol. i, pp. 128–9.
12. Ibid., vol. i, p. 100.
13. William Mackay, *Sidelights on Highland History* (Inverness, 1925), pp. 396–400.
14. *Gentleman's Magazine*, vol. xvi (1746), p. 382. I am grateful to W.A. Speck for this reference.
15. John van der Kiste, *King George II and Queen Caroline*, (Stroud, 1997), p. 98.
16. James Allardyce (ed.), *Historical Papers relating to the Jacobite Period*, (Aberdeen, 1895), vol. i, pp. 322–3.
17. M. Forster, *The Rash Adventurer*, p. 210.
18. Ibid., pp. 210–11.
19. Sir James Fergusson, *Argyll and the Forty-Five*, pp. 119 and 87.
20. Report of Lachlan MacLean, captain of the *May*, *Albemarle Papers*, pp. 236, 270–3.
21. Ibid., 278–81.
22. R. Forbes, *Lyon in Mourning*, vol. iii, pp. 90–3.
23. Ibid., vol. iii, p. 382.
24. *Albemarle Papers*, pp. 278–81, 236, 270–3.
25. R. Forbes, *Lyon in Mourning*, vol. i, p. 82.
26. F. Maclean, *Bonnie Prince Charlie*, p. 182.
27. John Selby, *Over the Sea to Skye* (London, 1973), p. 148.
28. A. Lang, *Companions of Pickle*, p. 123.
29. R. Forbes, *Lyon in Mourning*, vol. i, pp. 351–2.
30. Lachlan MacLean's report, *Albemarle Papers*, pp. 278–81, 236, 270–3.
31. M. Forster, *The Rash Adventurer*, p. 207.
32. B.G. Seton and J.G. Arnot (eds), *Prisoners of the '45*, vol. iii, p. 337.
33. Ibid., vol. iii, p. 338.
34. *The Trial of Simon, Lord Lovat of the '45*, p. 119, note.
35. Murray of Broughton, *Memorials*, p. 274.
36. *The Trial of Simon, Lord Lovat of the '45*, p. 294.
37. F. Maclean, *Bonnie Prince Charlie*, p. 291.
38. Ibid., p. 292.
39. Murray of Broughton, *Memorials*, p. xxxv.
40. Ibid., p. xxx.
41. *The Trial of Simon, Lord Lovat of the '45*, p. 144, note

42. A. Lang, *Companions of Pickle*, p. 89.
43. J. Brown, *History of the Highlands*, vol. iv, p. 101.
44. A. Lang, *Companions of Pickle*. p. 91.

12. One War – Three Campaigns

1. Robert Burns, *Complete Works*, ed. James Mackay (Ayr, 1986), p. 391.
2. F. Maclean, *Bonnie Prince Charlie*, p. 276.
3. Bruce Lenman, *The Jacobite Risings in Britain 1689–1746*, pp. 154–5.
4. Earl of Albemarle to Duke of Newcastle, 13 July 1746, *Albemarle Papers*, p. 9
5. Ibid.
6. Ibid., p. 318.
7. Ibid., pp. 300, 303–5, 371–4.
8. Ibid., p. 370.
9. Ibid., p. 348.
10. H. Douglas, *Charles Edward Stuart*, p. 108
11. Ibid., p. 109.
12. *Four New Songs, and a Prophecy*, Rosebery Pamphlets, NLS 1-2–85.
13. See William Donaldson, *The Jacobite Song*, pp. 55–61.
14. E. Charteris, *William Augustus, Duke of Cumberland*, p. 248.

13. 'Dealing with this Bloody Government'

1. Charles to James Stuart, 6 November 1746, quoted in Eileen Cassavetti, *The Lion and the Lilies*, pp. 115–20.
2. J.S. Gibson, *Ships of the Forty-Five*, p. 118.
3. J. Browne, *History of the Highlands*, vol. iii, p. 463.
4. Ibid., vol. iii, p. 463.
5. Marquis d'Argenson, *Journal et Mémoires*, ed. E.J.B. Rathery, vol. iv, p. 319. SP Domestic 81f.346. I am indebted to Frank McLynn for these references.
6. F. McLynn, *France and the Jacobite Rising of 1745*, p. 235.
7. Sir Thomas Sheridan to Charles Edward, 19 August 1746, in H. Tayler, *The Stuart Papers at Windsor Castle*, p. 148.
8. Duc de Luynes, *Mémoires du Duc de Luynes sur la Cour de Louis XV*, vol. vii, p. 463.
9. Sir Thomas Sheridan to Charles Edward, 19 August 1746, in H. Tayler, *Stuart Papers at Windsor Castle*, p. 148.
10. James to Sir Thomas Sheridan, 25 July 1746, in ibid.
11. Sir Thomas Sheridan to James, 14 August 1746, in ibid.
12. Sir Thomas Sheridan to Charles, 19 August 1746, in ibid.
13. Barisdale's story is told by Andrew Lang in *Companions of Pickle*, pp. 114–23.
14. Colonel Warren to James, 10 October 1746, in H. Tayler, *A Jacobite Miscellany*, p. 120.
15. Duc de Luynes, *Mémoires*, vol. vii, p. 450.
16. Ibid., vol. vii, pp. 449–66.
17. F. Maclean, *Bonnie Prince Charlie*, p. 300.
18. H. Douglas, *Charles Edward Stuart*, p. 201.
19. Sir John Graeme to James Stuart, 14 October 1746.
20. H. Tayler, *Stuart Papers at Windsor Castle*, p. 206
21. Duc de Luynes, *Mémoires*, vol. vii, pp. 462–3.
22. H. Douglas, *Charles Edward Stuart*, p. 201.
23. 'Le prince Edouard n'auroit pas, je crois, fort aimé le parfait incognito; il sent ce qu'il est, et quoiqu'il n'ait point de hauteur, il a la dignité; il désire même extrèmement d'être approuvé et de plaire. Il dit qu'il n'est qu'un montagnard, qu'il ne sait point les usages de ci pays-ci, que d'ailleurs il sait mal le françois, et que la fluxion qu'il a gagnée dans les montagnes l'empêche d'entendre aussi facilement qu'à son ordinaire.' Duc de Luynes, *Mémoires*, vol. vii, p. 462.

24. Duc de Luynes, *Mémoires*, vol. vii, pp. 460–1.
25. RA SP 11/356. See also E.J.F. Barbier, *Chronique de la Régence et du Règne de Louis XV*, vol. iii, p. 498.
26. RA SP 278/41.
27. J. Browne, *History of the Highlands*, vol. iii, pp. 466–7.
28. Ibid., vol. iii, pp. 469–71, 474–5.
29. RA SP 279/124.
30. F. McLynn, *Charles Edward Stuart*, p. 314.
31. AEMD Angleterre, Tome 80.
32. Charles to James Stuart, 6 November 1746, quoted in E. Cassavetti, *The Lion and the Lilies*, pp. 115–20.
33. Charles to James Edgar, 6 November 1746, quoted in J. Browne, *History of the Highlands*, vol. iii, p. 468.
34. James to Charles Edward, 25 November 1746, quoted in H. Tayler, *Stuart Papers at Windsor Castle*, p. 188.
35. AEMD 83 f.336.
36. RA SP 280/89B.
37. RA SP 279/71.
38. RA SP 279/34, 154.
39. H. Douglas, *Charles Edward Stuart*, p. 203.
40. J. Browne, *History of the Highlands*, vol. iii, p. 472. RA SP 279/114, 116.
41. Cardinal Albani to Sir Horace Mann, 27 December 1747. RA SP 98/52.
42. RA SP 282/128.
43. James to Charles, 17 April 1747, RA SP 283/7. J. Browne, *History of the Highlands*, vol. iii, pp. 472, 494–7.
44. J. Brown, *History of the Highlands*, vol. iii, pp. 498–9.
45. RA SP 284/103.
46. See F. McLynn, *Charles Edward Stuart*, pp. 326–8.
47. See Marquis d'Argenson, *Journal et Mémoires*, vol. v, pp. 98–9.
48. E. Morelli, *Le Lettre di Benedetto XIV a Tencin*, vol. i, p. 444. I am gateful to Frank McLynn for this reference.
49. F. McLynn, *Charles Edward Stuart*, p. 333.

14. Who Stole the Cursed Gold?

1. Charles to James, 6 November 1746, RA SP 289/4, quoted by Marion F. Hamilton in *The Loch Arkaig Treasure*, p. 145.
2. RA SP, 285/104.
3. A. Lang, *Pickle the Spy*, p. 1.
4. Duke of Cumberland to Duke of Newcastle, 5 June 1746, in B.G. Seton and J.G. Arnot, *Prisoners of the '45*, vol. i, p. 5.
5. Duke of Newcastle to Duke of Cumberland, 23 May 1746, in ibid., vol. i, p. 4.
6. A.I. Macinnes, *Clanship, Commerce and the House of Stuart, 1603–1788*, p. 210.
7. Captain Robert Duff of HMS *Terror* to Archibald Campbell of Ballimore, 4 May 1746, NLS 3373/327.
8. Donald Campbell of Auchindoun to General Campbell, n.d., NLS 3373/333.
9. Lord Milton to Duke of Newcastle, 29 June 1746. Murray of Broughton, *Memorials*, Appendix, p. 412.
10. *Albemarle Papers*, vol. i, pp. 304, 312, 326, 331, 371.
11. A. Lang, *Companions of Pickle*, p. 131.
12. Ibid., p. 135.
13. Undated note from Charles to Cluny; also various receipts from Lady Keppoch and others, SRO GD/52/79.
14. Colonel Napier's report, Cumberland Papers, RACP, quoted in A. Lang, *Companions of Pickle*, p. 137.
15. Report from Persons sent to Badenoch and Lochaber, 7 June 1749, SRO GD/52/79.
16. *Memoirs of Lochiel by a Balhaldy, member of Clan Alpin, written in 1735*, (Abbotsford Club, 1842).
17. Lord Albemarle to Duke of Newcastle, 1 September 1746, *Albemarle Papers*, vol. i, p. 212.
18. Young Glengarry to James, 22 January 1748, in J. Browne, *History of the Highlands*, vol. iv, p. 23.

19. James to Charles, 2 January 1748, in ibid.
20. James Edgar to Young Glengarry, 24 December 1748, in ibid., vol. iv, p. 51.
21. Ibid.
22. A. Lang, *Pickle the Spy*, p. 154.
23. Young Glengarry to Lord Lismore, 23 September 1749, in J. Browne, *History of the Highlands*, vol. iv, pp. 63–4.
24. *Correspondence of the Duke of Bedford* (London, 1843), vol. ii, p. 39.
25. A. Lang, *Companions of Pickle*, p. 139.
26. Ibid., pp. 138–9.
27. RA SP 289/4.
28. J. Browne, *History of the Highlands*, vol. iv, p. 60.
29. All four documents are in the Stuart Papers at Windsor, and are reprinted in *The Loch Arkaig Treasure*, Scottish History Society Miscellany, third series, vol. xxxv, pp. 146–68.
30. RA SP 300/80.
31. RA SP 310/82 and /83.
32. RA SP 358/28.
33. RA SP 350/50.
34. M.F. Hamilton, *The Loch Arkaig Treasure*, pp. 164–7.
35. A. Lang, *Pickle the Spy*, p. 158.
36. M.F. Hamilton, *The Loch Arkaig Treasure*, pp. 135–6.
37. RA SP 300/80.
38. A. Lang, *Companions of Pickle*, p. 145.
39. A. Lang, *Pickle the Spy*, p. 206.

15. To England via Fairyland

1. RA SP 285/104.
2. See H. Douglas, *The Private Passions of Bonnie Prince Charlie*, and L.L. Bongie, *The Love of a Prince, Bonnie Prince Charlie in France, 1744–48.*
3. AEMD, 101–4. RA SP 295/34.
4. See F. McLynn, *Charles Edward Stuart*, chapter 25.
5. Pickle the Spy, quoted by A. Lang, *Pickle the Spy*, p. 35.
6. Lettre de Madame de XXX à M. de XXX, December 1748, RA SP 295/104.
7. Lettre de M. Nugeon on the imprisonment of Charles, December 1748, RA SP 296/7.
8. RA SP 295/104.
9. E.C. Mossner, *The Life of David Hume* (Oxford, 1970), pp. 218–9.
10. MSS in Musée Calvet, Avignon, quoted in G. Dickson, *Des Ecossais à Avignon: Jacques III un Roi Sans Couronne*, p. 307. H. Tayler, *Jacobite Papers at Avignon*, p. 309.
11. Information from the Bibliothèque Municipale d'Avignon. See also H. Tayler, *Jacobite Papers at Avignon*, pp. 297–8 and F. McLynn, *Charles Edward Stuart*, pp. 374–5.
12. F. McLynn, *Charles Edward Stuart*, pp. 376.
13. BL Add. Mss 32,845 f.254.
14. A. Lang, *Pickle the Spy*, pp. 48–50.
15. Ibid., pp. 51–66.
16. Ibid., p. 61.
17. Maurice Tourneux, *Correspondence Littéraire, Philosophique et Critique par Grimm, Diderot, Rayal, Meiseter, etc.*, vol. xii, p,143.
18. H. Douglas, *The Private Passions of Bonnie Prince Charlie*, p. 221.
19. A. Lang, *Pickle the Spy*, chapter 3, pp. 44–66.
20. *Collections for a History of Staffordshire*, William Salt Archaeological Society (Birmingham, 1881), vol. ii, pp. 250–4.
21. P.K. Monod, *Jacobitism and the English People 1688–1788*, p. 199.
22. H. Douglas, *Charles Edward Stuart*, p. 222.
23. A.E.A. Axon, *The Annals of Manchester* (Manchester, 1886), p. 87.
24. RA SP 304/55.
25. William King, *Political and Literary Anecdotes*, p. 196. Mahon, *Decline of The Last Stuarts*, p. 96.
26. A. Lang, *Pickle the Spy*, p. 104
27. Ibid., pp. 103–4.
28. H. Douglas, *Charles Edward Stuart*, pp. 224–5.

16. How Pickle Was Trapped

1. A. Lang, *Pickle the Spy*, pp. 176–7.
2. Charles to Princesse de Talmont, n.d., RA SP 316/100.
3. RA SP 324/61, 86. I am indebted to Frank McLynn for this reference.
4. H. Walpole, *Correspondence*, vol. ii, p. 116
5. M. Forster, *The Rash Adventurer*, p. 262.
6. C.L. Berry, *The Young Pretender's Mistress*, pp. 73–4.
7. Duke of Newcastle to Joseph Yorke, British Envoy in Paris, September 1751, in E.E. Cuthell, *The Scottish Friend of Frederick the Great: the Last Earl Marischal*, vol, i, p. 256.
8. A. Lang, *Pickle the Spy*, p. 129.
9. Correspondence between Henry Goring and Earl Marischal during September 1751, quoted in J. Browne, *History of the Highlands*, vol. iv, pp. 89–90
10. A. Lang describes the movements of the Prince and spies during the latter part of 1751 in *Pickle the Spy*, pp. 132–5.
11. C. Petrie, *The Jacobite Movement*, pp. 424–5.
12. A. Lang, *Pickle the Spy*, pp. 160–1.
13. Ibid., p. 204.
14. C.L. Berry, *The Young Pretender's Mistress*, p. 39.
15. O'Sullivan to Charles, 29 May 1752, RA SP 332/51.
16. O'Sullivan to Clementine Walkinshaw, 31 May 1752, RA SP 332/65.
17. C.S. Terry, *Life of Prince Charles Stuart, the Young Pretender* (Aberdeen, 1900), p. 157.
18. Henry Goring to Charles, 7/10 June 1752. RA SP 1/347.
19. H. Tayler, *Prince Charlie's Daughter*, p. 28.
20. A. Lang, *Pickle the Spy*, p. 213.
21. Charles to John Waters, 12 November 1753, RA SP 344/161.
22. For the story of the Appin Murder see William Macarthur, *The Appin Murder* (London, 1960), and Seamus Carney, *The Appin Murder: The Killing of the Red Fox* (Edinburgh, 1989).
23. A. Lang, *Pickle the Spy*, p. 177.
24. F. Maclean, *Bonnie Prince Charlie*, p. 332.
25. A. Lang, *Pickle the Spy*, pp. 176–8.
26. Ibid., pp. 178–9.
27. Ibid., p. 201.
28. Ibid., p. 163.

17. Alone and Discarded by his Friends

1. M. Forster, *The Rash Adventurer*, p. 254
2. James Lees-Milne, *The Last Stuarts* (London, 1983), p. 85.
3. H. Goring to Charles, 8 May 1753, quoted in A. Lang, *Pickle the Spy*, p. 209.
4. J. Waters to James's secretary, 24 September 1755, RA SP 359/141.
5. A. Lang, *Pickle the Spy*, p. 126.
6. Ibid., p. 127.
7. R. Forbes, *Lyon in Mourning*, vol. i, pp. 54–5.
8. Ibid., vol. iii, pp. 132–5.
9. A. Lang, *Pickle the Spy*, p. 259.
10. Goring's correspondence of May 1745 is contained in A. Lang, *Pickle the Spy*, pp. 269–73.
11. BL. Add. Mss 32,734. Pickle to Gwynne Vaughan, 25 February 1754, quoted in A. Lang, *Pickle the Spy*, pp. 264–5.
12. Pickle to Vaughan, 8 April 1754, BL Add. Mss 32,755, quoted in A. Lang, *Pickle the Spy*, p. 266.
13. Pickle to Vaughan, 8 April 1754, quoted in A. Lang, *Pickle the Spy*, p. 268.
14. H. Goring to Charles, 5 May 1754, quoted in A. Lang, *Pickle the Spy*, p. 270.
15. Charles to H. Goring, 10 May 1754, quoted in A. Lang, *Pickle the Spy*, p. 270–1.
16. Goring to Charles, 16 May 1754, quoted in A. Lang, *Pickle the Spy*, pp. 271–3.
17. RA SP 348/88.
18. Alexander Murray to Charles, 29 September 1758. C. Petrie, *The*

Jacobite Movement, p. 420.
19. W. King, *Political and Literary Anecdotes*, p. 201.
20. J. Waters to Charles, 11 September 1754, RA SP 1/388.
21. H. Douglas, *Charles Edward Stuart*, p. 234.
22. C.L. Berry, *The Young Pretender's Mistress*, p. 62.
23. Dudley Bradstreet to Newcastle's secretary, Andrew Stone, 8 August, 1759, in D. Bradstreet, *The Life and Uncommon Adventures of Captain Dudley Bradstreet*, p. 168.
24. A. Lang, *Pickle the Spy*, p. 311
25. Ibid., pp. 306–8.
26. Clementine to Charles, 22 July 1760, original in West Highland Museum, Fort William.
27. Charles to Abbé Gordon, 26 July 1760. RA SP 404/144.
28. Abbé Gordon to Charles, 26 July 1760. RA SP 402/143.

Epilogue

1. A. Lang, *Pickle the Spy*, p. 287.
2. H. Douglas, *Bonnie Prince Charlie*, p. 274.
3. Mann to Duke of Newcastle, 29 November 1766, quoted in H. Douglas, *Charles Edward Stuart*, p. 244.
4. C. Petrie, *The Jacobite Movement* gives information on some of these clubs, pp. 441–4.
5. Stonor to James Edgar, May 1749, A. Lang, *Companions of Pickle*, p. 90.
6. Marischal's career is described by Edith E. Cuthell, in *The Scottish Friend of Frederick the Great.*
7. Pickle to Duke of Newcastle, 19 February 1760, BL Add. Mss 32,902, quoted in A. Lang, *Pickle the Spy*, p. 312.
8. Dudley Bradstreet to Andrew Stone, 8 August 1759, in D. Bradstreet, *The Life and Uncommon Adventures of Captain Dudley Bradstreet*, p. 168.
9. H. Douglas, *Charles Edward Stuart*, p. 267.

Bibliography

Albemarle Papers, C.S. Terry ed., 2 vols, London, 1902

Allardyce, J. (ed.), *Historical Papers relating to the Jacobite Period 1689–1750,* 2 vols, Aberdeen, 1895–6

Anderson, M.S., *Eighteenth-Century Europe 1713–89*, Oxford, 1966

Andrieux, Maurice, *Daily Life in Papal Rome in the Eighteenth Century*, London, 1968

Argenson, Marquis d', *Journal et Mémoires, 1747–8,* ed. E.J.B. Rathery, 9 vols, Paris, 1859–67

Atholl, 7th Duke of, *Chronicles of the Atholl and Tullibardine Families*, 5 vols, Edinburgh, 1908

Barbier, E.J.F., *Chronique de la Régence et du Règne de Louis XV*, 8 vols, Paris, 1847

Berry, C. Leo, *The Young Pretender's Mistress*, Edinburgh, 1977

Berwick, Duke of, *Mémoires du Maréchal de Berwick, écrit par lui-même*, Paris, 1778

Beaumont, G. du Bosq de, *La Cour des Stuarts à St Germain-en-Laye*, Paris, 1909

Bevan, Bryan, *Marlborough the Man*, London, 1973

Blaikie, W.B., *Itinerary of Prince Charles Edward Stuart from his Landing in Scotland July 1745 to his Departure September 1746*, Scottish History Society, Edinburgh, 1897

—— (ed.), *Origins of the Forty-Five and Other Papers Relating to the Rising*, Scottish History Society, Edinburgh, 1916

—— 'The Landing of Prince Charles Edward in Scotland', *Scottish Historical Review*, vol. xxiii, Glasgow, 1926.

Bongie, L.L., *The Love of a Prince, Bonnie Prince Charlie in France, 1744–48*, Vancouver, 1986

Bonstetten, Charles-Victor, *Souvenirs*, Paris, 1832

Bradstreet, D., *The Adventures of Captain Dudley Bradstreet*, 1755, ed. G.S. Taylor and E.H.W. Meyerstein, London, 1929

Brewer, J., *Party Ideology and Popular Politics at the Accession of George III*, Cambridge, 1976

Browne, James, *History of the Highlands and the Highland Clans*, 4 vols, Glasgow, 1832–3.

Broxap, Henry, *The Later Non-Jurors*, Cambridge, 1924

Burton, John Hill, *Jacobite Correspondence of the Atholl Family, 1745–6*, London, 1935

Byrom, Beppy, *Bonnie Price Charlie in Manchester: An Eye-witness Account*, Manchester n.d.,

Cameron, Archibald, *The Life of Dr Archibald Cameron*, brother to Donald Cameron of Lochiel to which is added *The Life of Jenny Cameron*, London, 1753

Carpio, M.J., *España y los Ultimos Estuardos*, Madrid, 1954

Cassavetti, Eileen, *The Lion & the Lilies. The Stewarts and France*, London, 1977

Chambers, Robert, *Jacobite Memoirs of the Rebellion of 1745, 1746, etc.*, Edinburgh, 1827

—— *History of the Rebellion of 1745–6*, Edinburgh, 1869

Christie, I.R., *Myth and Reality in Late Eighteenth-Century British Politics*, London, 1970

Churchill, Winston S., *Marlborough: his Life and Times*, Oxford, 1933

Cobban, Alfred, *A History of Modern France*, 3 vols, London, 1957

Cruickshanks, Eveline, *Political Untouchables: The Tories and the '45*, London, 1979

—— (ed.), *Ideology and Conspiracy: Aspects of Jacobitism, 1689–1759*, Edinburgh, 1982
Culloden Papers 1625–1748, ed. R.H. Duff, London, 1815. *See also* Forbes, Duncan of Culloden
Culloden Papers, (*More Culloden Papers*), ed. D. Warrand, 5 vols, Inverness, 1923–30
Cunningham, Audrey, *The Loyal Clans*, Cambridge, 1932
Cuthell, E.E., *The Scottish Friend of Frederick the Great*, 2 vols, London, 1915
Daiches, David, *Charles Edward Stuart: The Life and Times of Bonnie Prince Charlie*, London, 1973
Dickson, George (ed.), *Des Ecossais à Avignon: Jacques III Stuart, un Roi sans Couronne*, Paris, 1993
Donaldson, William, *The Jacobite Song: Political Myth and National Identity*, Aberdeen, 1988
Doran, John, *'Mann' and Manners at the court of Florence*, 2 vols, London, 1876
Douglas, Hugh, *Charles Edward Stuart: The Man, the King, the Legend*, London, 1975
—— *Flora MacDonald: The Most Loyal Rebel*, Stroud, 1993
—— *The Private Passions of Bonnie Prince Charlie*, Stroud, 1998
Duke, Winifred, *Lord George Murray and the Forty-Five*, Aberdeen, 1927
Dumont-Wilden, L., *The Wandering Prince*, London, 1934
Eardley-Simpson, Llewellyn, *Derby and the Forty-Five*, London, 1933
Elcho, David, Lord, *A Short Account of the Affairs of Scotland in the years 1744–6*, Edinburgh, 1907
—— *Diary*, in H. Tayler, *Jacobite Miscellany*, Roxburghe Club, Oxford, 1946
Eves, Charles Kenneth, *Matthew Prior: Poet and Diplomatist*, New York, 1939
Ewald, A.C., *Life and Times of Prince Charles Stuart*, 2 vols, London, 1875
Fergusson, Sir James, *Argyll in the Forty-Five*, London, 1951
Forbes, Duncan of Culloden, *Culloden Papers: Comprising an extensive and interesting correspondence for the years 1625 to 1748, including numerous letters from the unfortunate Lord Lovat and other distinguished persons of the time; with occasional State Papers*, ed. R.H. Duff, London, 1815
Forbes, Revd Robert, *The Lyon in Mourning*, ed. Henry Paton, 3 vols, Scottish History Society, Edinburgh, 1895–6
Forbes-Leith, A., *The Scots Guards in France*, 2 vols, London, 1899
Forster, Margaret, *The Rash Adventurer*, London, 1973
Fraser, Simon, Lord Lovat, *The Trial of Simon, Lord Lovat*, ed. D.N. Mackay, Edinburgh, 1911
Frederick the Great, *Politische Correspndenz*, 45 vols, Berlin, 1879–82
Fritz, P.S., *English Ministers and Jacobitism between the Rebellions of 1715 and 1745*, Toronto, 1975
Gibson, John Sibbald, *Ships of the Forty-Five*, London, 1967
—— *Lochiel of the '45*, Edinburgh, 1994
Grew, M. and S. (eds), *The English Court in Exile*, London, 1911
Hamilton, Marion F., *The Loch Arkaig Treasure*, Scottish History Society. Miscellany, vol. VII, Scottish History Society, third series, vol. XXXV, Edinburgh, 1941
Harkness, Douglas, *Bolingbroke, The Man and his Career*, London, 1957
Home, John, *History of the Rebellion in Scotland in the Year 1745*, Edinburgh, 1822
Hooke, Nathaniel, *Secret History of Colonel Hooke's Negociations in Scotland in 1707*, London, 1760
Horn, D.B., *Great Britain and Europe in the Eighteenth Century*, Oxford, 1961
Hughes, E.W., *North Country Life in the Eighteenth Century*, 2 vols, London, 1952
Hume, David, *History of the English Court during the reign of the Stuarts*, 6 vols, Paris, 1754–7
Irish, G.P., *The Scottish Jabcobite Movement*, London, 1952
Jarvis, Rupert C., *Collected Papers on the Jacobite Risings*, 2 vols, Manchester, 1971
Jesse, John Heneage, *Histoire de la Maison Royale de Stuart*, 3 vols, Paris, 1840

Johnstone, Chevalier de, *A Memoir of the Forty-Five*, Edinburgh, 1820
Jones, G.H., *The Main Stream of Jacobitism*, Cambridge, Mass., 1954
Jusserand, J.J., *Receuil des Instructions diplomatiques données aux Ambassadeurs: Angleterre*, Paris, 1929
Keith, George, 10th Earl Marischal, *Two Fragments of Autobiography*, ed. J.Y.T. Greig, Scottish History Society Miscellany, vol. VI, 1933
Lang, Andrew, *Pickle the Spy*, London, 1897
—— *The Companions of Pickle*, London, 1898
Lart, C.E. (ed), *The Parochial Registers of Saint-Germain-en-Laye*, 2 vols, Paris, 1912
Lecky, W.E.H., *Ireland in the Eighteenth Century*, 5 vols, London, 1892
Lenman, Bruce, *The Jacobite Clans of the Great Glen, 1650–1784*, London, 1984
—— *The Jacobite Risings in Britain 1689–1746*, London, 1980
Lewis, Lesley, *Connoisseurs and Secret agents in 18th Century Rome*, London, 1961
Lockhart of Carnwath, George, *Papers*, Edinburgh, 1817
Luynes, Duc de, *Mémoires du Duc de Luynes sur la Cour de Louis XV (1735–1758)*, vols IV–VII, Paris, 1861
Macallester, Oliver, *A series of Letters Discovering the Scheme Projected by France, in MDCCLIX, for an Intended Invasion upon England, etc. To which are prefixed the Secret Adventures of the Young Pretender*, 2 vols, London, 1767
McCorry, Helen C., 'Rats, Lice and Scotchmen', *Journal of the Society for Army Historical Research*, vol. LXXIV, no. 297, Spring 1996, 1–38
Macinnes, Allan I., *Clanship, Commerce and the House of Stuart, 1603–1788*, East Linton, 1996
Mackenzie, W.C., *Lovat of the Forty-Five*, Edinburgh, 1934
Macknight, James, *Life of Bolingbroke*, London, 1863
Maclean, Alasdair, *A Macdonald for the Prince, the story of Neil MacEachen*, Stornoway, 1982
Maclean, Sir Fitzroy, *Bonnie Prince Charlie*, London, 1988
McLynn, Frank, *Charles Edward Stuart: A Tragedy in Many Acts*, London, 1988
—— *The Jacobite Army in England, 1745: The Final Campaign*, Edinburgh, 1983
—— *France and the Jacobite Rising of 1745*, Edinburgh, 1981
—— *The Jacobites*, London, 1985
Mahon, Viscount, 5th Earl Stanhope (ed.), *The Decline of the Last Stuarts. Extracts from Despatches*, Oxford, 1843
Maxwell, James of Kirkconnell, *Narrative of Prince Charles's Expedition to Scotland (c. 1760)*, Edinburgh, 1841
Meikle, H.W., *Scotland and the French Revolution*, Glasgow, 1912
Miller, Lady Anne, *Letters from Italy*, 3 vols, London, 1776
Miller, Peggy, *James*, London, 1971.
Mitford, Nancy, *Madame de Pompadour*, London, 1954
Monod, Paul Kléber, *Jacobitism and the English People, 1688–1788*, Cambridge, 1989.
Morelli, Emilia, *Le Lettre di Benedetto XIV a Tencin*, 3 vols, Rome, 1955.
Murray, John, *Memorials of John Murray of Broughton*, ed. R. Fitzroy Bell, Scottish History Society, vol xxxvii, 1889
Murray, John, of Broughton, *Genuine Memoirs of John Murray of Broughton, 1747*, Edinburgh, 1898
Nobili-Vitelleschi, Marchesa, *A Court in Exile. Charles Edward Stuart and the Romance of the Countess d'Albanie*, 2 vols, London, 1903
Newman, Bernard, *Spy and Counter Spy*, London, 1970
Norrie, W. Drummond, *The Life and Adventures of Prince Charles Edward Stuart*, 4 vols, London, 1900
Oman, Carola, 'The Exiled Stuarts in Rome', *Parsons Journal*, vol 9, nos 53 and 54, 1961–2
O'Sullivan, Sir John W., *Journal of the 1745 Campaign and the Wanderings of Prince Charles Edward*, 1746

Overton, J.H., *The Non-Jurors*, London, 1902
Petrie, Sir Charles, *The Jacobite Movement*, London, 1959
—— *The Elibank Plot, 1752–3*, Royal Historical Society, fourth series, vol XIV, 1931
Pichot, Joseph, *Histoire de Charles Edward*, Paris, 1833
Pittock, Nurray G.H., *The Myth of the Jacobite Clans*, Edinburgh, 1995
Polnay, Peter de, *Death of a Legend*, London, 1952
Quynn, Dorothy Mackay, 'Philip von Stosch: Collector, Bibliophile, Spy, Thief', *Catholic Historical Review*, vol. xxvii, 1941
Richmond, H.W., *The Navy and the War of 1739–48*, London, 1920
Robson, R.J., *The Oxford Election of 1754*, London, 1949
Rudé, G., *Paris and London in the Eighteenth Century*, London, 1970
—— *Revolutionary Europe*, London, 1964
Seton, Sir Bruce Gordon and Jean Gordon Arnot, (eds.), *The Prisoners of the Forty-Five*, 3 vols, Scottish History Society, third series, vols XIII–XV, Edinburgh, 1928–9
Speck, W.A., *The Butcher. The Duke of Cumberland and the Suppression of the '45*, Oxford, 1981
Stewart, H.C., *The Exiled Stewarts in Italy 1717–1807*, Scottish History Society Miscellany, vol. VII, Edinburgh, 1941
'Stuarts In Italy', *Quarterly Review*, vol 107, 1846
Szechi, Daniel, *The Jacobites: Britain and Europe 1688–1788*, Manchester, 1994
Taillandier, Saint-René, Georges, *La Comtesse d'Albany*, Paris, 1862
Tayler, A. and H., *Introduction to the Stuart Papers at Windsor Castle*, Edinburgh, 1939
—— *Jacobites of Aberdeenshire and Banffshire in the '45*, Aberdeen, 1928
—— *A Jacobite Exile*, London, 1937
—— *1745 and After*, London, 1938
—— *Stuart Papers at Windsor*, London, 1939
Tayler, H., *Prince Charlie's Daughter*, London, 1950
—— (ed.), *Jacobite Miscellany*, London, 1948
—— *Jacobite Epilogue*, London, 1941
—— *Jacobite Papers at Avignon*, Scottish History Society Miscellany, vol. v, Edinburgh, 1933.
—— *Two Accounts of the Escape of Prince Charles Edward (with twelve letters from Lord George Murray to Andrew Lumisden)*, Oxford, 1951
Tomasson, Katherine, *The Jacobite General*, London, 1958
—— and Buist, Francis, *Battles of the '45*, London, 1962
Thompson, Mrs, *Memoirs of the Jacobites*, 1846
Ure, John, *A Bird on the Wing*, London, 1992
Walpole, Horace, *Correspondence*, eds, G.L. Lam, W.S. Lewis, W. Hunting Smith, 45 vols, London, 1960
Waugh, Mary, *Smuggling in Kent and Sussex 1700–1840*, Newbury, 1998
White, Jon Manchip, *Marshal of France; Life and Times of Maurice de Saxe*, London, 1962
Wood, Stephen, *The Auld Alliance; Scotland And France, The Military Connection*, Edinburgh, 1989
Woodhouselee Manuscript, *A Narrative of Events in Edinburgh and District During the Jacobite Occupation, September to November, 1745*, Edinburgh, 1907
Youngson, A.J., *After the Forty-Five*, London, 1973

Index